Shojo Beat

VAMPIRE KNIGHT

Story & Art by
Matsuri
Hino

Vol. 9

The Story of VAMPIRE KNIGHT

1 Cross Academy, a private boarding school, is where the Day Class and the Night Class coexist. The Night Class—a group of beautiful elite students—are all vampires!

2 Four years ago, the pureblood Shizuka Hio bit Zero and turned him into a vampire. Kaname killed Shizuka, but the source may still exist. Meanwhile, Yuki suffers from her lost memories. When Kaname sinks his fangs into her neck, her memories return!

3 Yuki is the princess of the Kuran family—and a pureblood vampire!! Ten years ago, her mother exchanged her life to seal away Yuki's vampire nature. Yuki's Uncle Rido killed her father. Rido takes over Shiki's body and arrives at the Academy. He targets Yuki for her blood. Kaname gives his own blood to resurrect Rido. Kaname confesses that he's the progenitor of the Kurans, and that Rido is the master who awakened him!

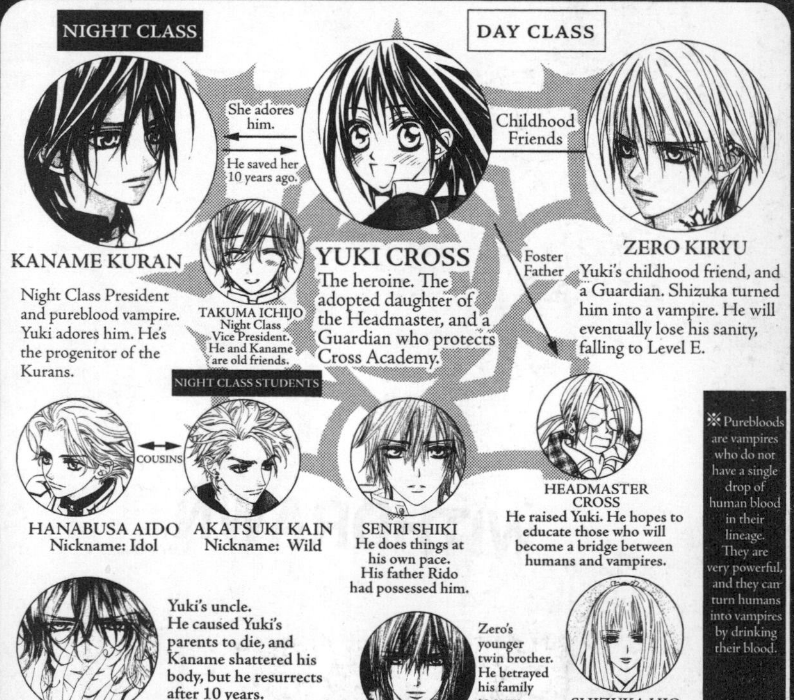

NIGHT CLASS
DAY CLASS
She adores him.
He saved her 10 years ago.
Childhood Friends
Foster Father
KANAME KURAN
Night Class President and pureblood vampire. Yuki adores him. He's the progenitor of the Kurans.
TAKUMA ICHIJO
Night Class Vice President. He and Kaname are old friends.
YUKI CROSS
The heroine. The adopted daughter of the Headmaster, and a Guardian who protects Cross Academy.
ZERO KIRYU
Yuki's childhood friend, and a Guardian. Shizuka turned him into a vampire. He will eventually lose his sanity, falling to Level E.
NIGHT CLASS STUDENTS
COUSINS
HANABUSA AIDO
Nickname: Idol
AKATSUKI KAIN
Nickname: Wild
SENRI SHIKI
He does things at his own pace. His father Rido had possessed him.
HEADMASTER CROSS
He raised Yuki. He hopes to educate those who will become a bridge between humans and vampires.
※Purebloods are vampires who do not have a single drop of human blood in their lineage. They are very powerful, and they can turn humans into vampires by drinking their blood.
RIDO KURAN
Yuki's uncle. He caused Yuki's parents to die, and Kaname shattered his body, but he resurrects after 10 years. He took over his son Shiki's body and came to Cross Academy.
ICHIRU
Zero's younger twin brother. He betrayed his family to serve Shizuka.
SHIZUKA HIO
The pureblood who robbed Zero of his family. Kaname killed her.

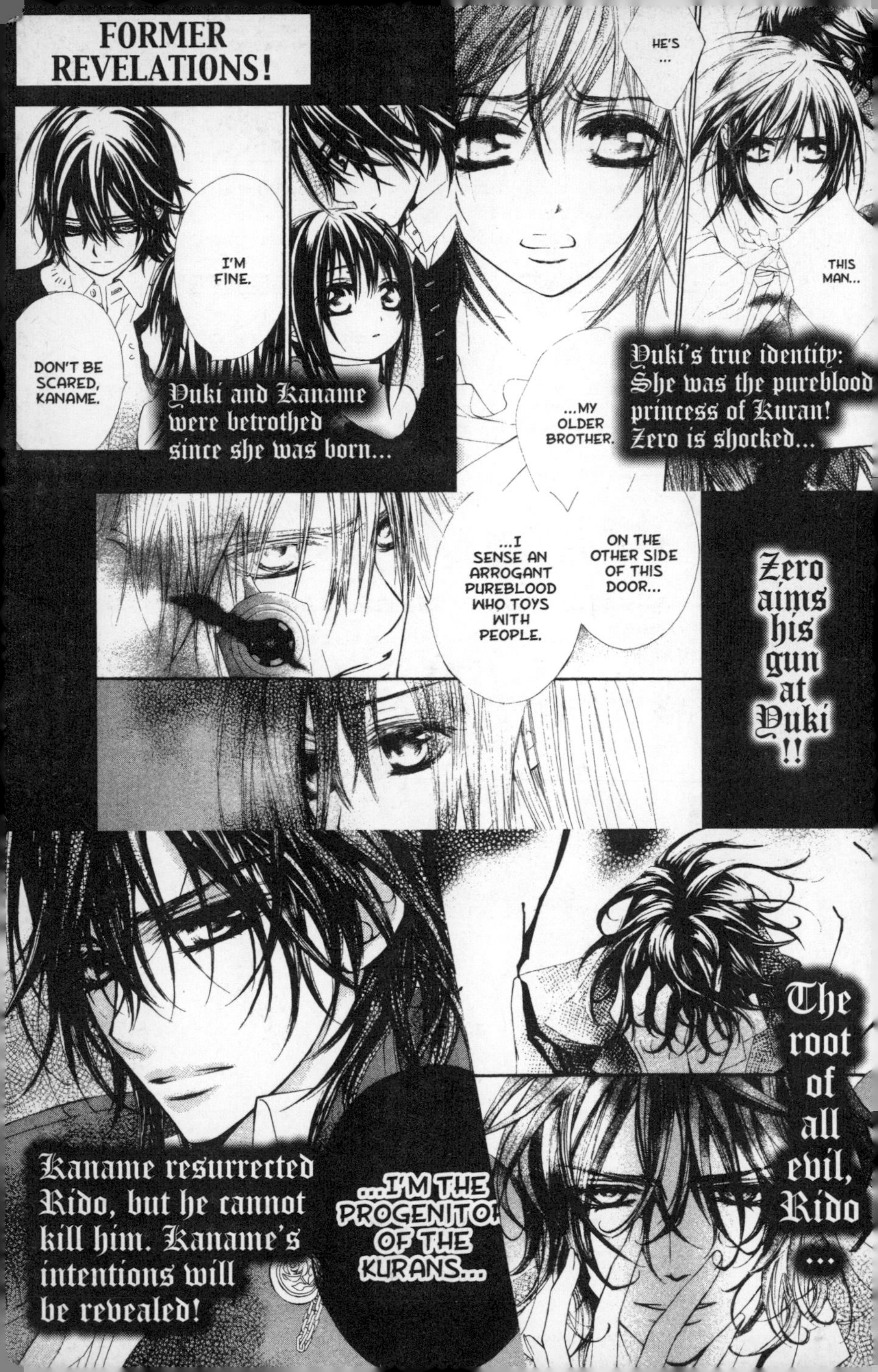
FORMER REVELATIONS!
HE'S ...
THIS MAN...
...MY OLDER BROTHER.
Yuki's true identity: She was the pureblood princess of Kuran! Zero is shocked...
I'M FINE.
DON'T BE SCARED, KANAME.
Yuki and Kaname were betrothed since she was born...
Zero aims his gun at Yuki!!
ON THE OTHER SIDE OF THIS DOOR...
...I SENSE AN ARROGANT PUREBLOOD WHO TOYS WITH PEOPLE.
The root of all evil, Rido...
...I'M THE PROGENITO OF THE KURANS...
Kaname resurrected Rido, but he cannot kill him. Kaname's intentions will be revealed!

VAMPIRE KNIGHT

Contents

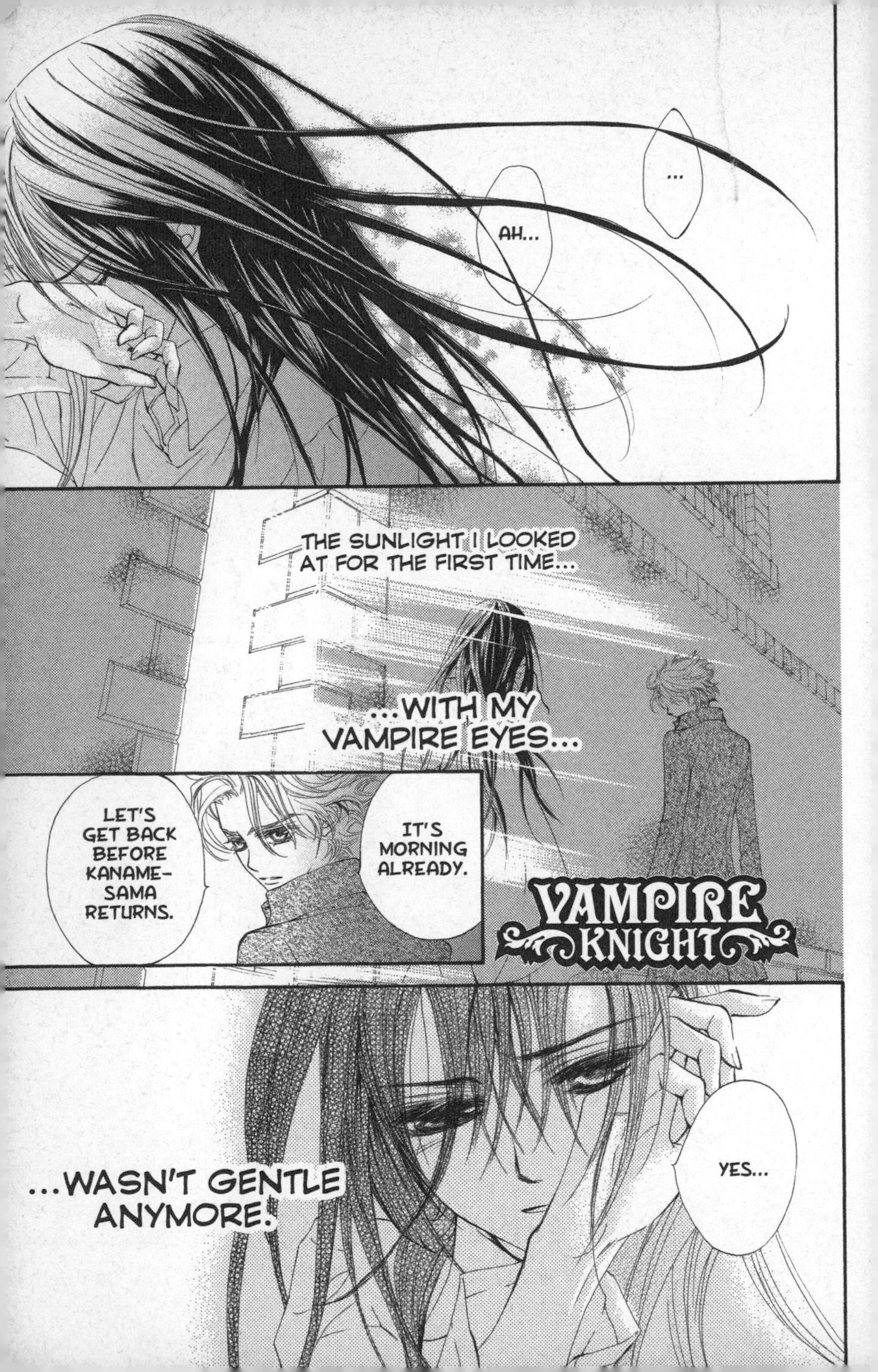
...
AH...
THE SUNLIGHT I LOOKED AT FOR THE FIRST TIME...
...WITH MY VAMPIRE EYES...
VAMPIRE KNIGHT
IT'S MORNING ALREADY.
LET'S GET BACK BEFORE KANAME-SAMA RETURNS.
YES...
...WASN'T GENTLE ANYMORE.

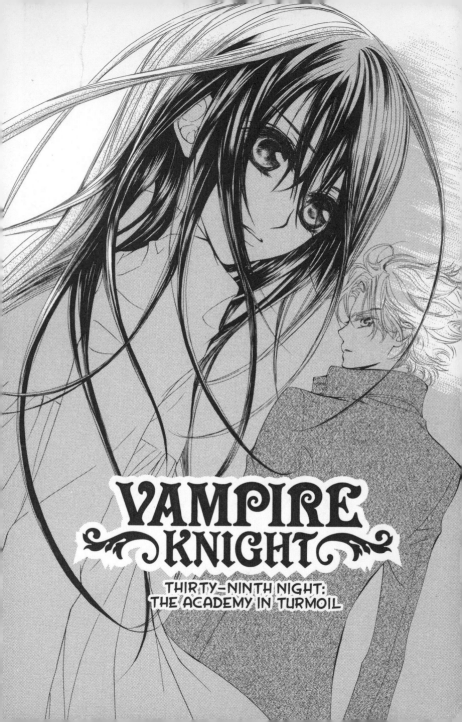

VAMPIRE KNIGHT

THIRTY-NINTH NIGHT:
THE ACADEMY IN TURMOIL

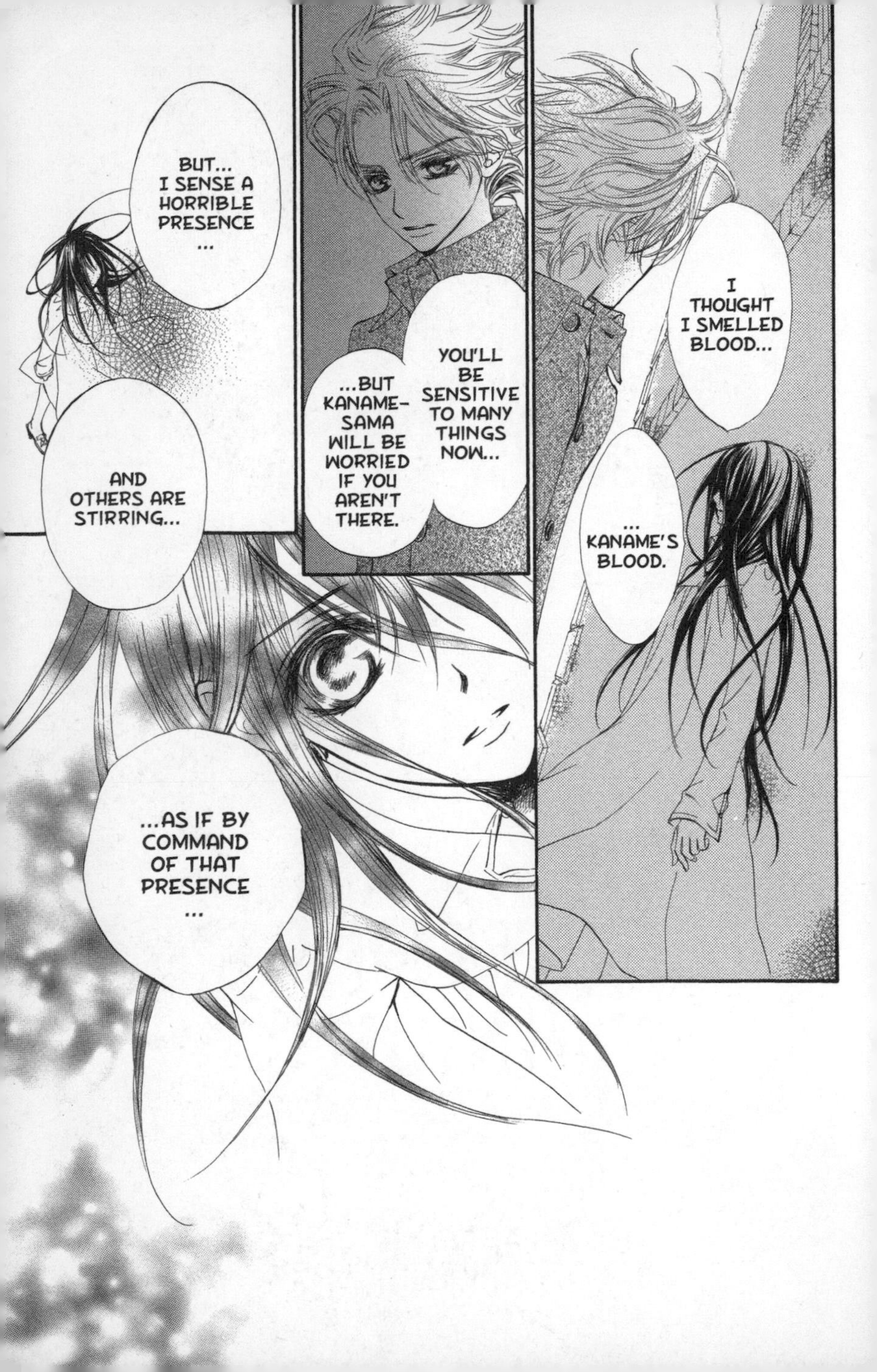
I THOUGHT I SMELLED BLOOD...
... KANAME'S BLOOD.
YOU'LL BE SENSITIVE TO MANY THINGS NOW...
...BUT KANAME-SAMA WILL BE WORRIED IF YOU AREN'T THERE.
BUT... I SENSE A HORRIBLE PRESENCE ...
AND OTHERS ARE STIRRING...
...AS IF BY COMMAND OF THAT PRESENCE ...

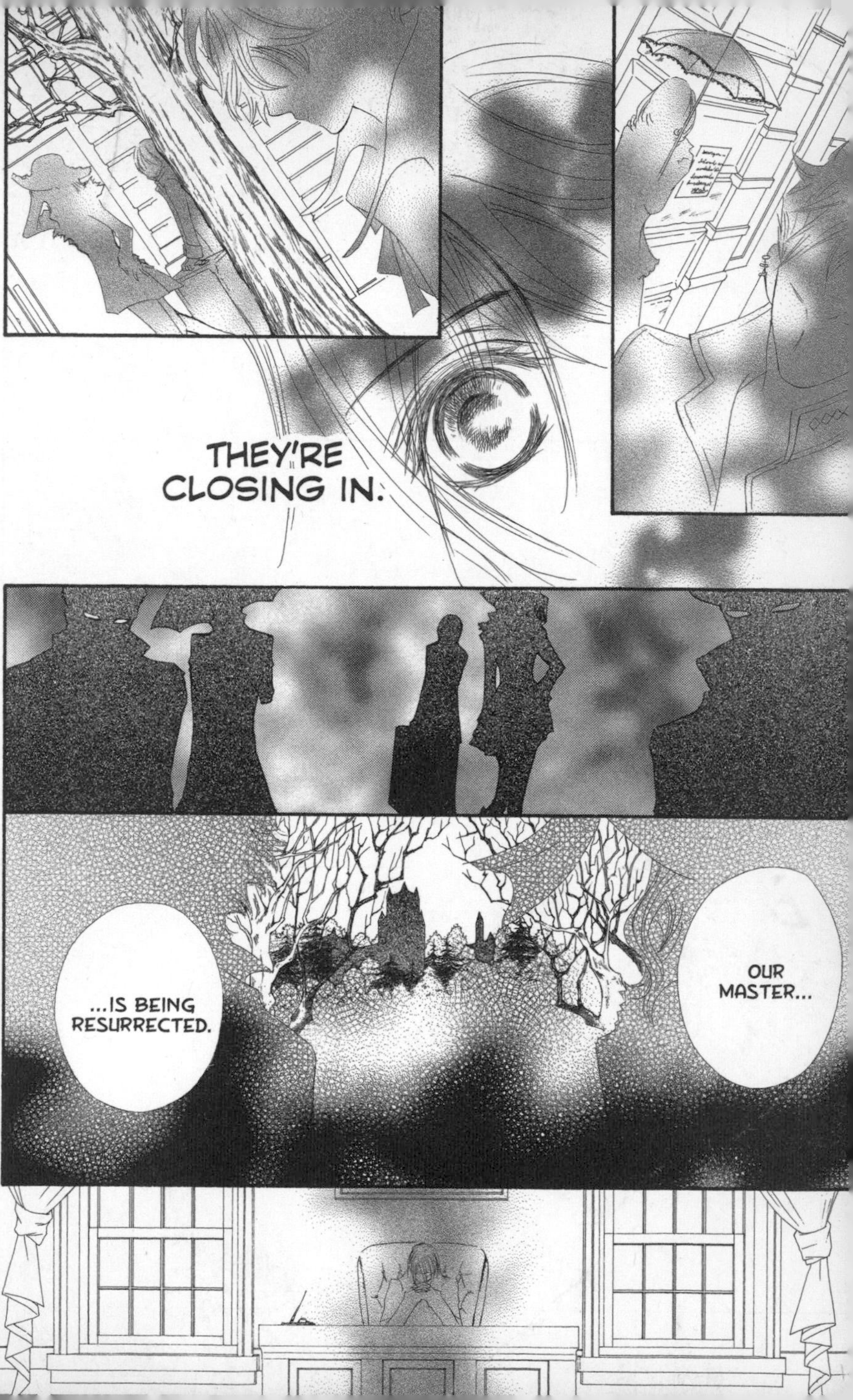
THEY'RE CLOSING IN.
OUR MASTER...
...IS BEING RESURRECTED.

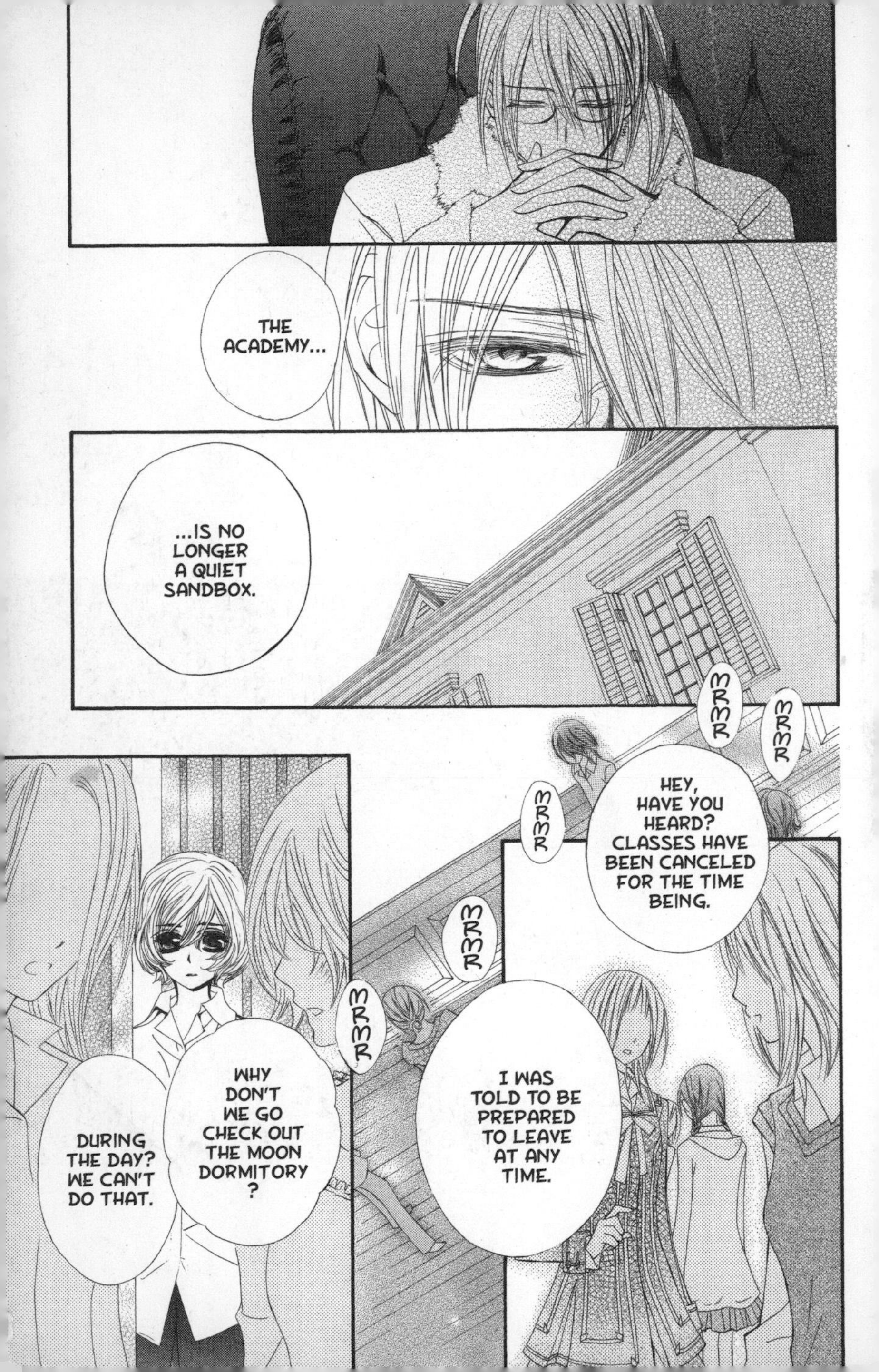
THE ACADEMY...
...IS NO LONGER A QUIET SANDBOX.
MRMR
MRMR
MRMR
HEY, HAVE YOU HEARD? CLASSES HAVE BEEN CANCELED FOR THE TIME BEING.
MRMR
MRMR
I WAS TOLD TO BE PREPARED TO LEAVE AT ANY TIME.
WHY DON'T WE GO CHECK OUT THE MOON DORMITORY?
DURING THE DAY? WE CAN'T DO THAT.

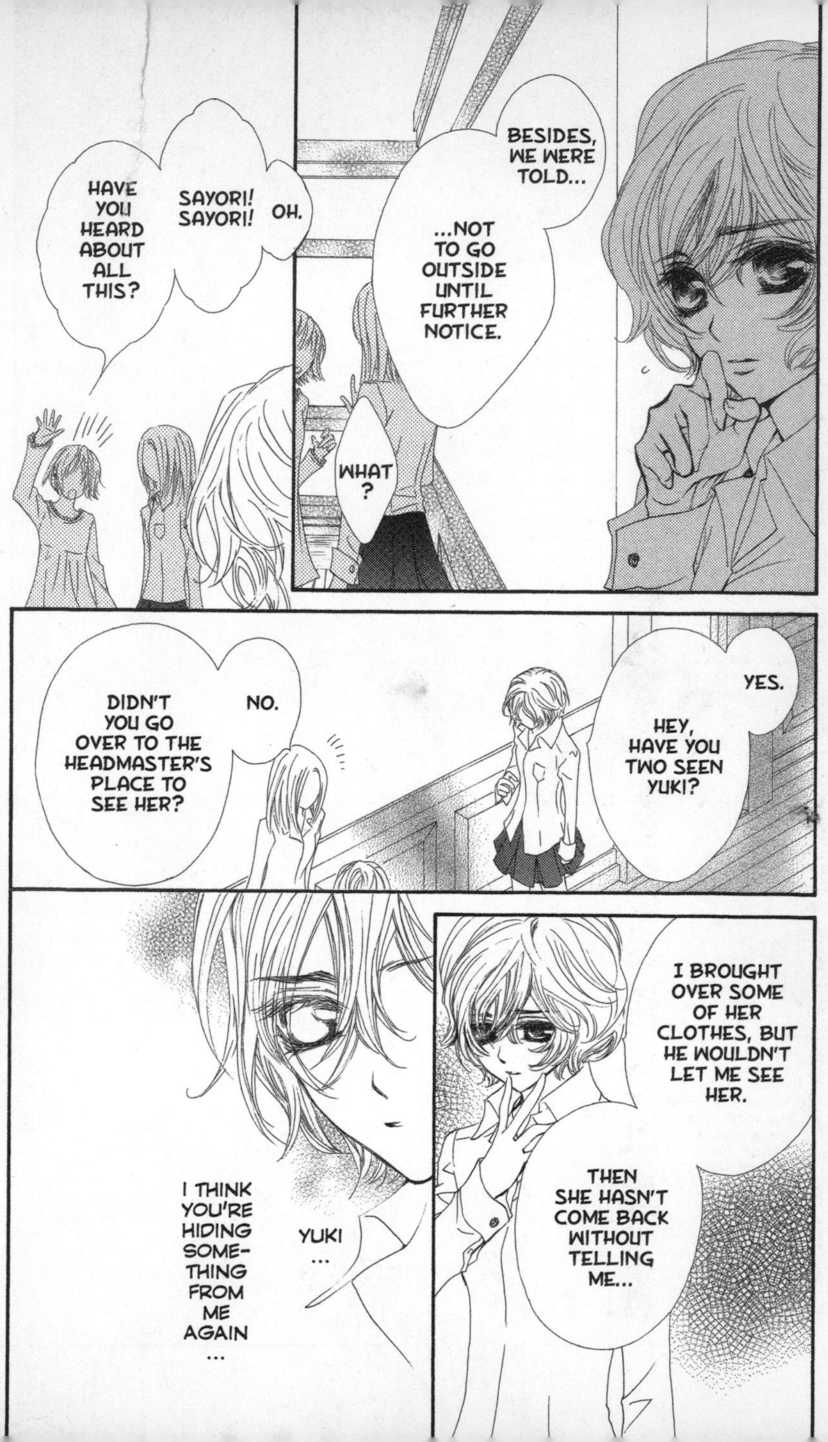
BESIDES, WE WERE TOLD...
...NOT TO GO OUTSIDE UNTIL FURTHER NOTICE.
WHAT?
OH.
SAYORI! SAYORI!
HAVE YOU HEARD ABOUT ALL THIS?
YES.
HEY, HAVE YOU TWO SEEN YUKI?
NO.
DIDN'T YOU GO OVER TO THE HEADMASTER'S PLACE TO SEE HER?
I BROUGHT OVER SOME OF HER CLOTHES, BUT HE WOULDN'T LET ME SEE HER.
THEN SHE HASN'T COME BACK WITHOUT TELLING ME...
YUKI ...
I THINK YOU'RE HIDING SOME-THING FROM ME AGAIN ...

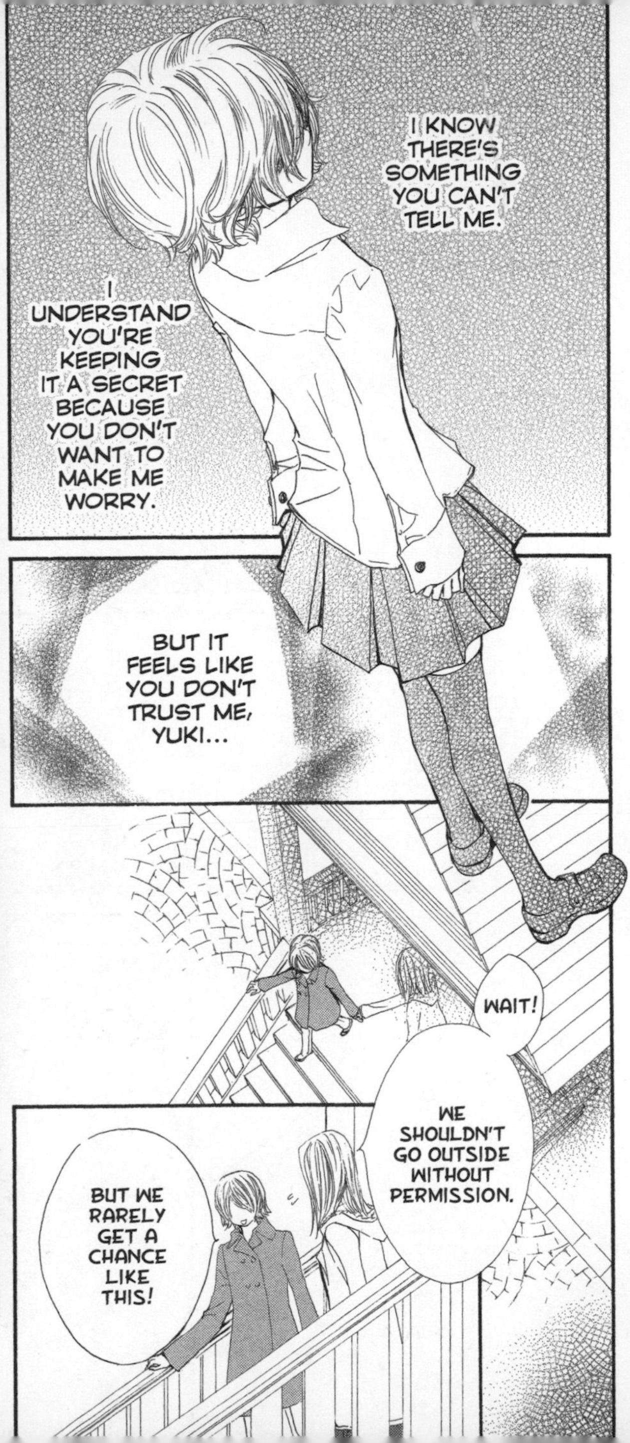
I KNOW THERE'S SOMETHING YOU CAN'T TELL ME.
I UNDERSTAND YOU'RE KEEPING IT A SECRET BECAUSE YOU DON'T WANT TO MAKE ME WORRY.
BUT IT FEELS LIKE YOU DON'T TRUST ME, YUKI...
WAIT!
WE SHOULDN'T GO OUTSIDE WITHOUT PERMISSION.
BUT WE RARELY GET A CHANCE LIKE THIS!

I

Hello! This is Matsuri Hino. Pant, wheeze... What is this feeling of achievement, like I've climbed a mountain? I remember... working on two volumes while supervising and drawing new illustrations for the novel and fan book, working on the game in between drawing my manga manuscripts... (I'm not involved with the anime anymore.) Then I've also been drawing various illustrations and helping judge the LMG (LaLa Manga Grand Prix) contest, increasing pages for the monthly chapters, and giving it my all to make seven color illustrations for covers and title pages...

It was an intense three months. But I was able to survive, thanks to my editor and everyone at *LaLa*, and thanks to lots of cooperation from the people at the printer. (It may be more accurate to say I inconvenienced them a lot)... And thanks to the support of the people around me, and all the readers cheering me on!! Thank you!!

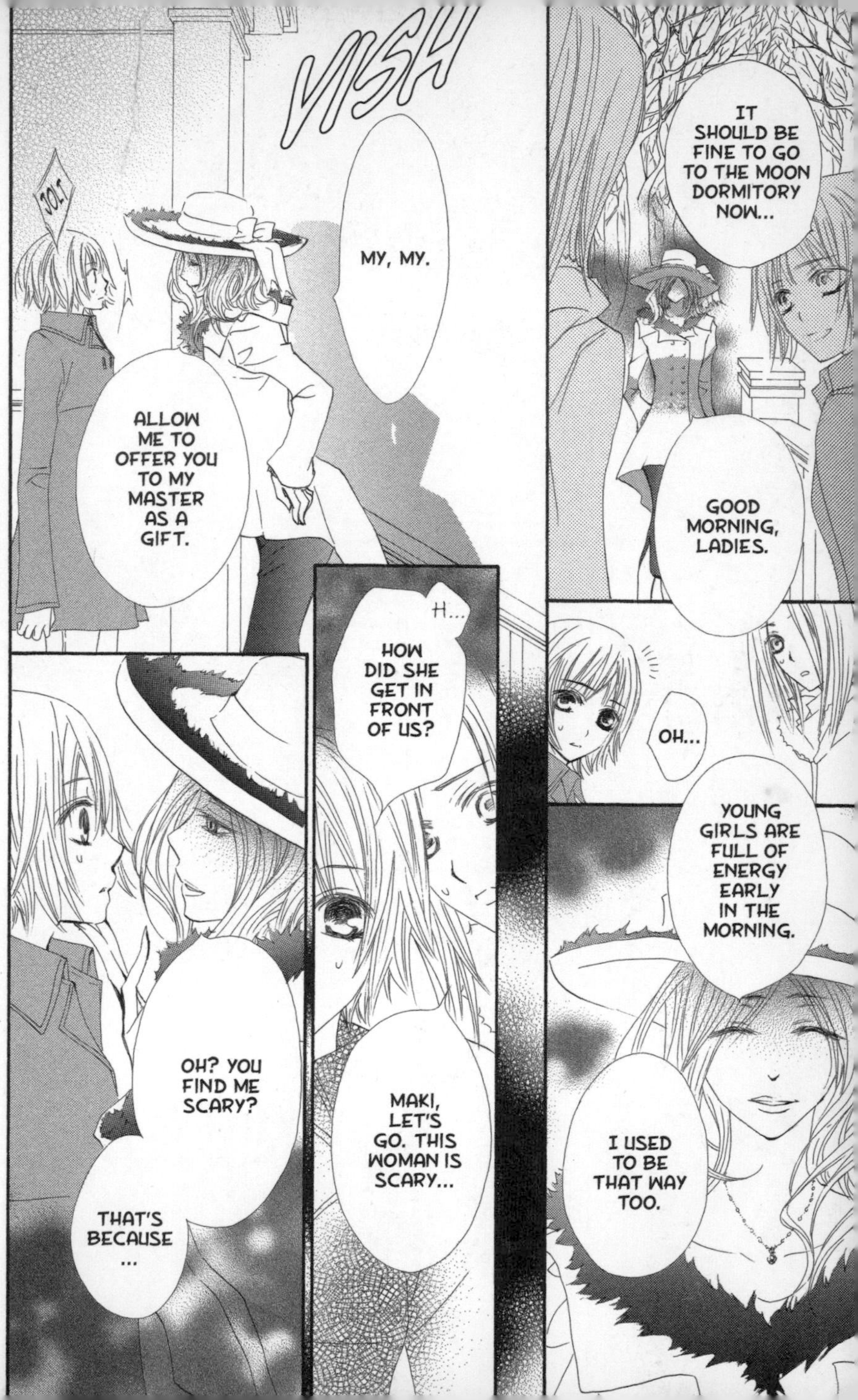

IT SHOULD BE FINE TO GO TO THE MOON DORMITORY NOW...
GOOD MORNING, LADIES.
OH...
YOUNG GIRLS ARE FULL OF ENERGY EARLY IN THE MORNING.
I USED TO BE THAT WAY TOO.
VISH
MY, MY.
JOLT
ALLOW ME TO OFFER YOU TO MY MASTER AS A GIFT.
H...
HOW DID SHE GET IN FRONT OF US?
MAKI, LET'S GO. THIS WOMAN IS SCARY...
OH? YOU FIND ME SCARY?
THAT'S BECAUSE ...

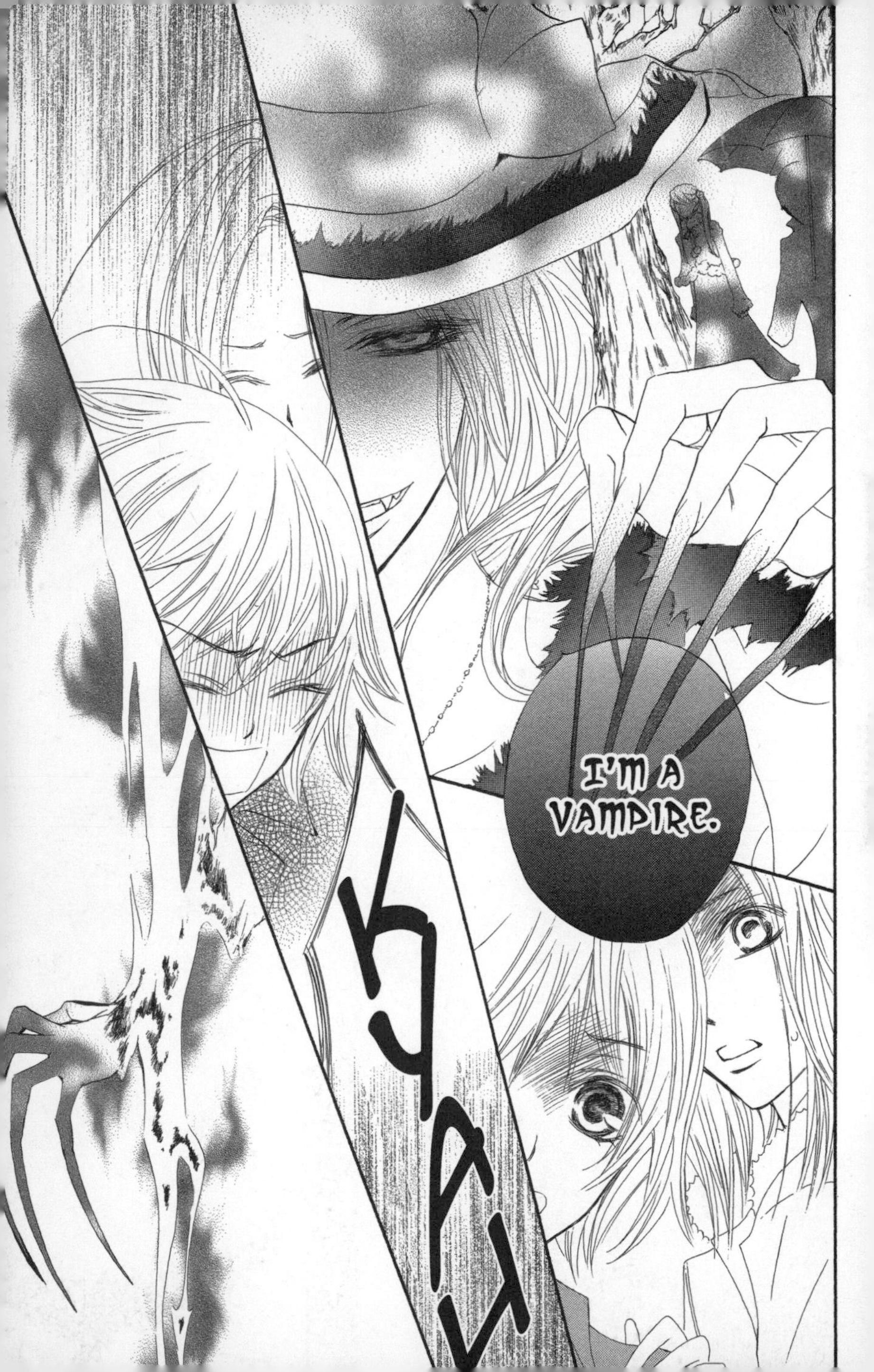
I'M A VAMPIRE.
KYAA

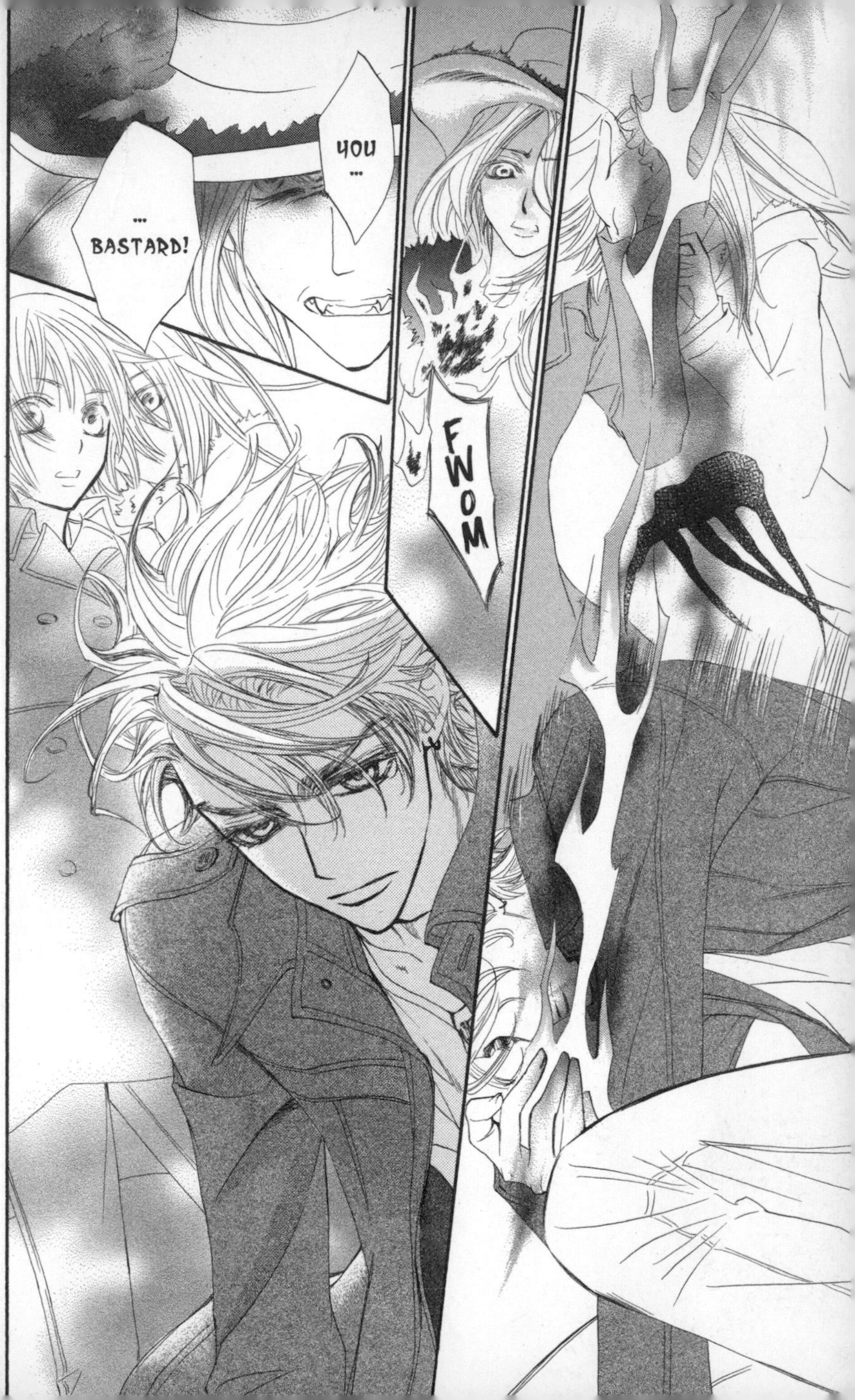
FWOM
YOU ...
... BASTARD!

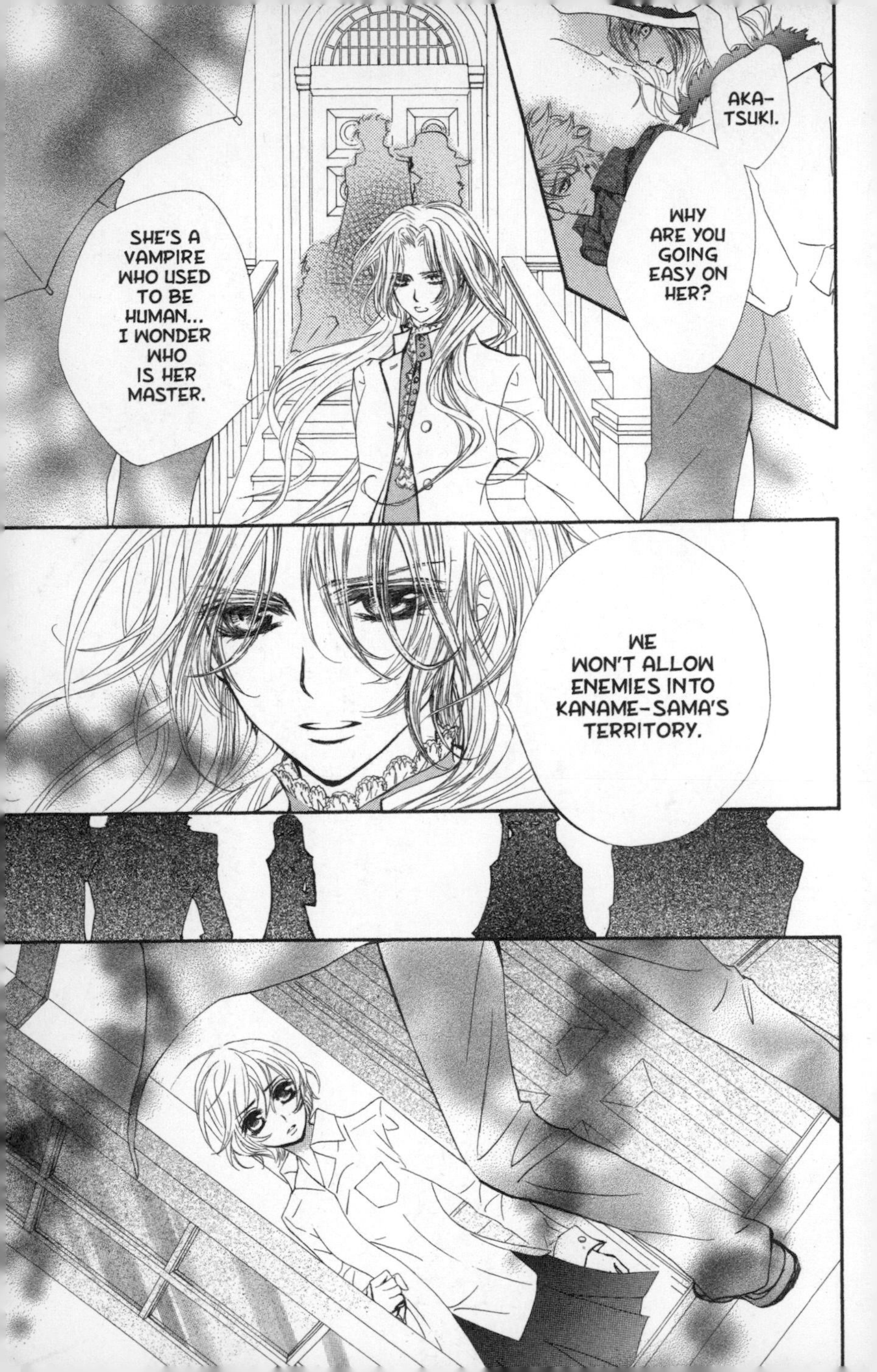
AKA-TSUKI.
WHY ARE YOU GOING EASY ON HER?
SHE'S A VAMPIRE WHO USED TO BE HUMAN... I WONDER WHO IS HER MASTER.
WE WON'T ALLOW ENEMIES INTO KANAME-SAMA'S TERRITORY.

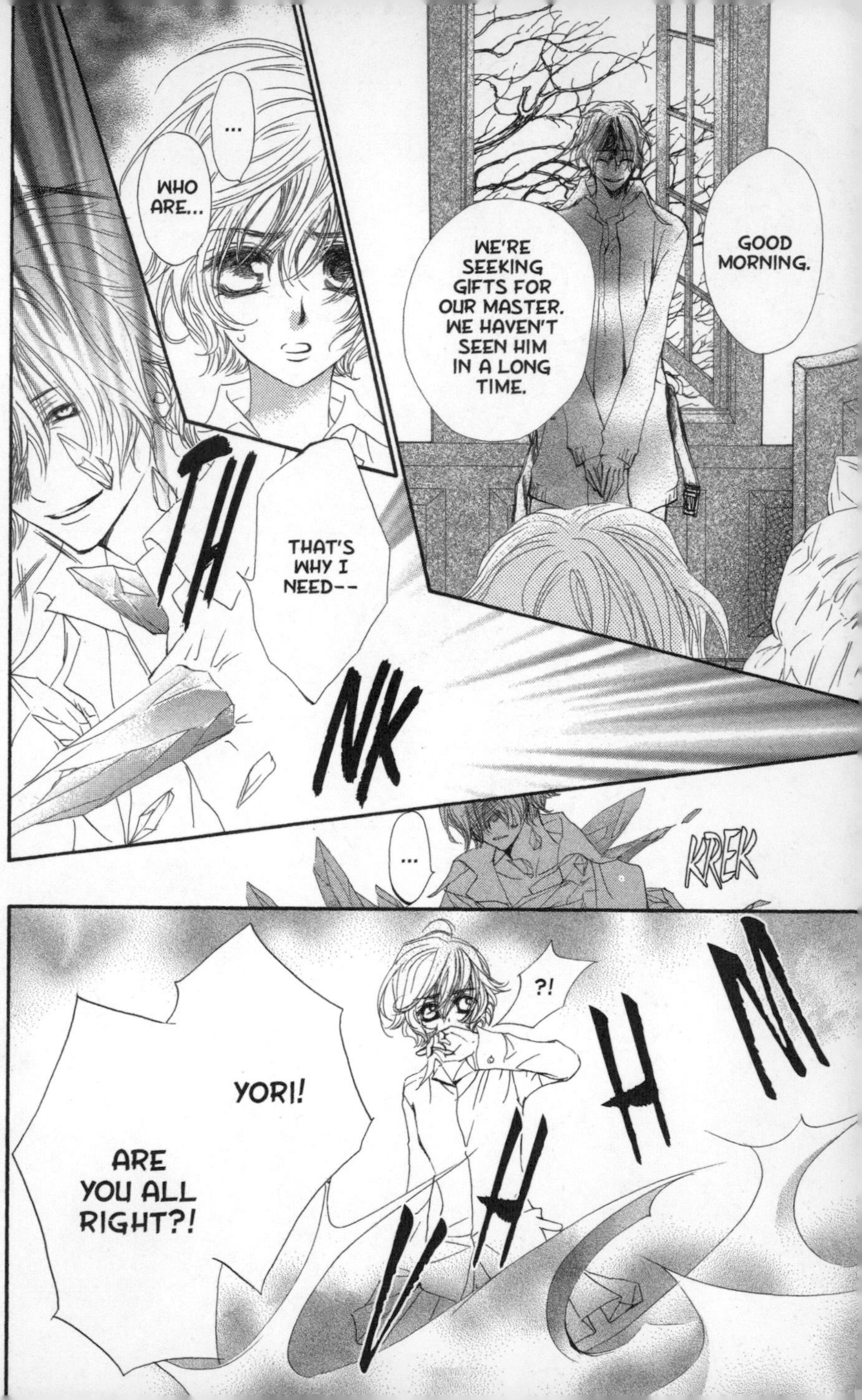
GOOD MORNING.
WE'RE SEEKING GIFTS FOR OUR MASTER. WE HAVEN'T SEEN HIM IN A LONG TIME.
...
WHO ARE...
THAT'S WHY I NEED--
THNK
KREK
...
?!
YORI!
ARE YOU ALL RIGHT?!
WHHM

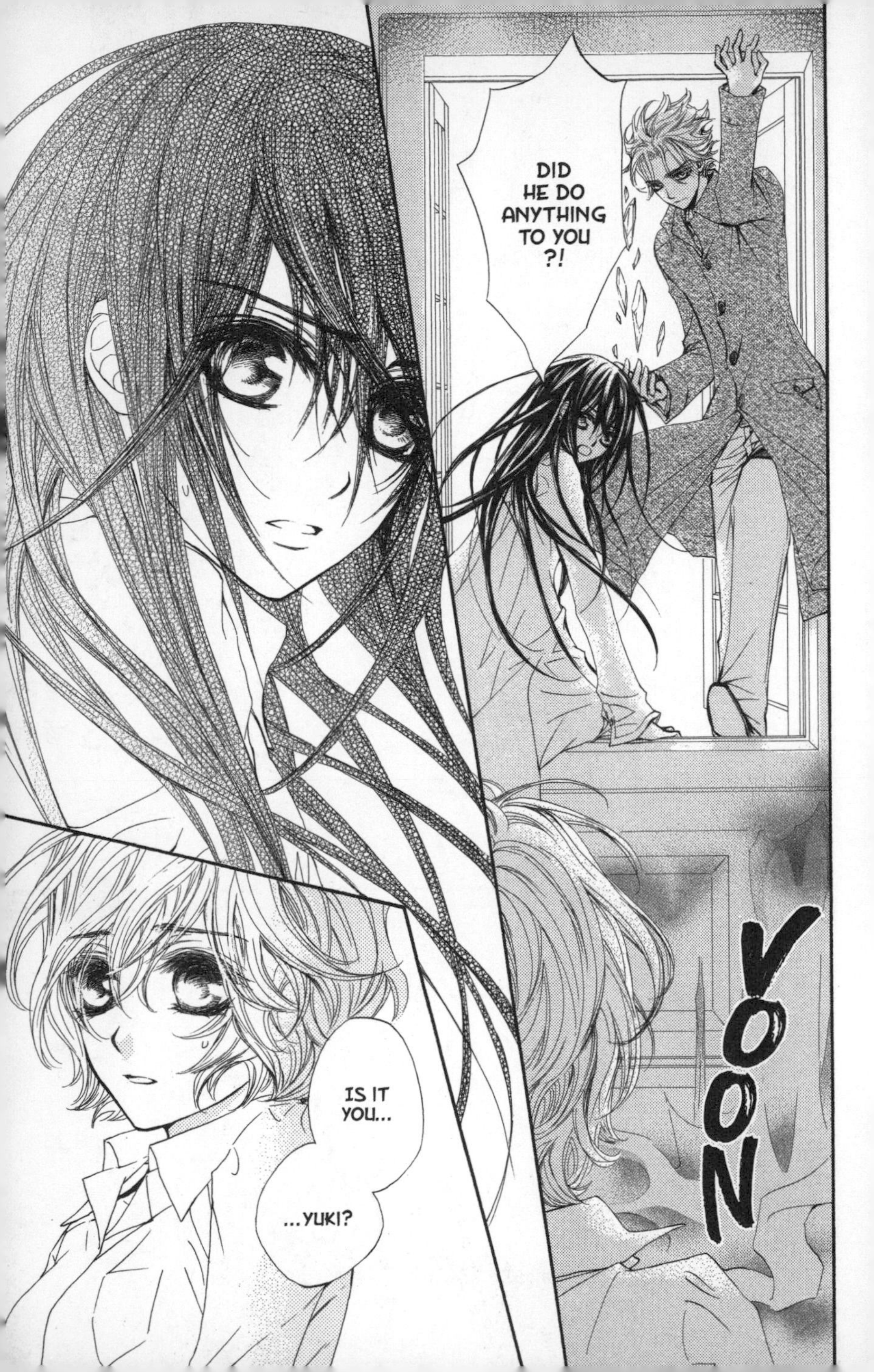
DID HE DO ANYTHING TO YOU ?!
VOON
IS IT YOU...
...YUKI?

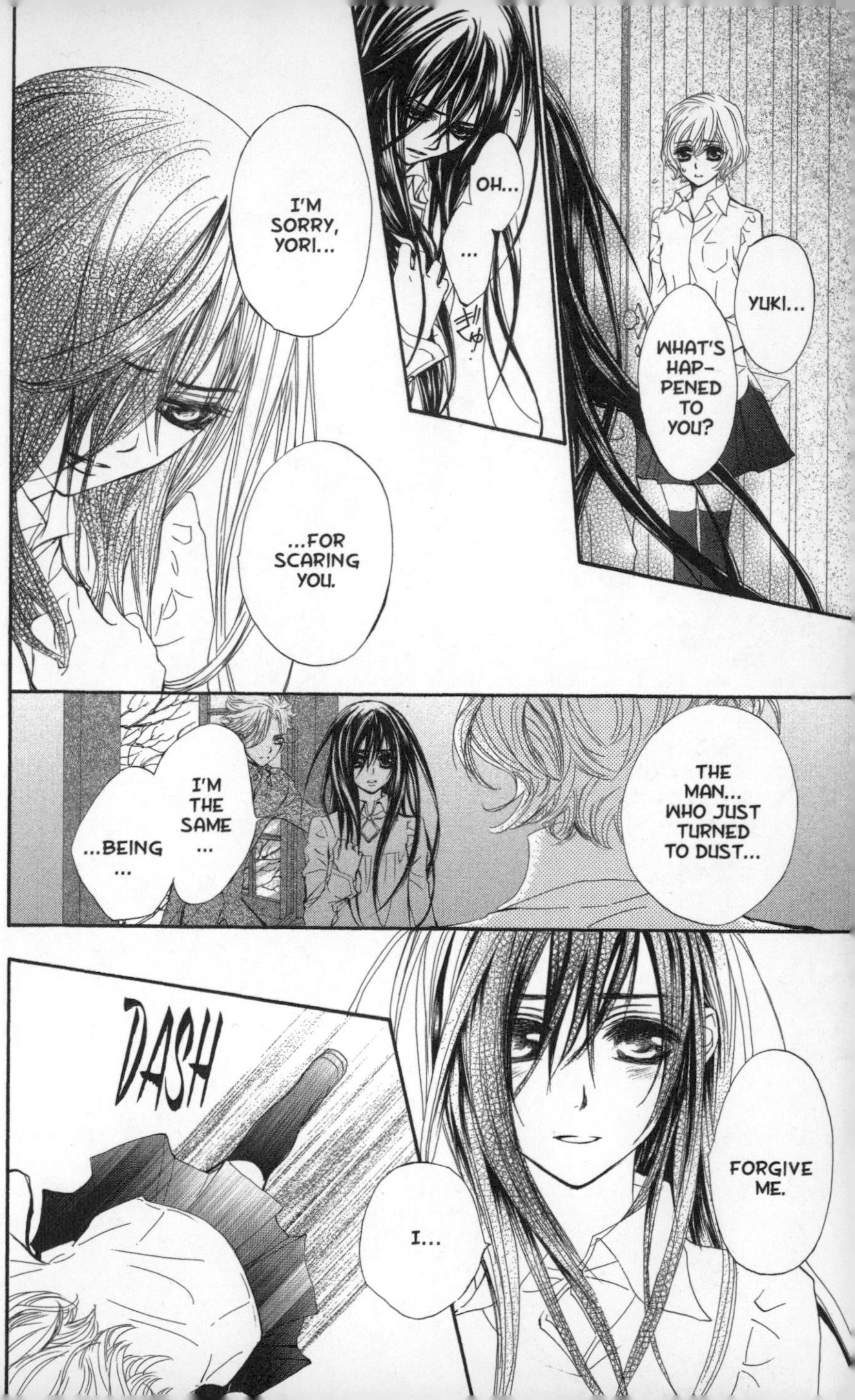
YUKI...
WHAT'S HAP-PENED TO YOU?
OH...
...
I'M SORRY, YORI...
...FOR SCARING YOU.
THE MAN... WHO JUST TURNED TO DUST...
I'M THE SAME ...
...BEING ...
FORGIVE ME.
I...
DASH

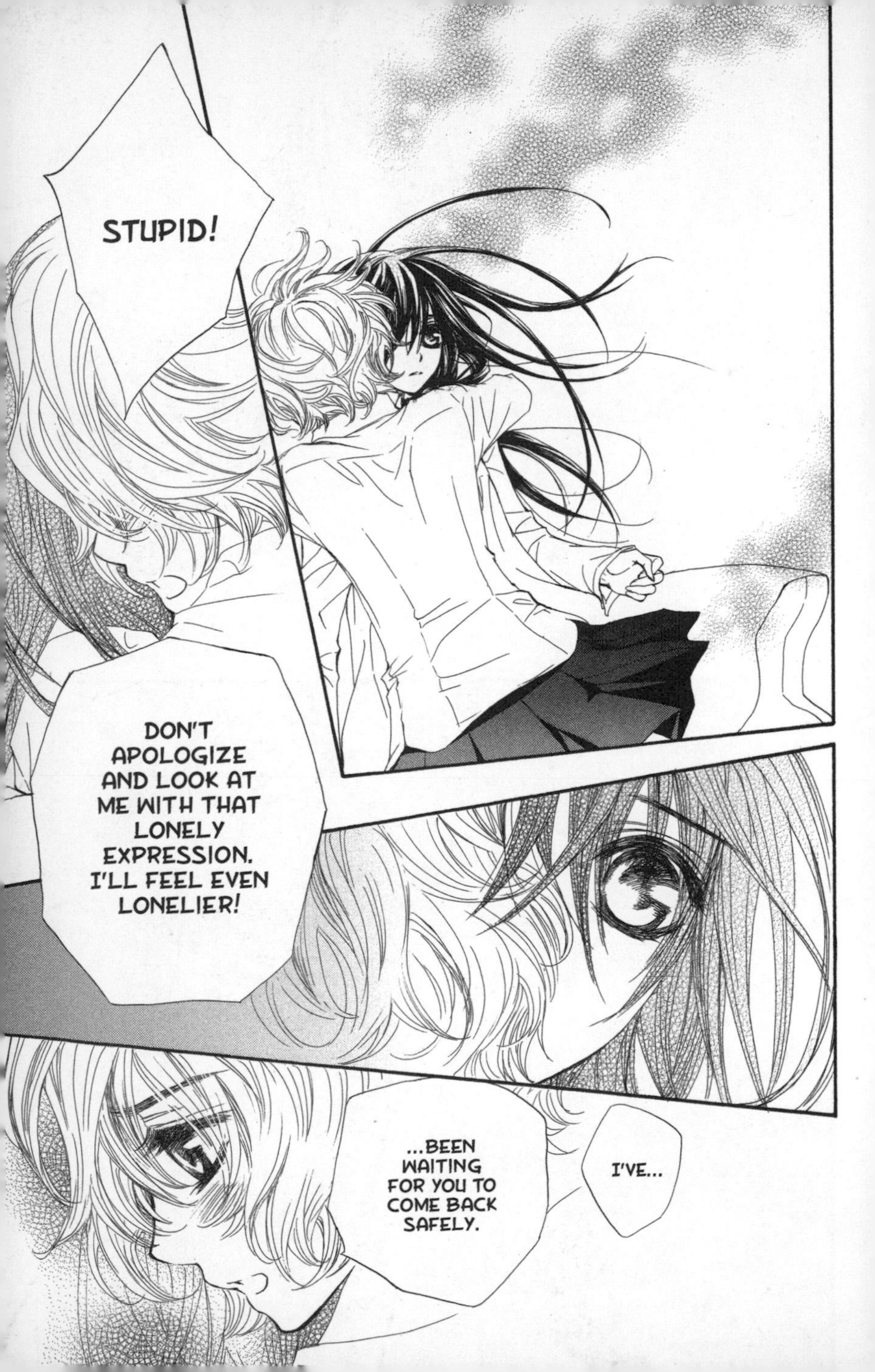
STUPID!
DON'T APOLOGIZE AND LOOK AT ME WITH THAT LONELY EXPRESSION. I'LL FEEL EVEN LONELIER!
I'VE...
...BEEN WAITING FOR YOU TO COME BACK SAFELY.

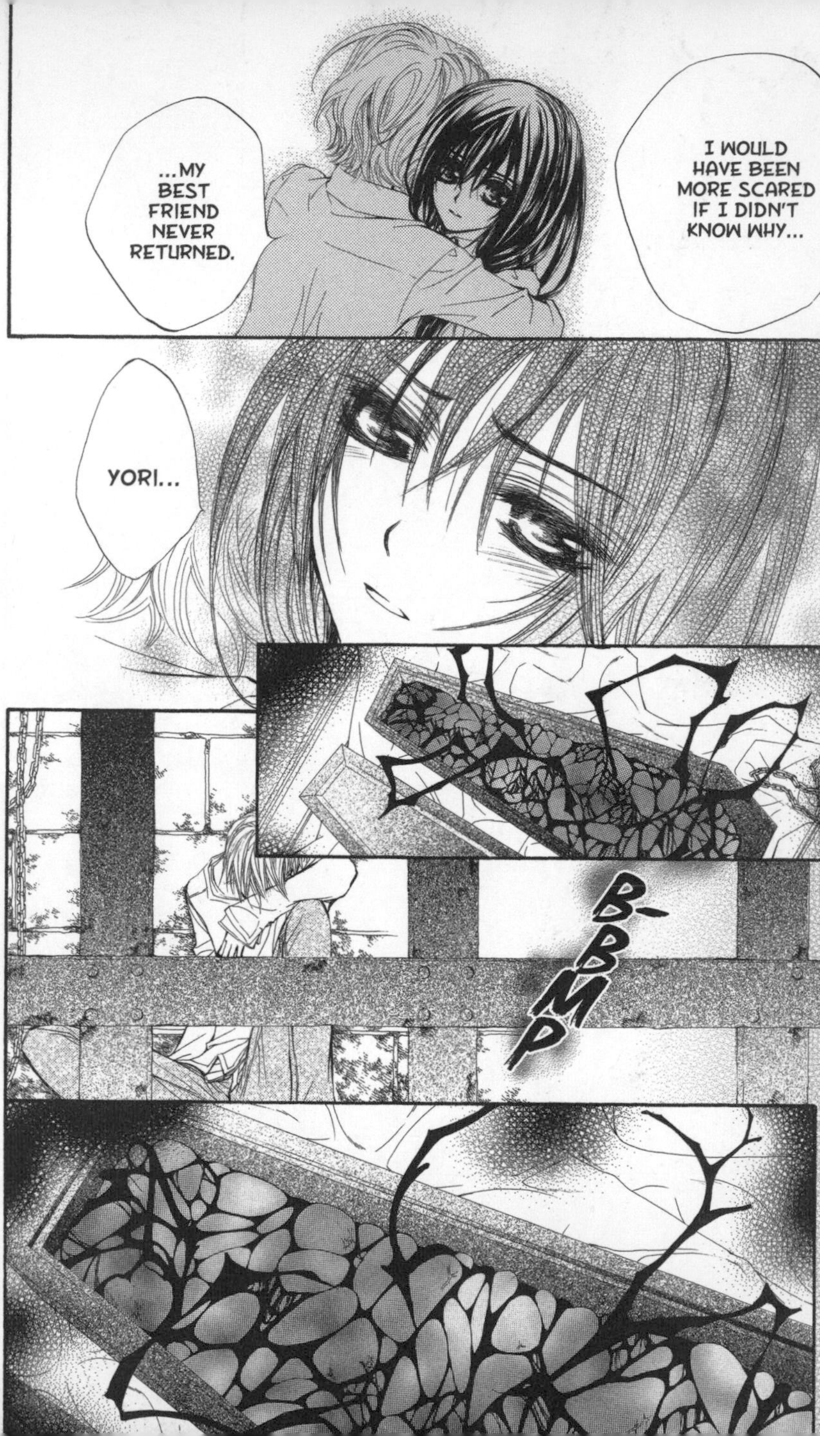
I WOULD HAVE BEEN MORE SCARED IF I DIDN'T KNOW WHY...
...MY BEST FRIEND NEVER RETURNED.
YORI...
B-BMP

B-
BBMP

RIDO-
SAMA...

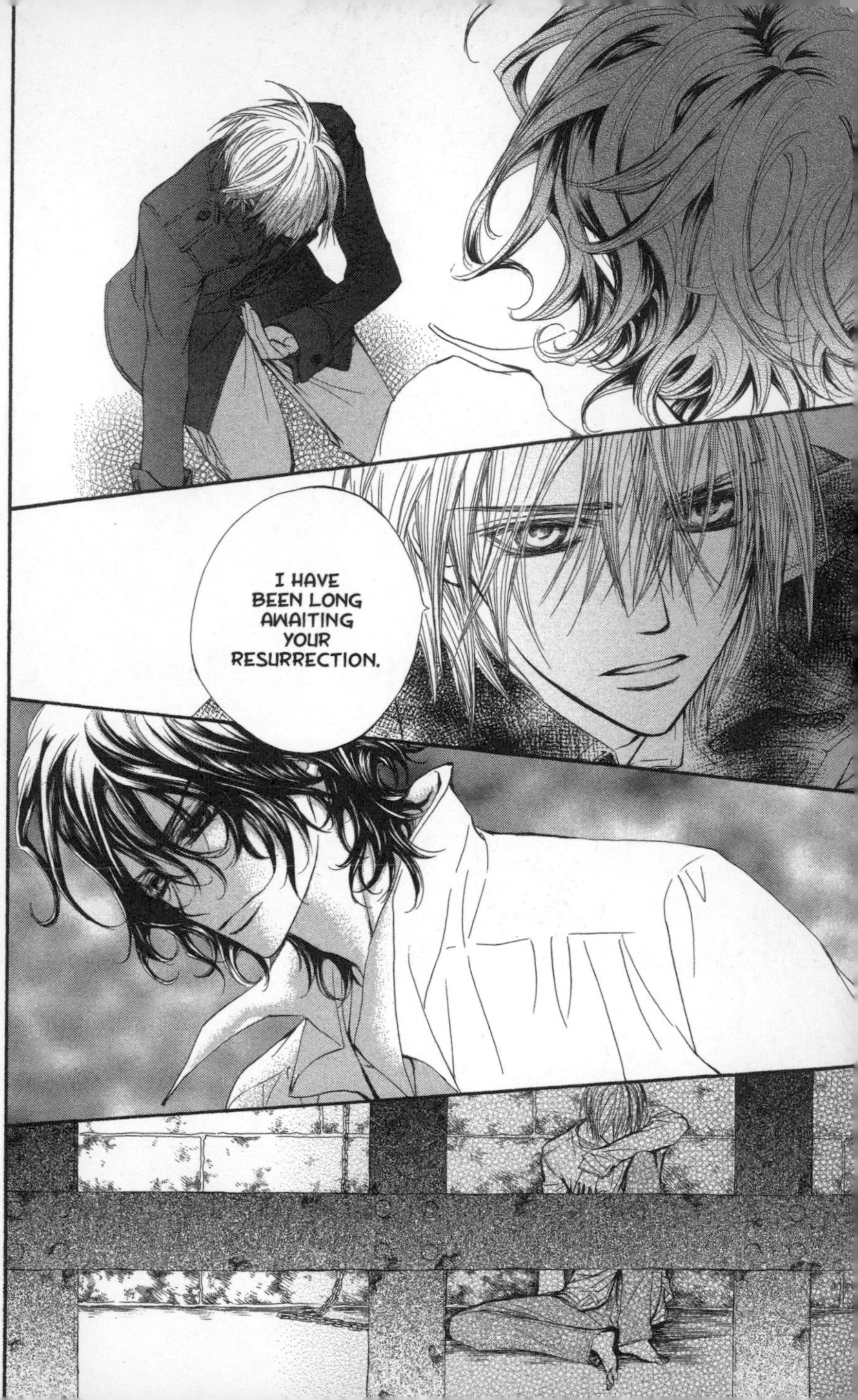
I HAVE BEEN LONG AWAITING YOUR RESURRECTION.

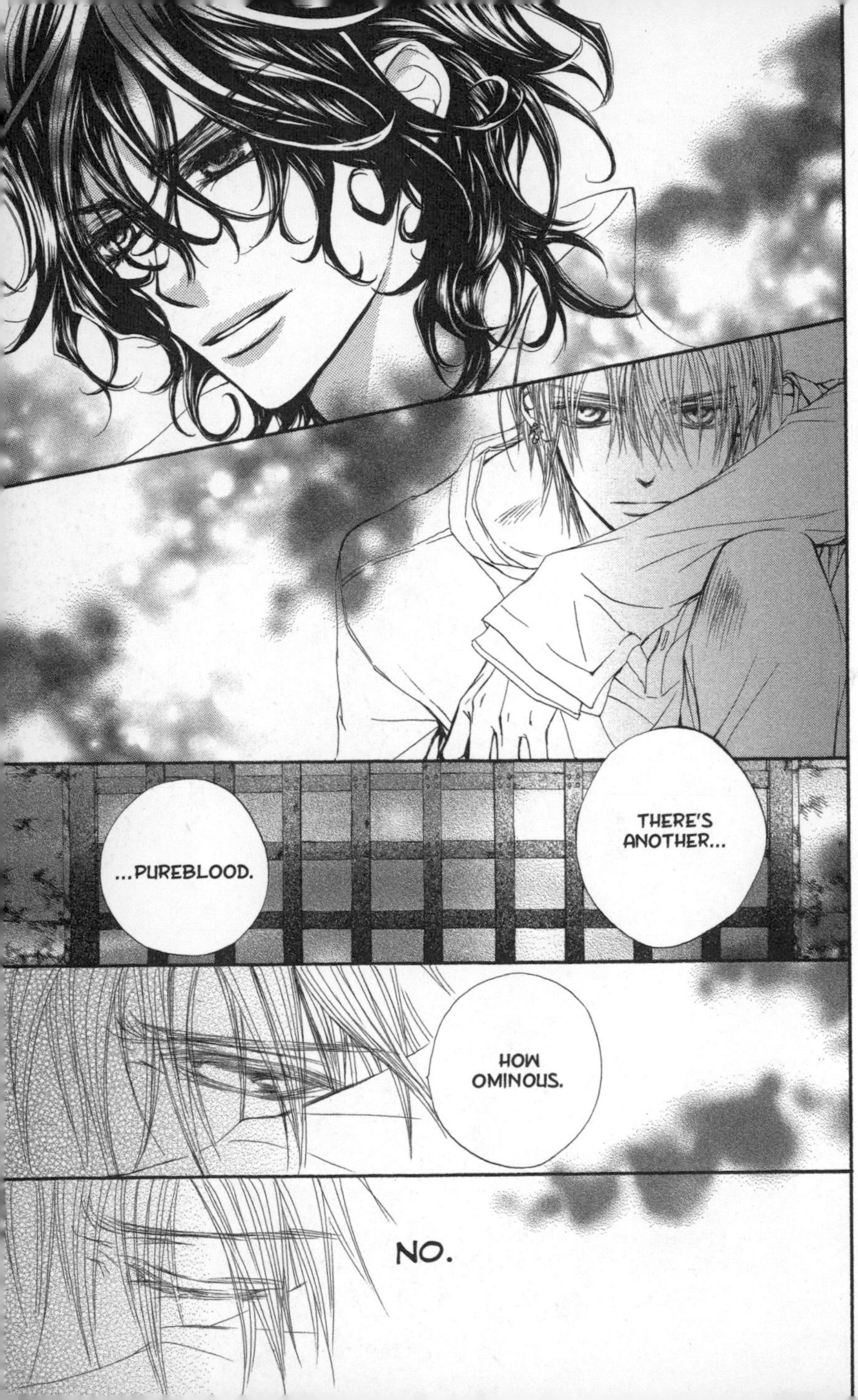
THERE'S ANOTHER...
...PUREBLOOD.
HOW OMINOUS.
NO.

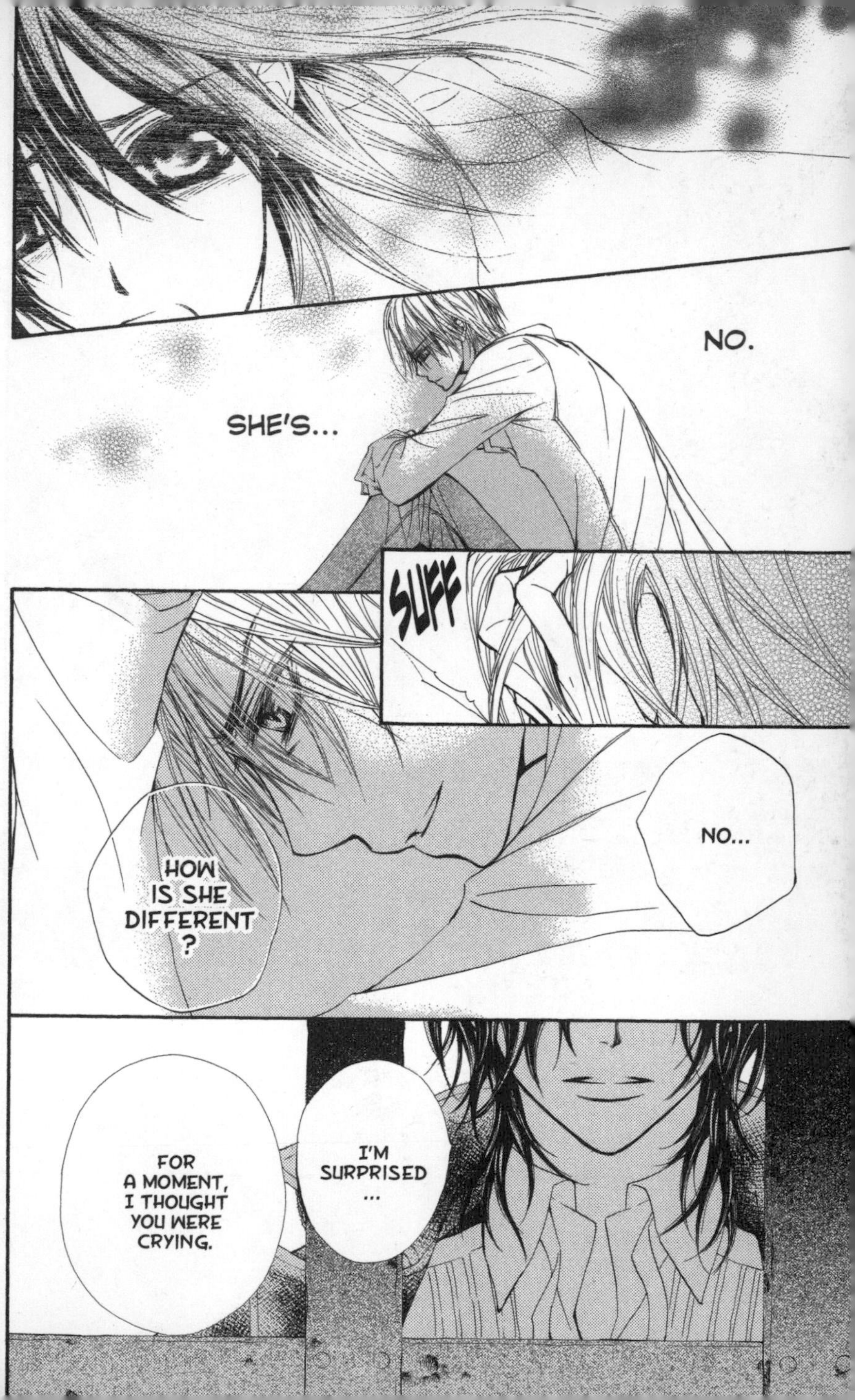
NO.
SHE'S...
SUFF
NO...
HOW IS SHE DIFFERENT?
I'M SURPRISED...
FOR A MOMENT, I THOUGHT YOU WERE CRYING.

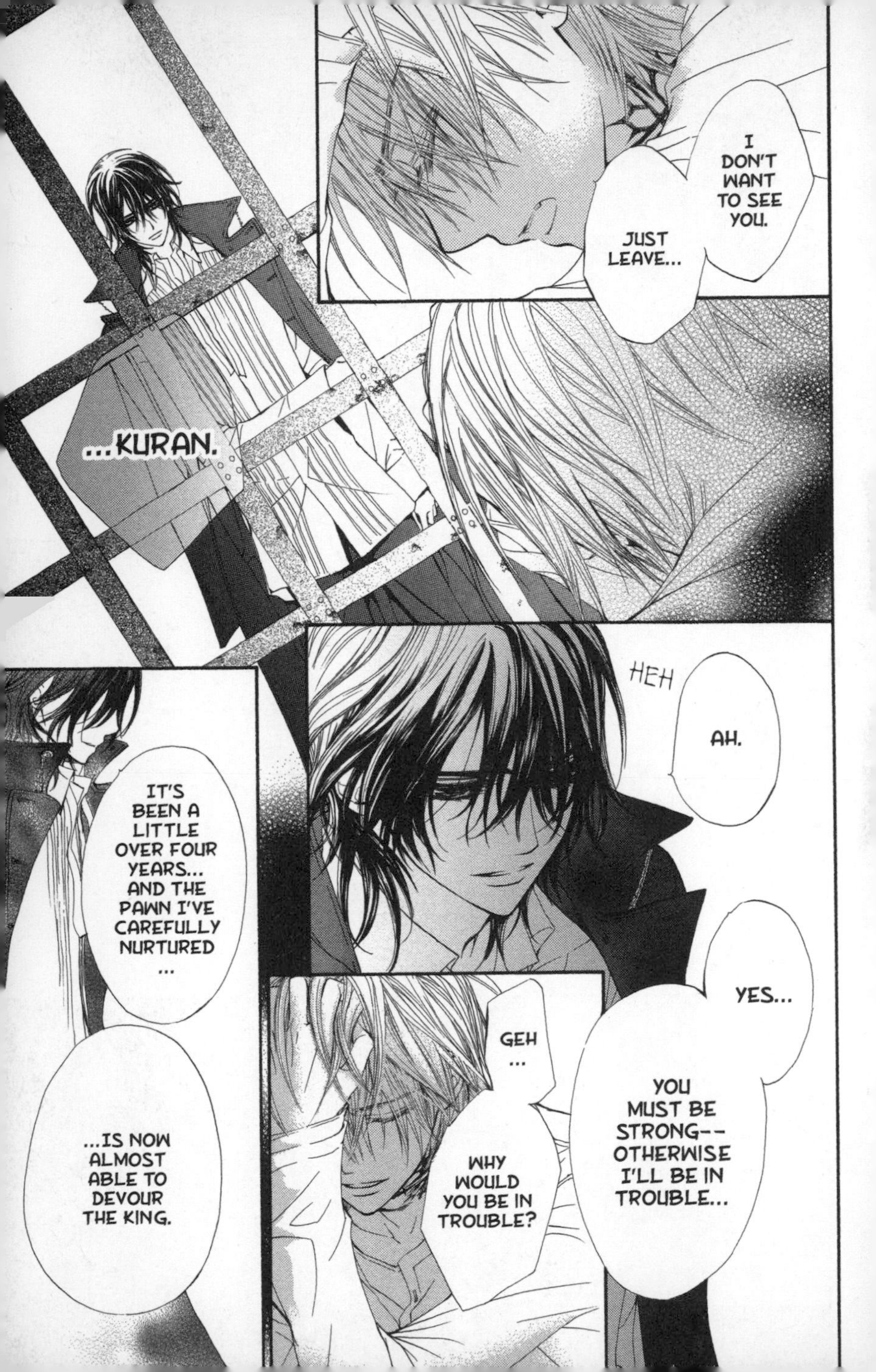
I DON'T WANT TO SEE YOU.
JUST LEAVE...
...KURAN.
HEH
AH.
YES...
YOU MUST BE STRONG-- OTHERWISE I'LL BE IN TROUBLE...
GEH ...
WHY WOULD YOU BE IN TROUBLE?
IT'S BEEN A LITTLE OVER FOUR YEARS... AND THE PAWN I'VE CAREFULLY NURTURED ...
...IS NOW ALMOST ABLE TO DEVOUR THE KING.

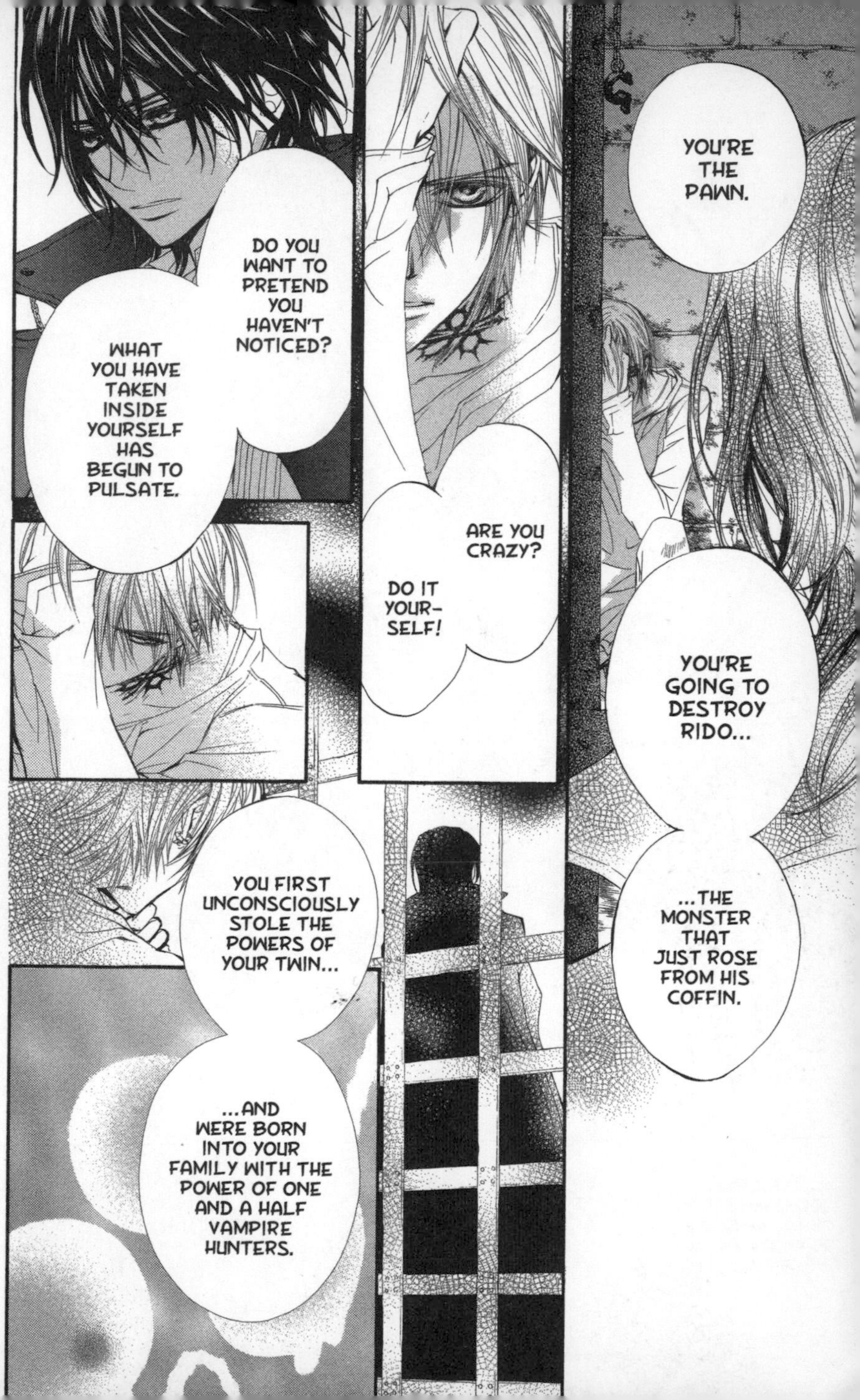
YOU'RE THE PAWN.
YOU'RE GOING TO DESTROY RIDO...
...THE MONSTER THAT JUST ROSE FROM HIS COFFIN.
ARE YOU CRAZY?
DO IT YOUR-SELF!
DO YOU WANT TO PRETEND YOU HAVEN'T NOTICED?
WHAT YOU HAVE TAKEN INSIDE YOURSELF HAS BEGUN TO PULSATE.
YOU FIRST UNCONSCIOUSLY STOLE THE POWERS OF YOUR TWIN...
...AND WERE BORN INTO YOUR FAMILY WITH THE POWER OF ONE AND A HALF VAMPIRE HUNTERS.

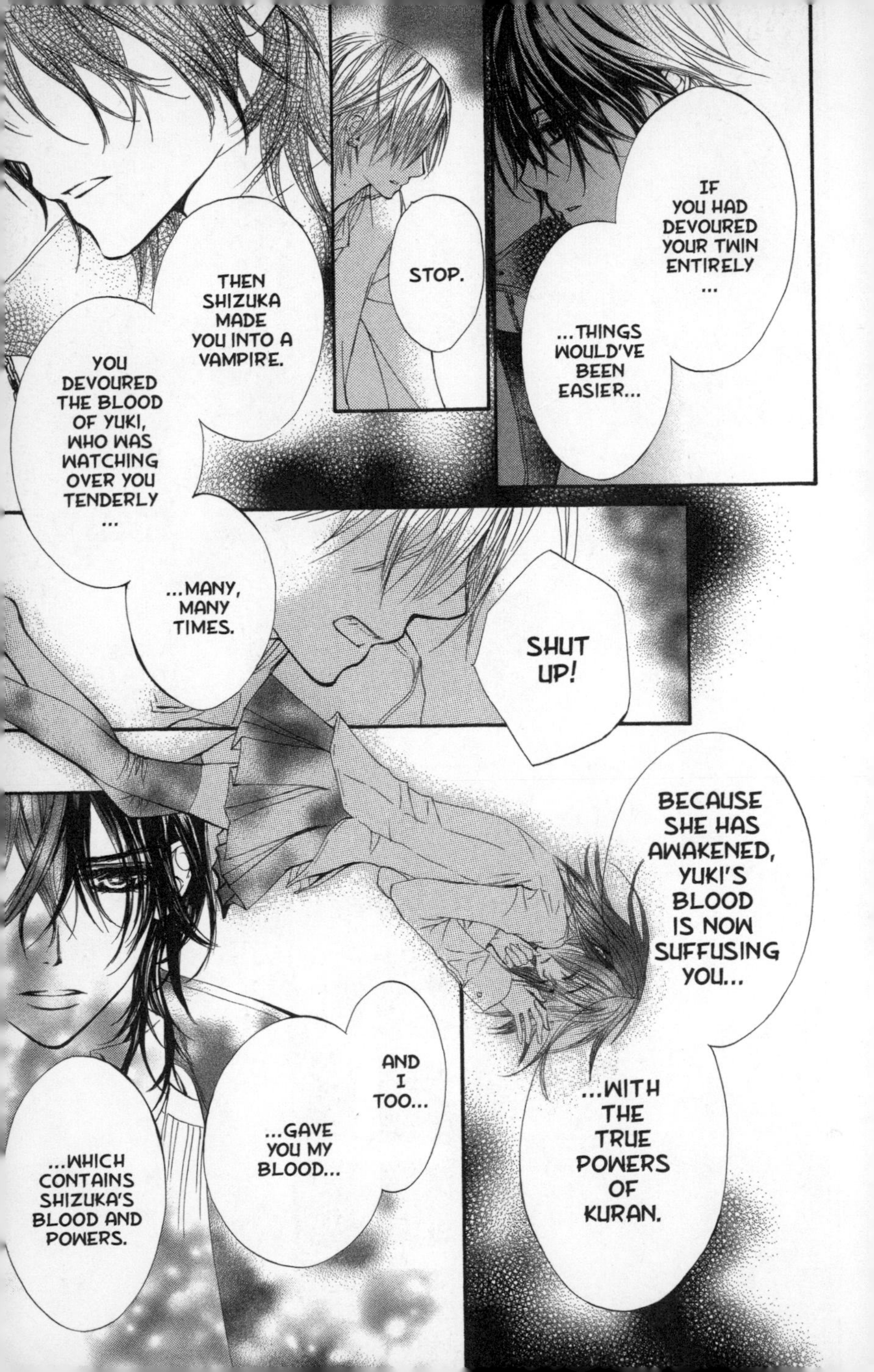
IF YOU HAD DEVOURED YOUR TWIN ENTIRELY ...
...THINGS WOULD'VE BEEN EASIER...
STOP.
THEN SHIZUKA MADE YOU INTO A VAMPIRE.
YOU DEVOURED THE BLOOD OF YUKI, WHO WAS WATCHING OVER YOU TENDERLY ...
...MANY, MANY TIMES.
SHUT UP!
BECAUSE SHE HAS AWAKENED, YUKI'S BLOOD IS NOW SUFFUSING YOU...
...WITH THE TRUE POWERS OF KURAN.
AND I TOO...
...GAVE YOU MY BLOOD...
...WHICH CONTAINS SHIZUKA'S BLOOD AND POWERS.

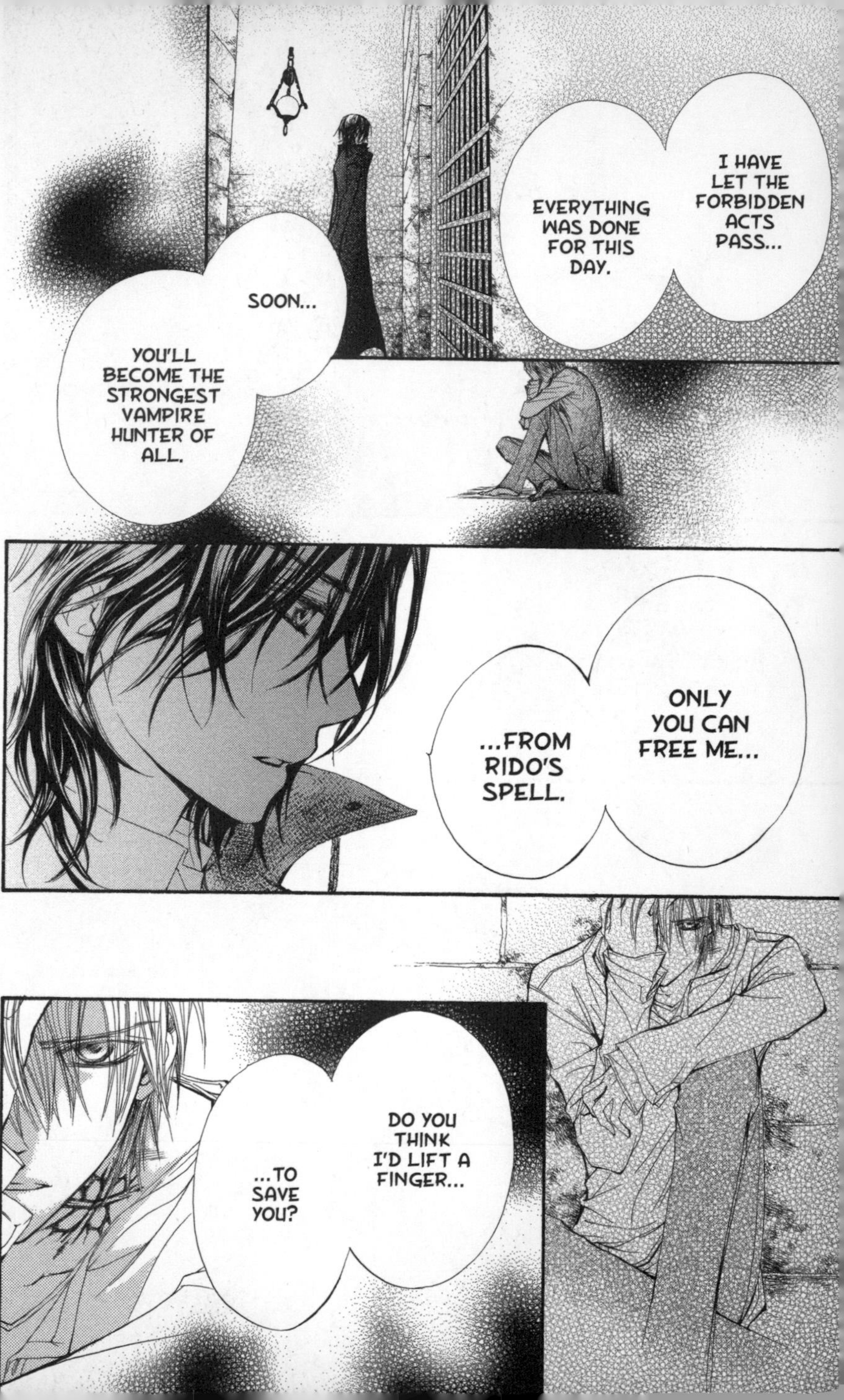
I HAVE LET THE FORBIDDEN ACTS PASS...
EVERYTHING WAS DONE FOR THIS DAY.
SOON...
YOU'LL BECOME THE STRONGEST VAMPIRE HUNTER OF ALL.
ONLY YOU CAN FREE ME...
...FROM RIDO'S SPELL.
DO YOU THINK I'D LIFT A FINGER...
...TO SAVE YOU?

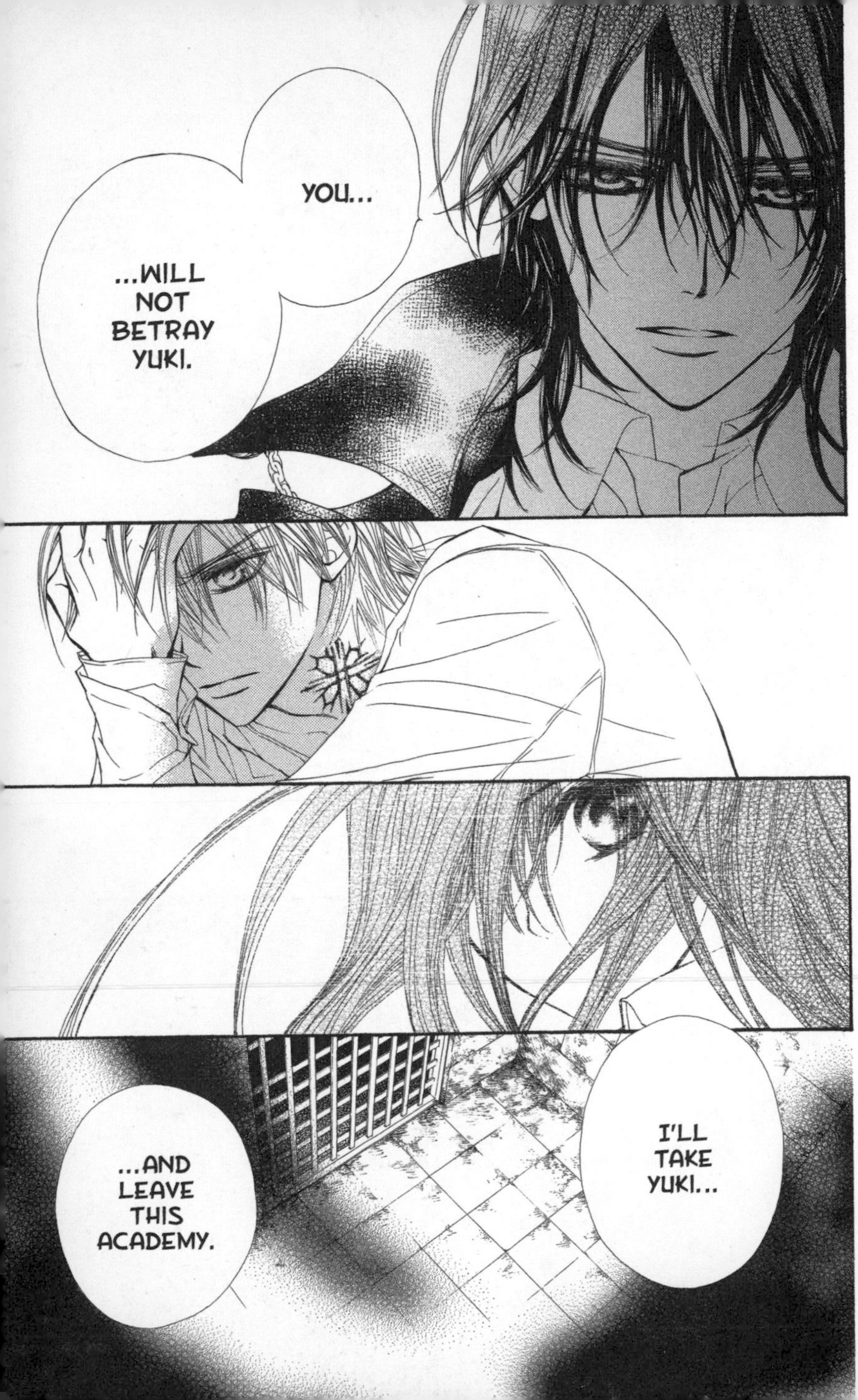
YOU...
...WILL NOT BETRAY YUKI.
I'LL TAKE YUKI...
...AND LEAVE THIS ACADEMY.

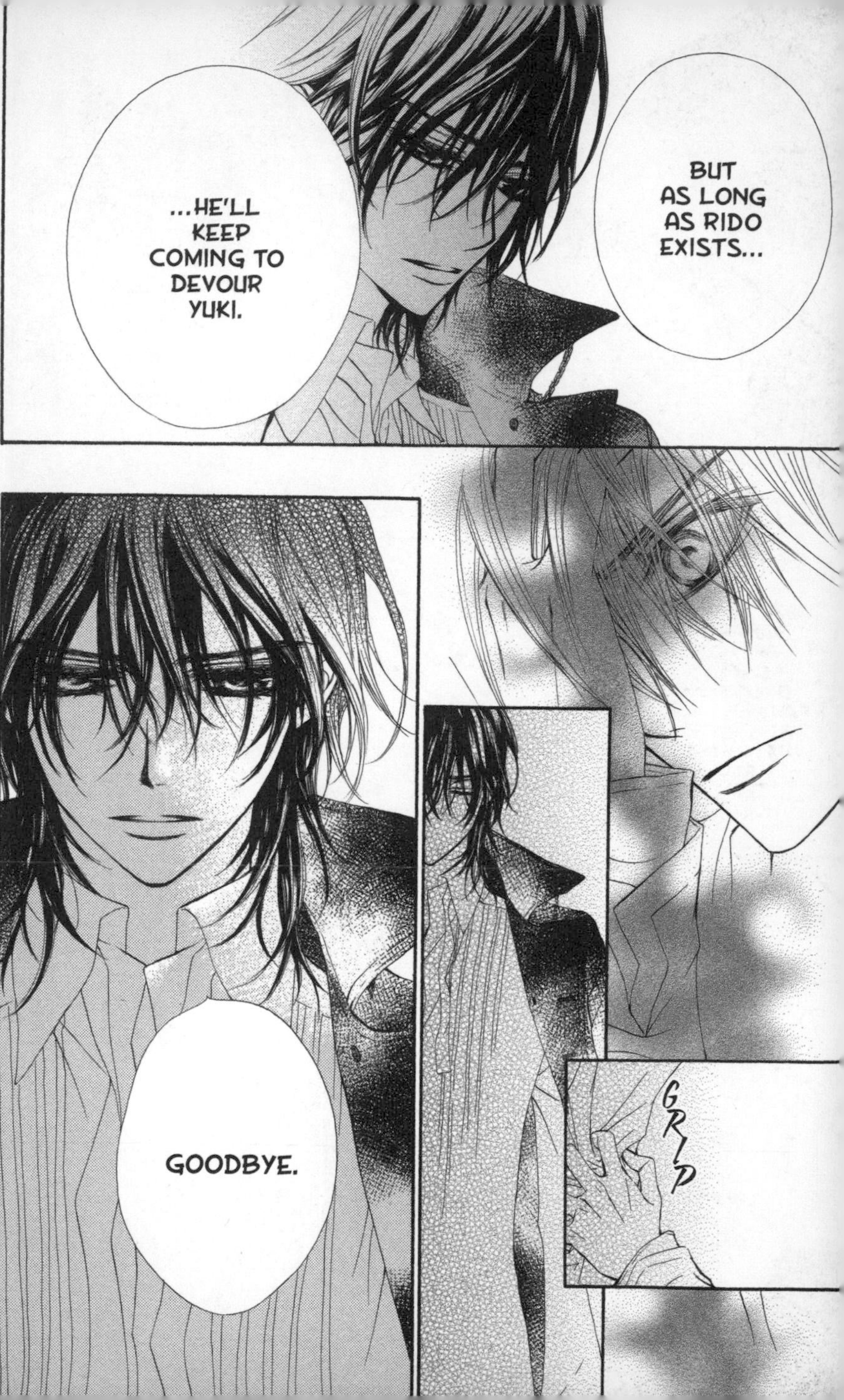
BUT AS LONG AS RIDO EXISTS...
...HE'LL KEEP COMING TO DEVOUR YUKI.
GRIP
GOODBYE.

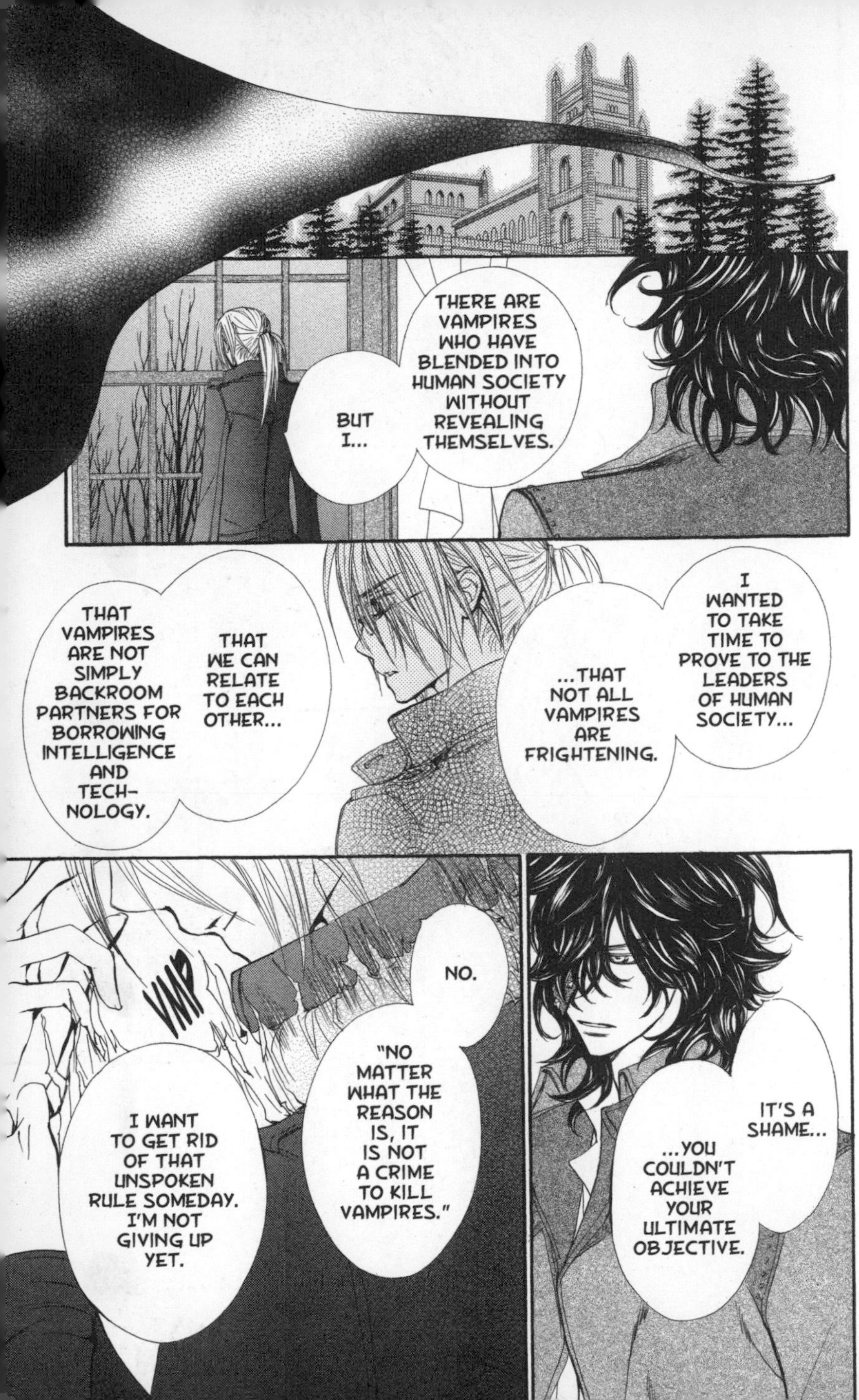
THERE ARE VAMPIRES WHO HAVE BLENDED INTO HUMAN SOCIETY WITHOUT REVEALING THEMSELVES.
BUT I...
I WANTED TO TAKE TIME TO PROVE TO THE LEADERS OF HUMAN SOCIETY...
...THAT NOT ALL VAMPIRES ARE FRIGHTENING.
THAT WE CAN RELATE TO EACH OTHER...
THAT VAMPIRES ARE NOT SIMPLY BACKROOM PARTNERS FOR BORROWING INTELLIGENCE AND TECH-NOLOGY.
IT'S A SHAME...
...YOU COULDN'T ACHIEVE YOUR ULTIMATE OBJECTIVE.
NO.
VMP
"NO MATTER WHAT THE REASON IS, IT IS NOT A CRIME TO KILL VAMPIRES."
I WANT TO GET RID OF THAT UNSPOKEN RULE SOMEDAY. I'M NOT GIVING UP YET.

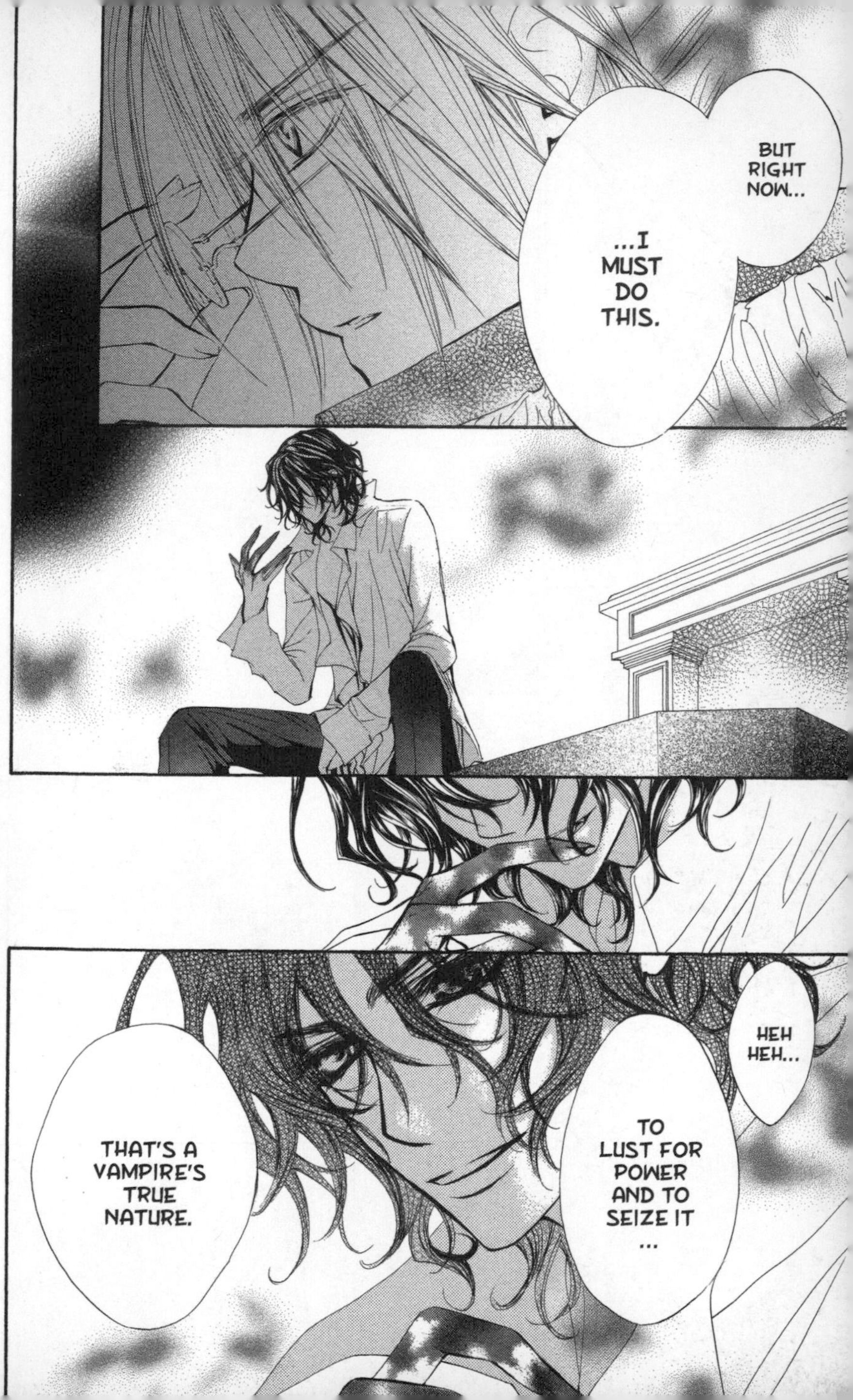
BUT RIGHT NOW...
...I MUST DO THIS.
HEH HEH...
TO LUST FOR POWER AND TO SEIZE IT ...
THAT'S A VAMPIRE'S TRUE NATURE.

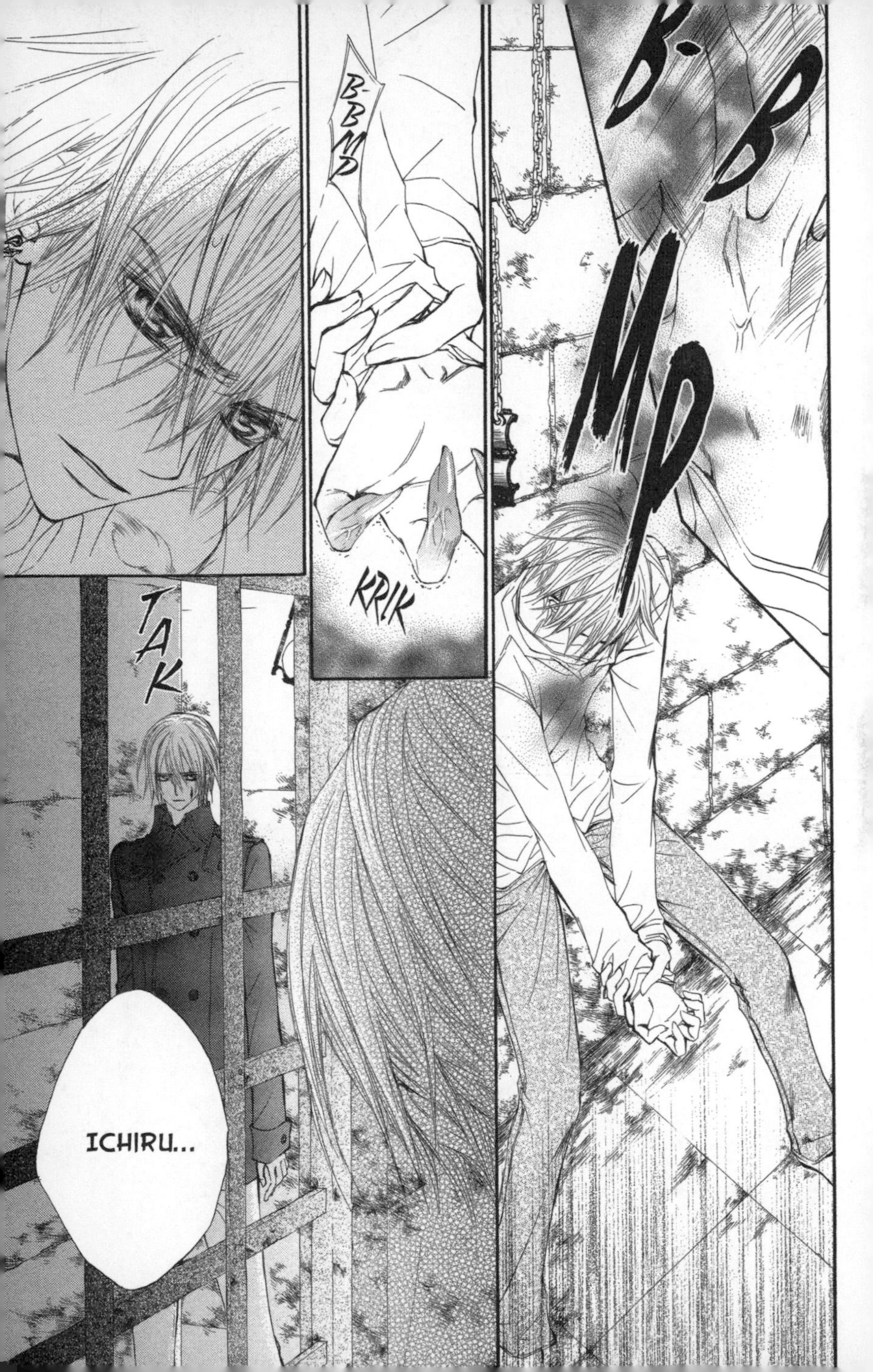
B-BMP
B-BBMP
KRIK
TAK
ICHIRU...

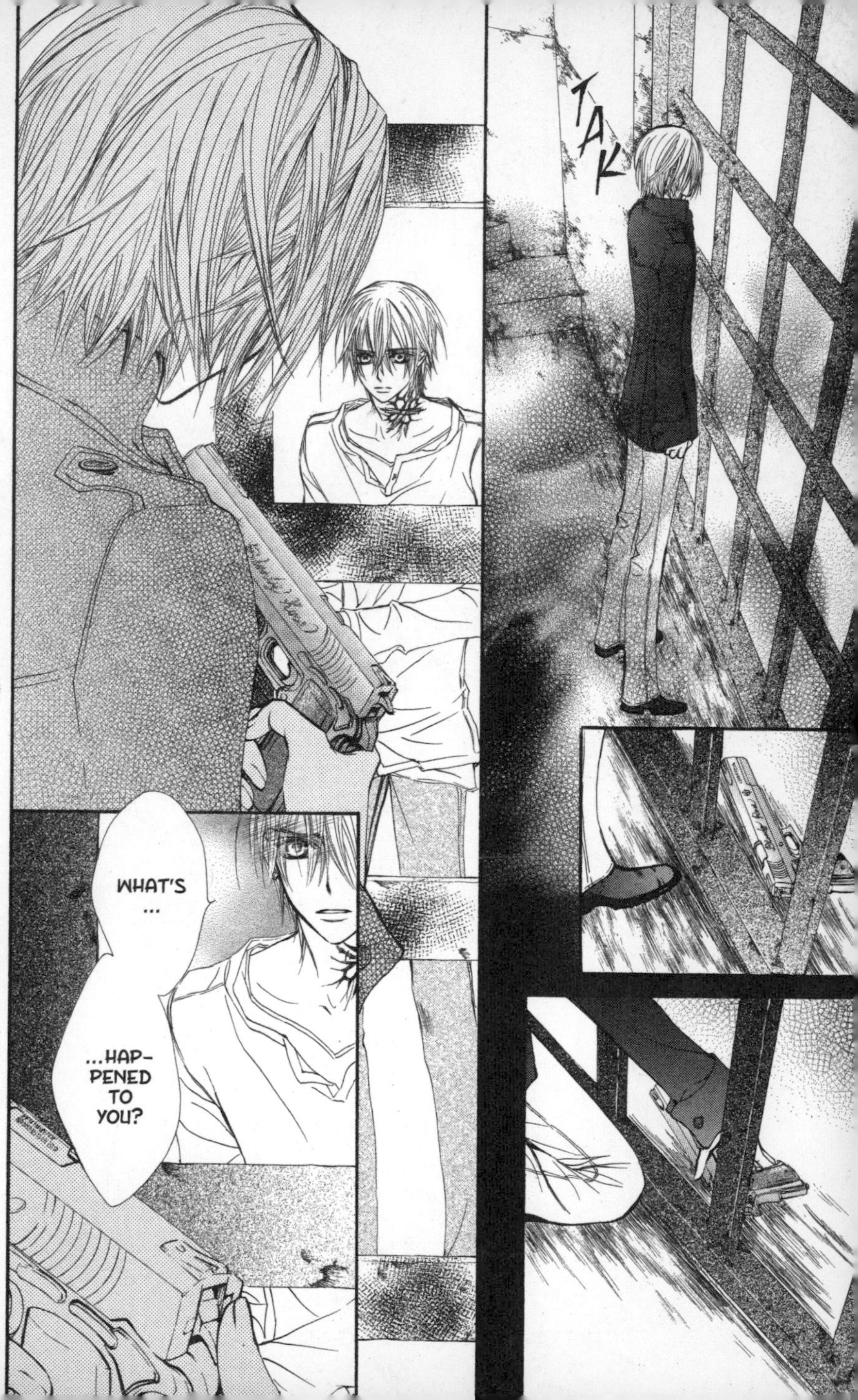
TAK
WHAT'S ...
...HAP-PENED TO YOU?

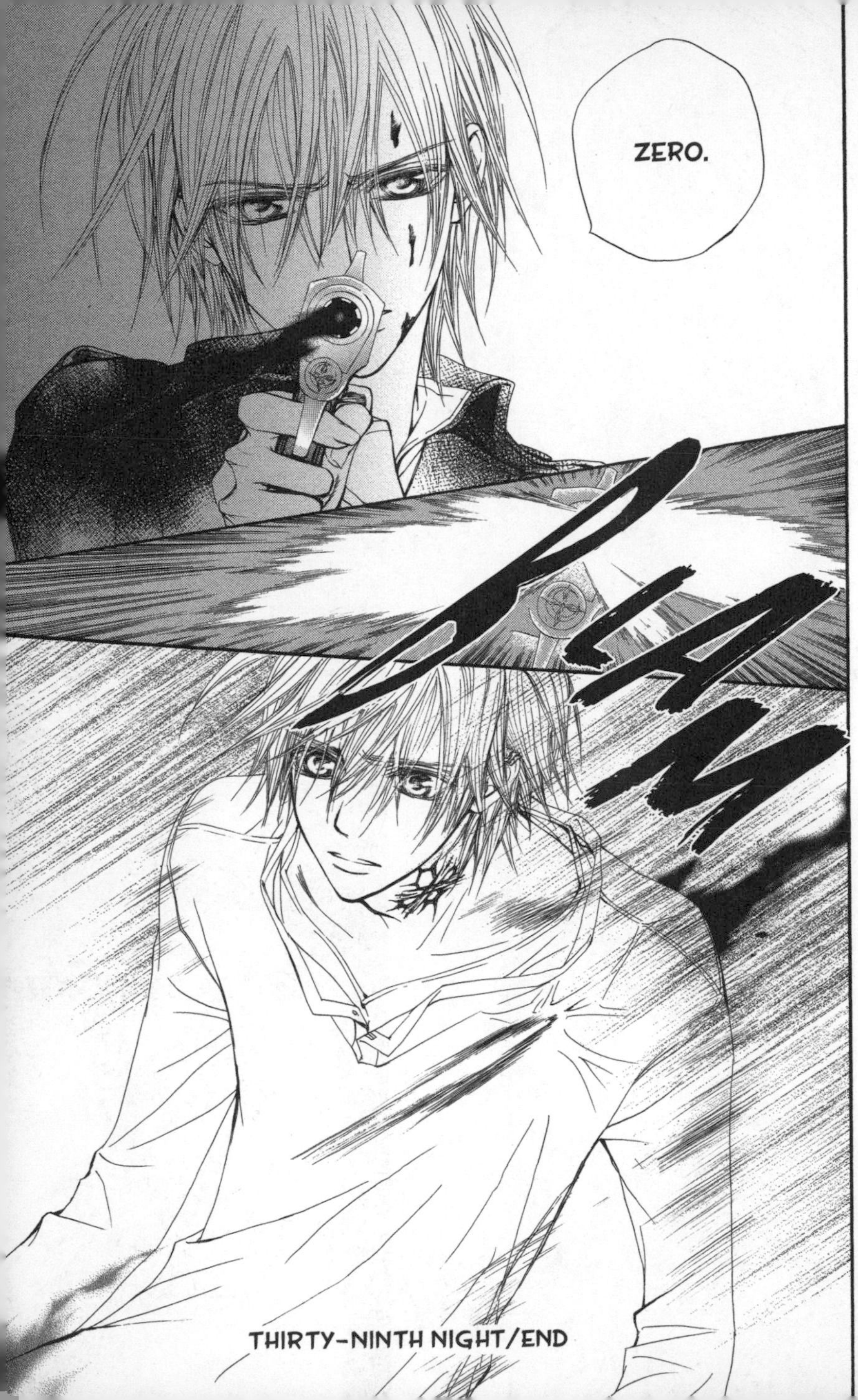
ZERO.
BLAM
THIRTY-NINTH NIGHT/END

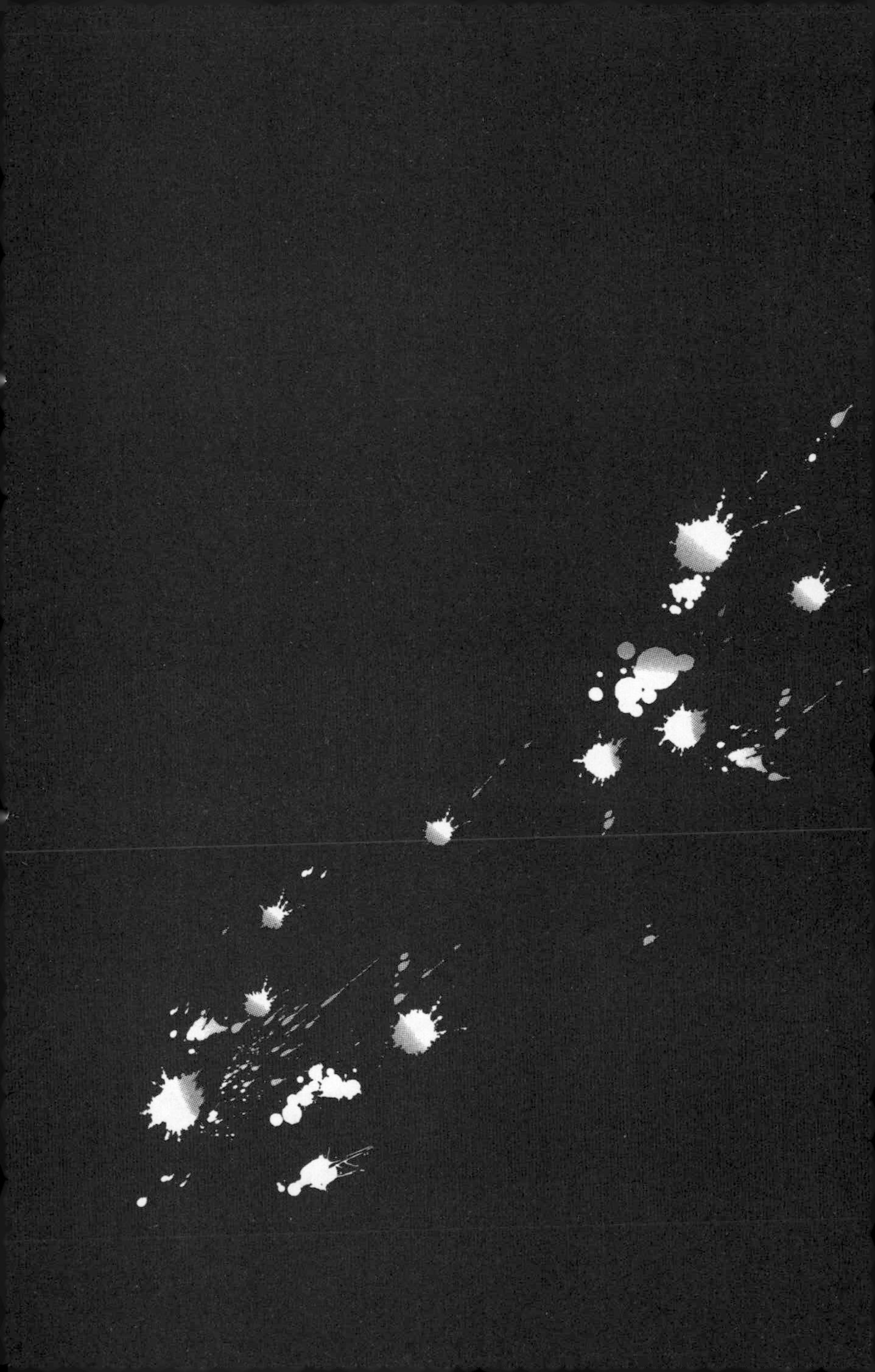

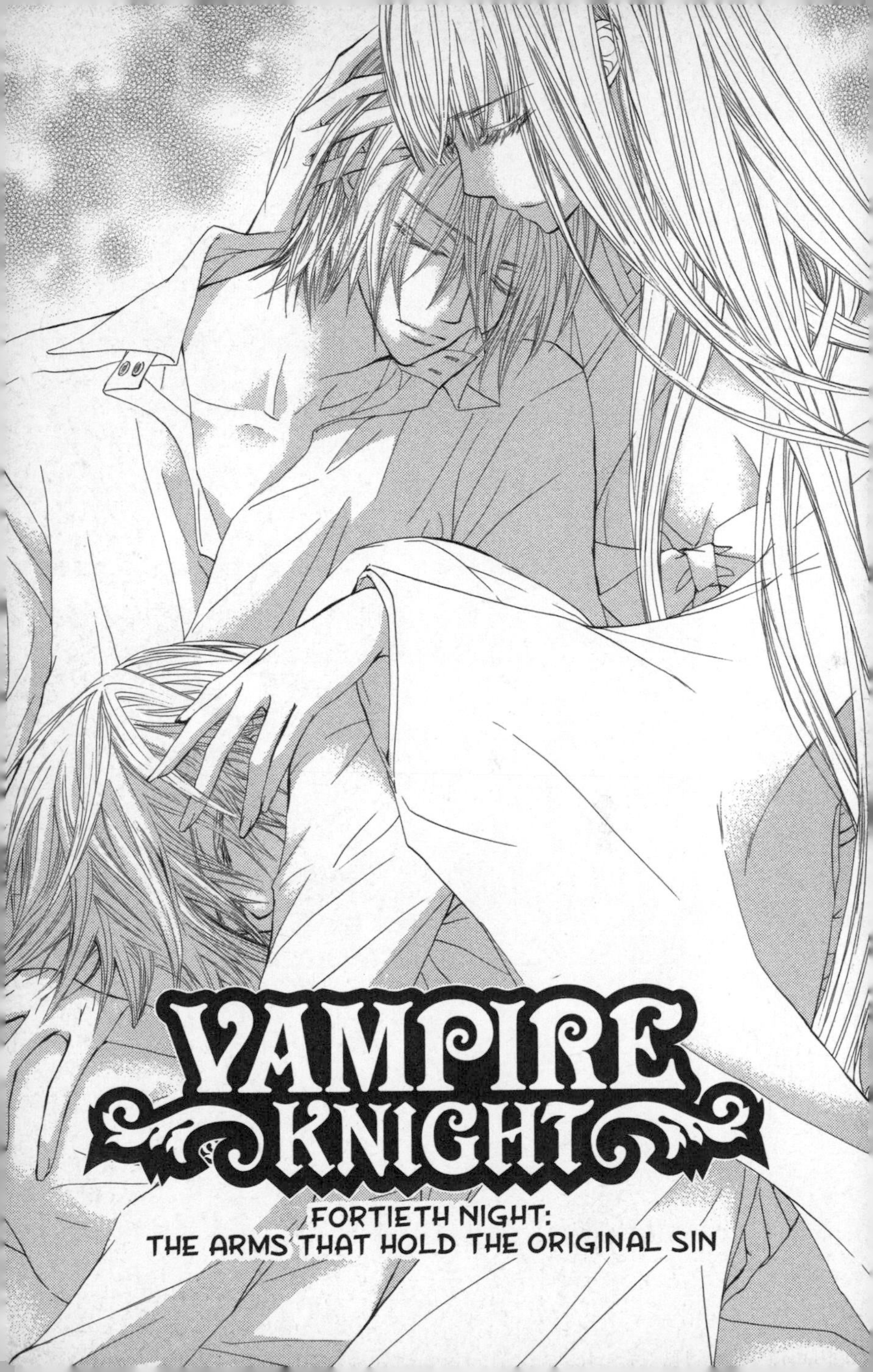
VAMPIRE KNIGHT
FORTIETH NIGHT:
THE ARMS THAT HOLD THE ORIGINAL SIN

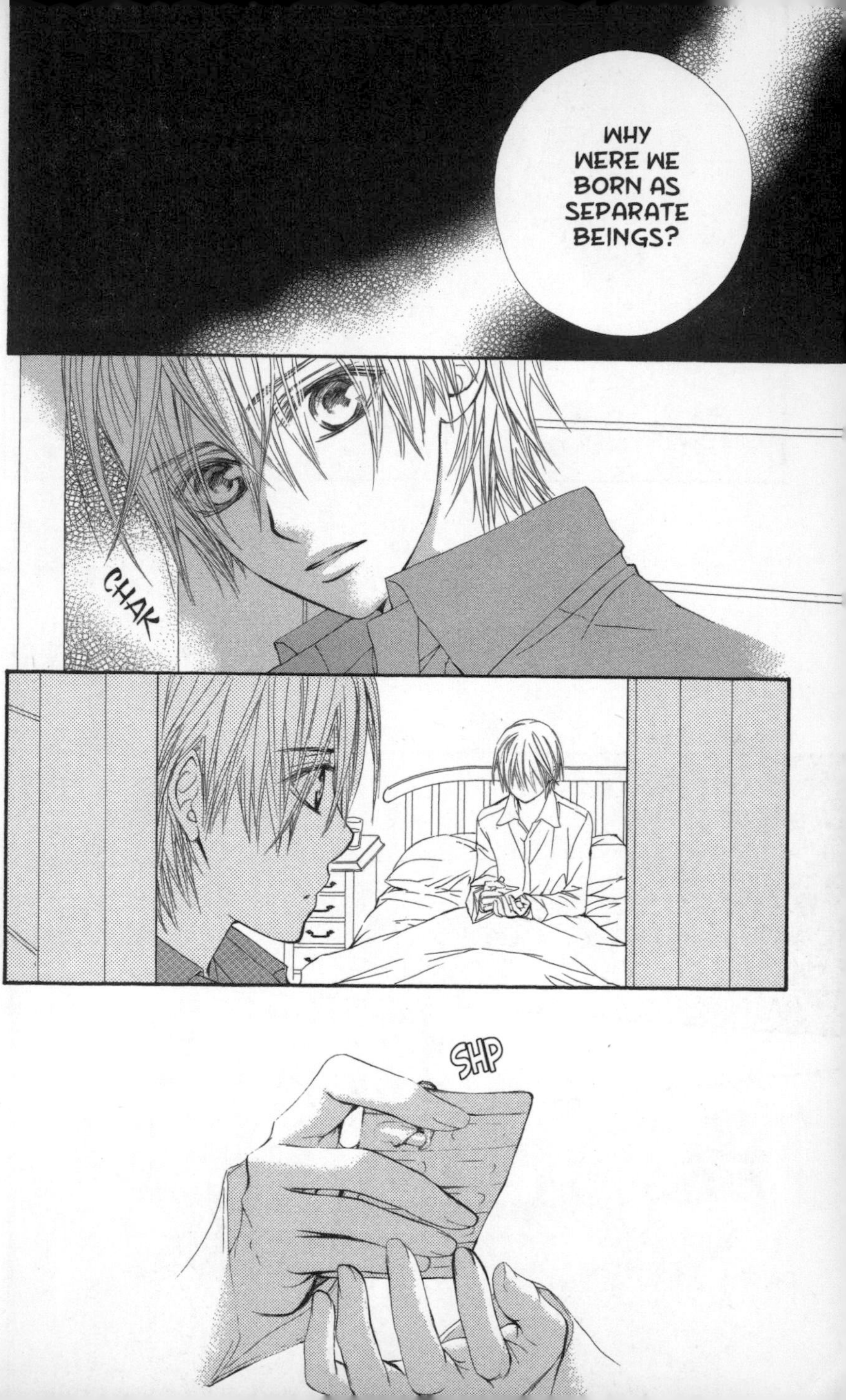
WHY WERE WE BORN AS SEPARATE BEINGS?
CHAK
SHP

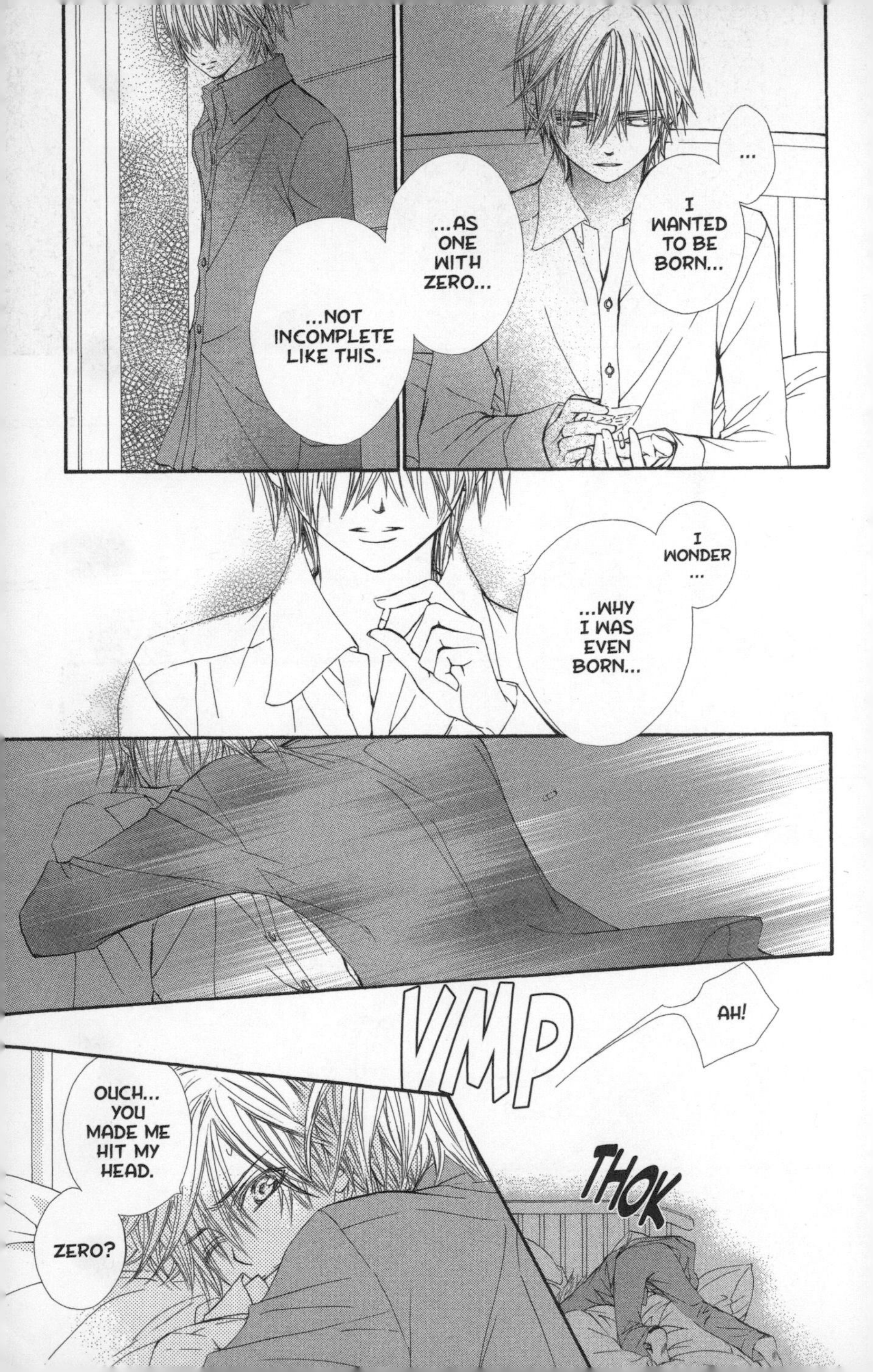
...
I WANTED TO BE BORN...
...AS ONE WITH ZERO...
...NOT INCOMPLETE LIKE THIS.
I WONDER...
...WHY I WAS EVEN BORN...
VMP
AH!
THOK
OUCH... YOU MADE ME HIT MY HEAD.
ZERO?

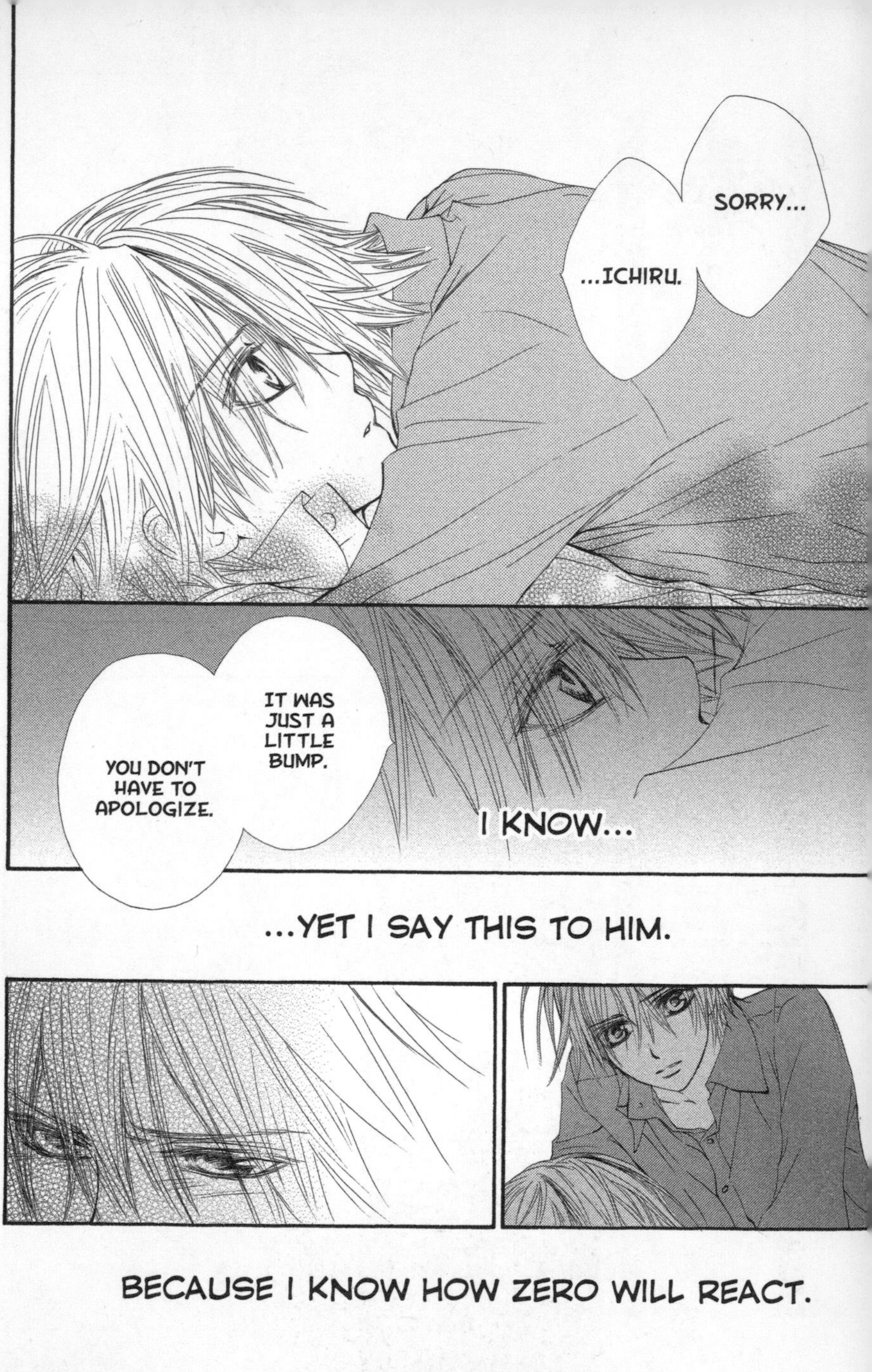
SORRY...
...ICHIRU.
IT WAS JUST A LITTLE BUMP.
YOU DON'T HAVE TO APOLOGIZE.
I KNOW...
...YET I SAY THIS TO HIM.
BECAUSE I KNOW HOW ZERO WILL REACT.

This past year, I had a whole lot of work to do. I was thankful 95% of the time, felt my life was in danger 3% of the time, and felt that I wanted to be rewarded 2% of the time. The reward was a "free ticket to all anime-related parties and events!"...And, well, since they were being held...you know, I wanted to go to them. But I had so much work, there was no way I could finish and attend too...

I draw slowly. I've improved enough to be able to draw 50% faster, but I still couldn't finish my work...and my rewards slipped away from me. But I did my best, believing that I'd be able to reap my rewards someday. What a great system!!...Uh, what I learned was that you need to be able to do your work very quickly in order to utilize your free tickets. (smile)

...ONLY IN MOMENTS WHEN I HURT HIM.

I FELT I COULD BE ZERO'S OTHER HALF...

YOU ALREADY REALIZE IT...

...ZERO.

I DON'T KNOW WHAT TO DO ...

...ICHIRU.

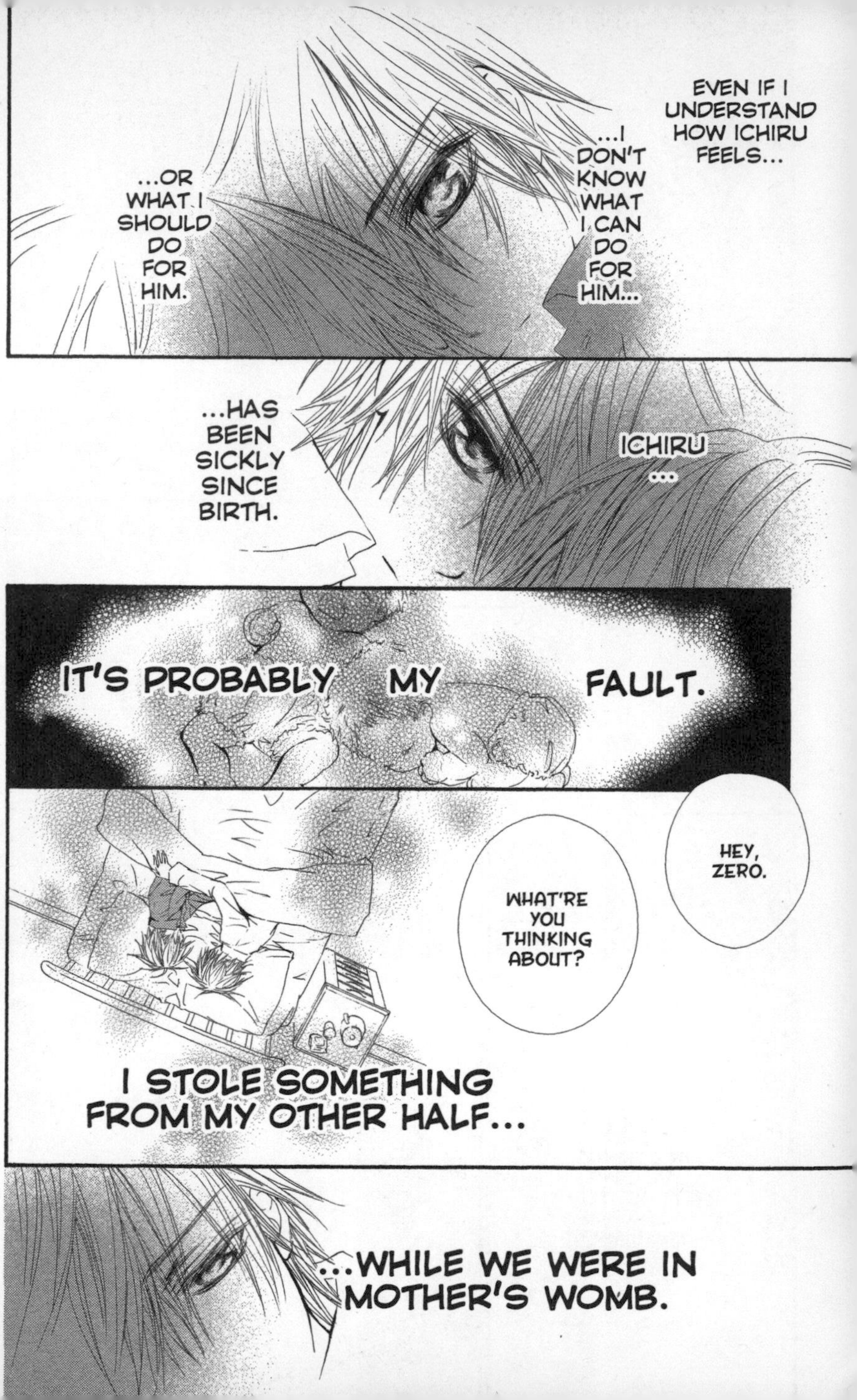
EVEN IF I UNDERSTAND HOW ICHIRU FEELS...
...I DON'T KNOW WHAT I CAN DO FOR HIM...
...OR WHAT I SHOULD DO FOR HIM.
ICHIRU ...
...HAS BEEN SICKLY SINCE BIRTH.
IT'S PROBABLY MY FAULT.
HEY, ZERO.
WHAT'RE YOU THINKING ABOUT?
I STOLE SOMETHING FROM MY OTHER HALF...
...WHILE WE WERE IN MOTHER'S WOMB.

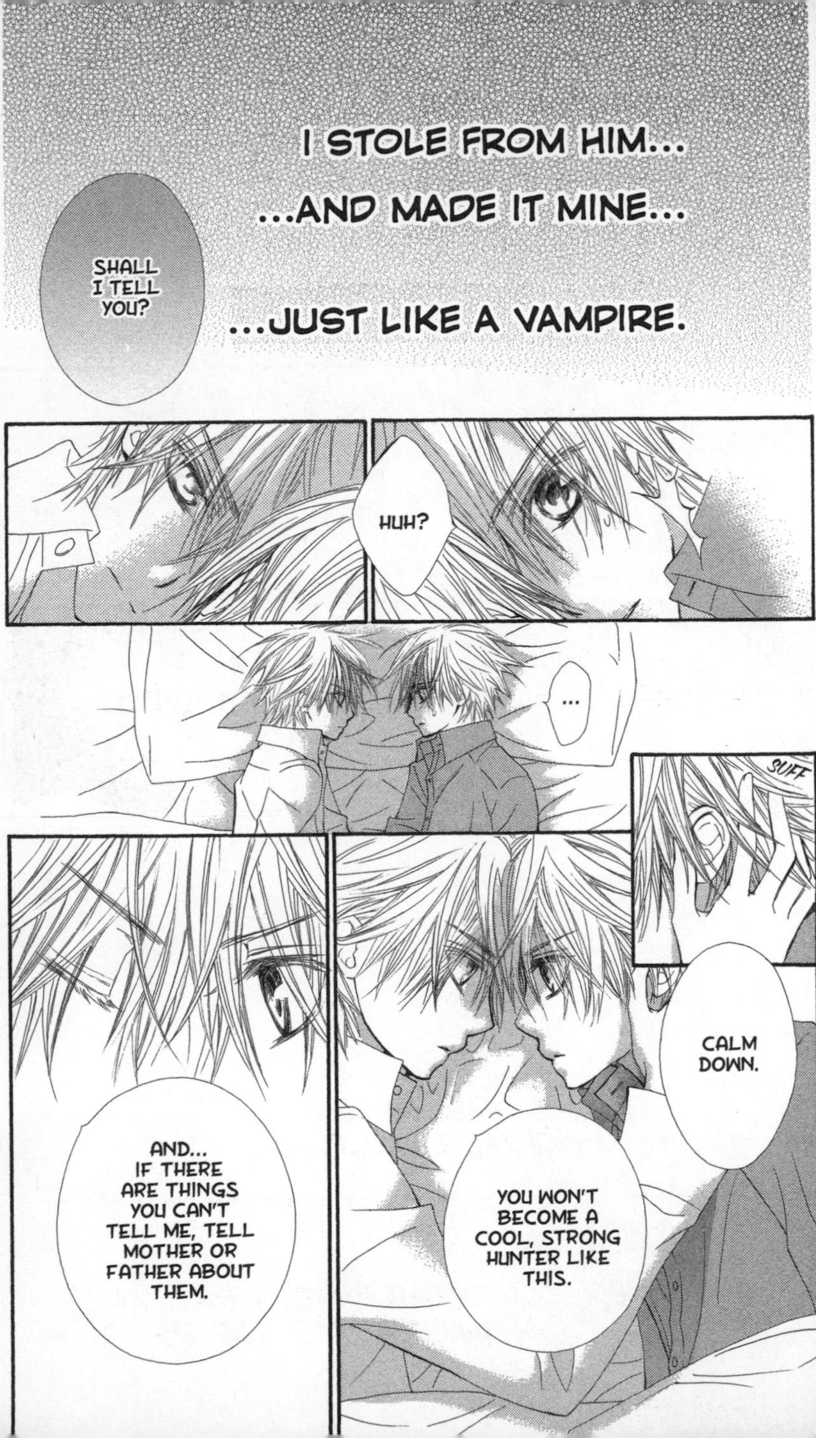
I STOLE FROM HIM...
...AND MADE IT MINE...
...JUST LIKE A VAMPIRE.
SHALL I TELL YOU?
HUH?
...
SUFF
CALM DOWN.
YOU WON'T BECOME A COOL, STRONG HUNTER LIKE THIS.
AND... IF THERE ARE THINGS YOU CAN'T TELL ME, TELL MOTHER OR FATHER ABOUT THEM.

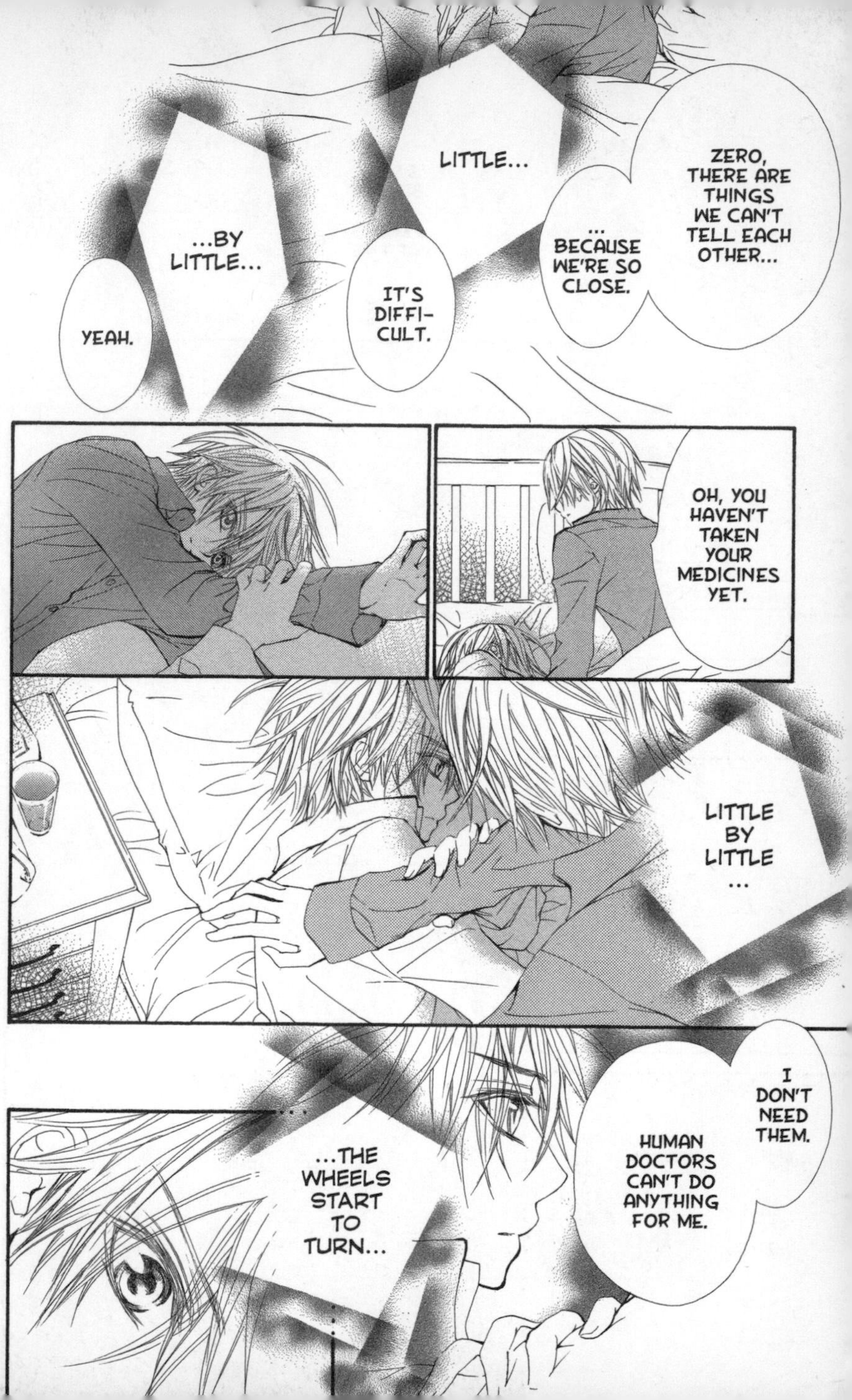
ZERO, THERE ARE THINGS WE CAN'T TELL EACH OTHER...
...BECAUSE WE'RE SO CLOSE.
LITTLE...
IT'S DIFFI-CULT.
...BY LITTLE...
YEAH.
OH, YOU HAVEN'T TAKEN YOUR MEDICINES YET.
LITTLE BY LITTLE ...
I DON'T NEED THEM.
HUMAN DOCTORS CAN'T DO ANYTHING FOR ME.
...THE WHEELS START TO TURN...

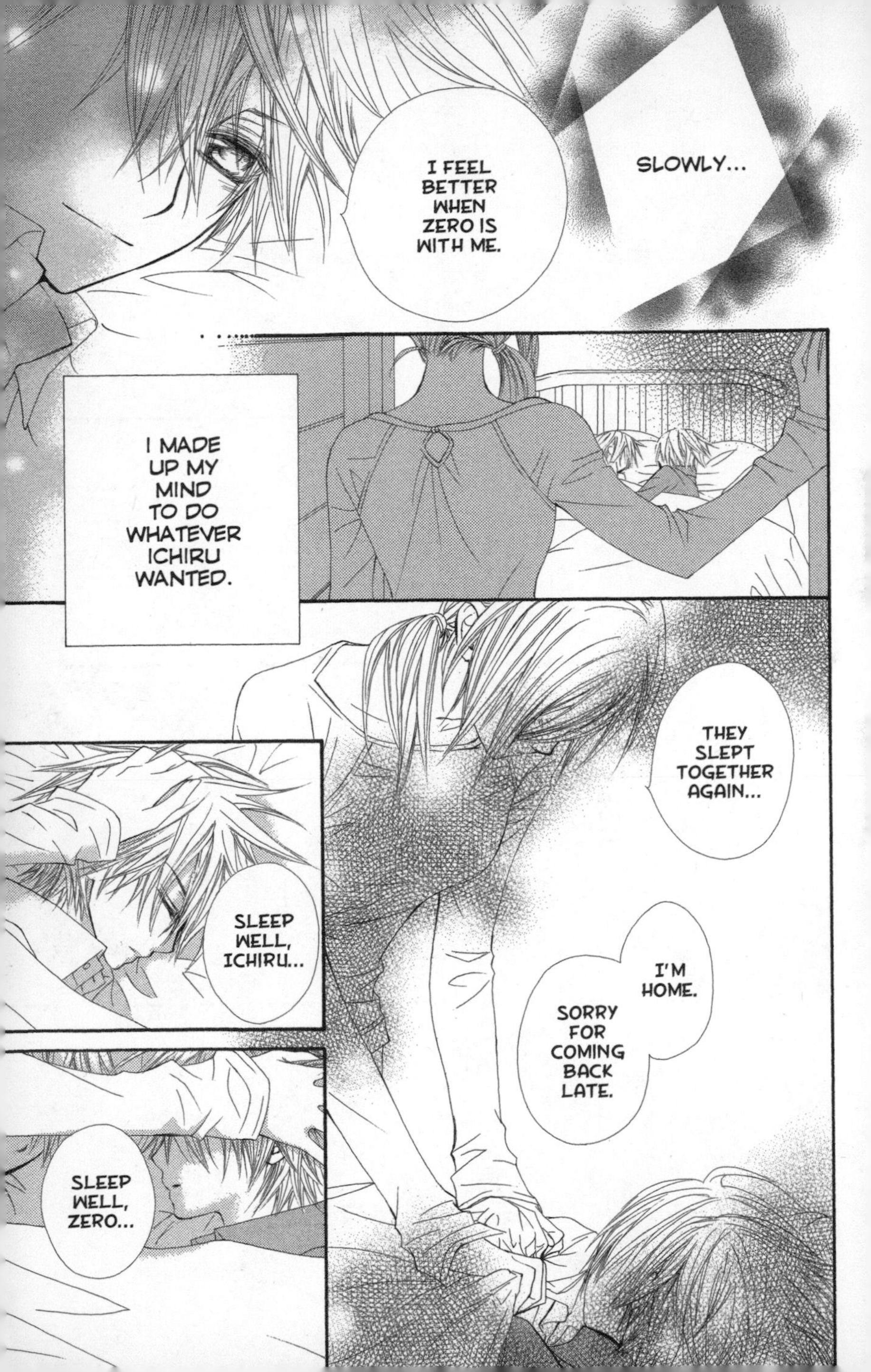
SLOWLY...
I FEEL BETTER WHEN ZERO IS WITH ME.
I MADE UP MY MIND TO DO WHATEVER ICHIRU WANTED.
THEY SLEPT TOGETHER AGAIN...
I'M HOME. SORRY FOR COMING BACK LATE.
SLEEP WELL, ICHIRU...
SLEEP WELL, ZERO...

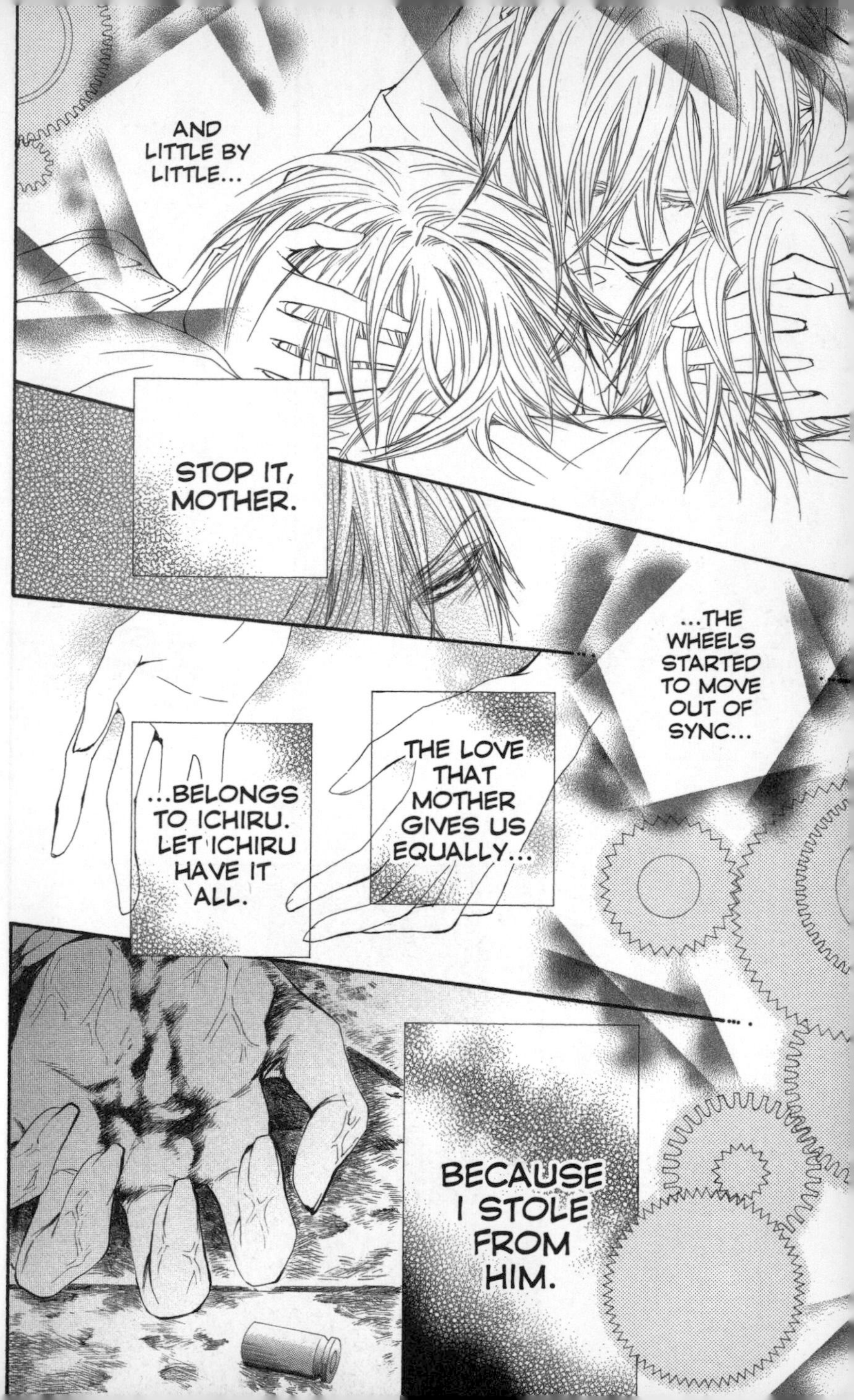
AND LITTLE BY LITTLE...
STOP IT, MOTHER.
...THE WHEELS STARTED TO MOVE OUT OF SYNC...
THE LOVE THAT MOTHER GIVES US EQUALLY...
...BELONGS TO ICHIRU. LET ICHIRU HAVE IT ALL.
BECAUSE I STOLE FROM HIM.

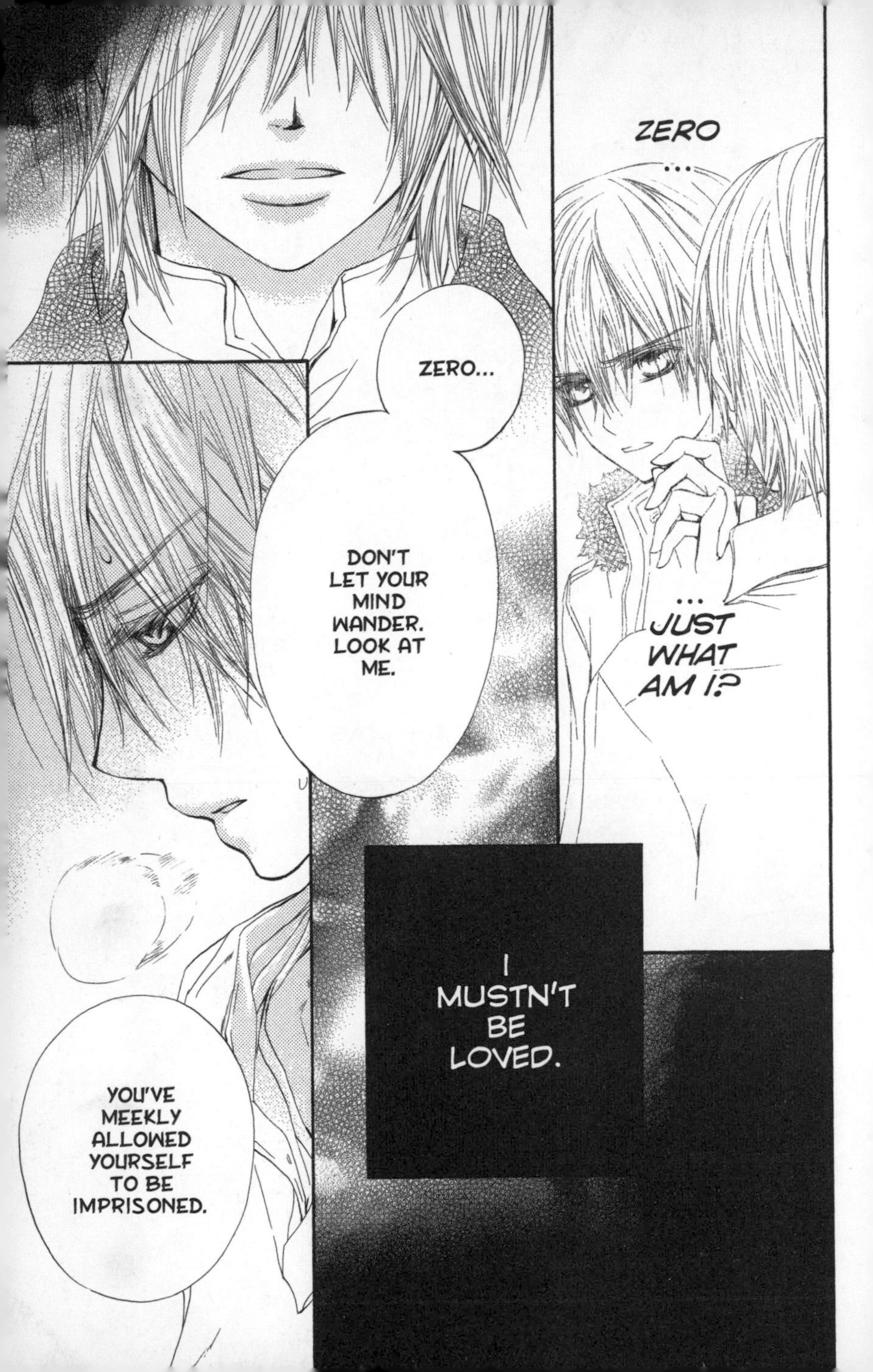
ZERO ...
... JUST WHAT AM I?
ZERO...
DON'T LET YOUR MIND WANDER. LOOK AT ME.
I MUSTN'T BE LOVED.
YOU'VE MEEKLY ALLOWED YOURSELF TO BE IMPRISONED.

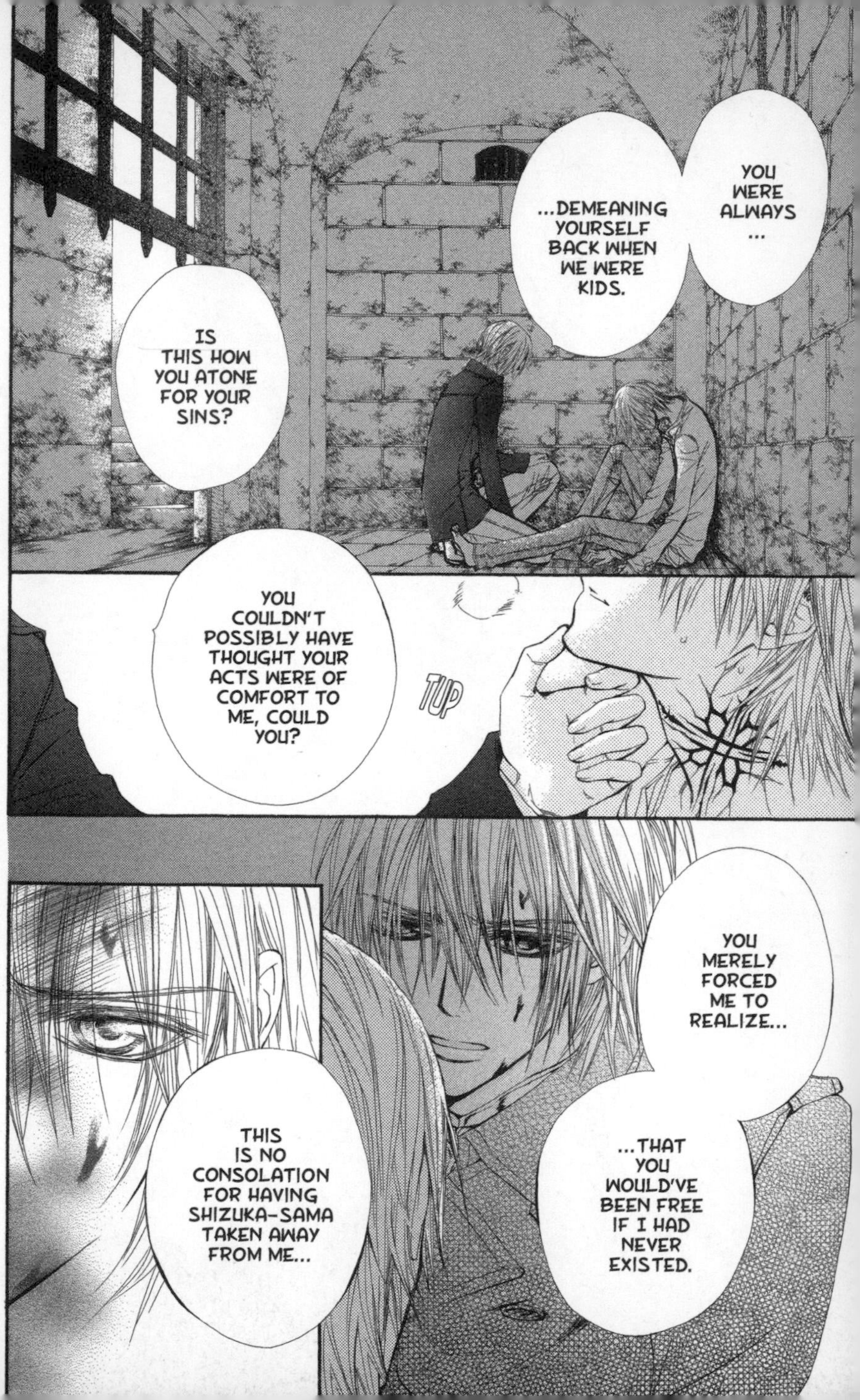
YOU WERE ALWAYS...
...DEMEANING YOURSELF BACK WHEN WE WERE KIDS.
IS THIS HOW YOU ATONE FOR YOUR SINS?
TUP
YOU COULDN'T POSSIBLY HAVE THOUGHT YOUR ACTS WERE OF COMFORT TO ME, COULD YOU?
YOU MERELY FORCED ME TO REALIZE...
...THAT YOU WOULD'VE BEEN FREE IF I HAD NEVER EXISTED.
THIS IS NO CONSOLATION FOR HAVING SHIZUKA-SAMA TAKEN AWAY FROM ME...

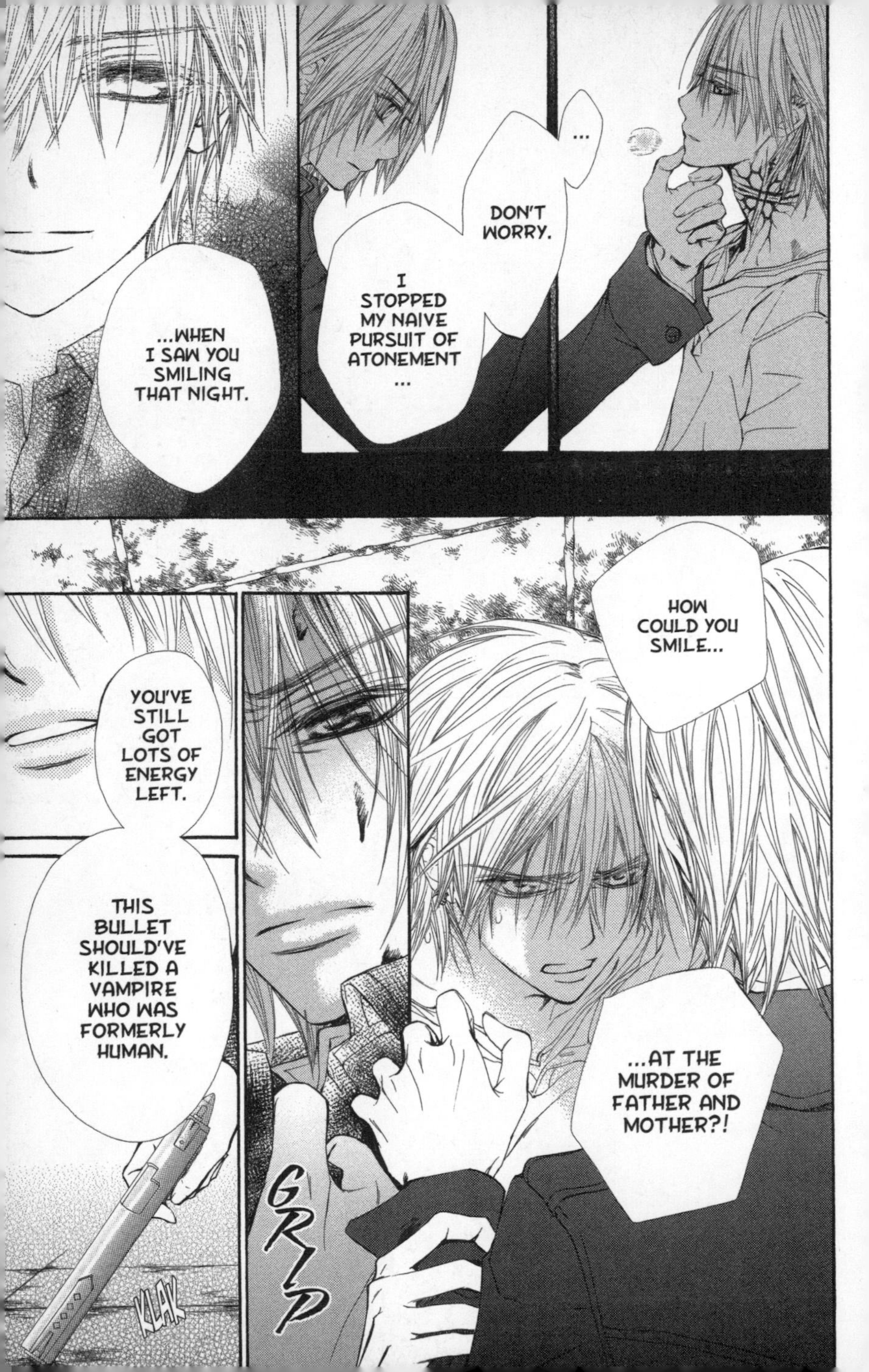
...
DON'T WORRY.
I STOPPED MY NAIVE PURSUIT OF ATONEMENT ...
...WHEN I SAW YOU SMILING THAT NIGHT.
HOW COULD YOU SMILE...
...AT THE MURDER OF FATHER AND MOTHER?!
GRIP
YOU'VE STILL GOT LOTS OF ENERGY LEFT.
THIS BULLET SHOULD'VE KILLED A VAMPIRE WHO WAS FORMERLY HUMAN.
KLAK

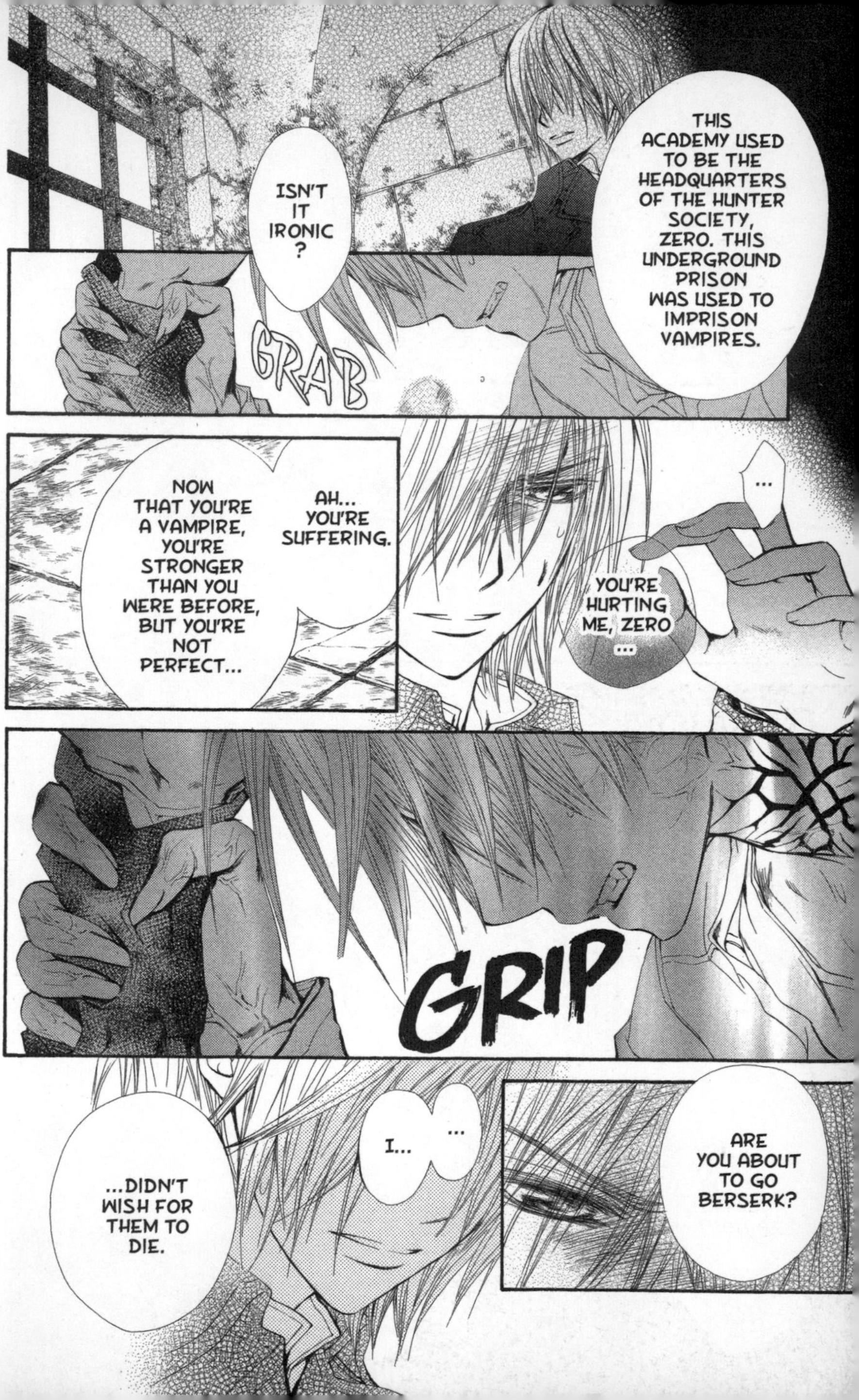
THIS ACADEMY USED TO BE THE HEADQUARTERS OF THE HUNTER SOCIETY, ZERO. THIS UNDERGROUND PRISON WAS USED TO IMPRISON VAMPIRES.
ISN'T IT IRONIC?
GRAB
...
YOU'RE HURTING ME, ZERO...
AH... YOU'RE SUFFERING.
NOW THAT YOU'RE A VAMPIRE, YOU'RE STRONGER THAN YOU WERE BEFORE, BUT YOU'RE NOT PERFECT...
GRIP
ARE YOU ABOUT TO GO BERSERK?
...
I...
...DIDN'T WISH FOR THEM TO DIE.

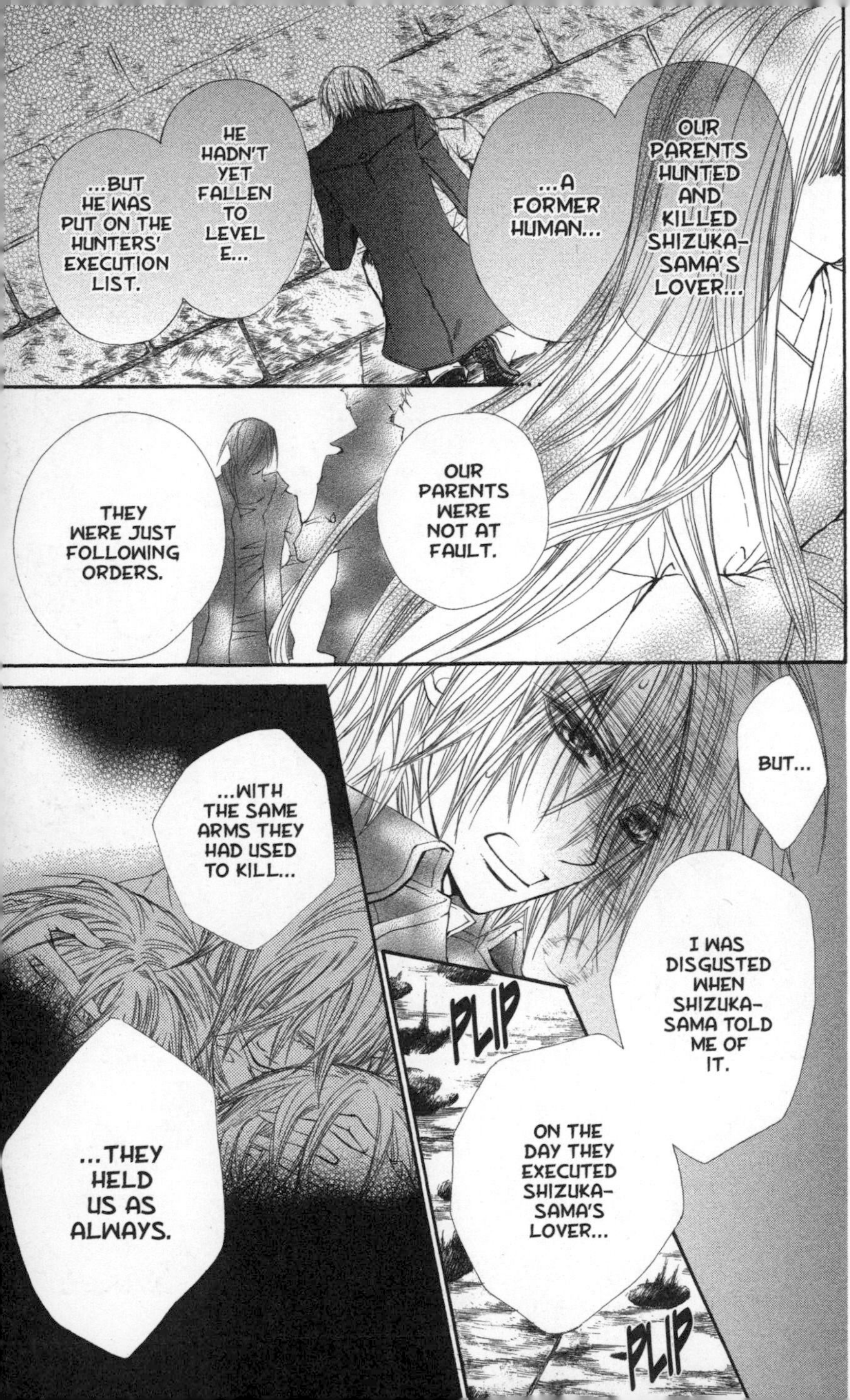
OUR PARENTS HUNTED AND KILLED SHIZUKA-SAMA'S LOVER...
...A FORMER HUMAN...
HE HADN'T YET FALLEN TO LEVEL E...
...BUT HE WAS PUT ON THE HUNTERS' EXECUTION LIST.
OUR PARENTS WERE NOT AT FAULT.
THEY WERE JUST FOLLOWING ORDERS.
BUT...
I WAS DISGUSTED WHEN SHIZUKA-SAMA TOLD ME OF IT.
PLIP
ON THE DAY THEY EXECUTED SHIZUKA-SAMA'S LOVER...
PLIP
...WITH THE SAME ARMS THEY HAD USED TO KILL...
...THEY HELD US AS ALWAYS.

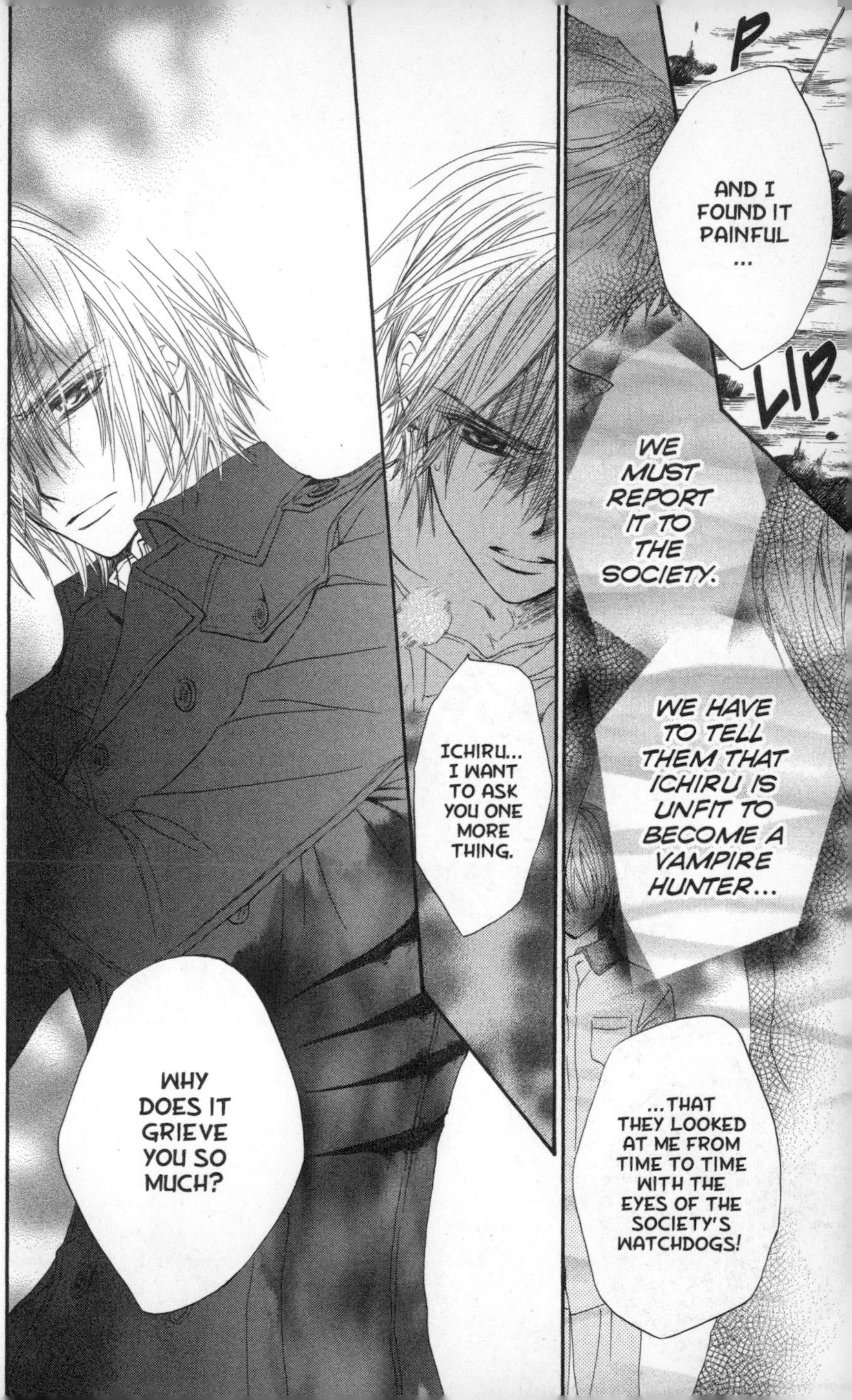
P
LIP
AND I FOUND IT PAINFUL ...
WE MUST REPORT IT TO THE SOCIETY.
WE HAVE TO TELL THEM THAT ICHIRU IS UNFIT TO BECOME A VAMPIRE HUNTER...
...THAT THEY LOOKED AT ME FROM TIME TO TIME WITH THE EYES OF THE SOCIETY'S WATCHDOGS!
ICHIRU... I WANT TO ASK YOU ONE MORE THING.
WHY DOES IT GRIEVE YOU SO MUCH?

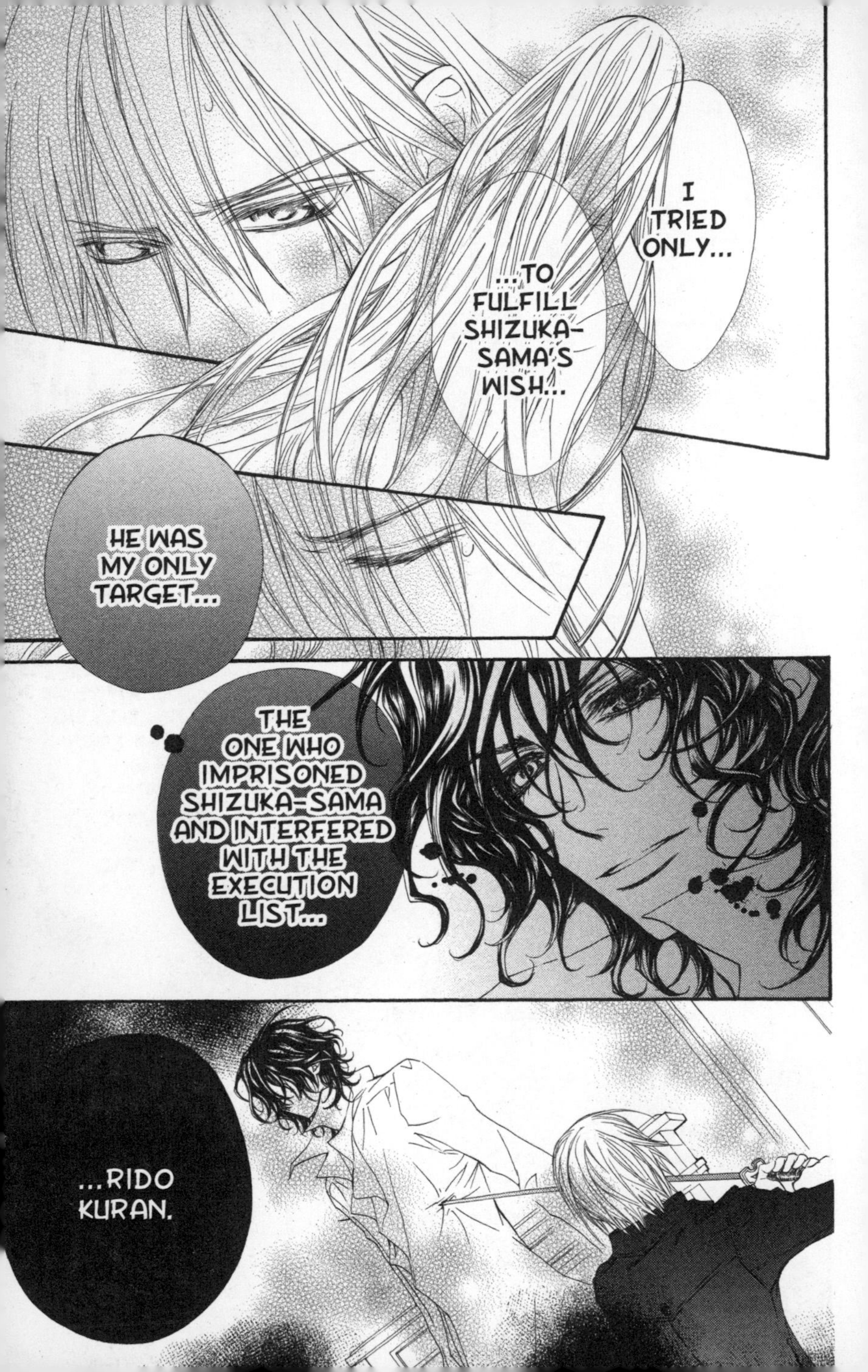
I TRIED ONLY...
...TO FULFILL SHIZUKA-SAMA'S WISH...
HE WAS MY ONLY TARGET...
THE ONE WHO IMPRISONED SHIZUKA-SAMA AND INTERFERED WITH THE EXECUTION LIST...
...RIDO KURAN.

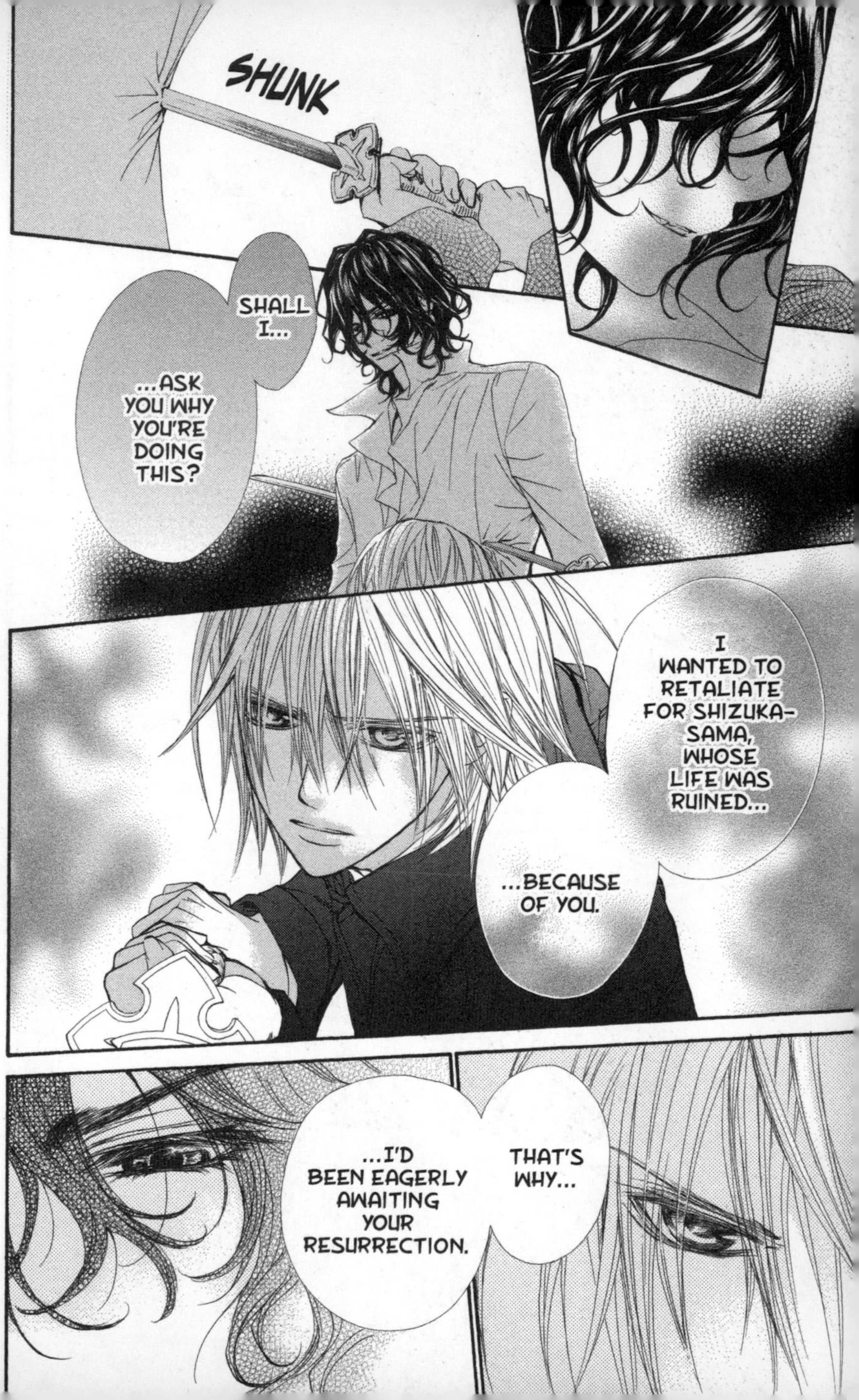
SHUNK
SHALL I...
...ASK YOU WHY YOU'RE DOING THIS?
I WANTED TO RETALIATE FOR SHIZUKA-SAMA, WHOSE LIFE WAS RUINED...
...BECAUSE OF YOU.
THAT'S WHY...
...I'D BEEN EAGERLY AWAITING YOUR RESURRECTION.

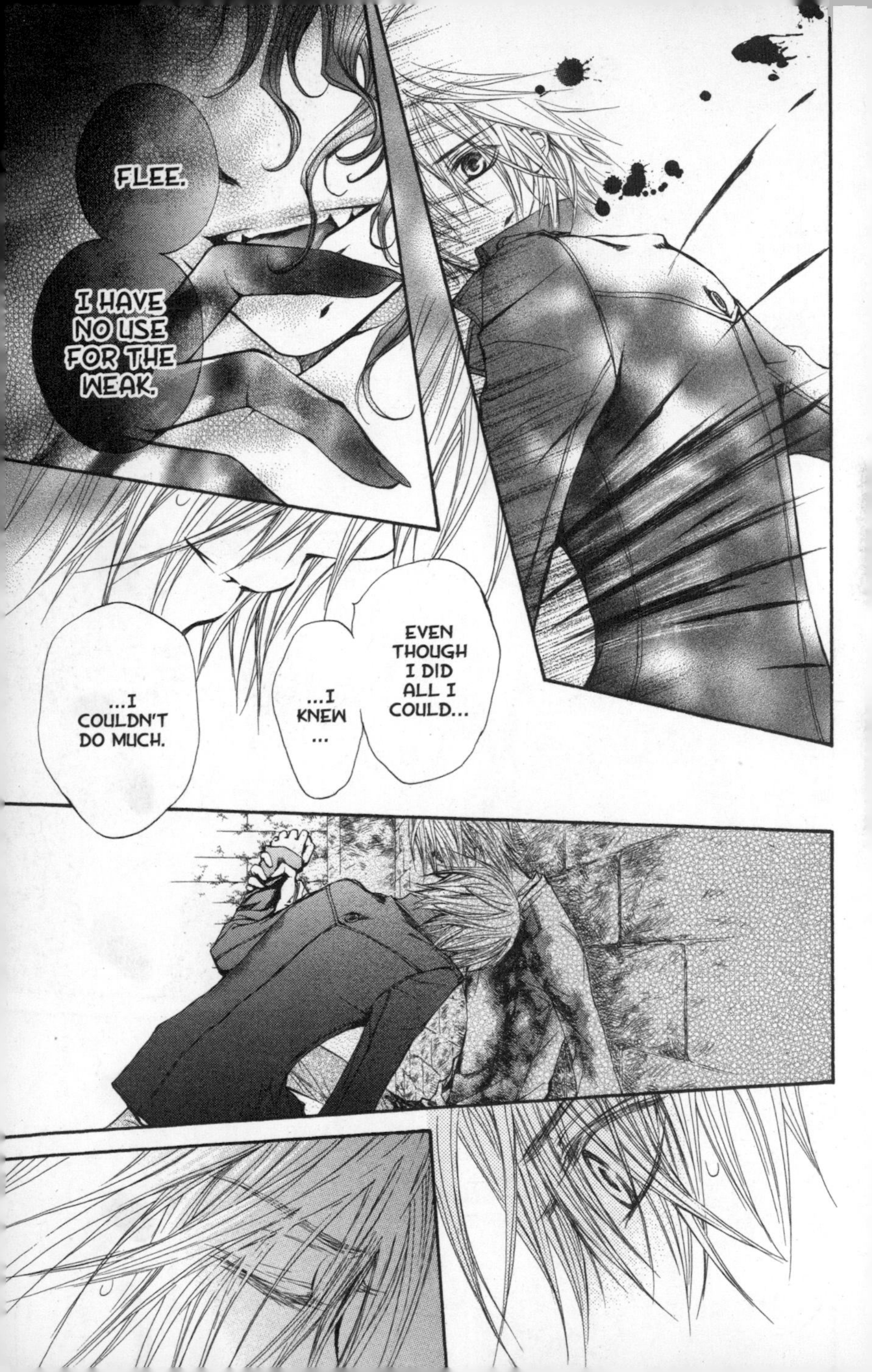
FLEE.
I HAVE NO USE FOR THE WEAK.
EVEN THOUGH I DID ALL I COULD...
...I KNEW...
...I COULDN'T DO MUCH.

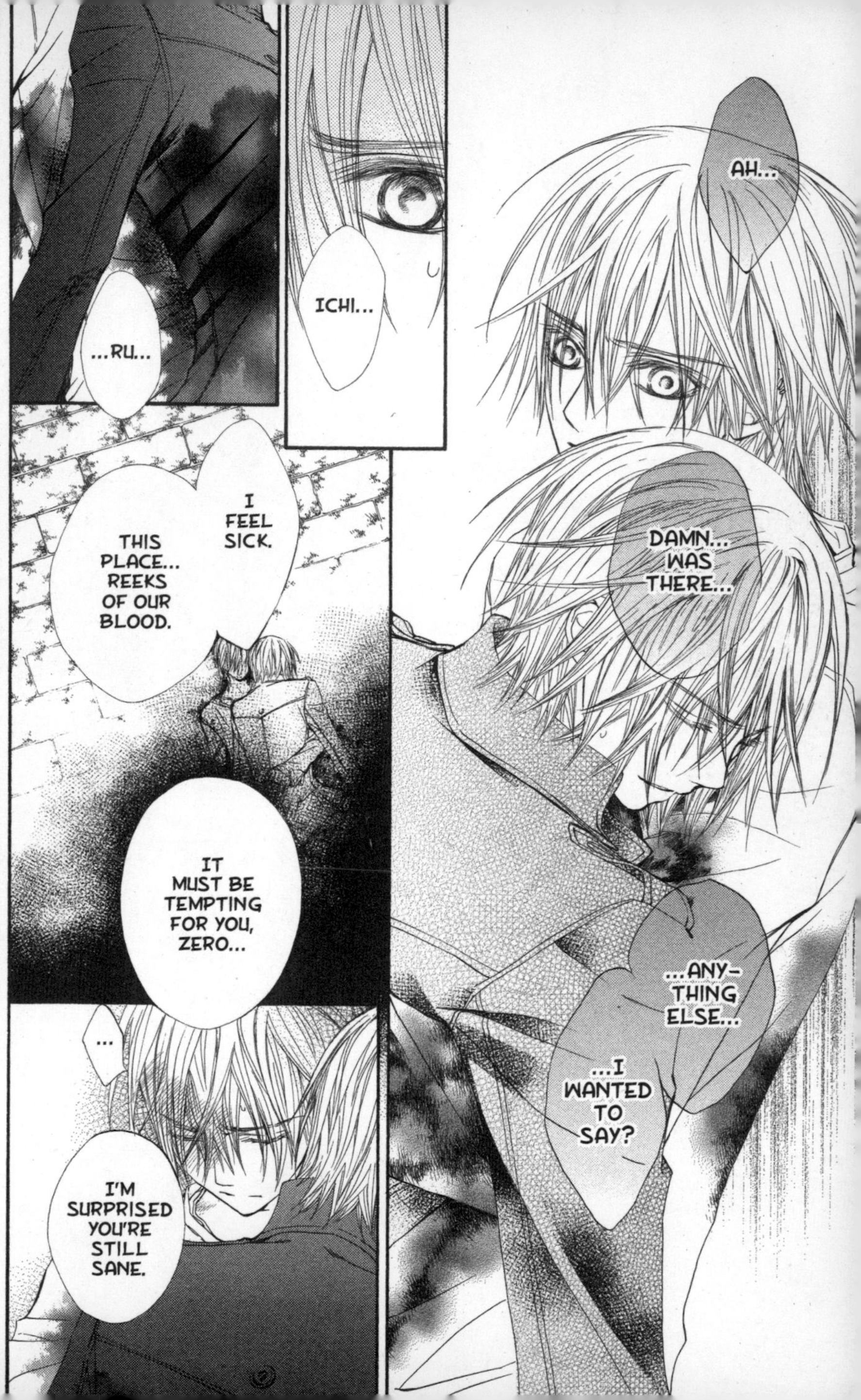
AH...
DAMN... WAS THERE...
...ANY-THING ELSE...
...I WANTED TO SAY?
ICHI...
...RU...
I FEEL SICK.
THIS PLACE... REEKS OF OUR BLOOD.
IT MUST BE TEMPTING FOR YOU, ZERO...
...
I'M SURPRISED YOU'RE STILL SANE.

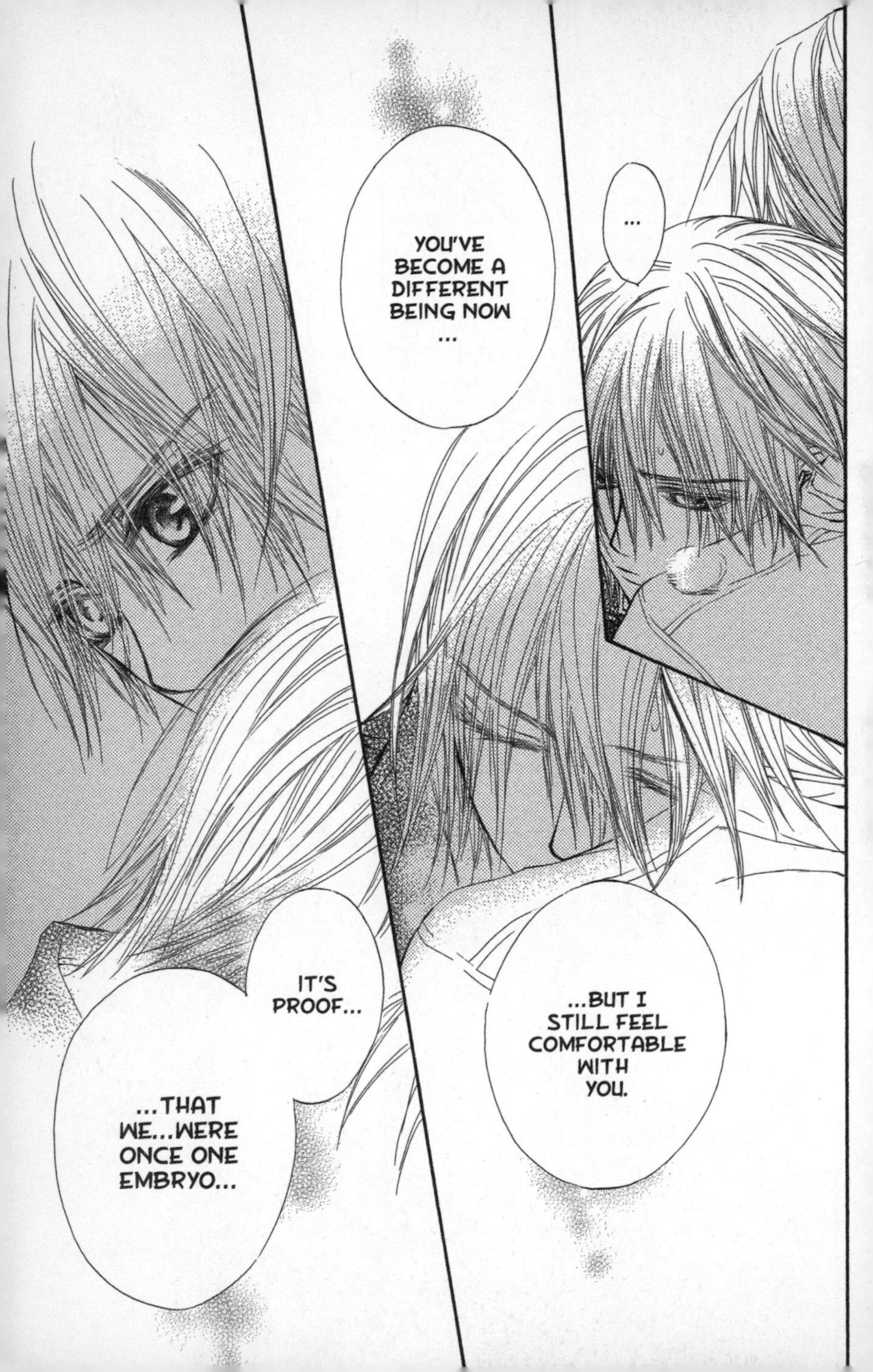
...
YOU'VE BECOME A DIFFERENT BEING NOW ...
...BUT I STILL FEEL COMFORTABLE WITH YOU.
IT'S PROOF...
...THAT WE...WERE ONCE ONE EMBRYO...

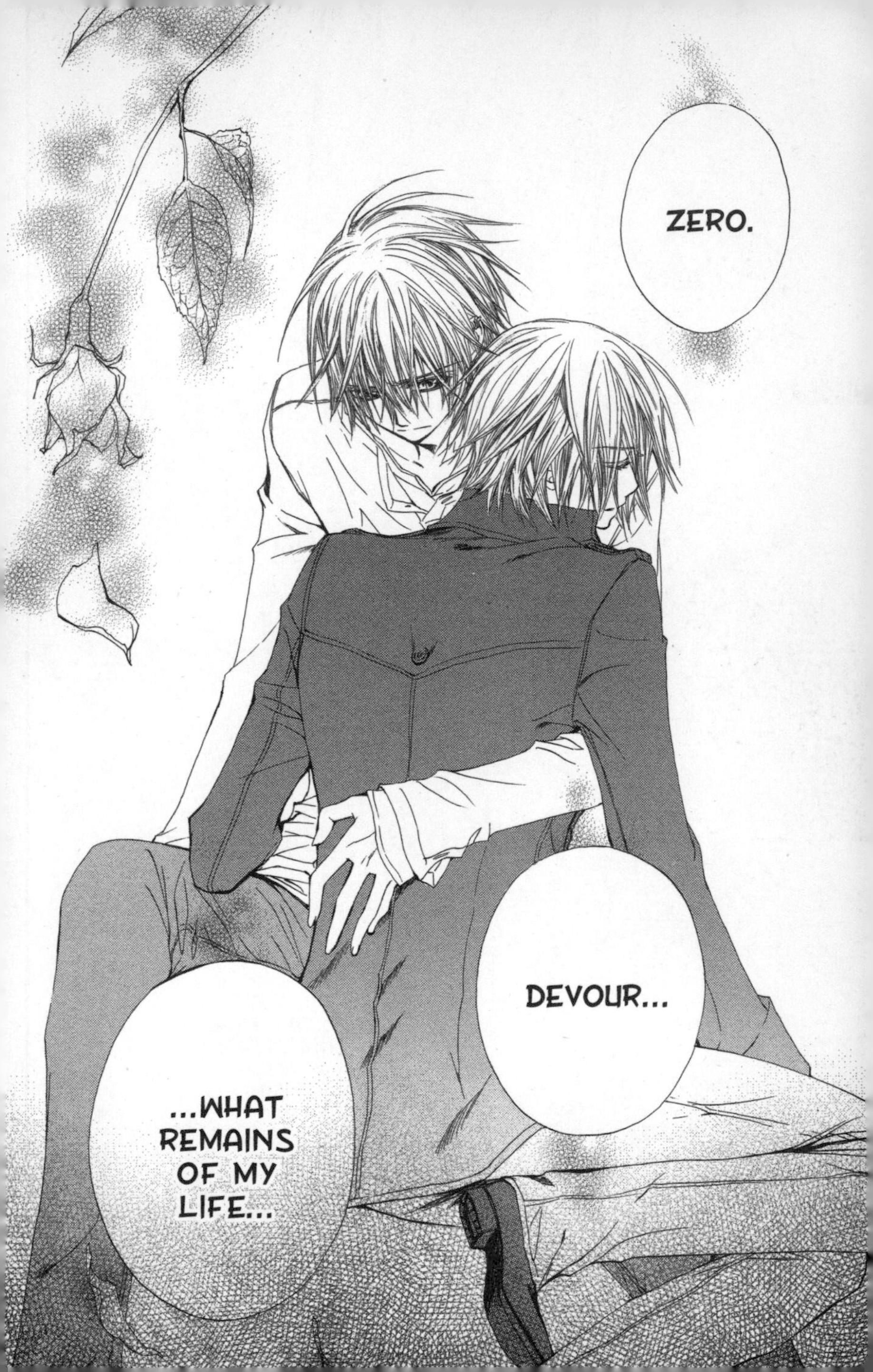
ZERO.
DEVOUR...
...WHAT REMAINS OF MY LIFE...

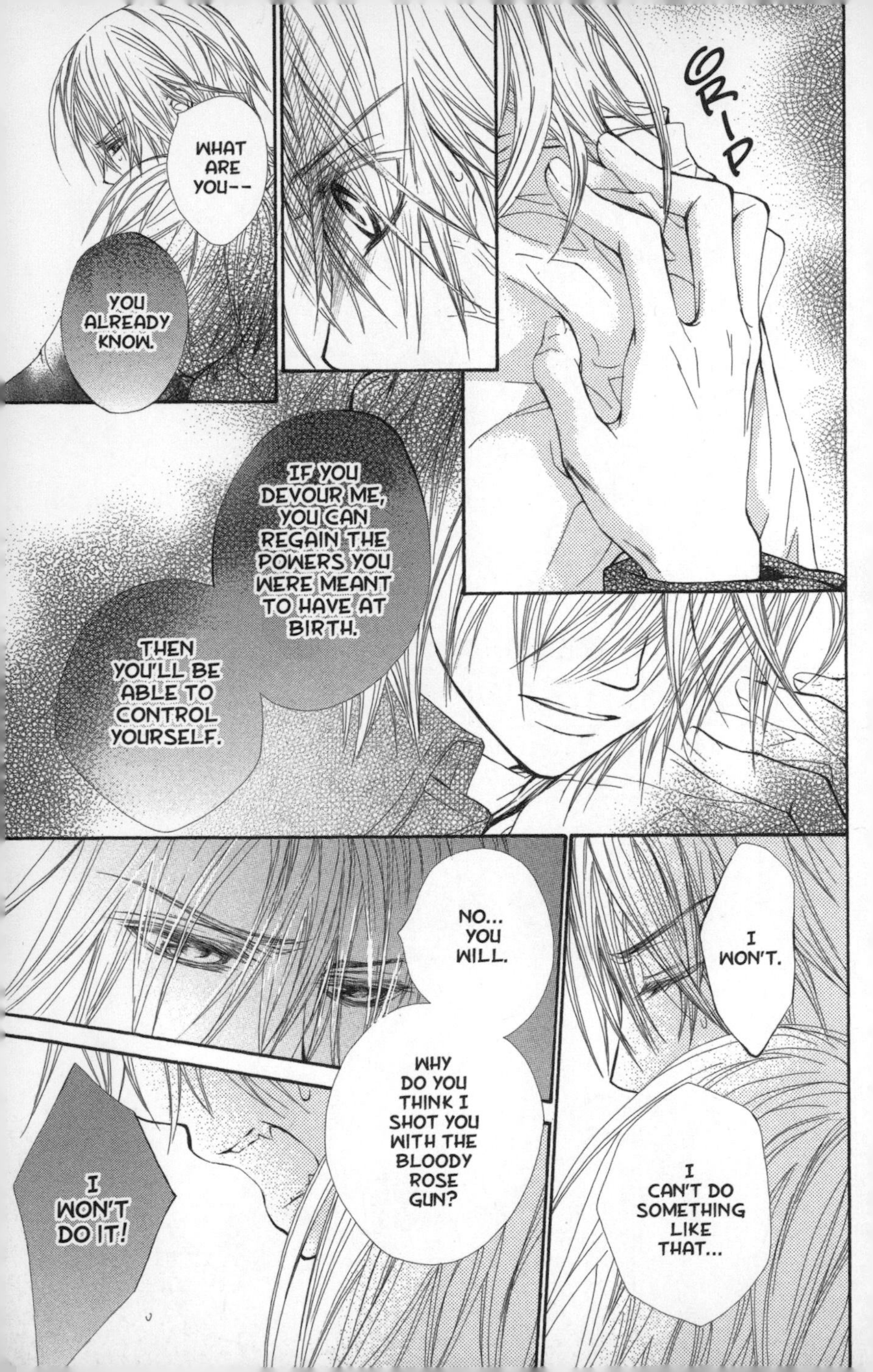
GRIP
WHAT ARE YOU--
YOU ALREADY KNOW.
IF YOU DEVOUR ME, YOU CAN REGAIN THE POWERS YOU WERE MEANT TO HAVE AT BIRTH.
THEN YOU'LL BE ABLE TO CONTROL YOURSELF.
I WON'T.
I CAN'T DO SOMETHING LIKE THAT...
NO... YOU WILL.
WHY DO YOU THINK I SHOT YOU WITH THE BLOODY ROSE GUN?
I WON'T DO IT!

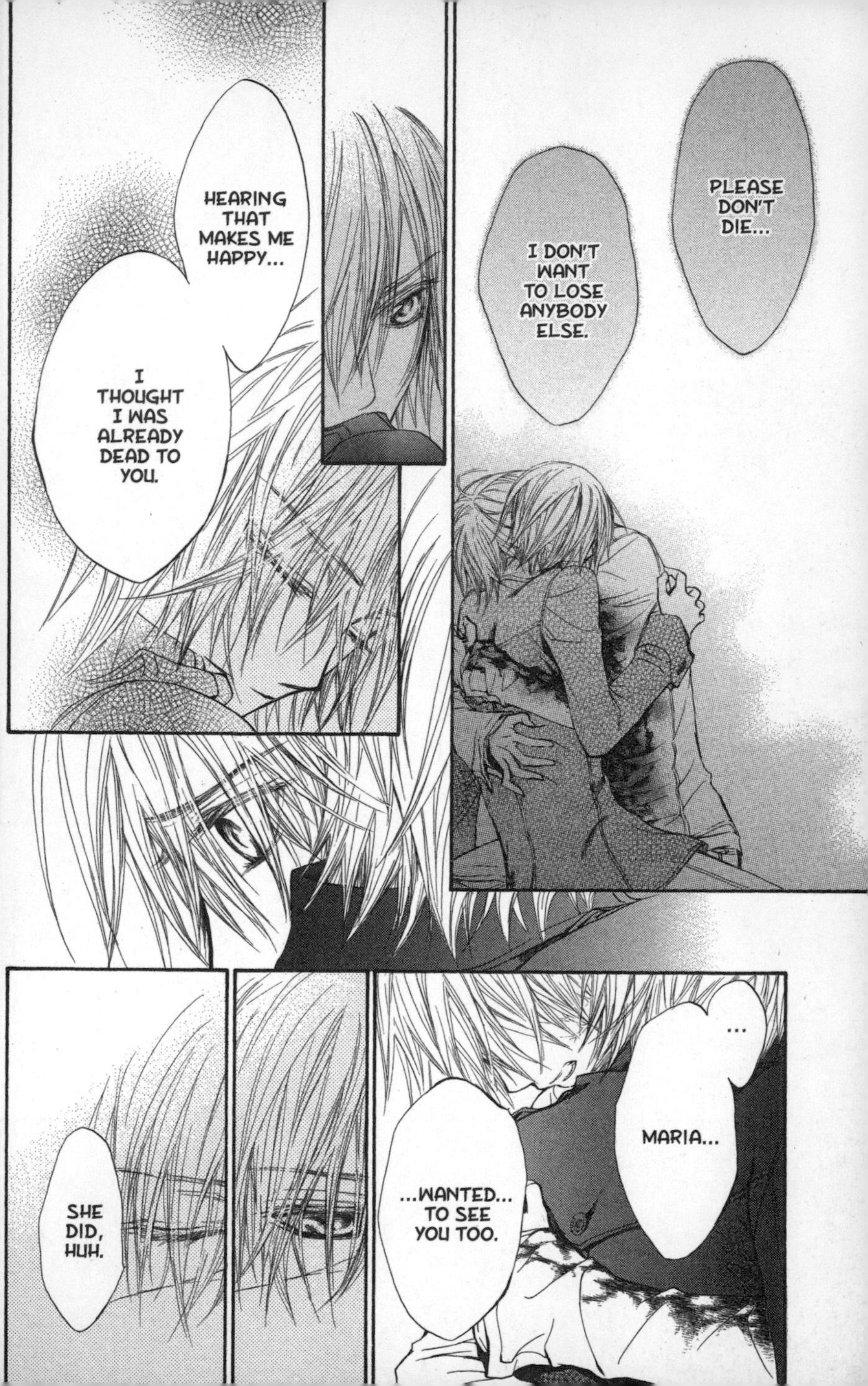
PLEASE DON'T DIE...
I DON'T WANT TO LOSE ANYBODY ELSE.
HEARING THAT MAKES ME HAPPY...
I THOUGHT I WAS ALREADY DEAD TO YOU.
...
MARIA...
...WANTED... TO SEE YOU TOO.
SHE DID, HUH.

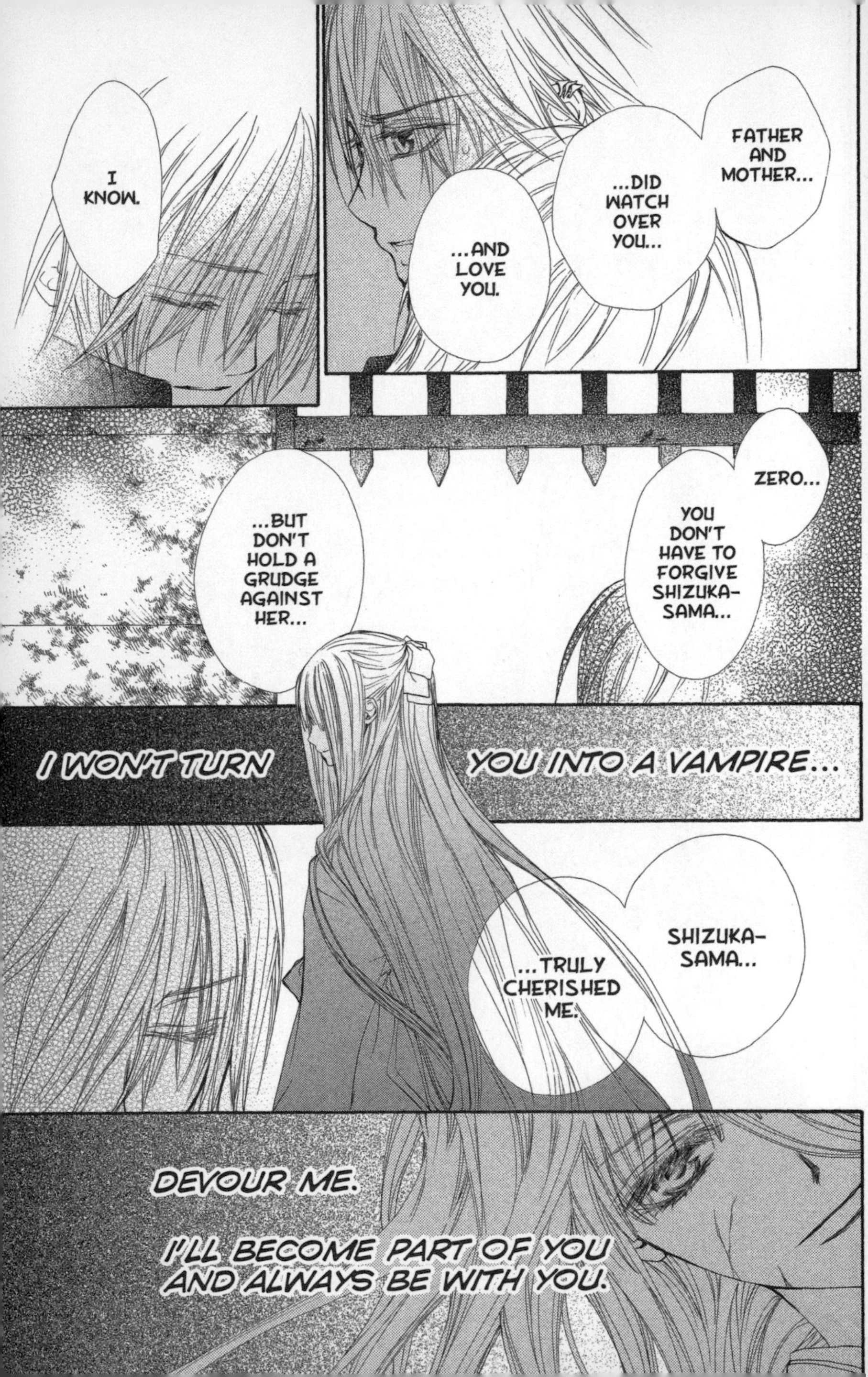
FATHER AND MOTHER...
...DID WATCH OVER YOU...
...AND LOVE YOU.
I KNOW.
ZERO...
YOU DON'T HAVE TO FORGIVE SHIZUKA-SAMA...
...BUT DON'T HOLD A GRUDGE AGAINST HER...
I WON'T TURN YOU INTO A VAMPIRE...
SHIZUKA-SAMA...
...TRULY CHERISHED ME.
DEVOUR ME.
I'LL BECOME PART OF YOU AND ALWAYS BE WITH YOU.

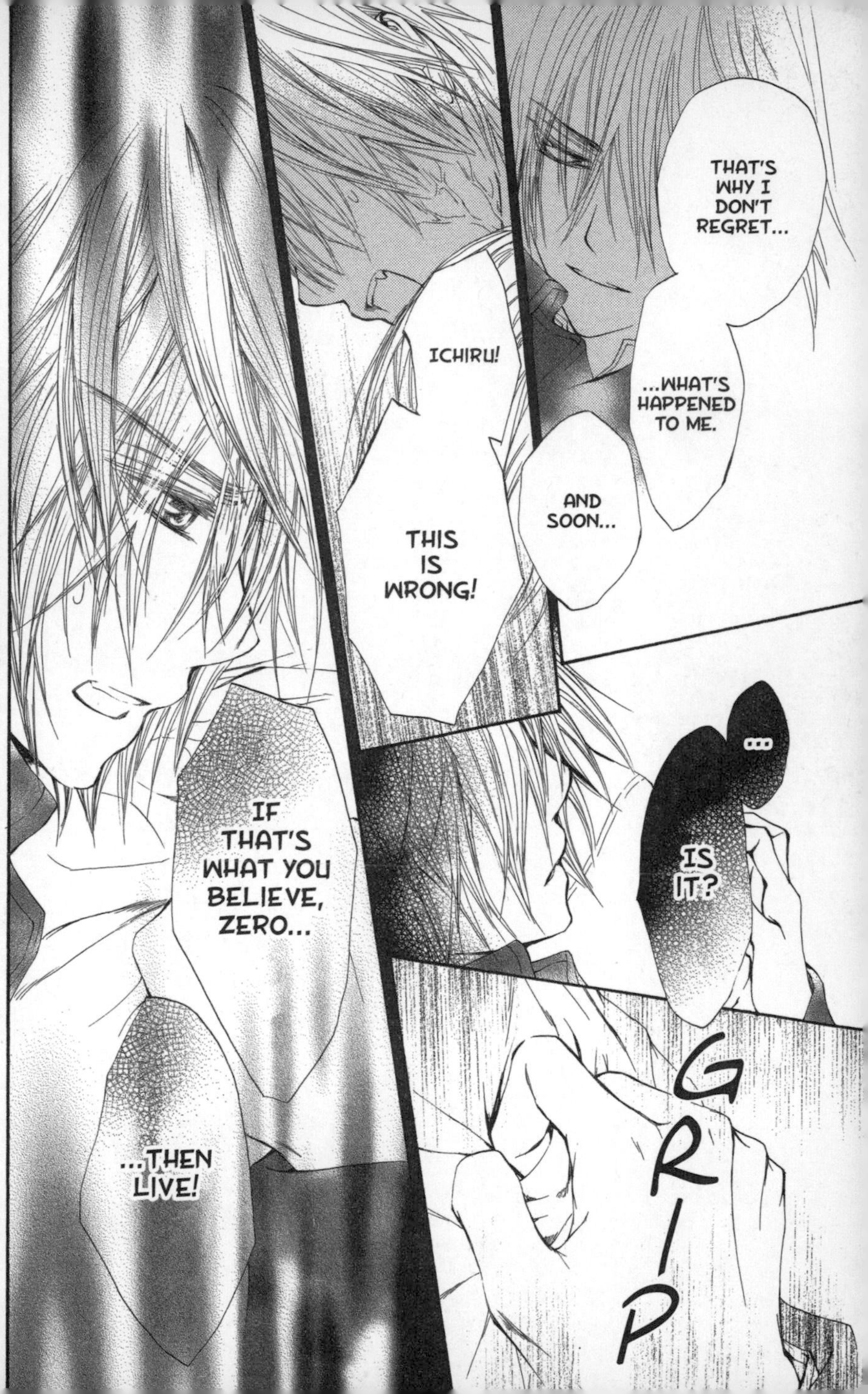
THAT'S WHY I DON'T REGRET...
...WHAT'S HAPPENED TO ME.
AND SOON...
ICHIRU!
THIS IS WRONG!
...
IS IT?
GRIP
IF THAT'S WHAT YOU BELIEVE, ZERO...
...THEN LIVE!

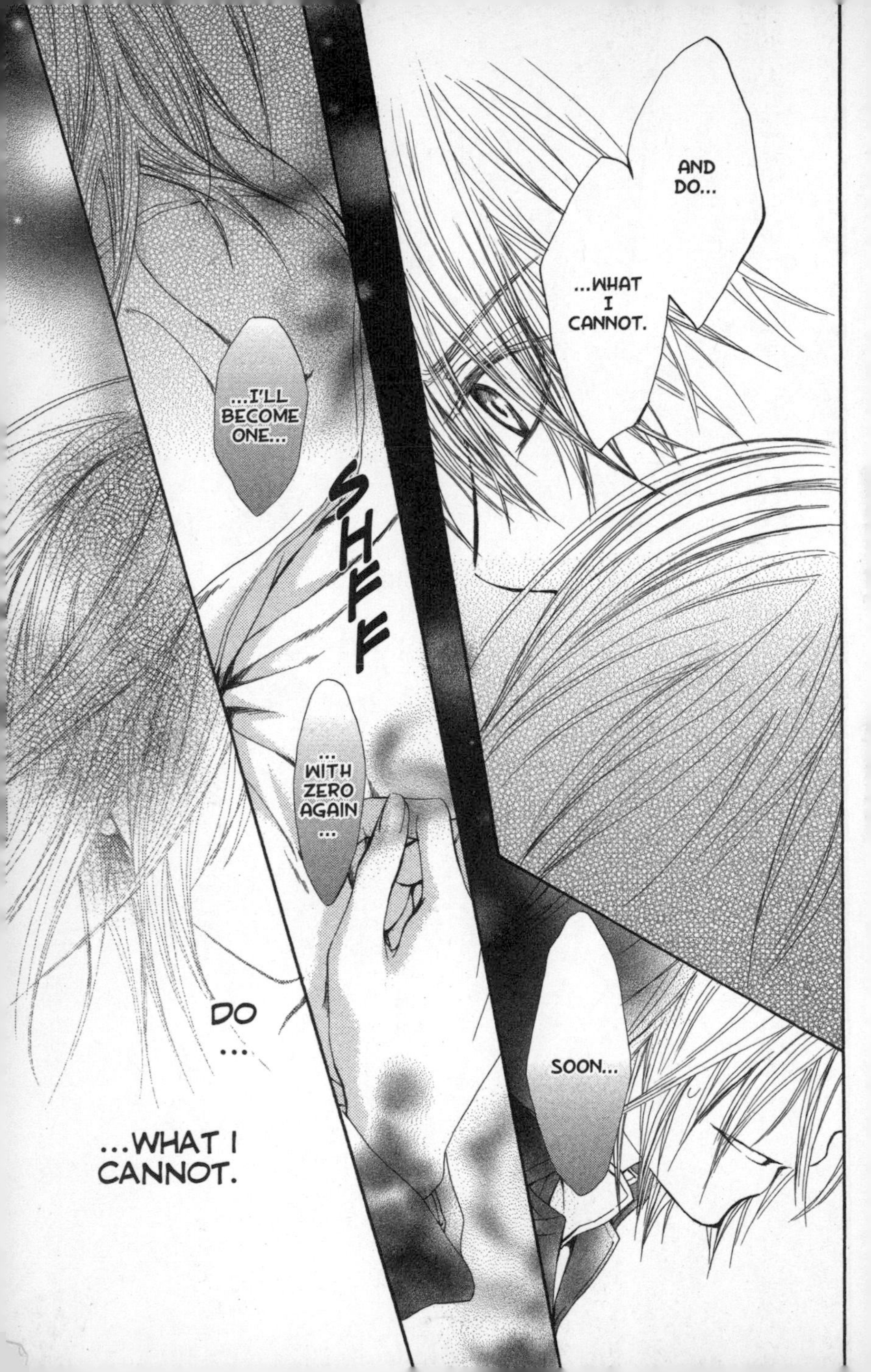
AND DO...
...WHAT I CANNOT.
...I'LL BECOME ONE...
SHFF
...WITH ZERO AGAIN...
SOON...
DO...
...WHAT I CANNOT.

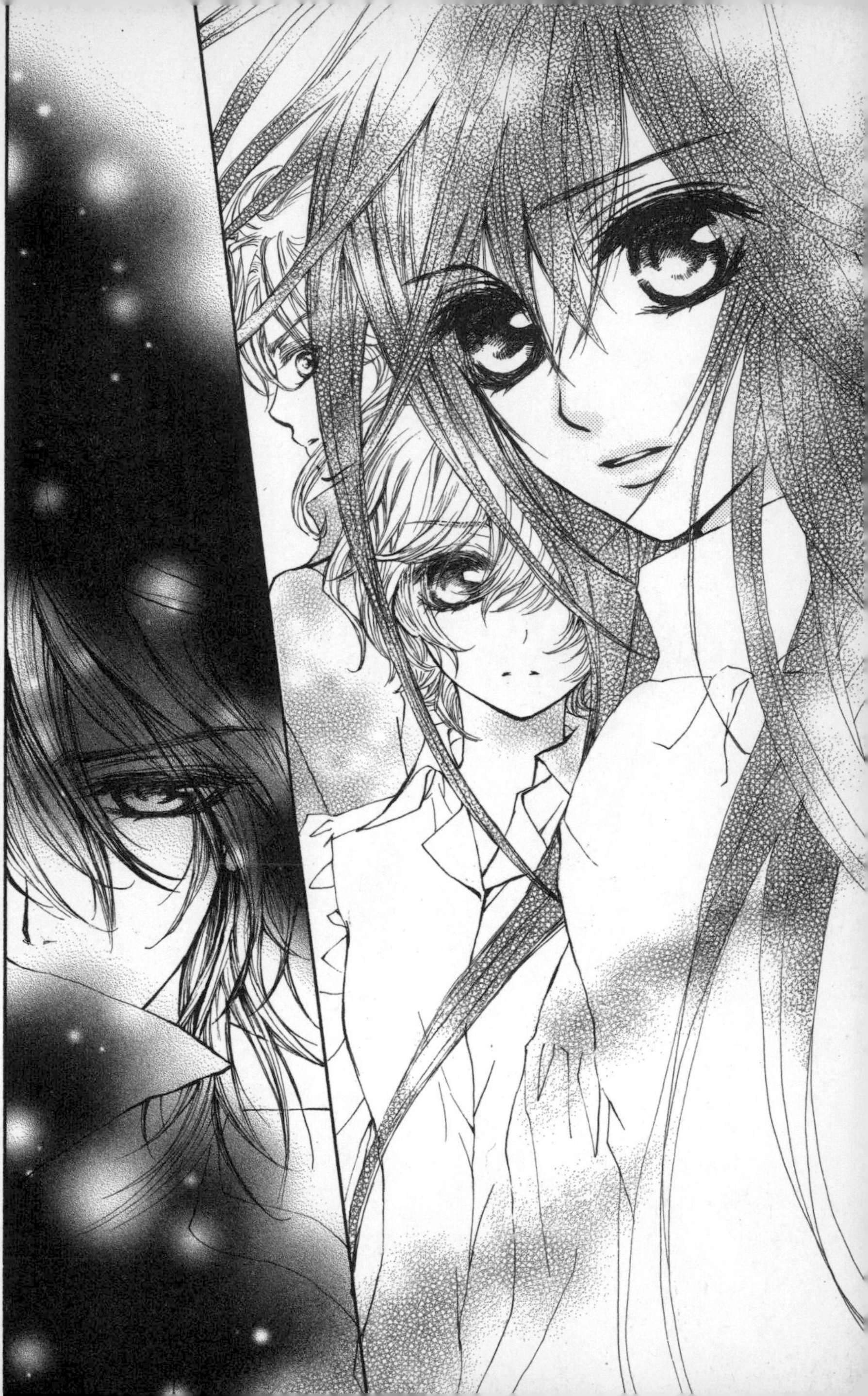

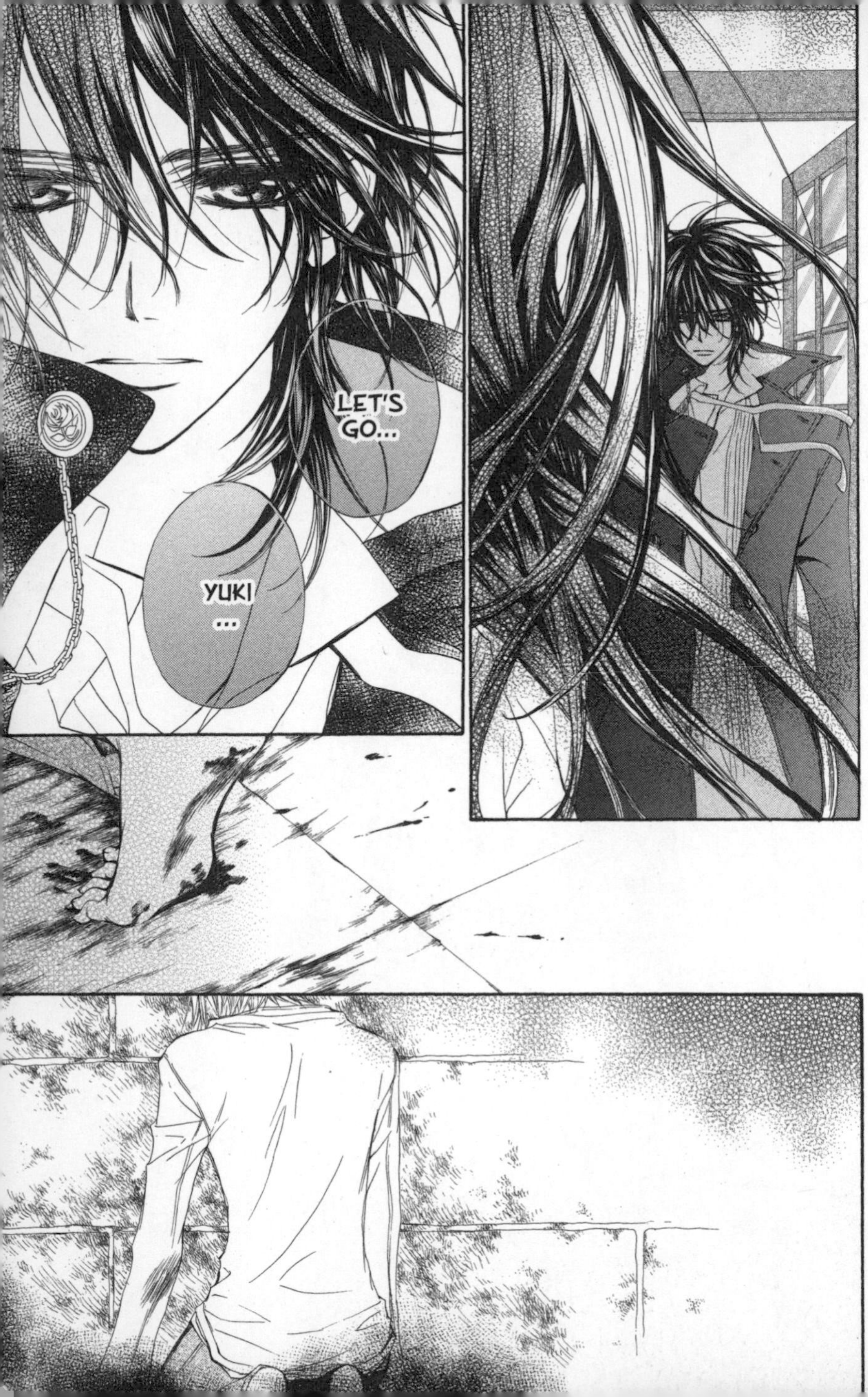
LET'S GO...
YUKI ...

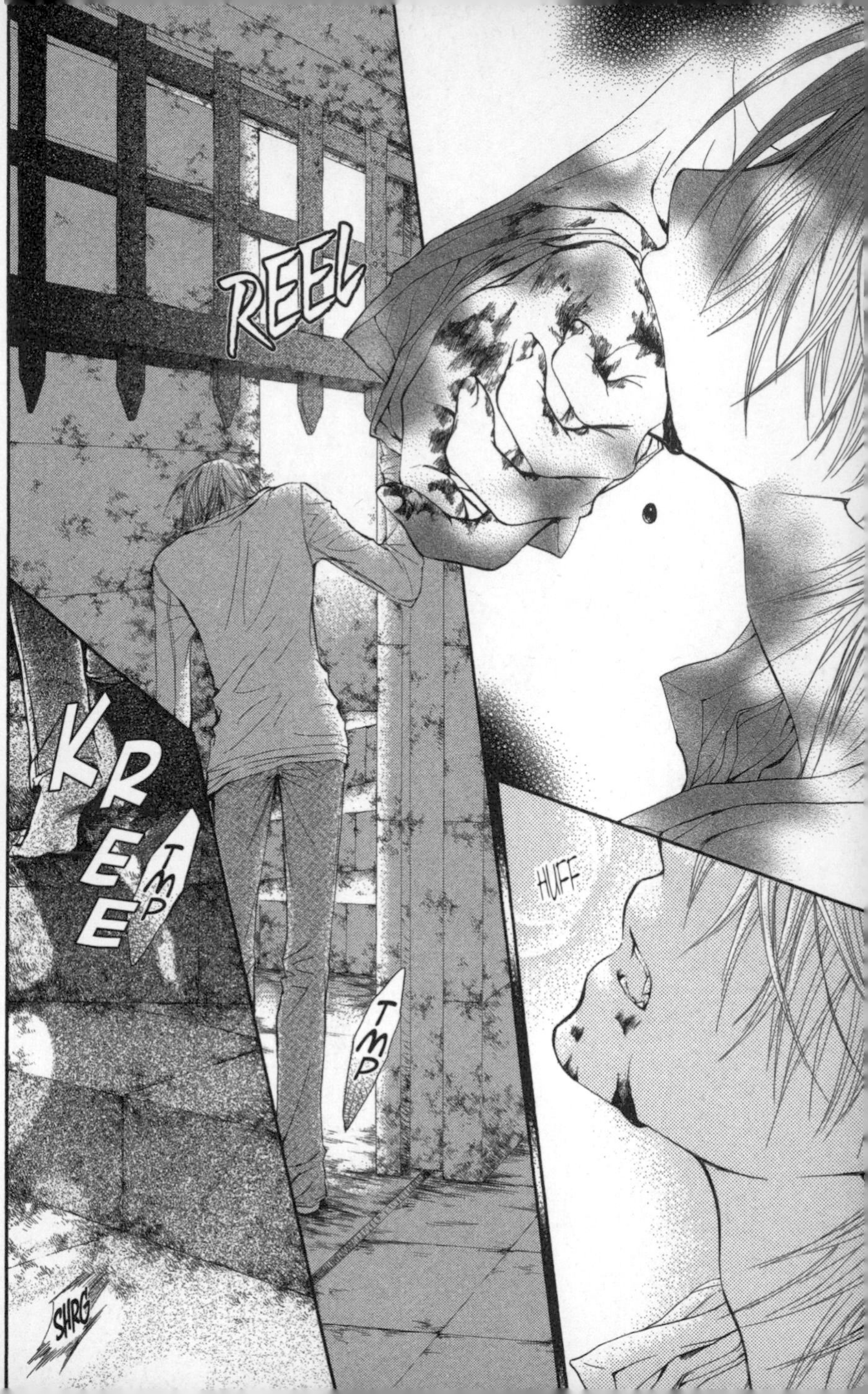
HUFF
REEL
KREEE
TMP
TMP
SHRG

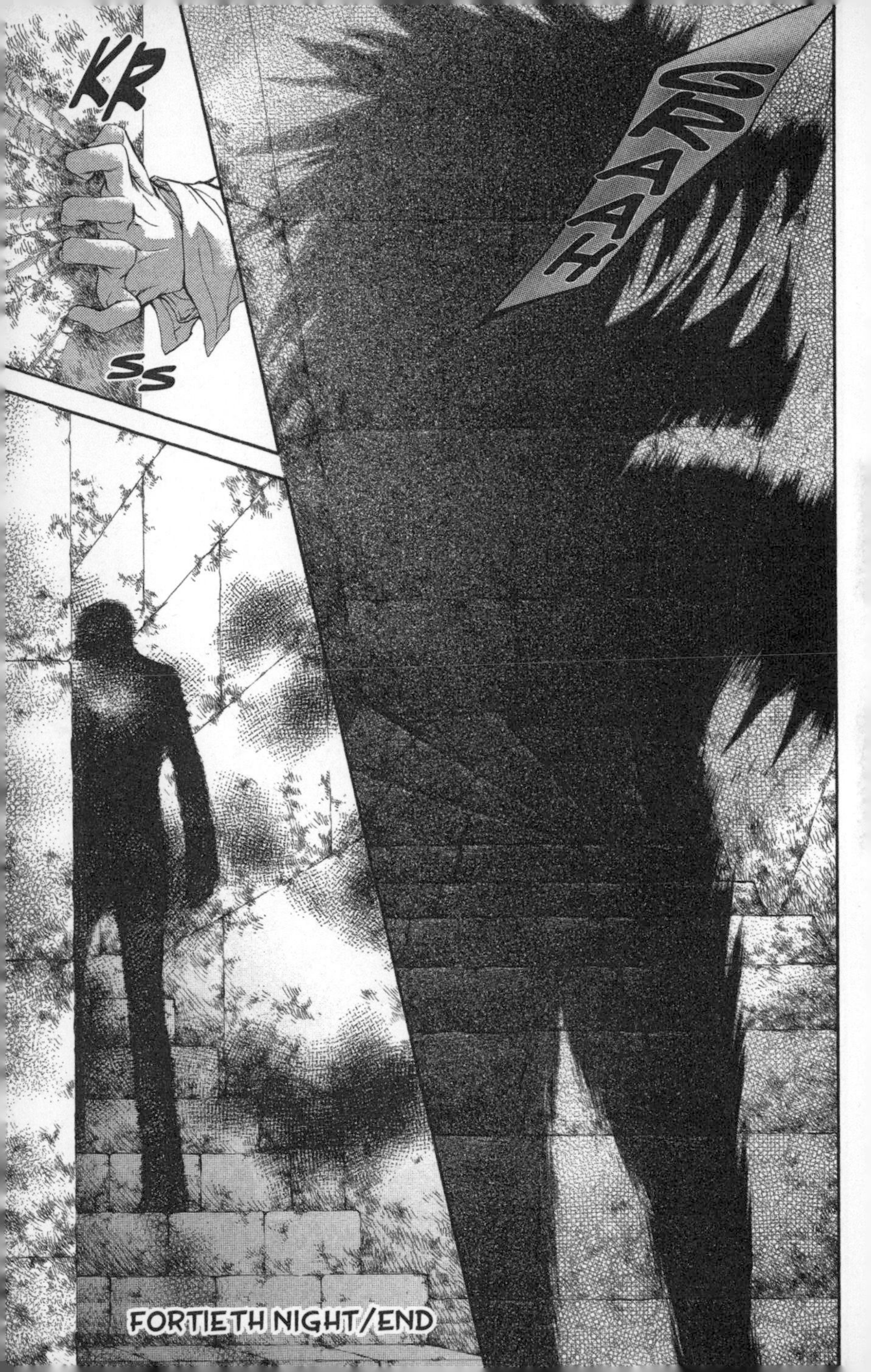
GRAAH
KR
SS
FORTIETH NIGHT/END

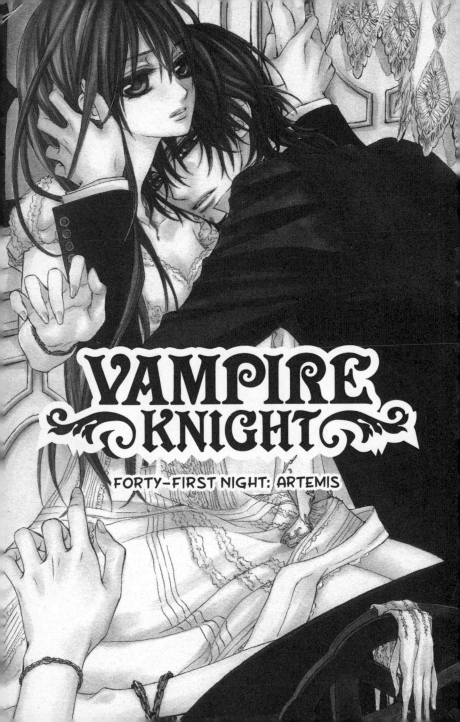

VAMPIRE KNIGHT

FORTY-FIRST NIGHT: ARTEMIS

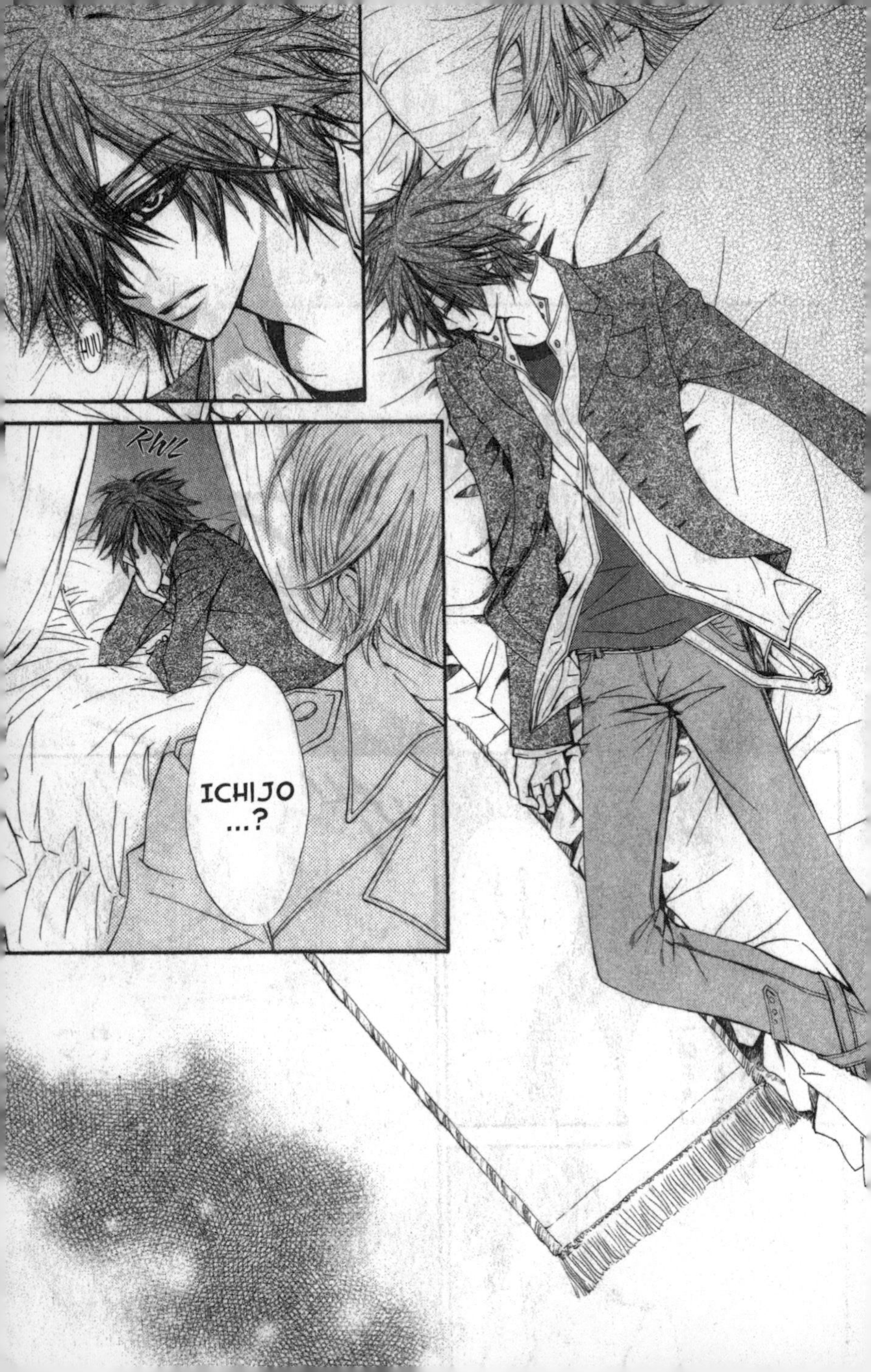
HUU
RWL
ICHIJO ...?

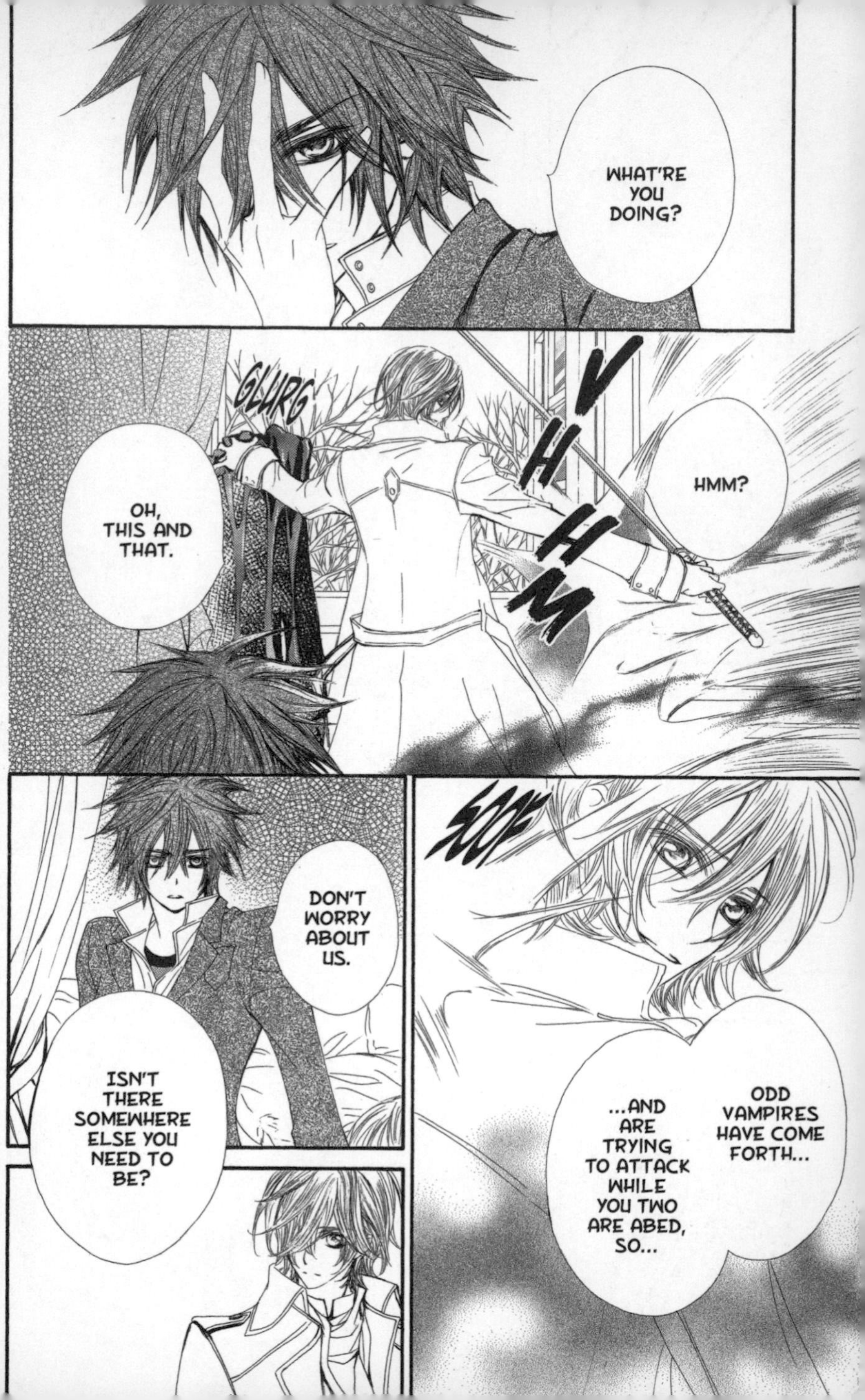
WHAT'RE YOU DOING?
VHHHM
HMM?
GLURG
OH, THIS AND THAT.
ODD VAMPIRES HAVE COME FORTH...
...AND ARE TRYING TO ATTACK WHILE YOU TWO ARE ABED, SO...
DON'T WORRY ABOUT US.
ISN'T THERE SOMEWHERE ELSE YOU NEED TO BE?

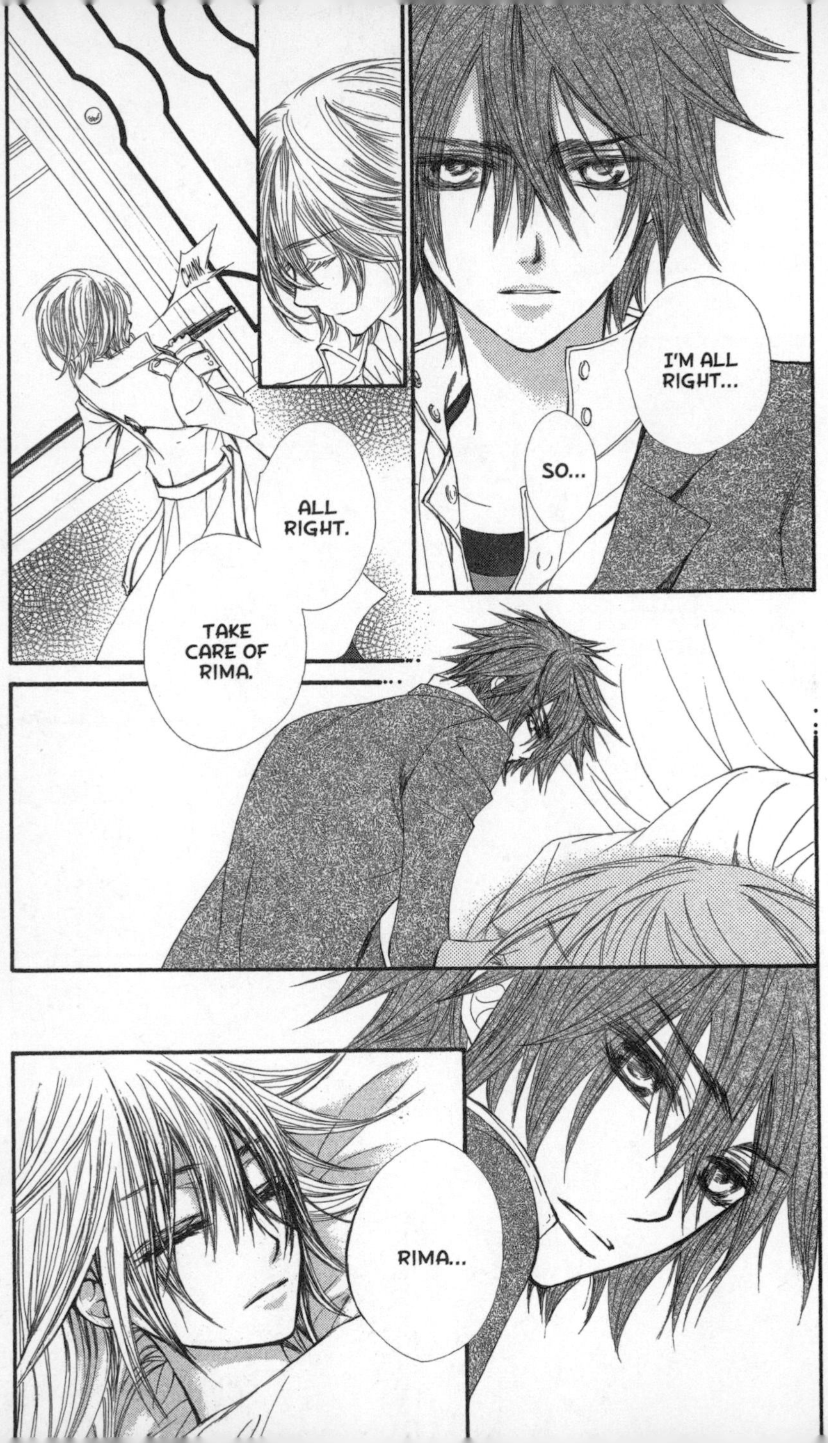
I'M ALL RIGHT...
SO...
CHINK
ALL RIGHT.
TAKE CARE OF RIMA.
RIMA...

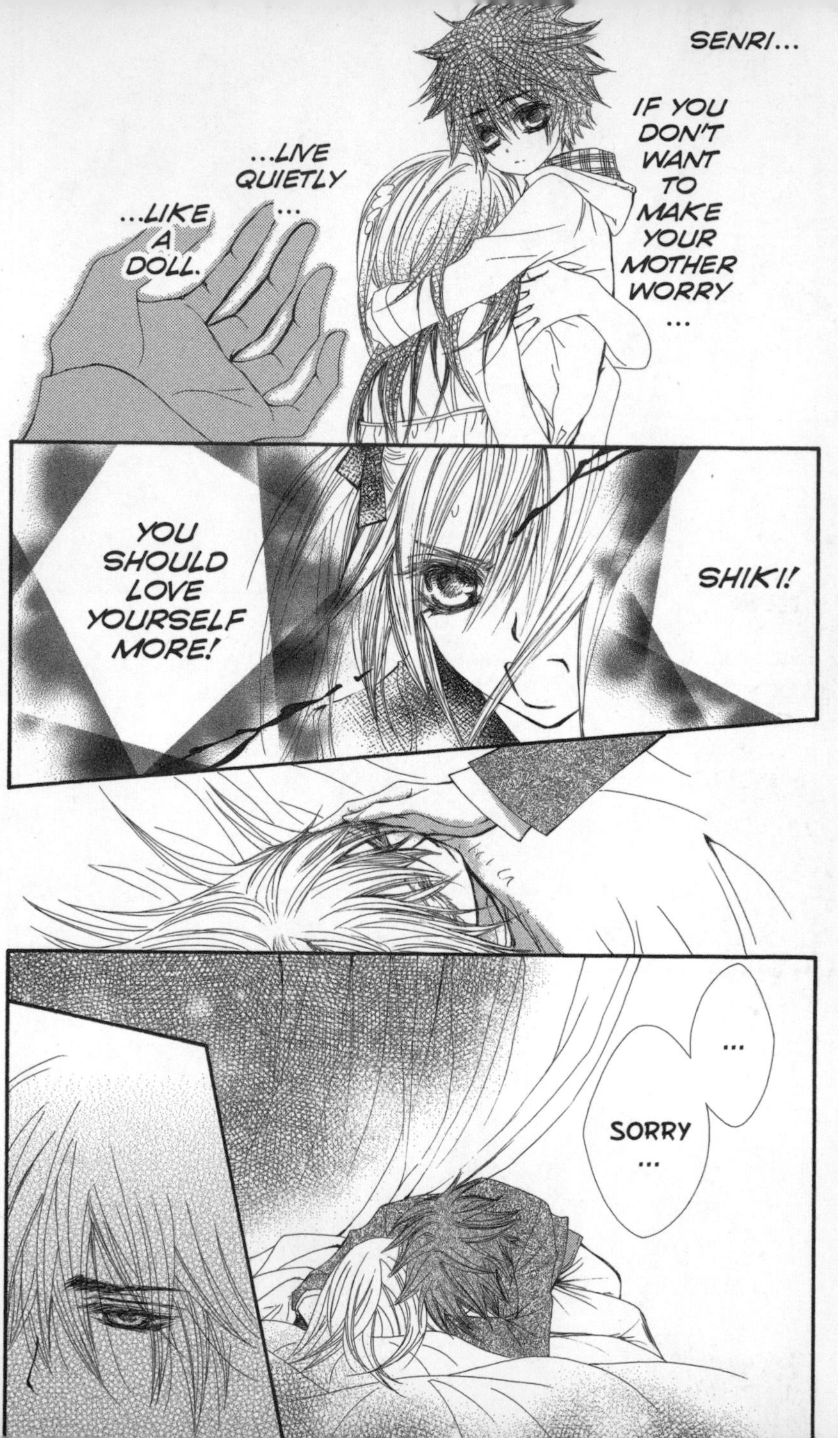
SENRI...
IF YOU DON'T WANT TO MAKE YOUR MOTHER WORRY ...
...LIVE QUIETLY ...
...LIKE A DOLL.
SHIKI!
YOU SHOULD LOVE YOURSELF MORE!
... SORRY ...

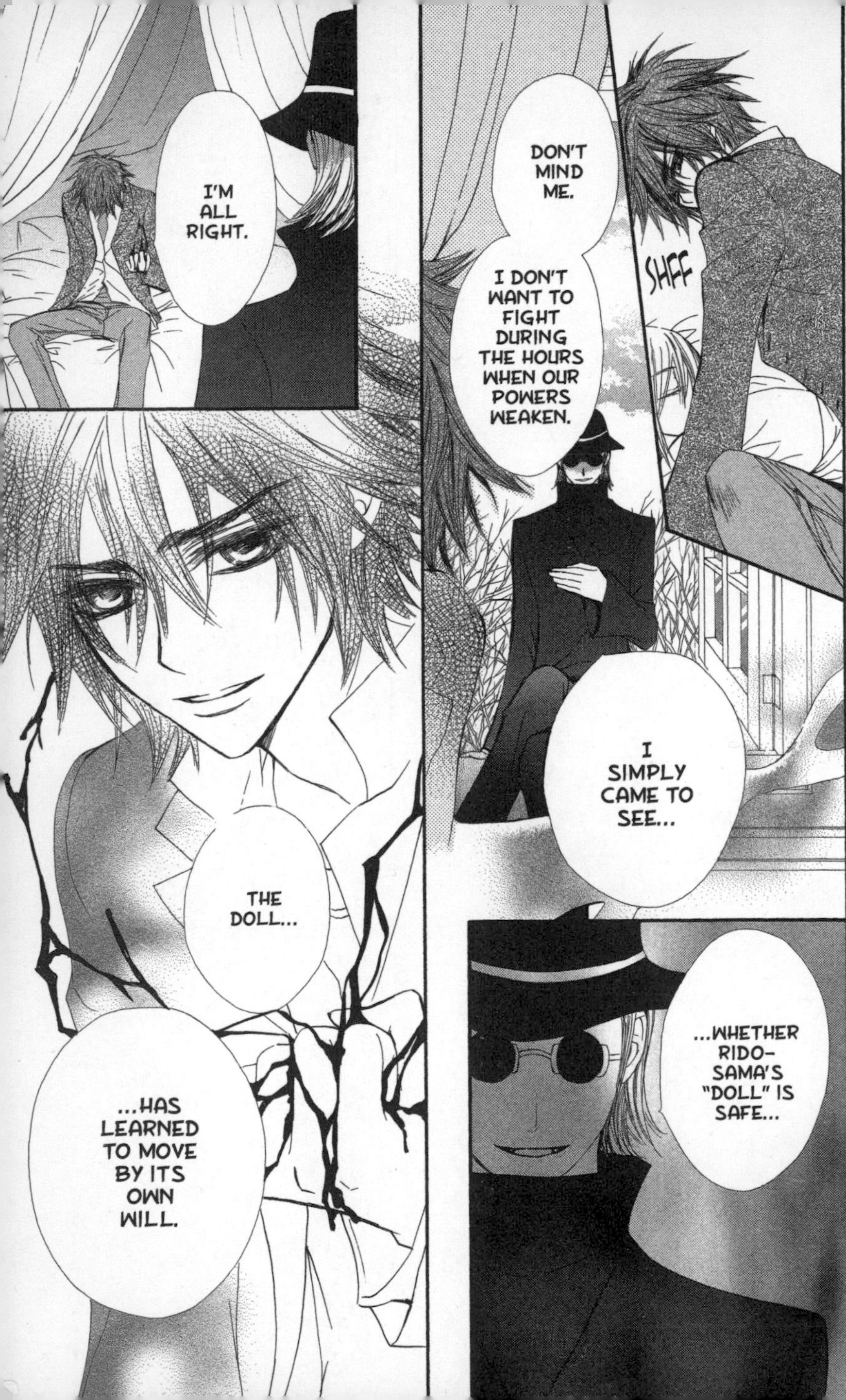
DON'T MIND ME.
SHFF
I DON'T WANT TO FIGHT DURING THE HOURS WHEN OUR POWERS WEAKEN.
I SIMPLY CAME TO SEE...
...WHETHER RIDO-SAMA'S "DOLL" IS SAFE...
I'M ALL RIGHT.
THE DOLL...
...HAS LEARNED TO MOVE BY ITS OWN WILL.

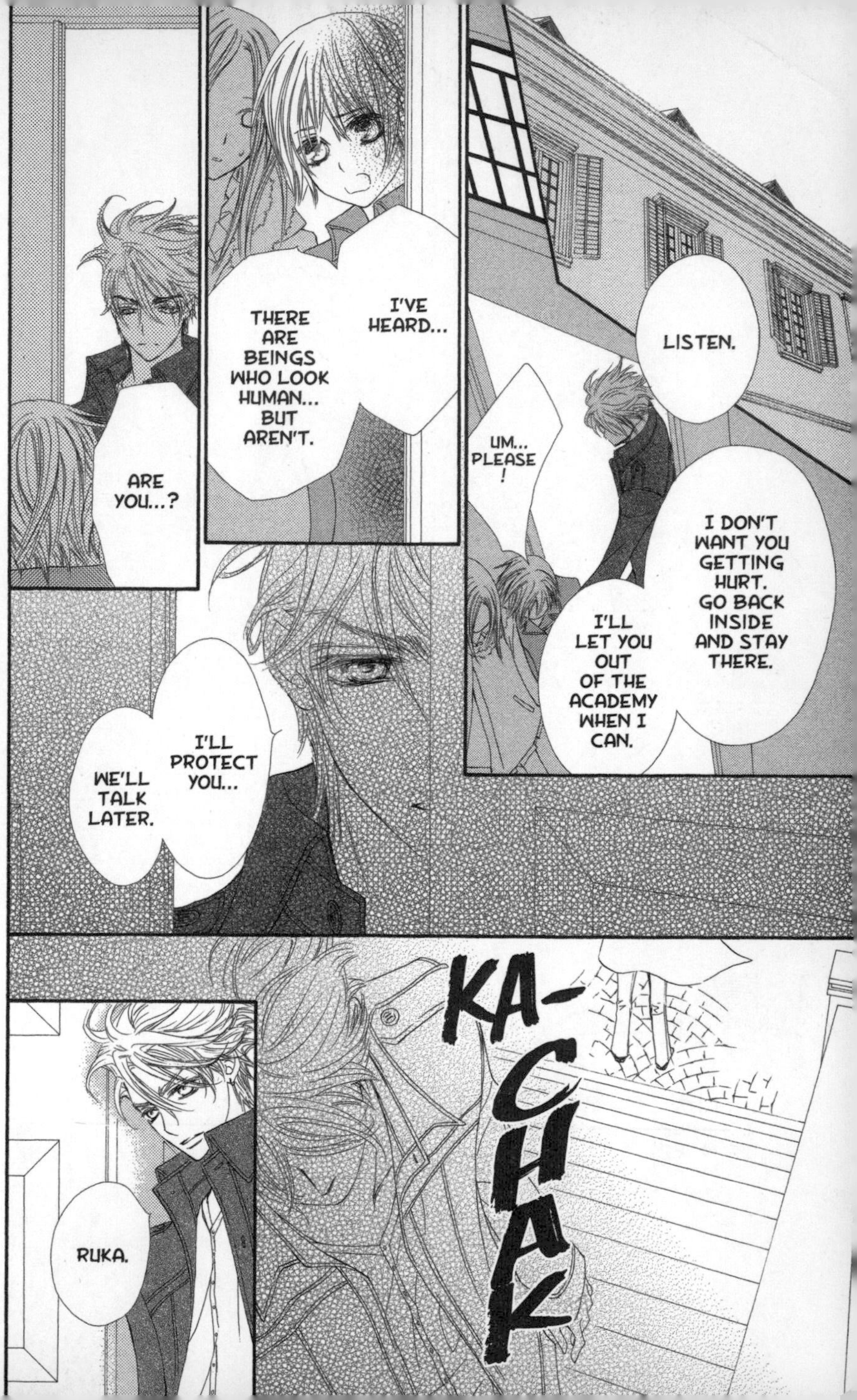
LISTEN.
UM... PLEASE!
I DON'T WANT YOU GETTING HURT. GO BACK INSIDE AND STAY THERE.
I'LL LET YOU OUT OF THE ACADEMY WHEN I CAN.
I'VE HEARD...
THERE ARE BEINGS WHO LOOK HUMAN... BUT AREN'T.
ARE YOU...?
I'LL PROTECT YOU...
WE'LL TALK LATER.
KA-CHAK
RUKA.

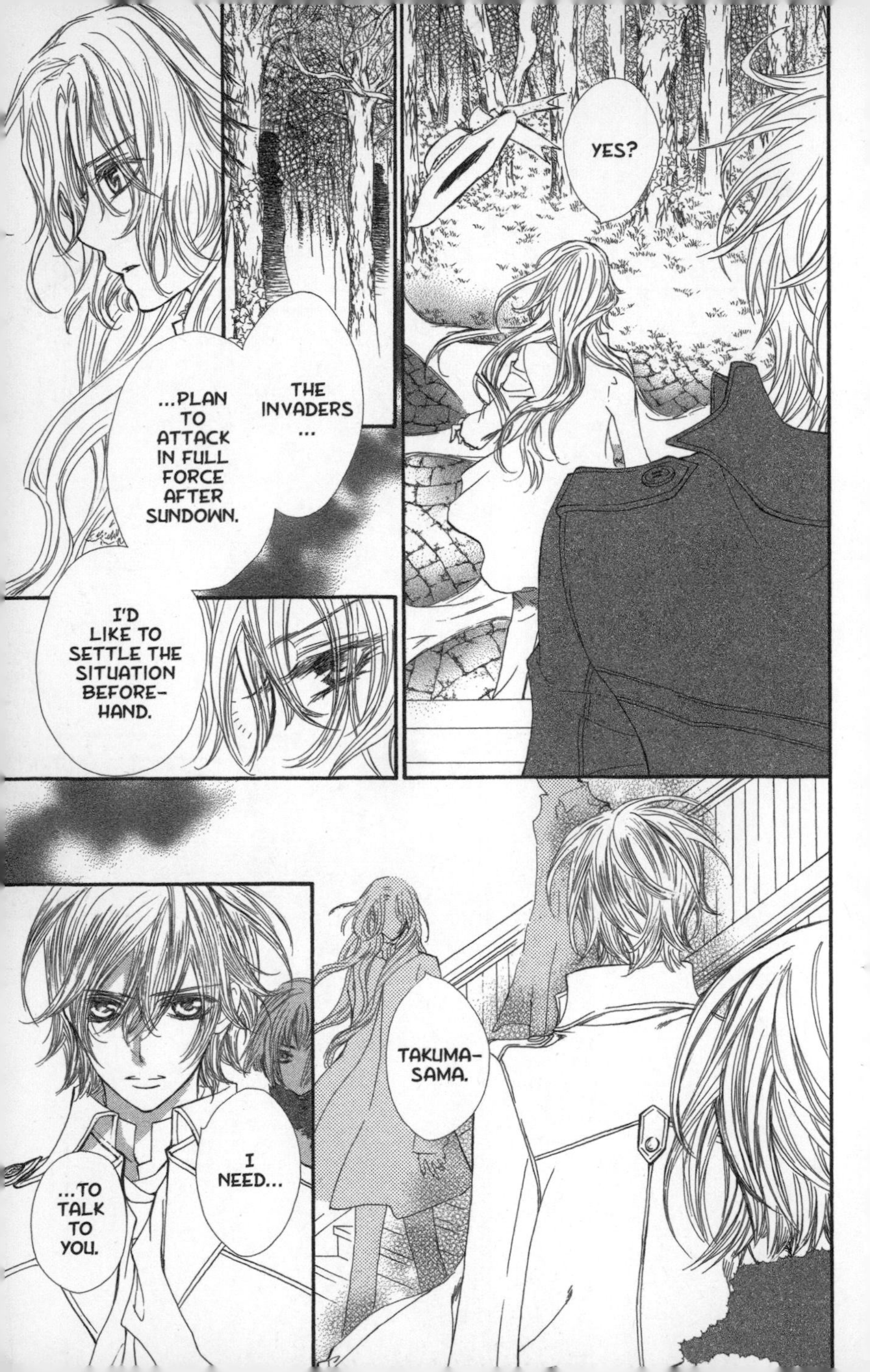
YES?
THE INVADERS...
...PLAN TO ATTACK IN FULL FORCE AFTER SUNDOWN.
I'D LIKE TO SETTLE THE SITUATION BEFOREHAND.
TAKUMA-SAMA.
I NEED...
...TO TALK TO YOU.

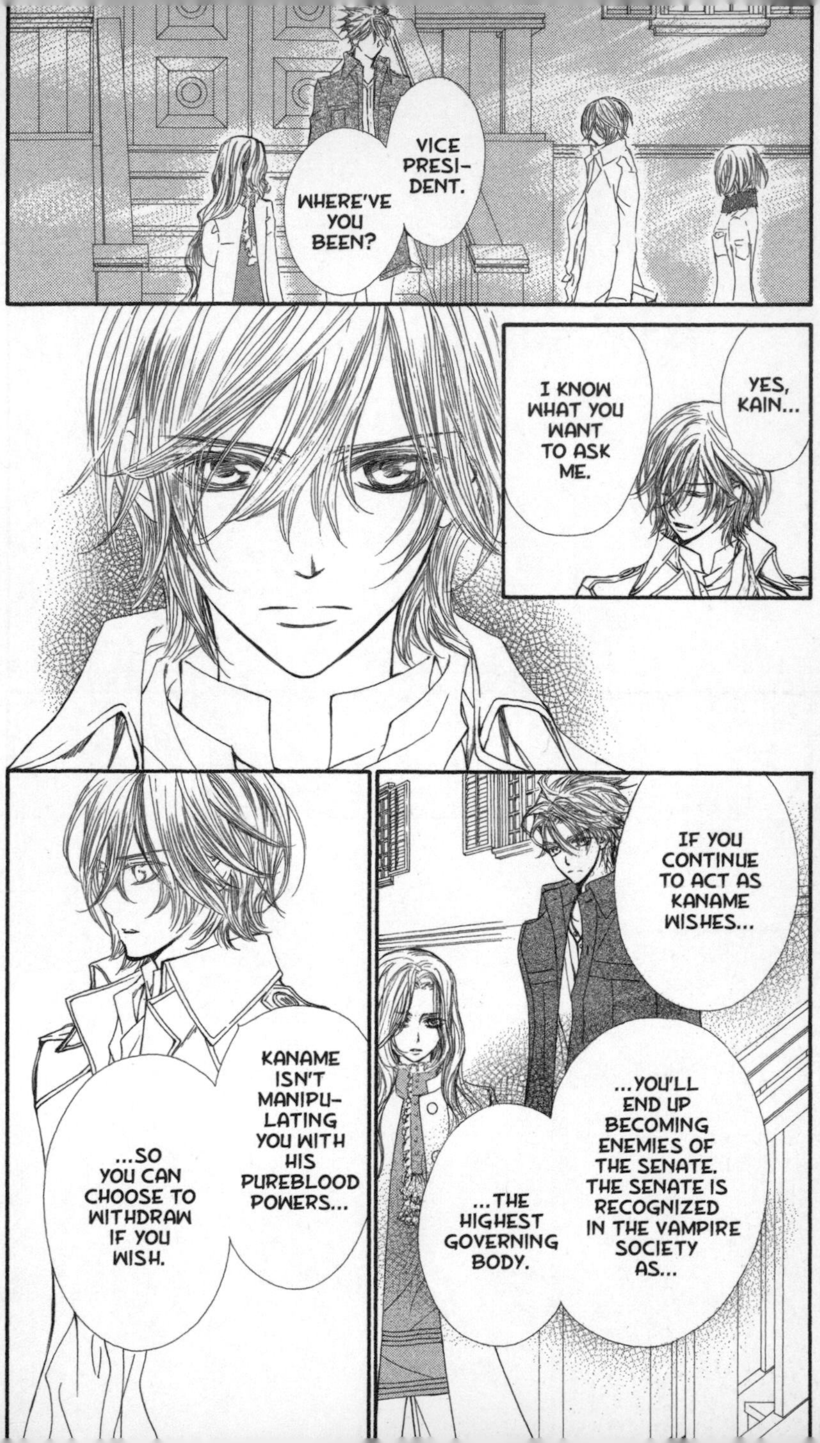
VICE PRESI-DENT.
WHERE'VE YOU BEEN?
YES, KAIN...
I KNOW WHAT YOU WANT TO ASK ME.
IF YOU CONTINUE TO ACT AS KANAME WISHES...
...YOU'LL END UP BECOMING ENEMIES OF THE SENATE. THE SENATE IS RECOGNIZED IN THE VAMPIRE SOCIETY AS...
...THE HIGHEST GOVERNING BODY.
KANAME ISN'T MANIPU-LATING YOU WITH HIS PUREBLOOD POWERS...
...SO YOU CAN CHOOSE TO WITHDRAW IF YOU WISH.

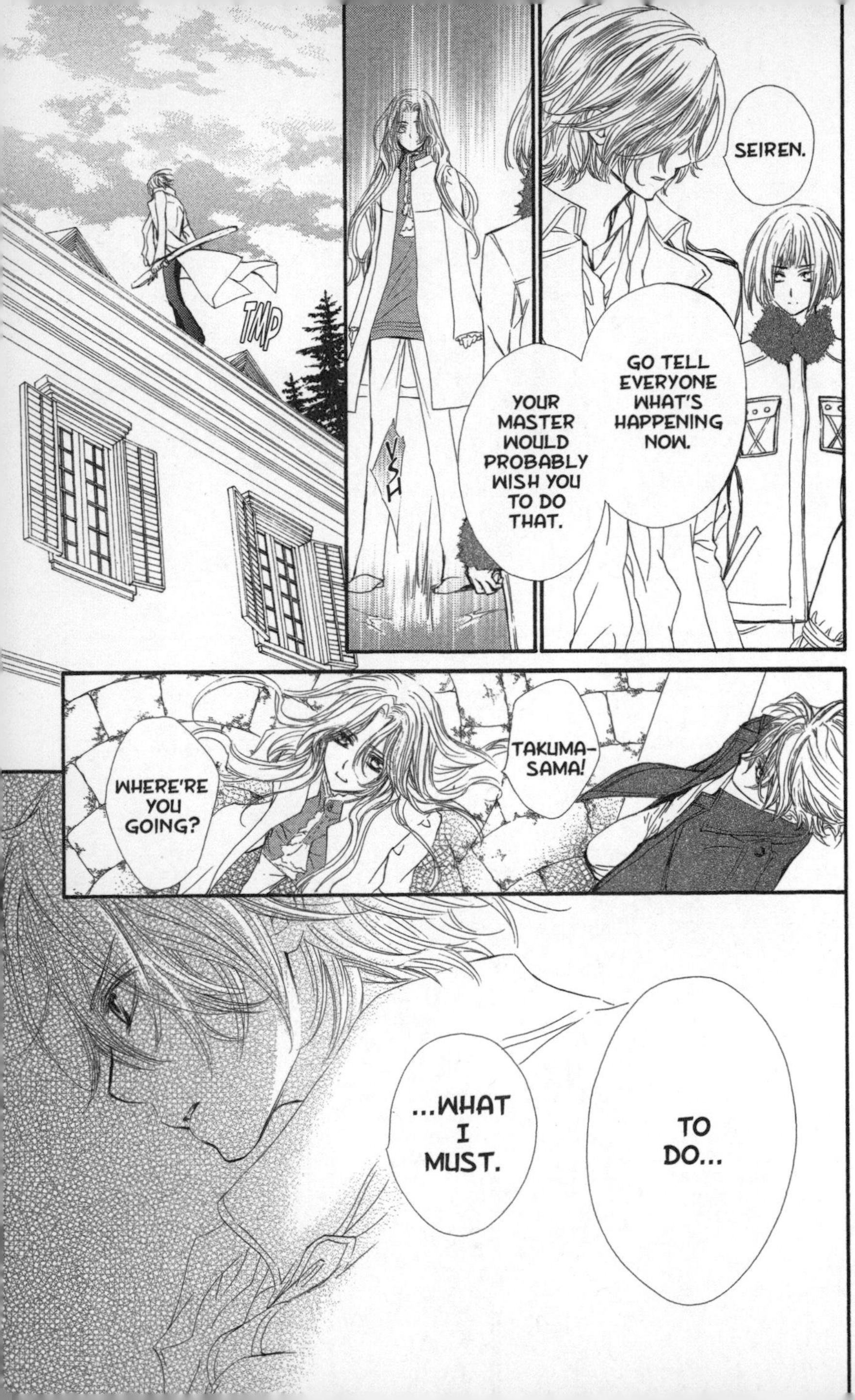
SEIREN.
GO TELL EVERYONE WHAT'S HAPPENING NOW.
YOUR MASTER WOULD PROBABLY WISH YOU TO DO THAT.
VSH
TMP
TAKUMA-SAMA!
WHERE'RE YOU GOING?
TO DO...
...WHAT I MUST.

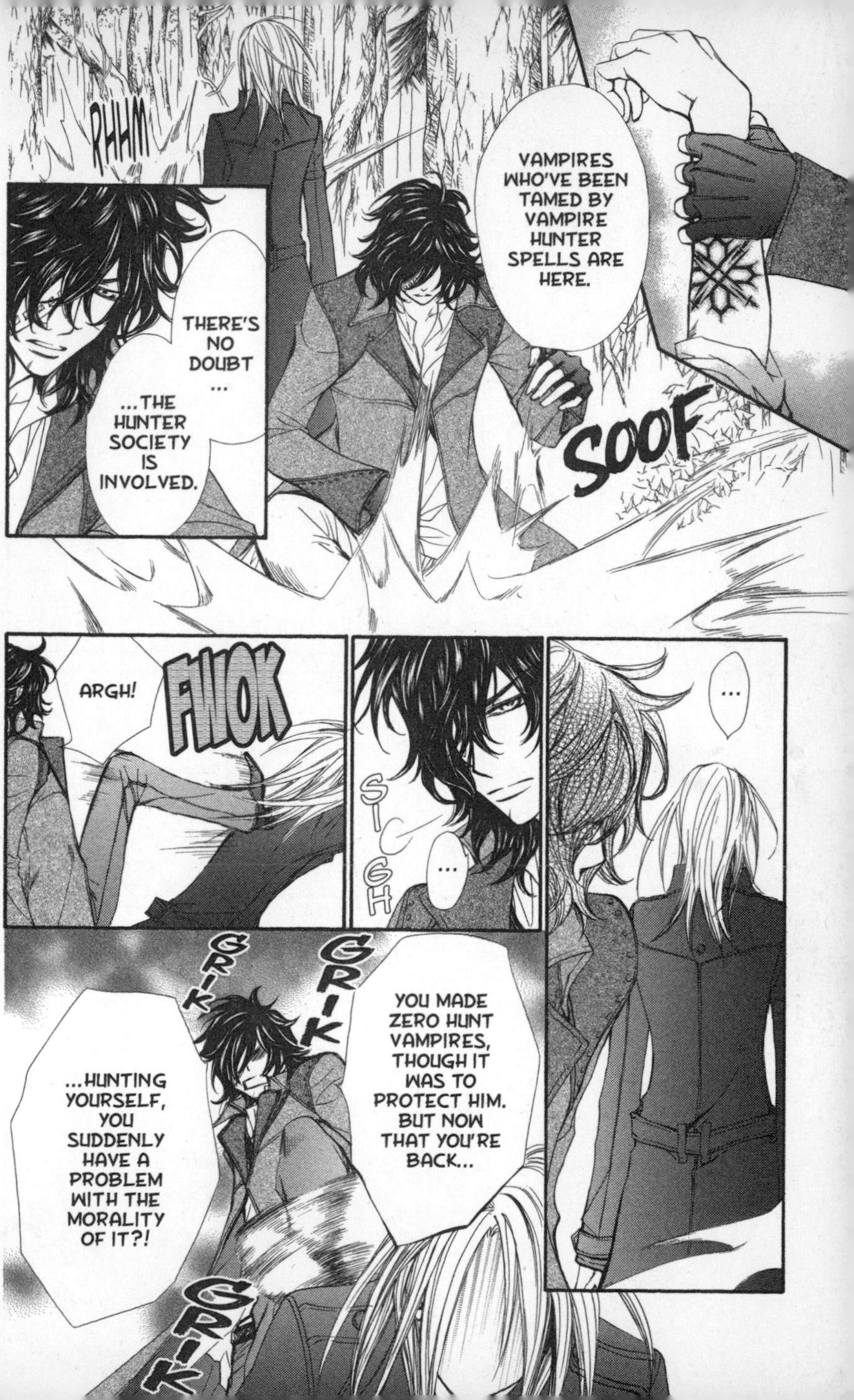
VAMPIRES WHO'VE BEEN TAMED BY VAMPIRE HUNTER SPELLS ARE HERE.
RHHM
SOOF
THERE'S NO DOUBT...
...THE HUNTER SOCIETY IS INVOLVED.
...
SIGH
...
FWOK
ARGH!
YOU MADE ZERO HUNT VAMPIRES, THOUGH IT WAS TO PROTECT HIM. BUT NOW THAT YOU'RE BACK...
GRIK
GRIK
...HUNTING YOURSELF, YOU SUDDENLY HAVE A PROBLEM WITH THE MORALITY OF IT?!
GRIK

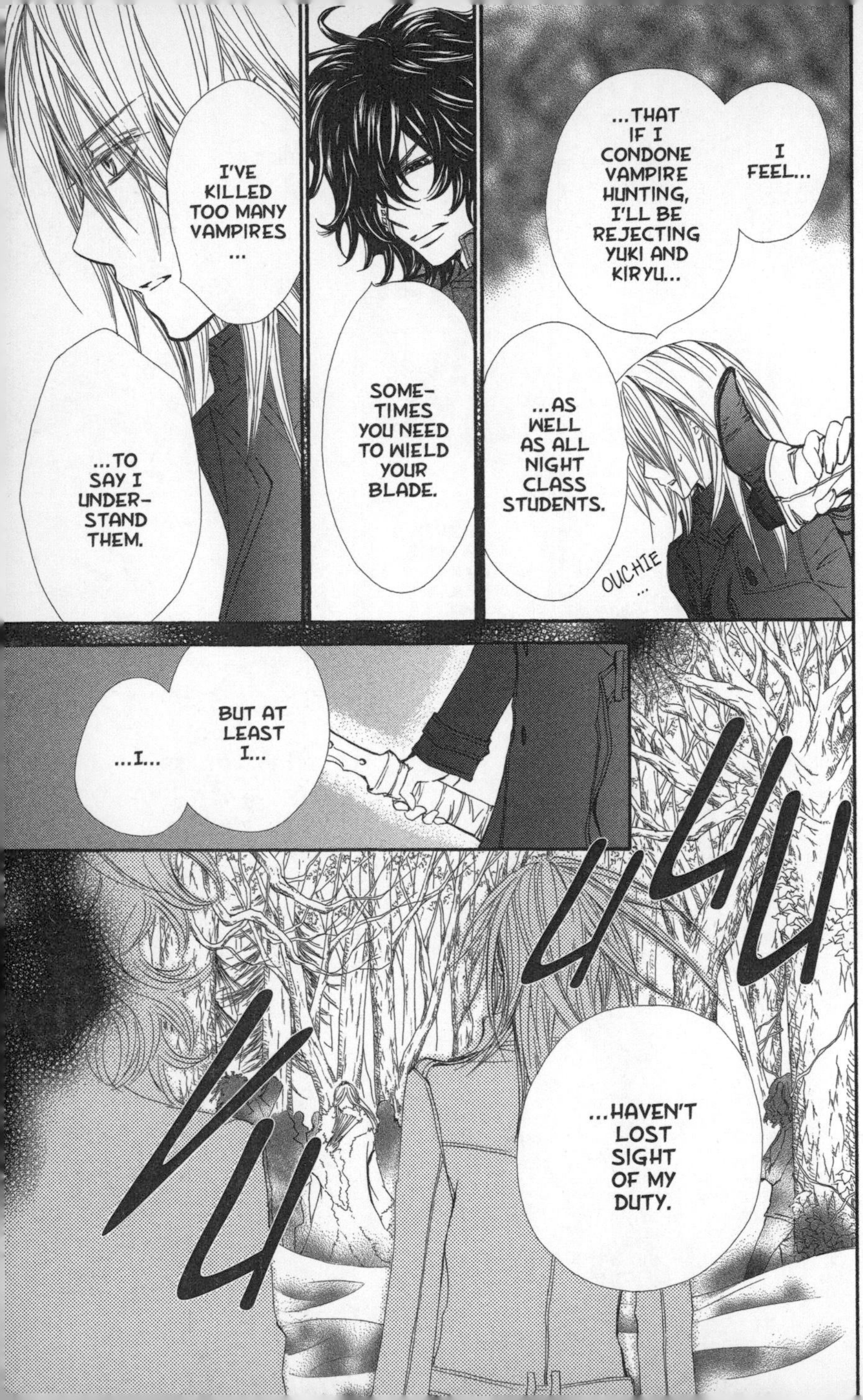
I FEEL...
...THAT IF I CONDONE VAMPIRE HUNTING, I'LL BE REJECTING YUKI AND KIRYU...
...AS WELL AS ALL NIGHT CLASS STUDENTS.
OUCHIE ...
SOME-TIMES YOU NEED TO WIELD YOUR BLADE.
I'VE KILLED TOO MANY VAMPIRES ...
...TO SAY I UNDER-STAND THEM.
BUT AT LEAST I...
...I...
...HAVEN'T LOST SIGHT OF MY DUTY.

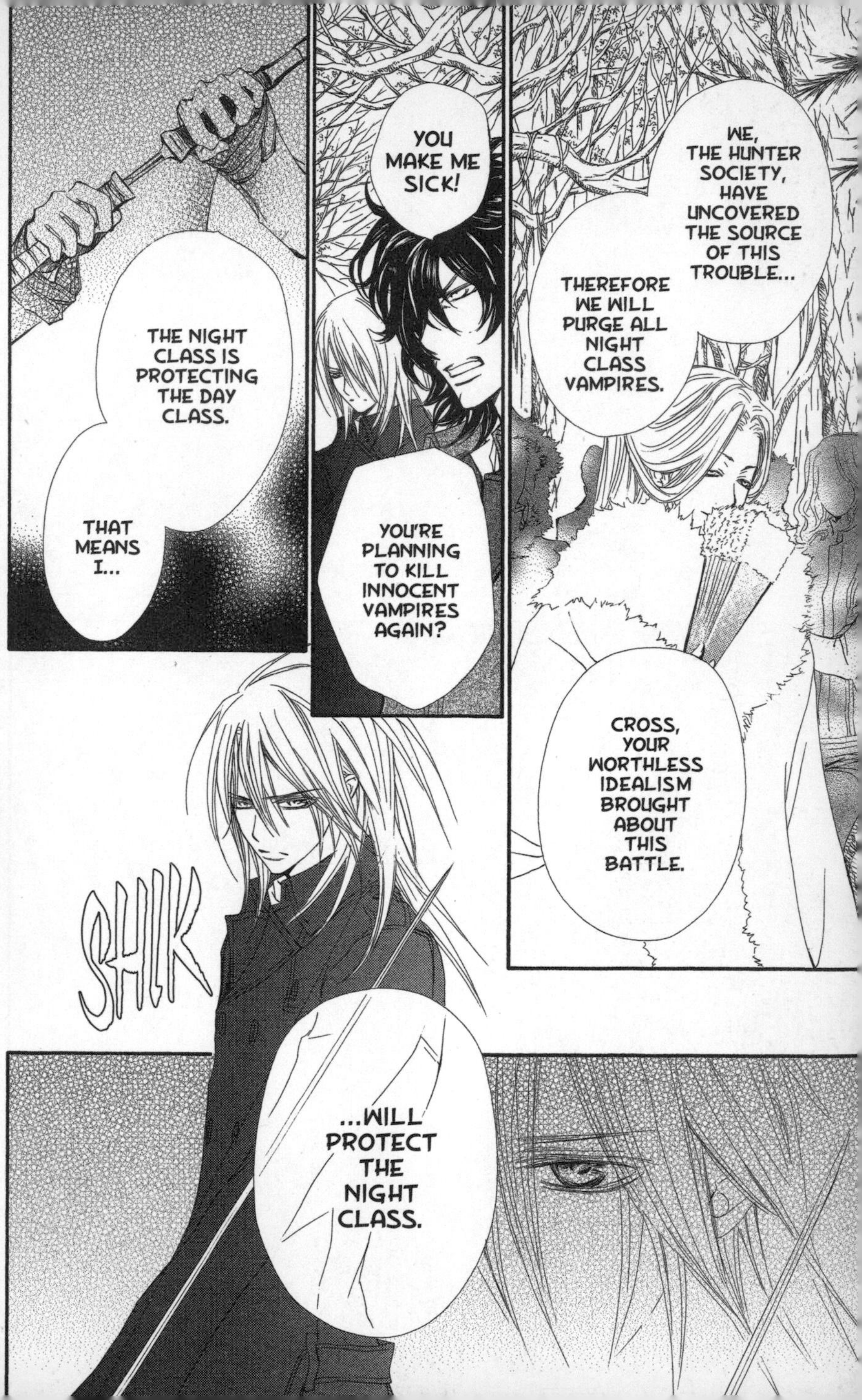
WE, THE HUNTER SOCIETY, HAVE UNCOVERED THE SOURCE OF THIS TROUBLE...
THEREFORE WE WILL PURGE ALL NIGHT CLASS VAMPIRES.
CROSS, YOUR WORTHLESS IDEALISM BROUGHT ABOUT THIS BATTLE.
YOU MAKE ME SICK!
YOU'RE PLANNING TO KILL INNOCENT VAMPIRES AGAIN?
THE NIGHT CLASS IS PROTECTING THE DAY CLASS.
THAT MEANS I...
SHIK
...WILL PROTECT THE NIGHT CLASS.

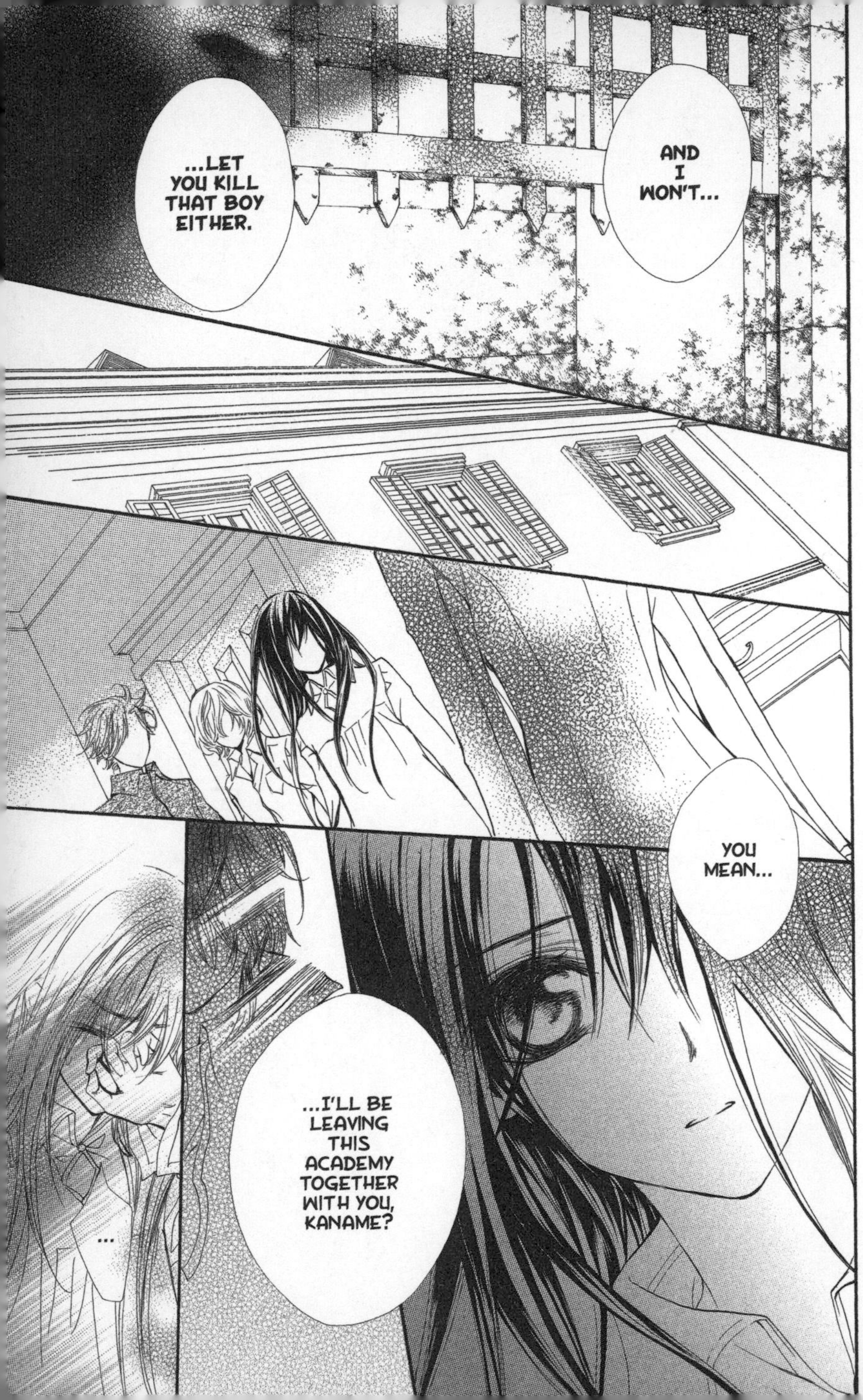
AND I WON'T...
...LET YOU KILL THAT BOY EITHER.
YOU MEAN...
...I'LL BE LEAVING THIS ACADEMY TOGETHER WITH YOU, KANAME?
...

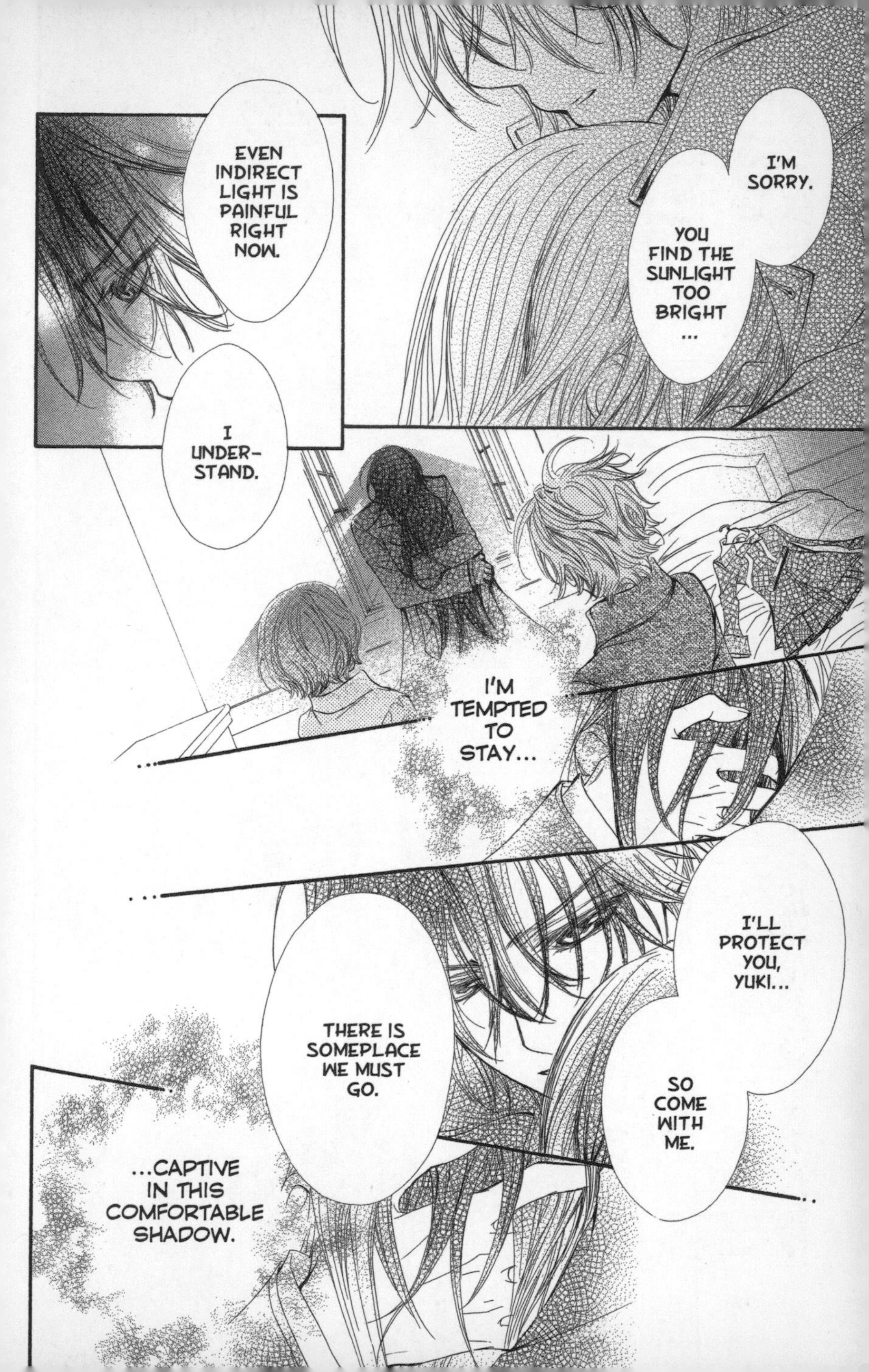
I'M SORRY.
YOU FIND THE SUNLIGHT TOO BRIGHT...
EVEN INDIRECT LIGHT IS PAINFUL RIGHT NOW.
I UNDER-STAND.
I'M TEMPTED TO STAY...
I'LL PROTECT YOU, YUKI...
SO COME WITH ME.
THERE IS SOMEPLACE WE MUST GO.
...CAPTIVE IN THIS COMFORTABLE SHADOW.

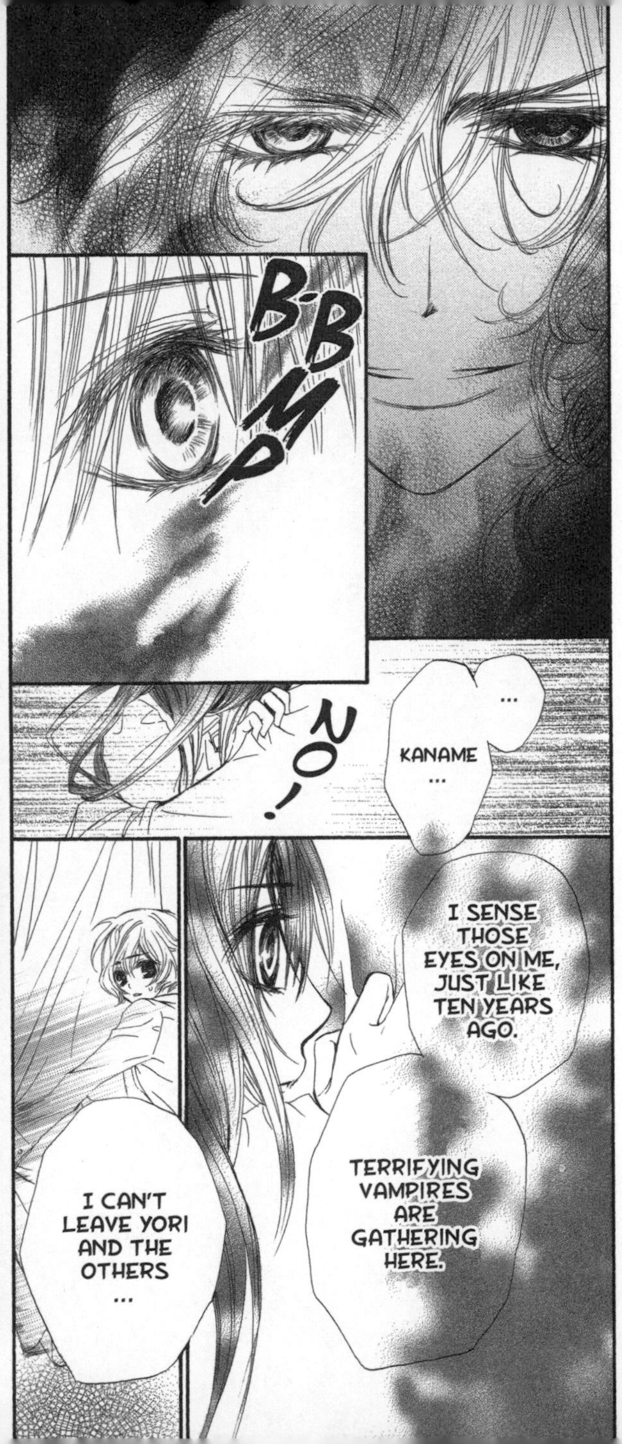
B-BMP
... KANAME ...
NO...!
I SENSE THOSE EYES ON ME, JUST LIKE TEN YEARS AGO.
TERRIFYING VAMPIRES ARE GATHERING HERE.
I CAN'T LEAVE YORI AND THE OTHERS ...

VII

If I end with what I wrote in the second sidebar, people will misunderstand, so let me explain a little more.

There were super-wonderful opportunities.

I had dinner with the anime staff and the voice actors that I adore. I met the ON/OFF pair who are singing the opening theme... (I was so nervous I was acting...weird...) I'm truly thankful to the people who made arrangements and gave me moments that were like a dream.

◆

The fan book came out on the same day as this tankobon. There are a few questions I couldn't answer in the Q&A section because we ran out of space... Q. "Please tell me what tools you use." This is a question that people often ask, so I think I'll answer it here.

Well then.

A. Here's what I use: current tools

(↓ continues)

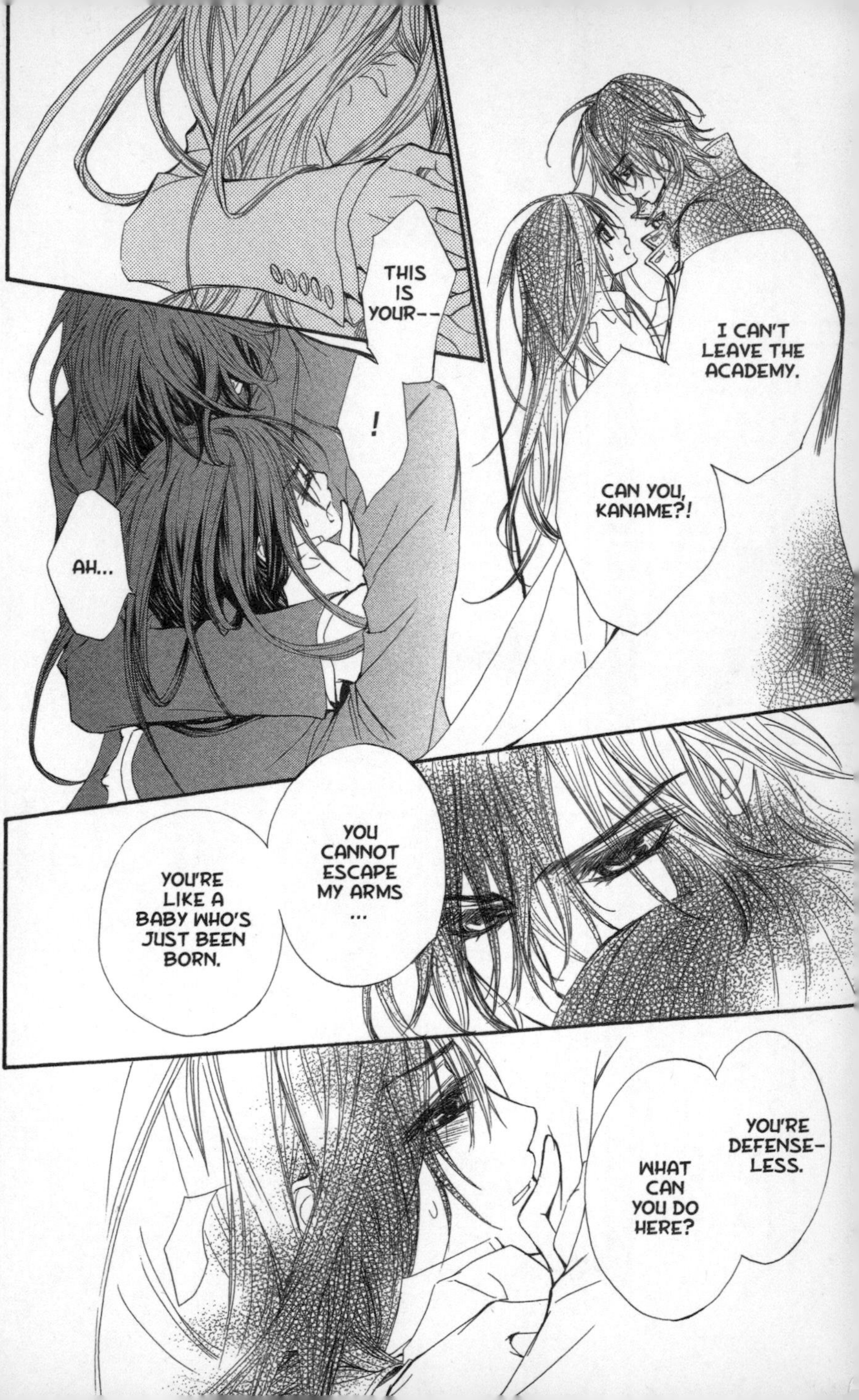
I CAN'T LEAVE THE ACADEMY.
CAN YOU, KANAME?!
THIS IS YOUR--
!
AH...
YOU CANNOT ESCAPE MY ARMS ...
YOU'RE LIKE A BABY WHO'S JUST BEEN BORN.
YOU'RE DEFENSE-LESS.
WHAT CAN YOU DO HERE?

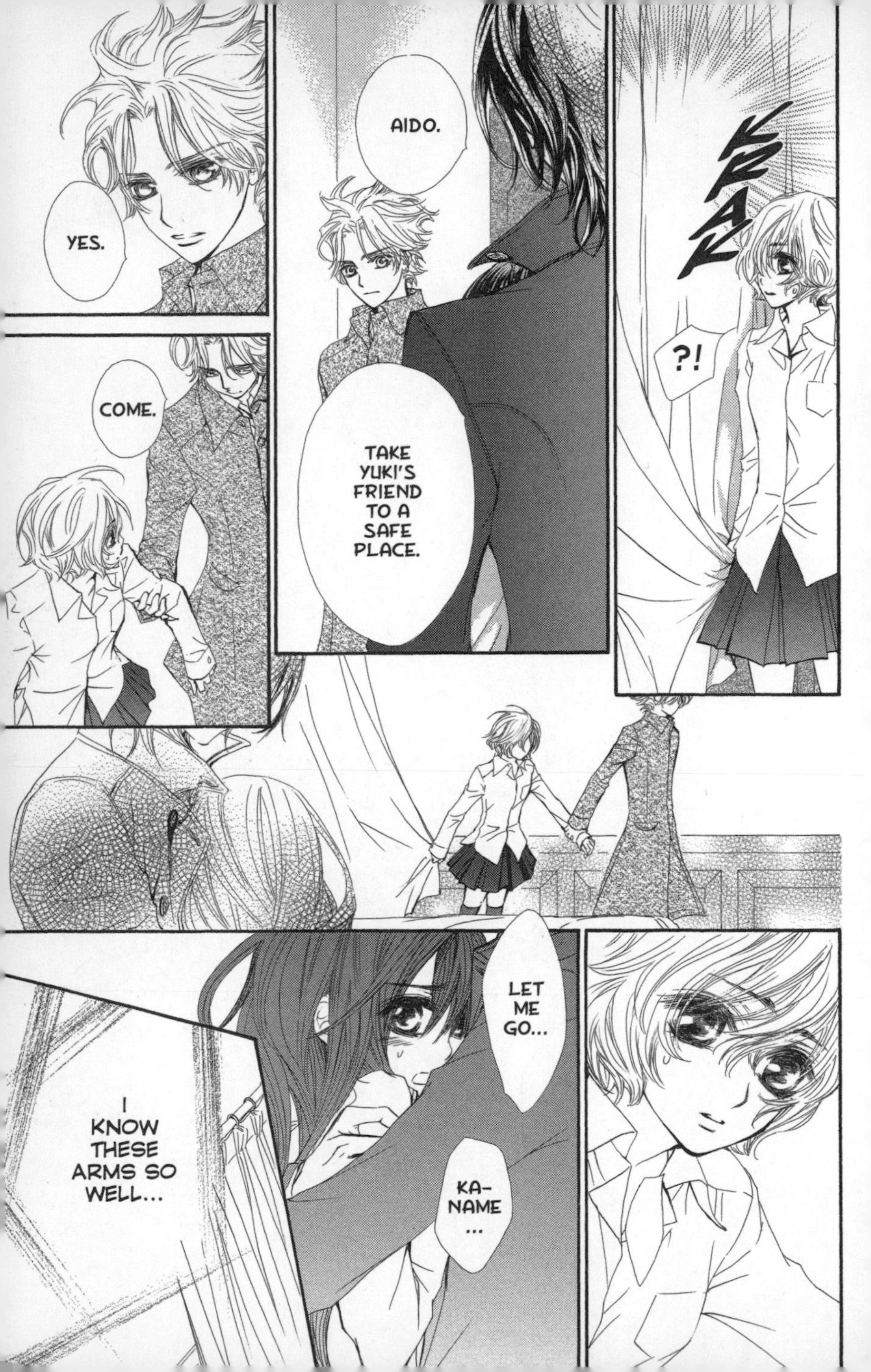
KRAK
?!
AIDO.
TAKE YUKI'S FRIEND TO A SAFE PLACE.
YES.
COME.
LET ME GO...
KA-NAME...
I KNOW THESE ARMS SO WELL...

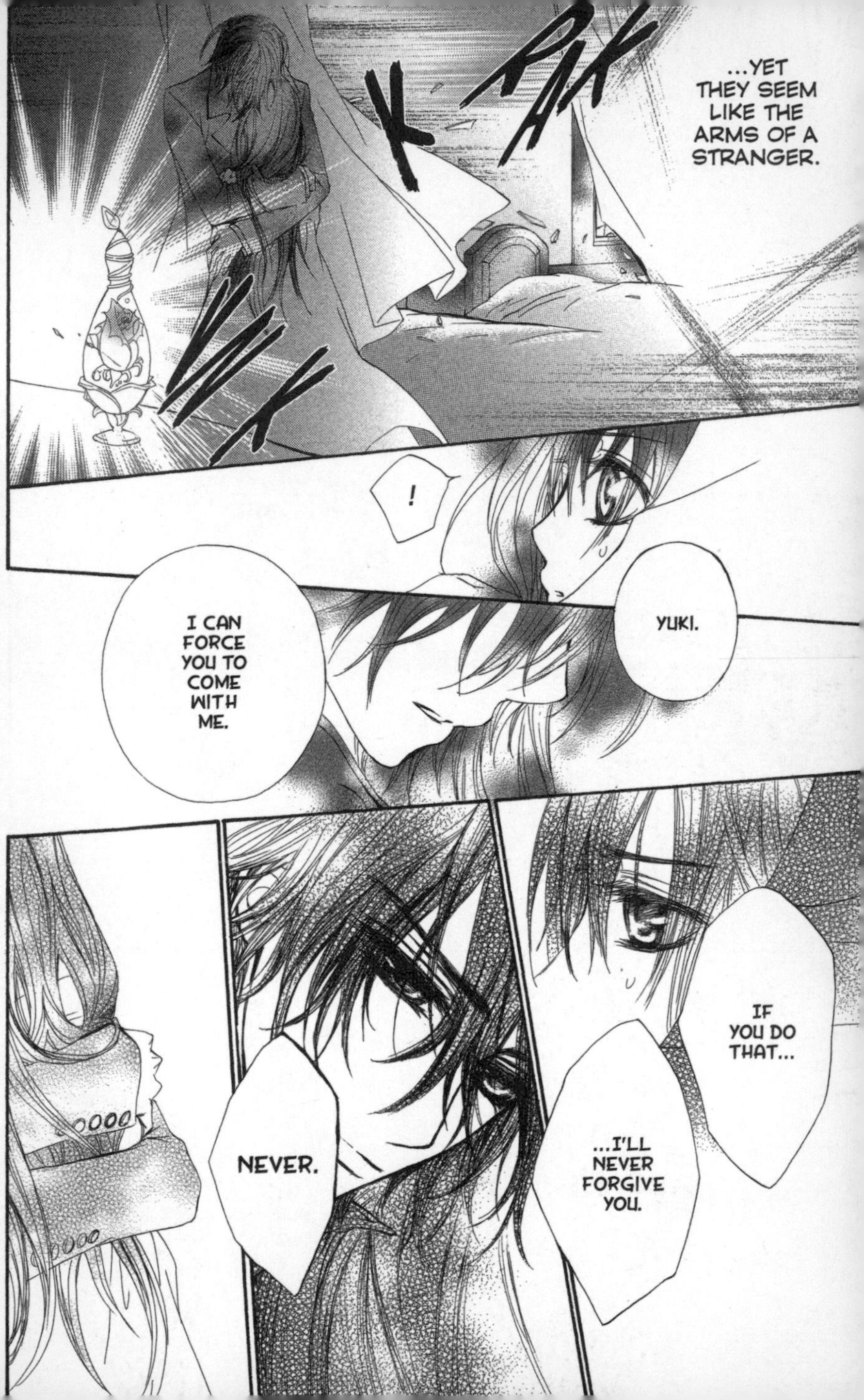
...YET THEY SEEM LIKE THE ARMS OF A STRANGER.
!
YUKI.
I CAN FORCE YOU TO COME WITH ME.
IF YOU DO THAT...
...I'LL NEVER FORGIVE YOU.
NEVER.

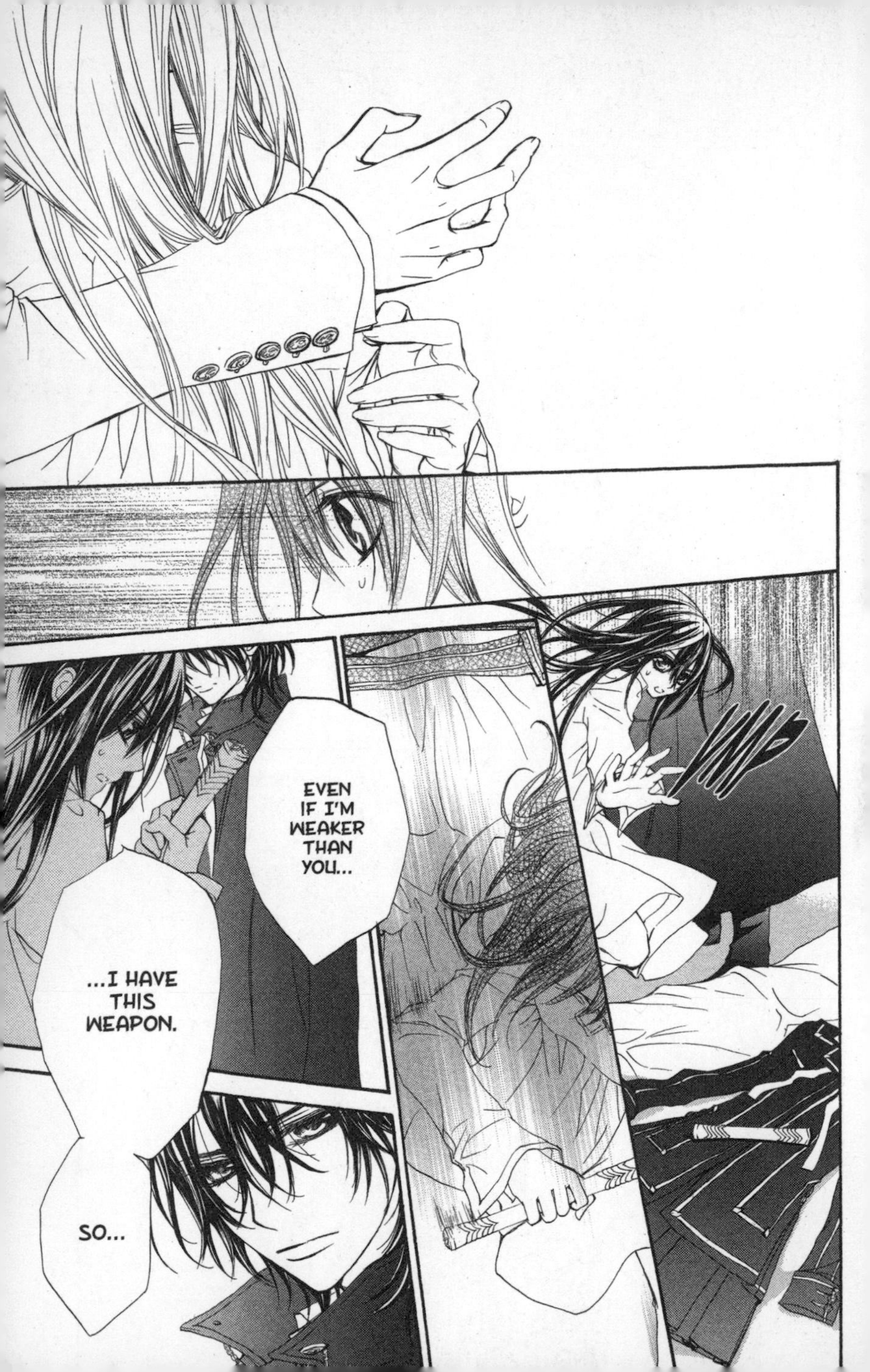
EVEN IF I'M WEAKER THAN YOU...
...I HAVE THIS WEAPON.
SO...

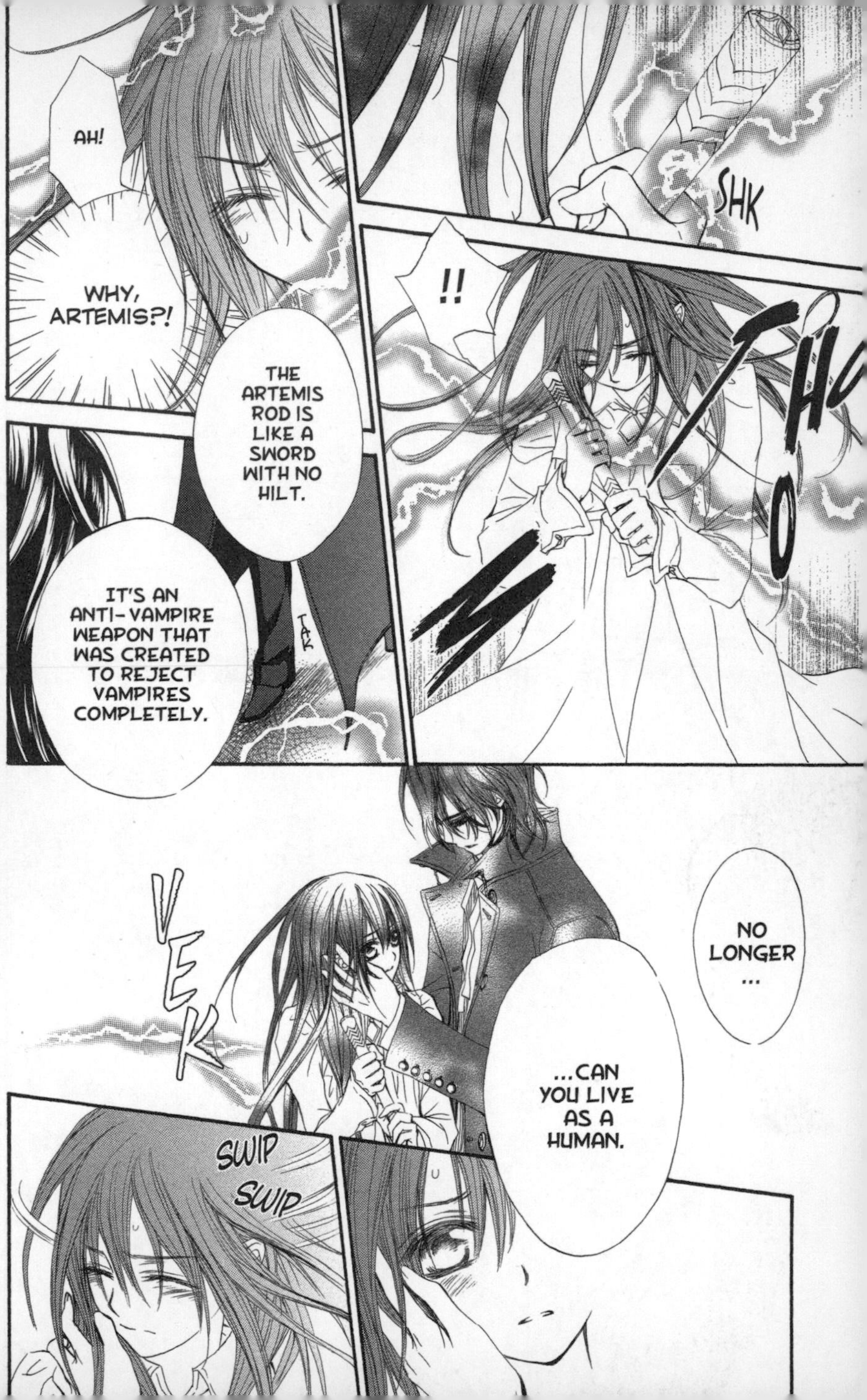
SHK
AH!
WHY, ARTEMIS?!
!!
THOOM
THE ARTEMIS ROD IS LIKE A SWORD WITH NO HILT.
IT'S AN ANTI-VAMPIRE WEAPON THAT WAS CREATED TO REJECT VAMPIRES COMPLETELY.
TAK
NO LONGER...
VEK
...CAN YOU LIVE AS A HUMAN.
SWIP
SWIP

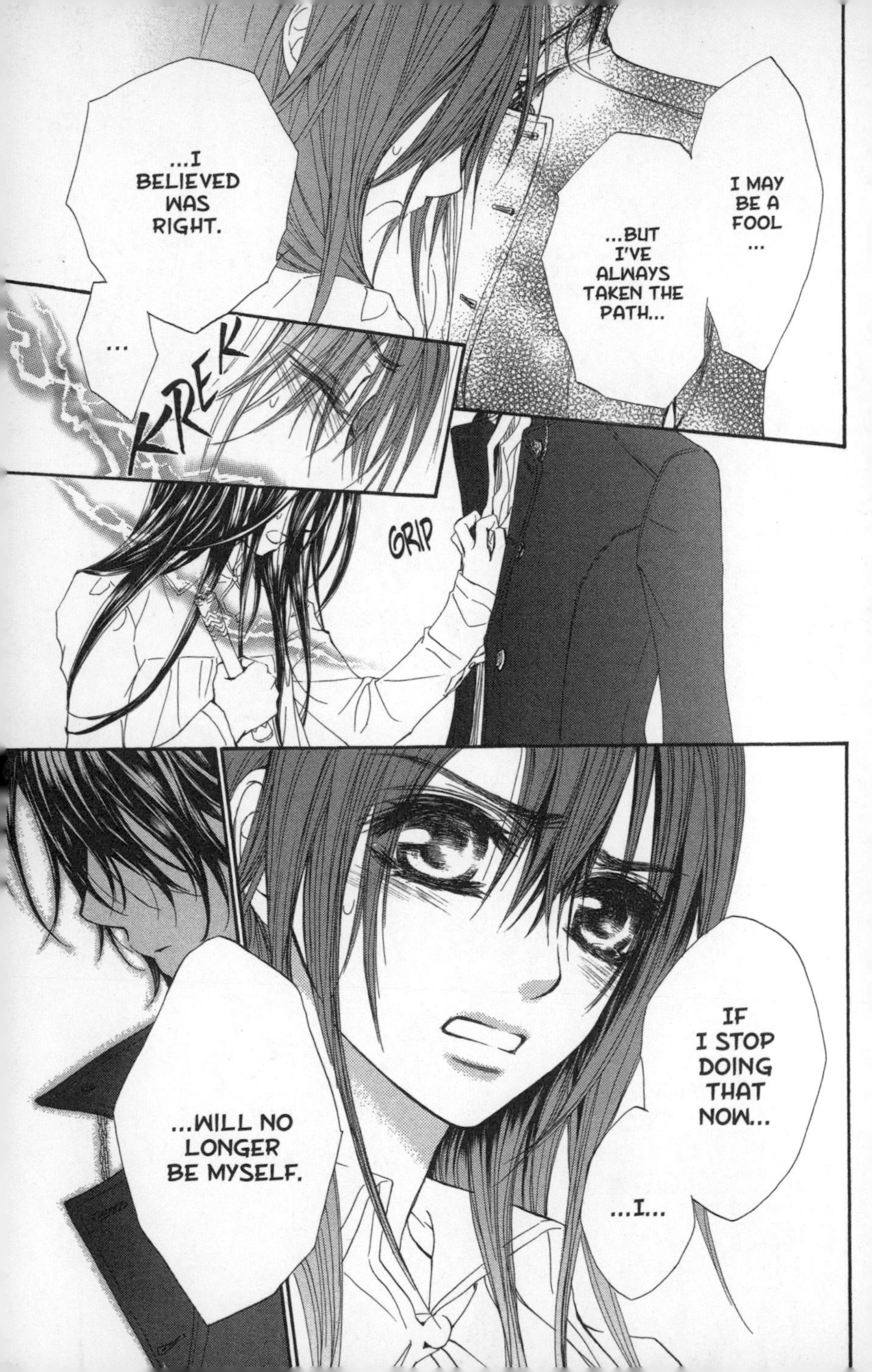
I MAY BE A FOOL...
...BUT I'VE ALWAYS TAKEN THE PATH...
...I BELIEVED WAS RIGHT.
...
KREK
GRIP
IF I STOP DOING THAT NOW...
...I...
...WILL NO LONGER BE MYSELF.

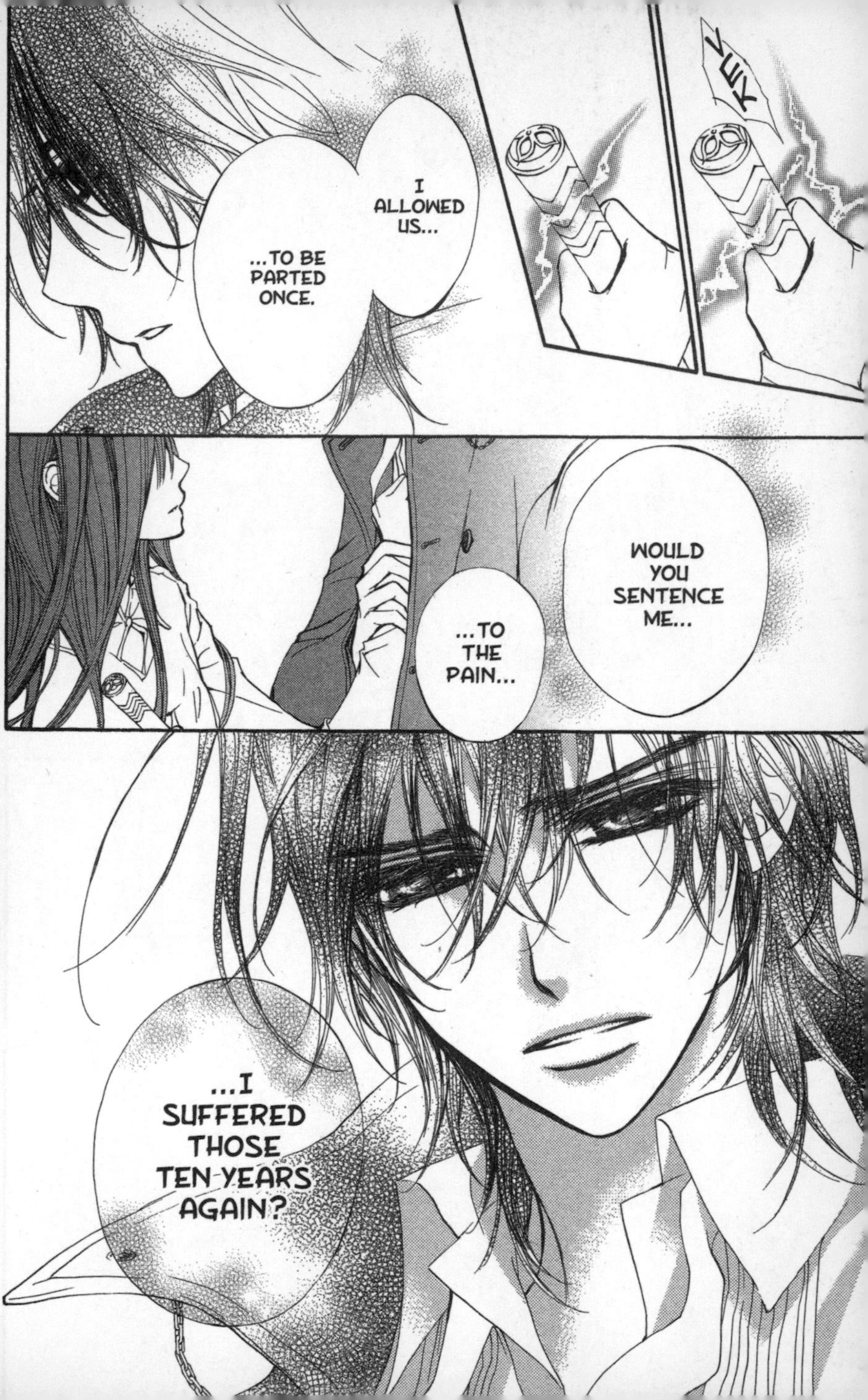
VEK
I ALLOWED US...
...TO BE PARTED ONCE.
WOULD YOU SENTENCE ME...
...TO THE PAIN...
...I SUFFERED THOSE TEN YEARS AGAIN?

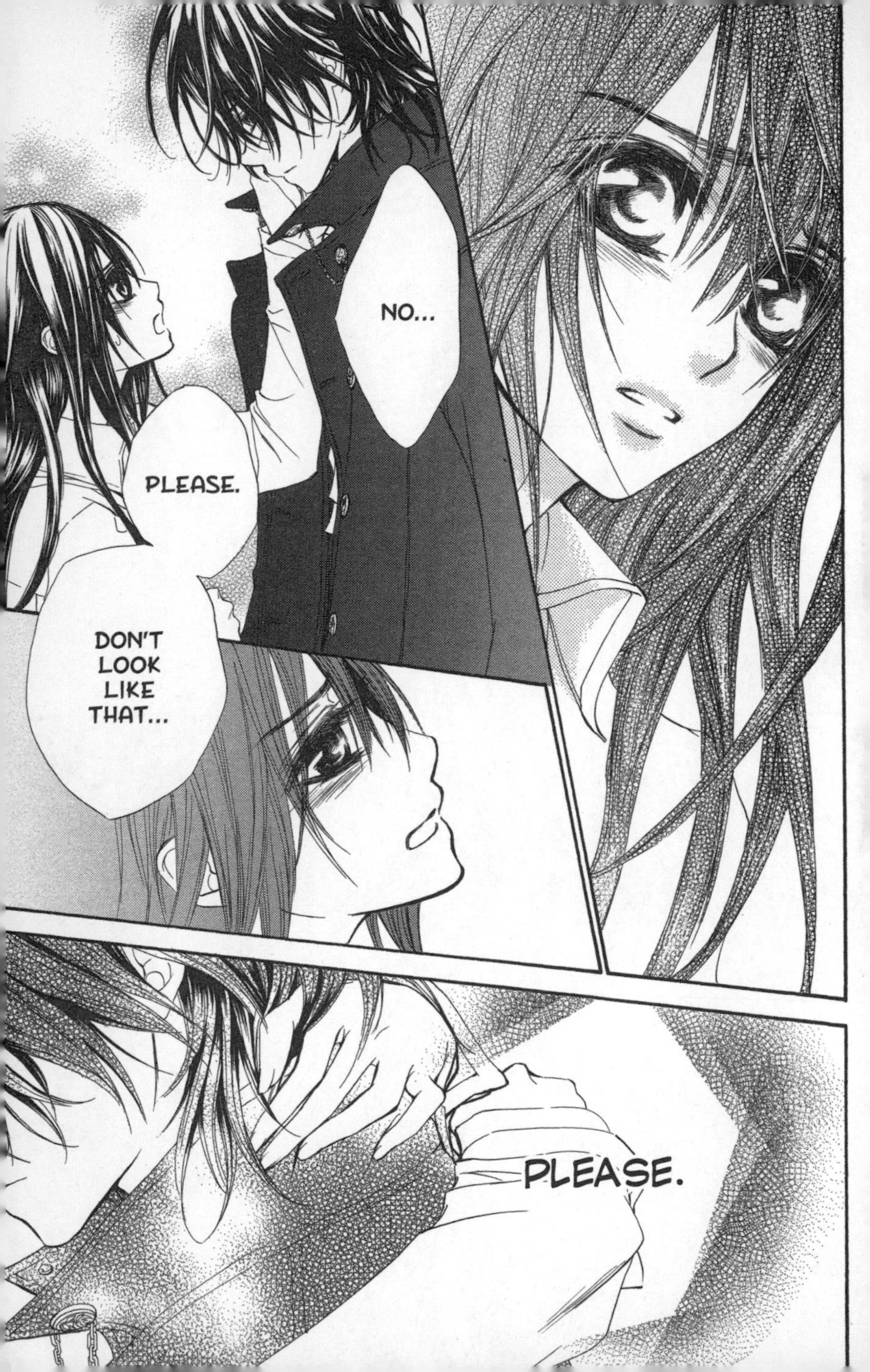
NO...
PLEASE.
DON'T LOOK LIKE THAT...
PLEASE.

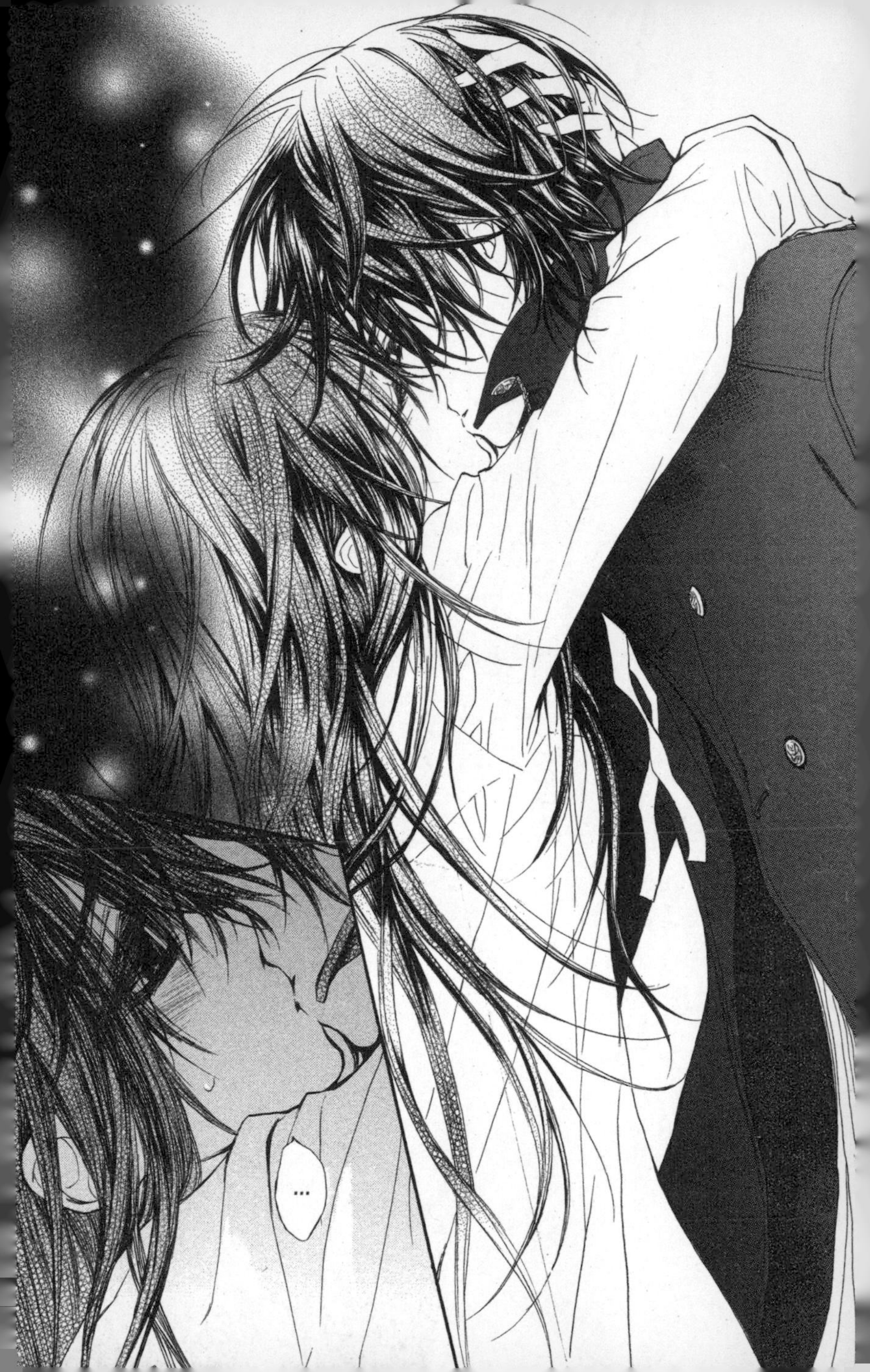
...

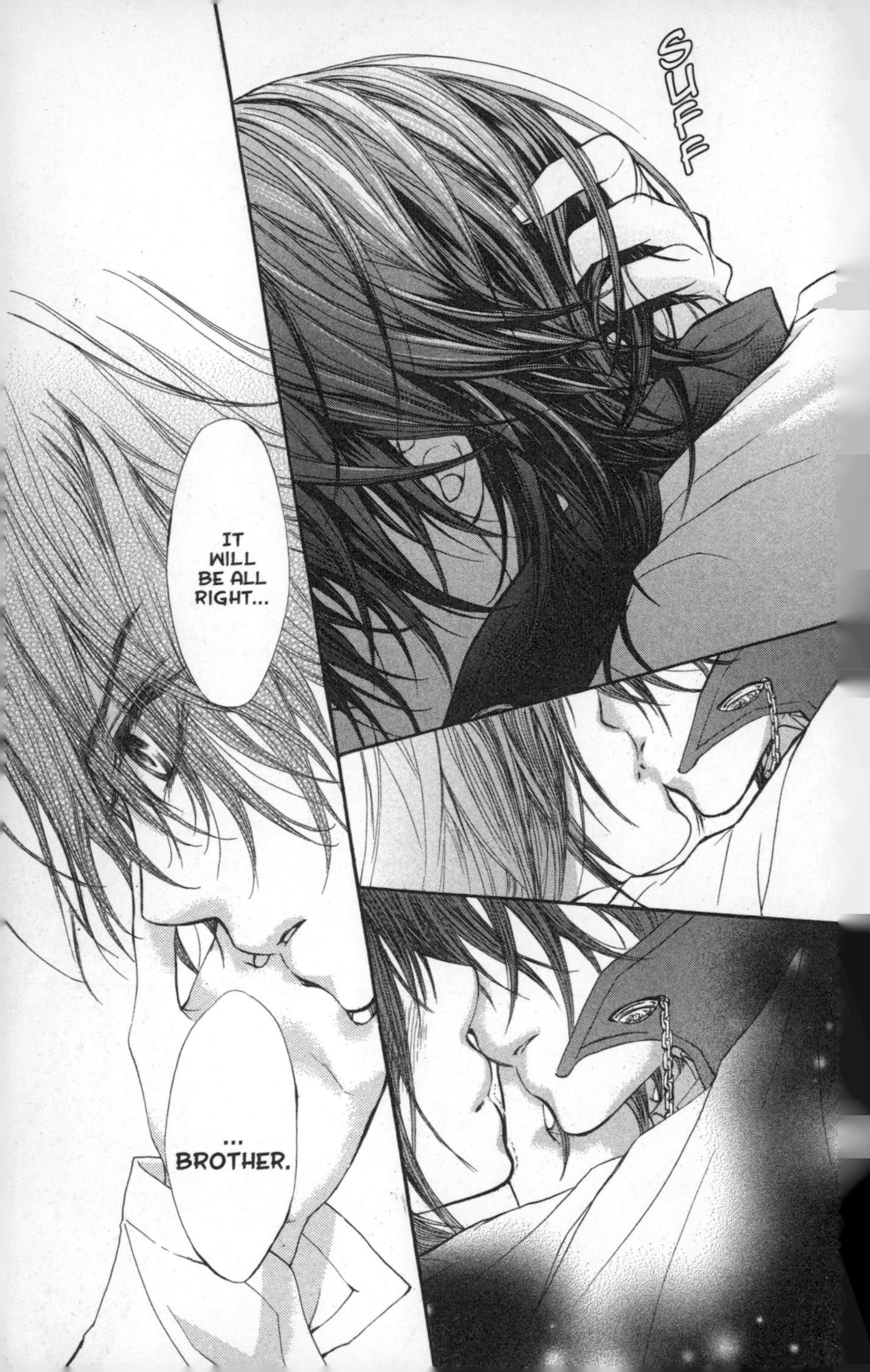
SUFF
IT WILL BE ALL RIGHT...
... BROTHER.

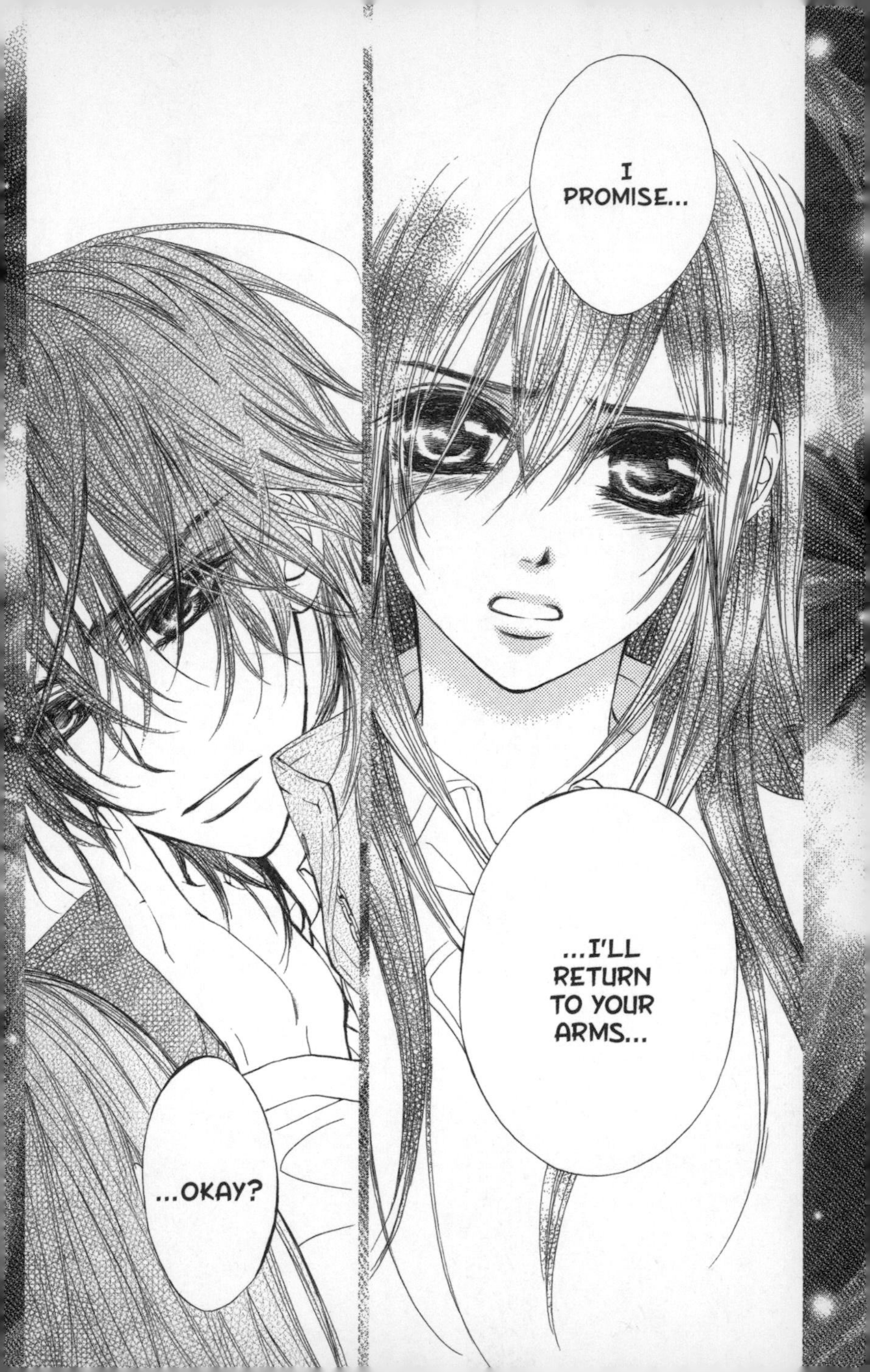
I PROMISE...
...I'LL RETURN TO YOUR ARMS...
...OKAY?

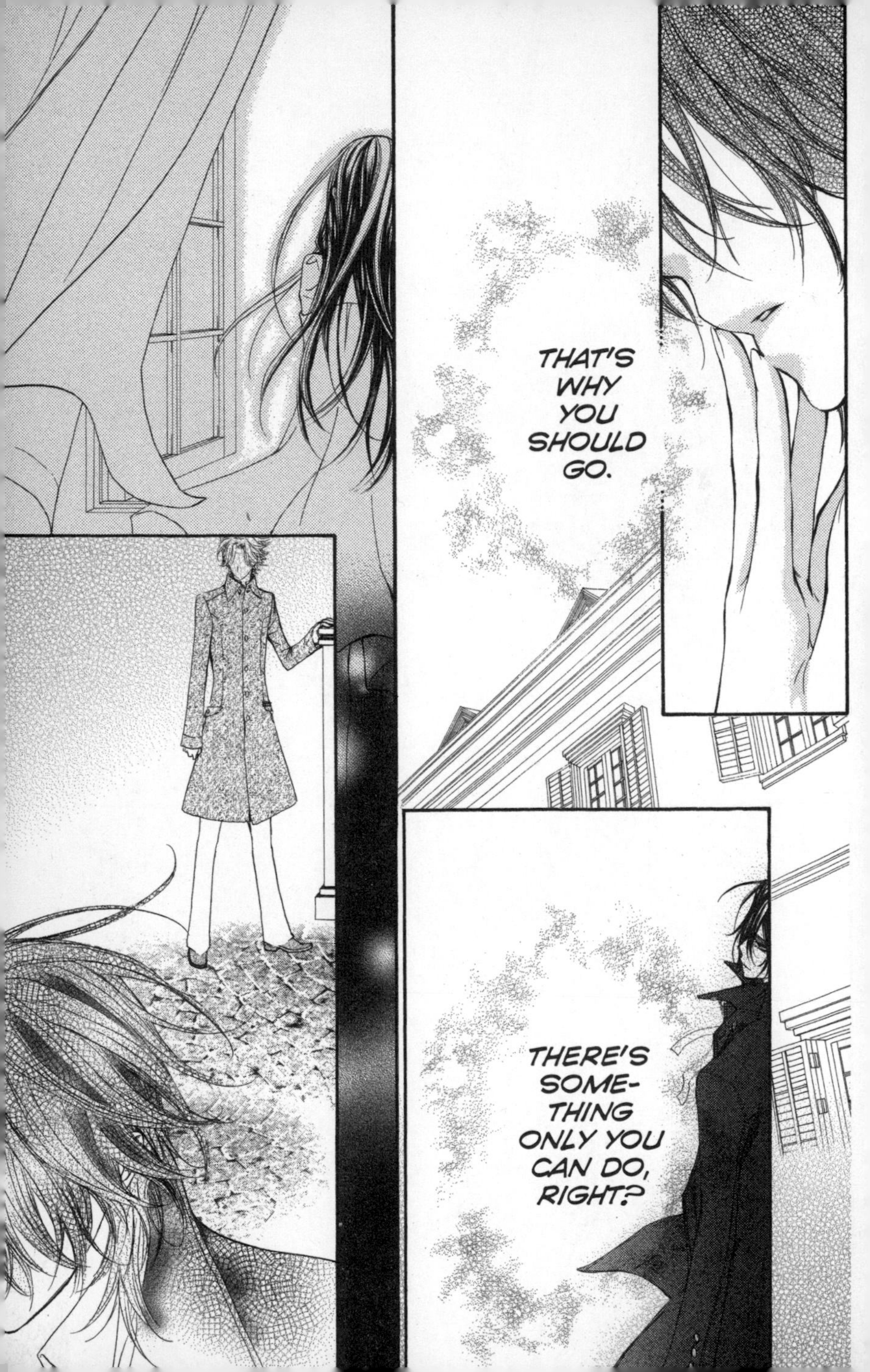
THAT'S WHY YOU SHOULD GO.
THERE'S SOME-THING ONLY YOU CAN DO, RIGHT?

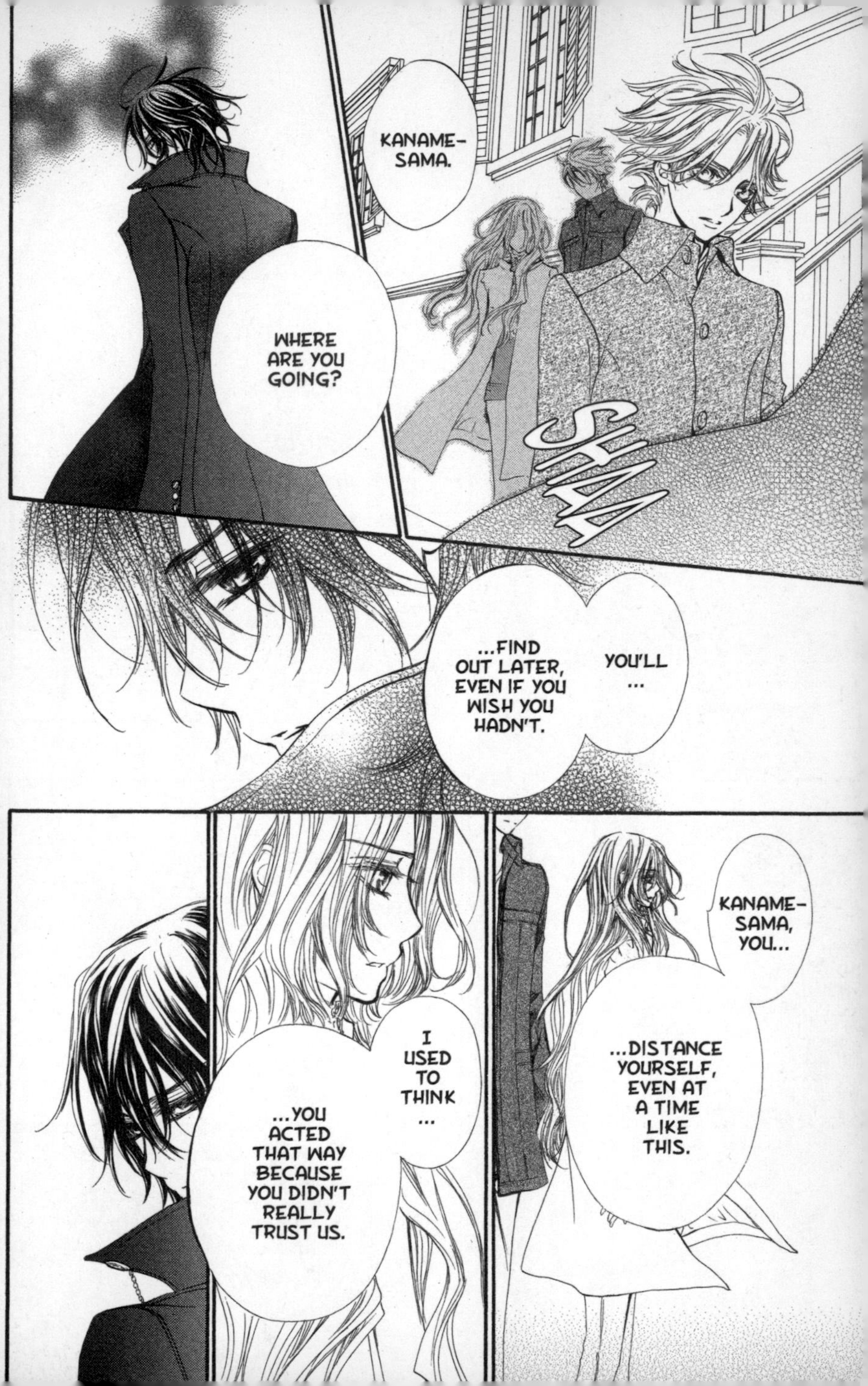
KANAME-SAMA.
WHERE ARE YOU GOING?
SHAA
YOU'LL ...
...FIND OUT LATER, EVEN IF YOU WISH YOU HADN'T.
KANAME-SAMA, YOU...
...DISTANCE YOURSELF, EVEN AT A TIME LIKE THIS.
I USED TO THINK ...
...YOU ACTED THAT WAY BECAUSE YOU DIDN'T REALLY TRUST US.

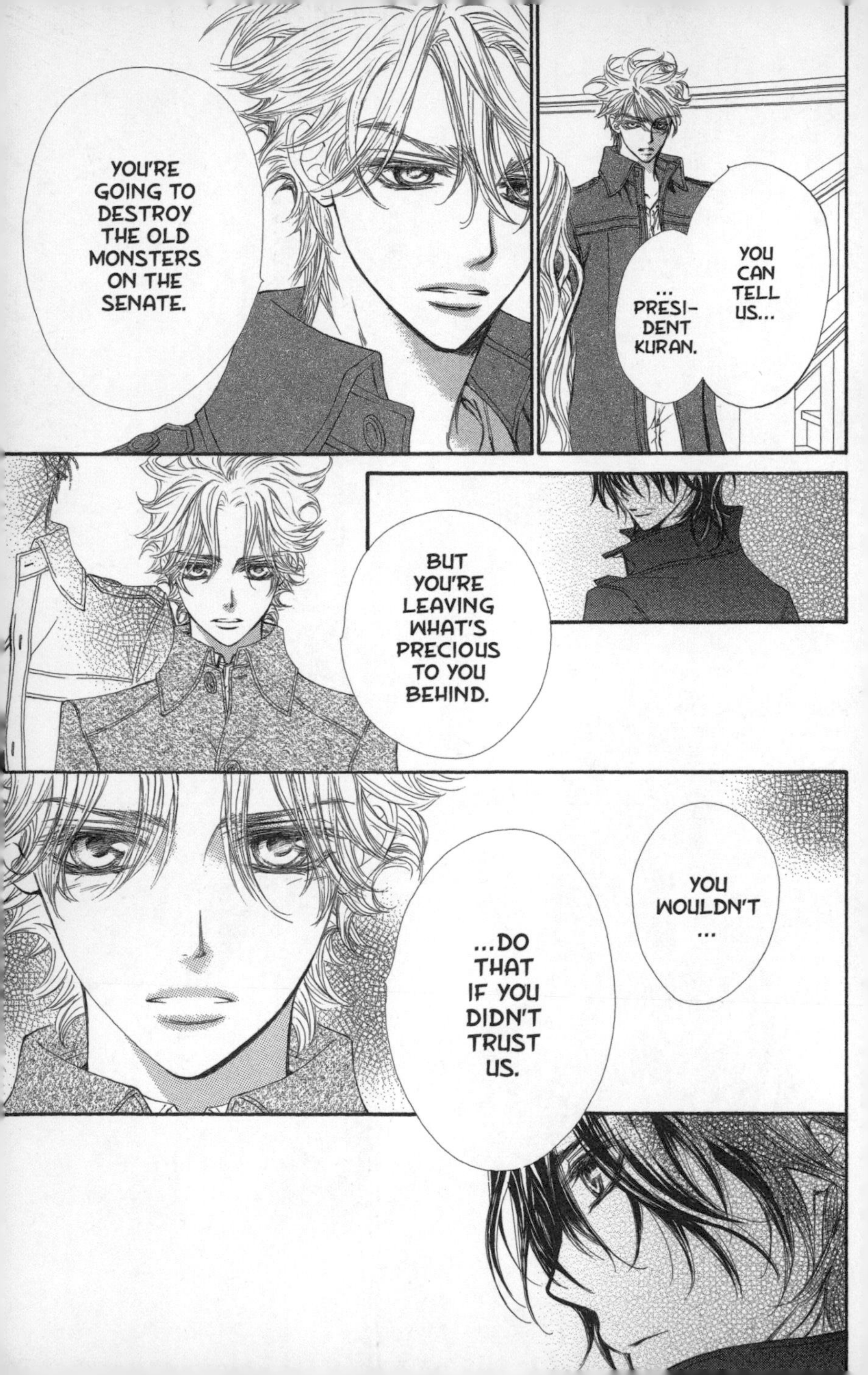
YOU CAN TELL US...
... PRESI-DENT KURAN.
YOU'RE GOING TO DESTROY THE OLD MONSTERS ON THE SENATE.
BUT YOU'RE LEAVING WHAT'S PRECIOUS TO YOU BEHIND.
YOU WOULDN'T ...
...DO THAT IF YOU DIDN'T TRUST US.

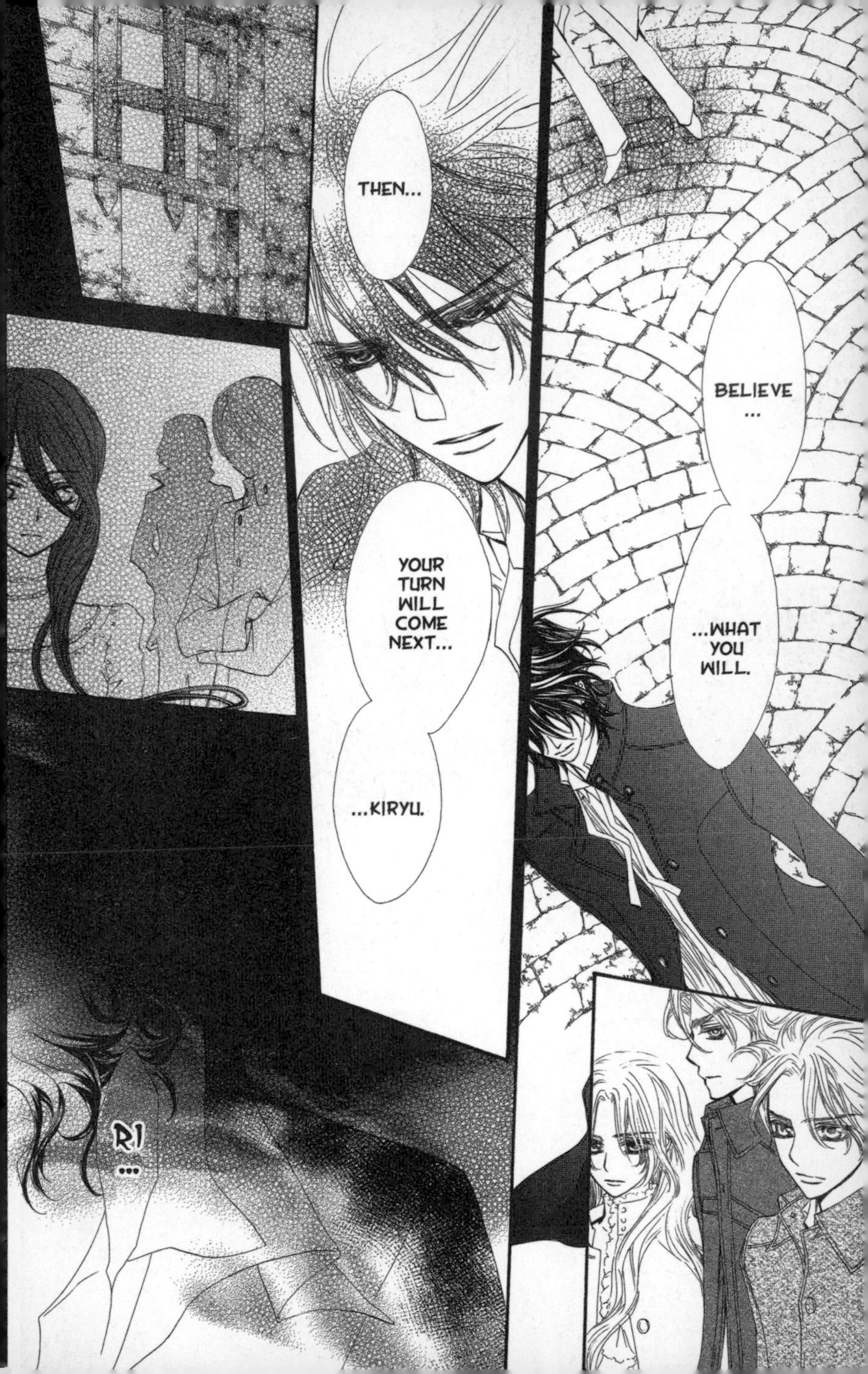
BELIEVE ...
...WHAT YOU WILL.
THEN...
YOUR TURN WILL COME NEXT...
...KIRYU.
RI ...

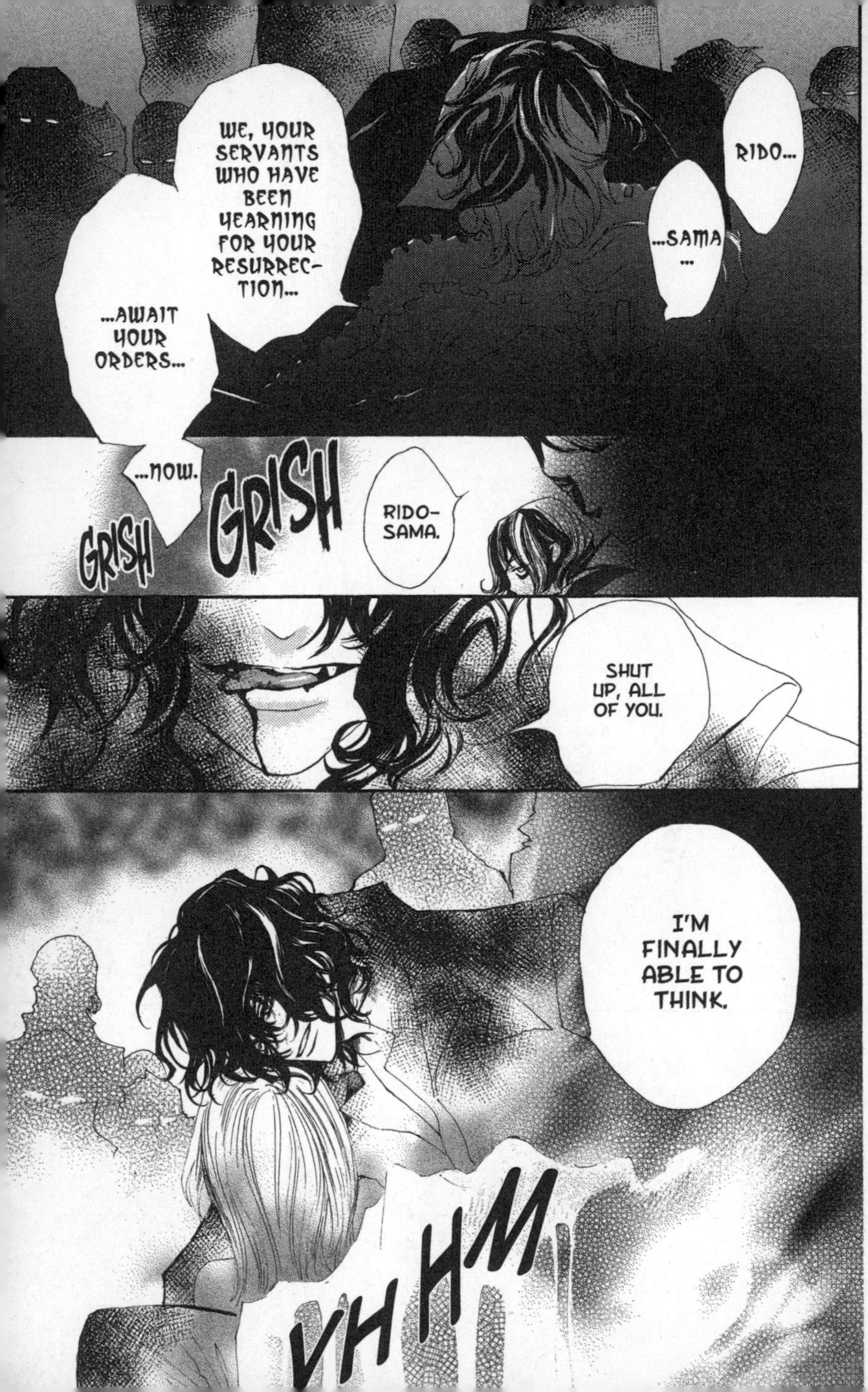
RIDO...
...SAMA ...
WE, YOUR SERVANTS WHO HAVE BEEN YEARNING FOR YOUR RESURREC-TION...
...AWAIT YOUR ORDERS...
...now.
RIDO-SAMA.
GRISH
GRISH
SHUT UP, ALL OF YOU.
I'M FINALLY ABLE TO THINK.
VHHM

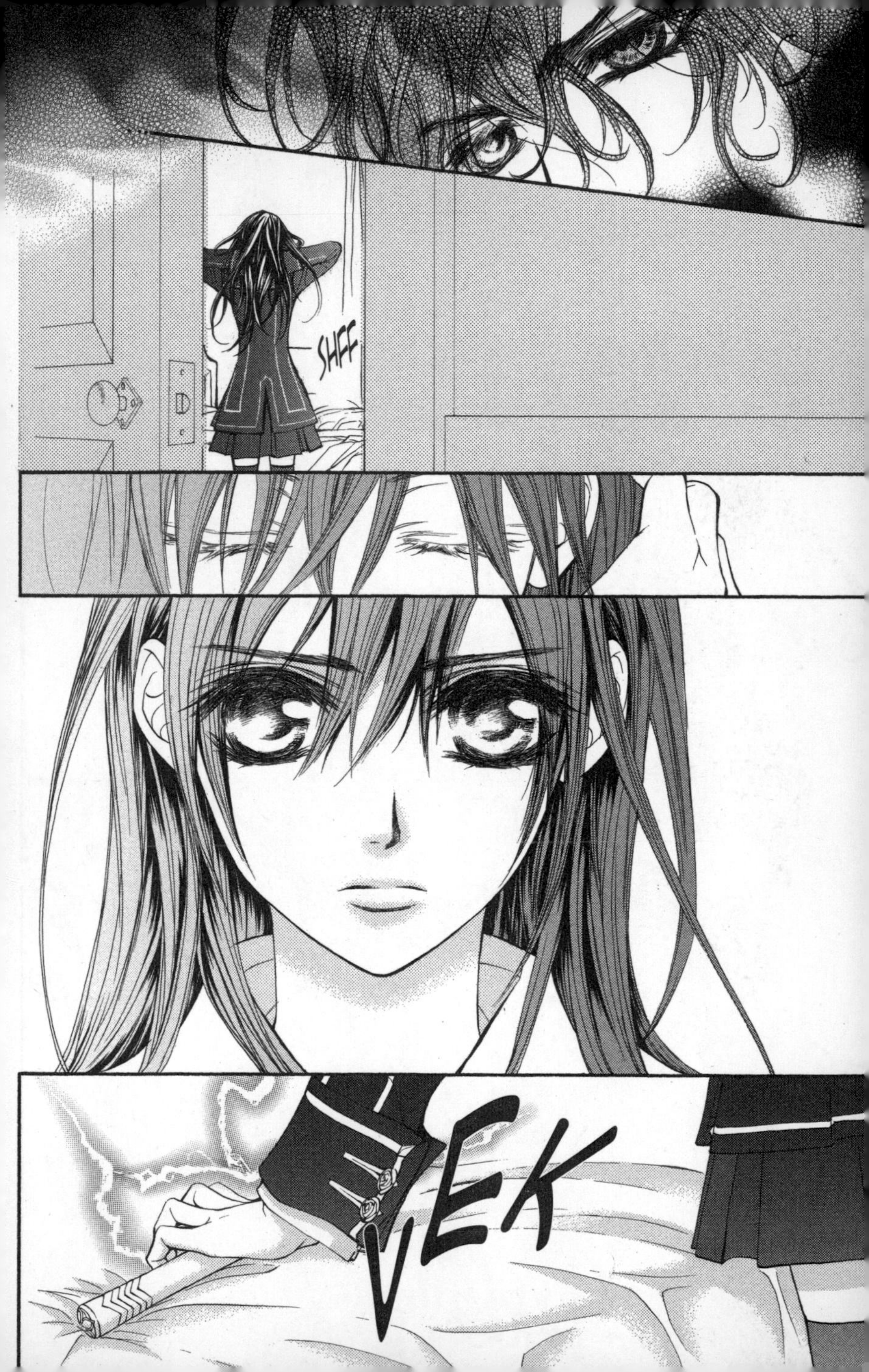
SHFF
VEK

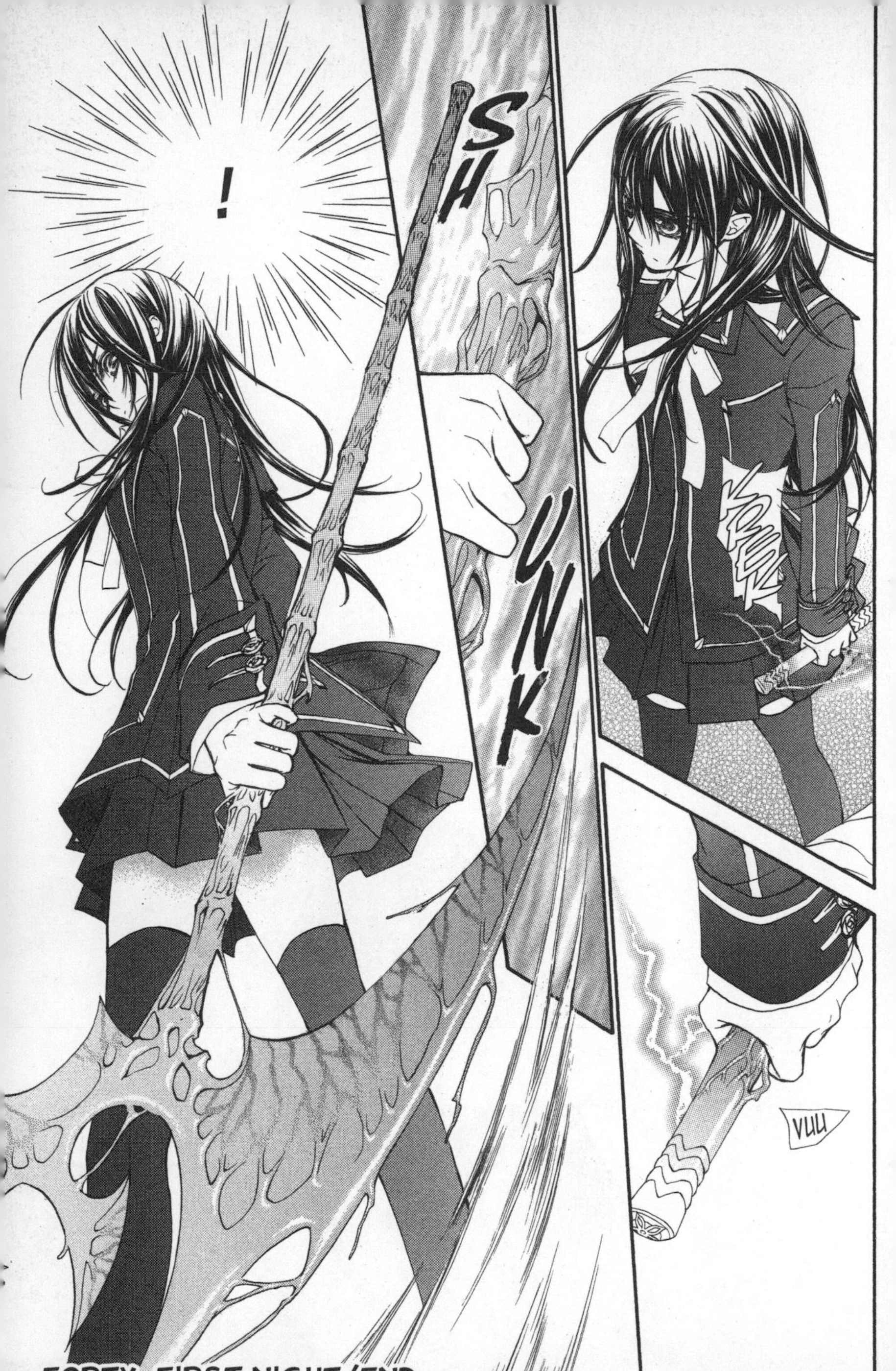
VUU
SHUNK
!

FORTY-FIRST NIGHT/END

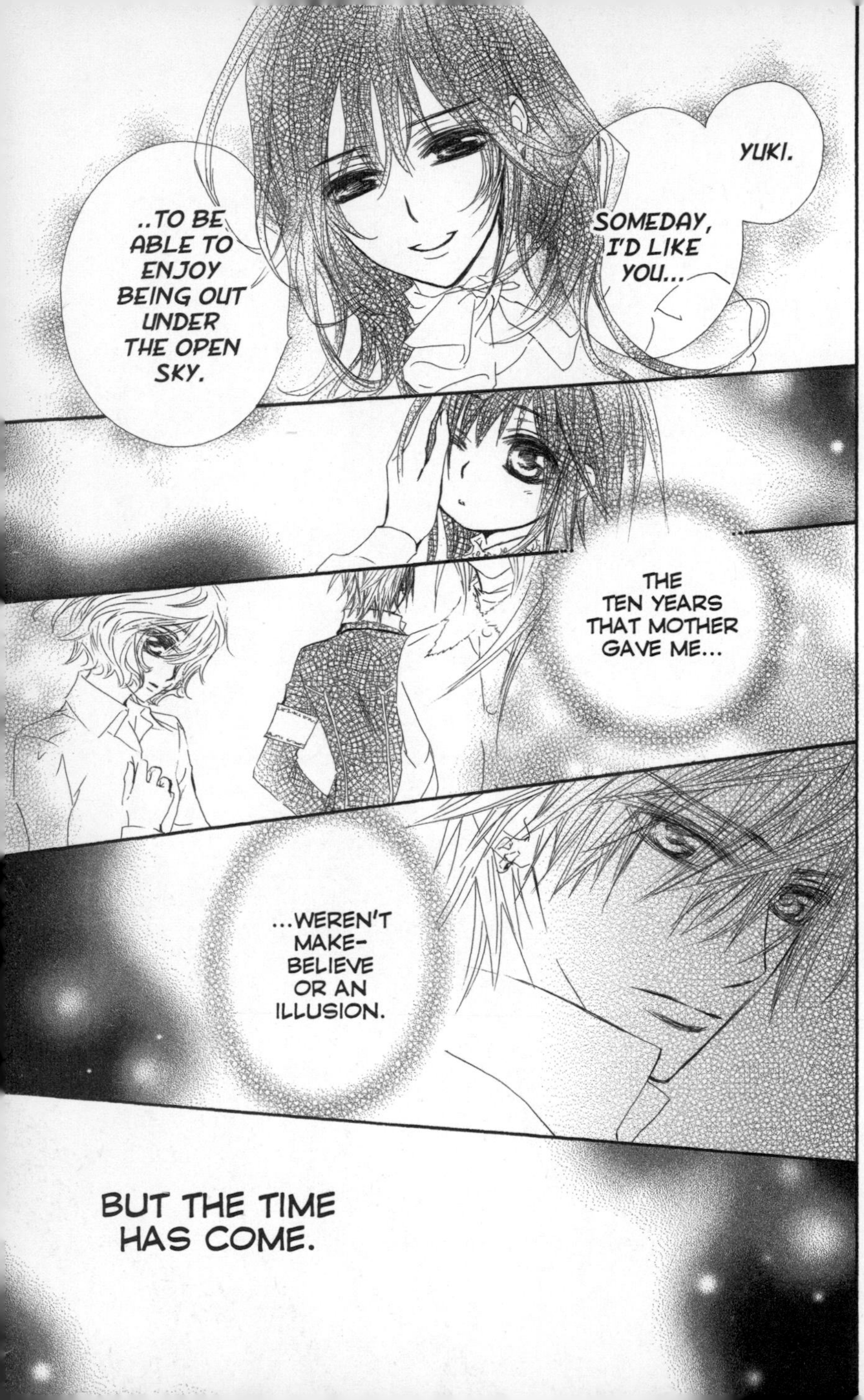
YUKI.
SOMEDAY, I'D LIKE YOU...
..TO BE ABLE TO ENJOY BEING OUT UNDER THE OPEN SKY.
THE TEN YEARS THAT MOTHER GAVE ME...
...WEREN'T MAKE-BELIEVE OR AN ILLUSION.
BUT THE TIME HAS COME.

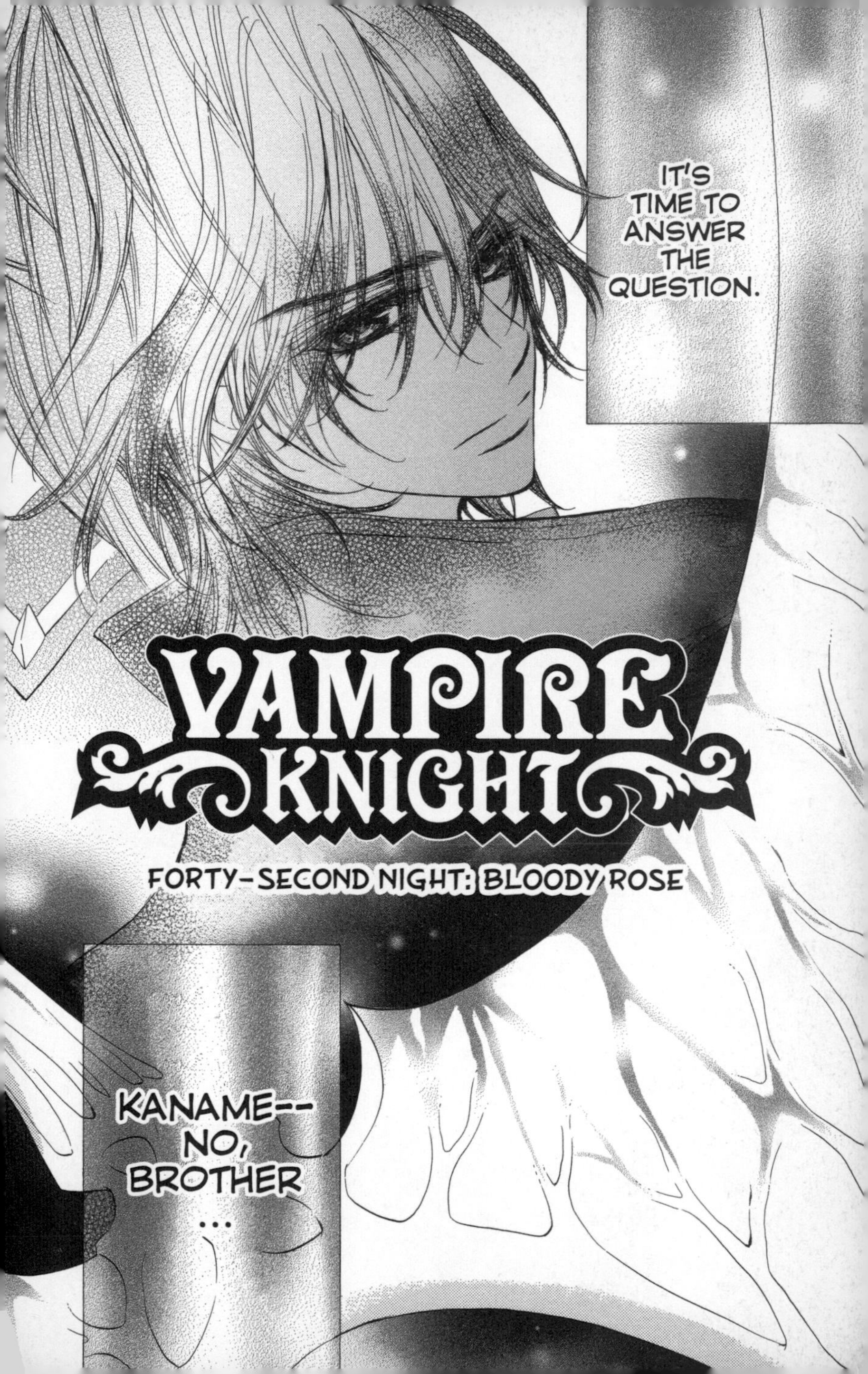
IT'S TIME TO ANSWER THE QUESTION.
VAMPIRE KNIGHT
FORTY-SECOND NIGHT: BLOODY ROSE
KANAME-- NO, BROTHER ...

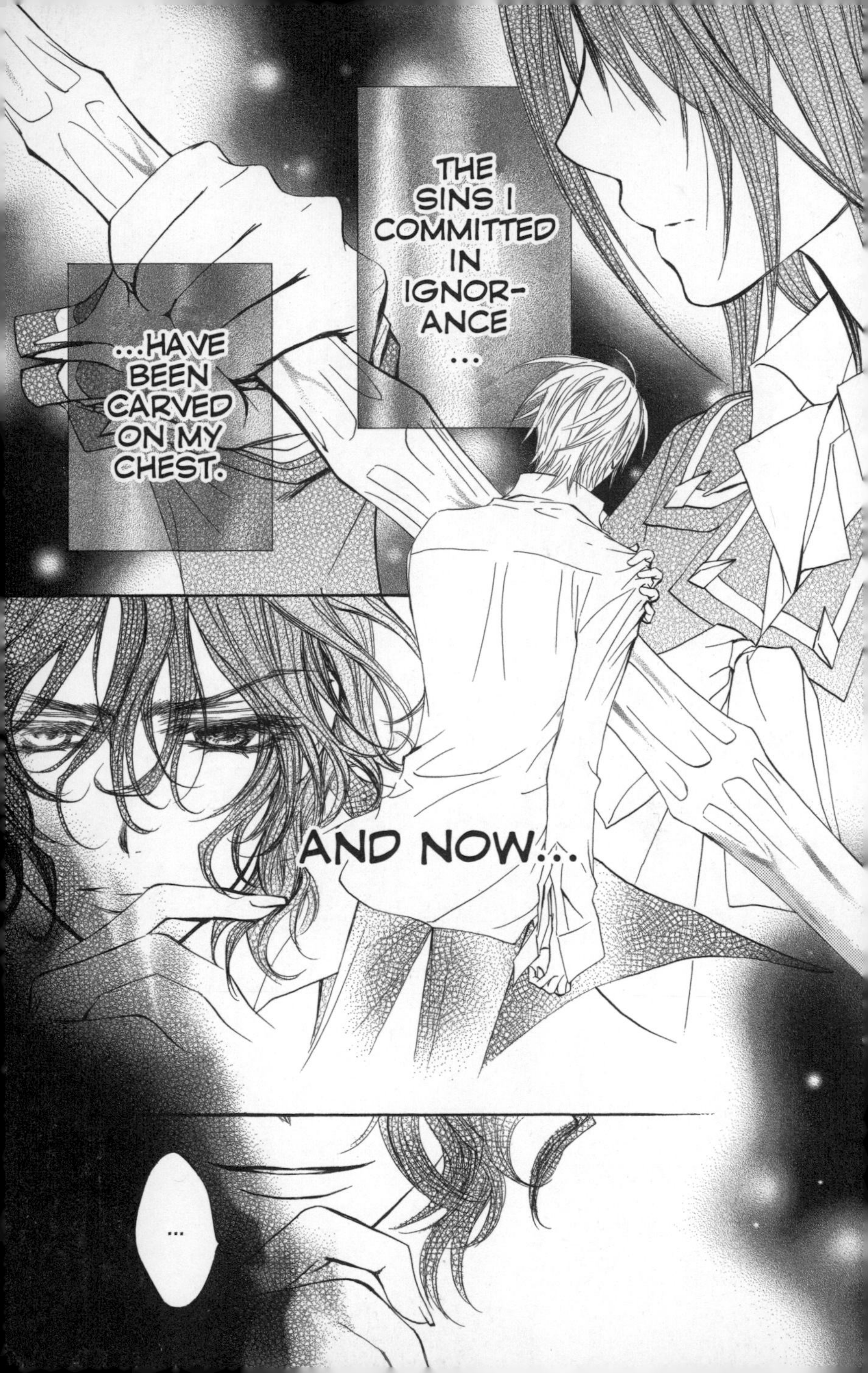
THE SINS I COMMITTED IN IGNORANCE...
...HAVE BEEN CARVED ON MY CHEST.
AND NOW...
...

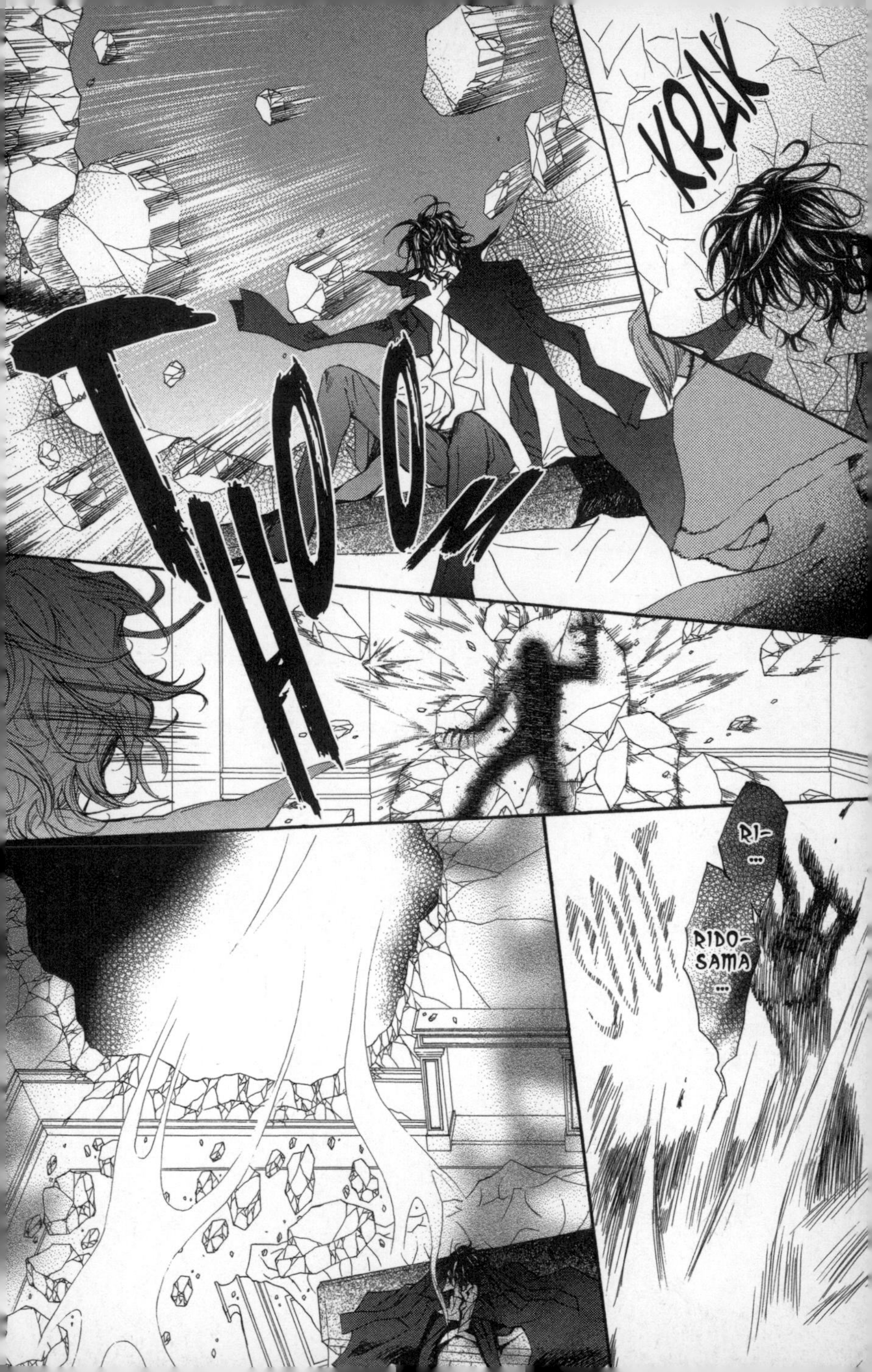
KRAK
THOOM
RI-...
RIDO-SAMA...

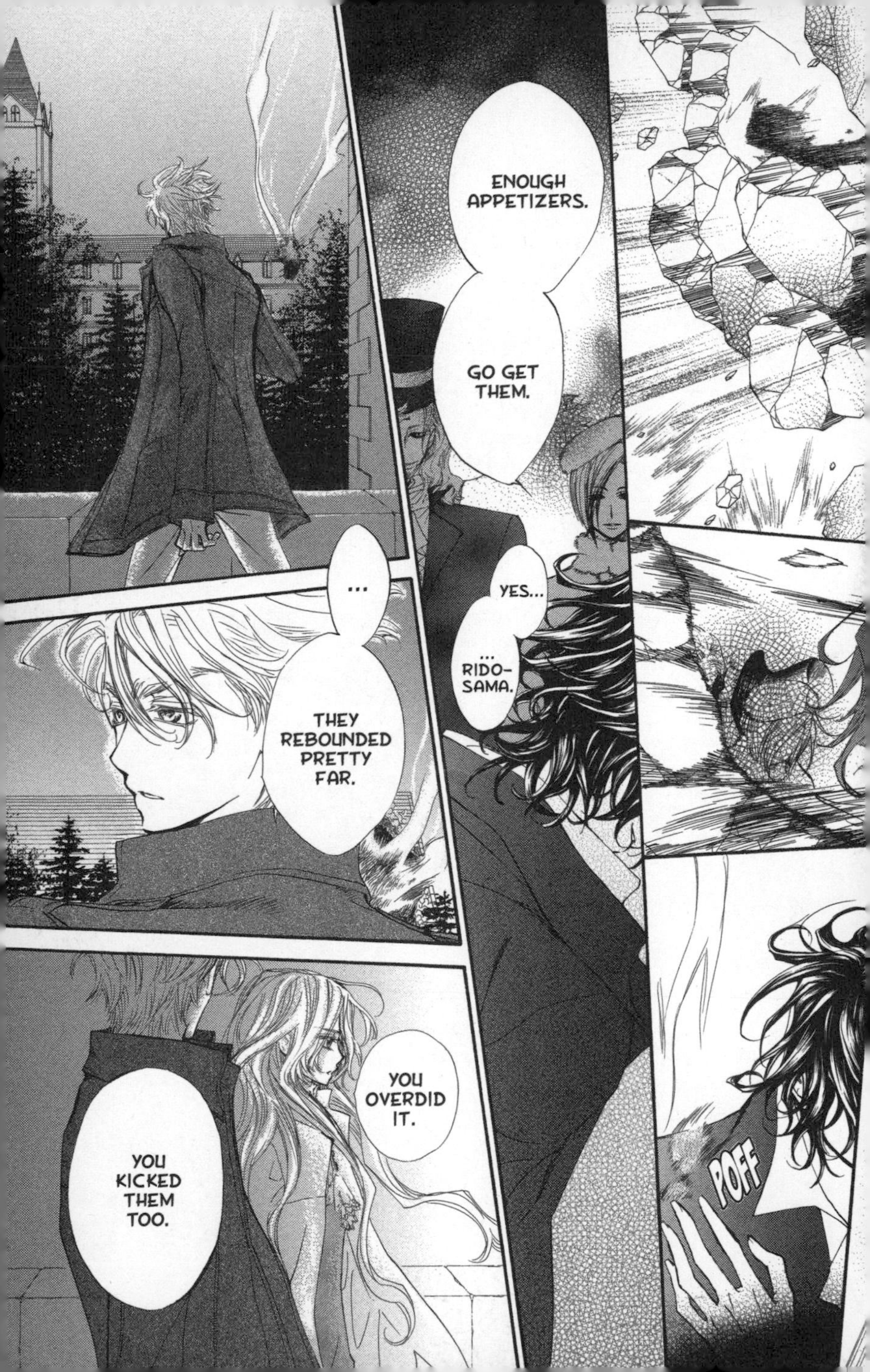
POFF
ENOUGH APPETIZERS.
GO GET THEM.
YES...
... RIDO-SAMA.
...
THEY REBOUNDED PRETTY FAR.
YOU OVERDID IT.
YOU KICKED THEM TOO.

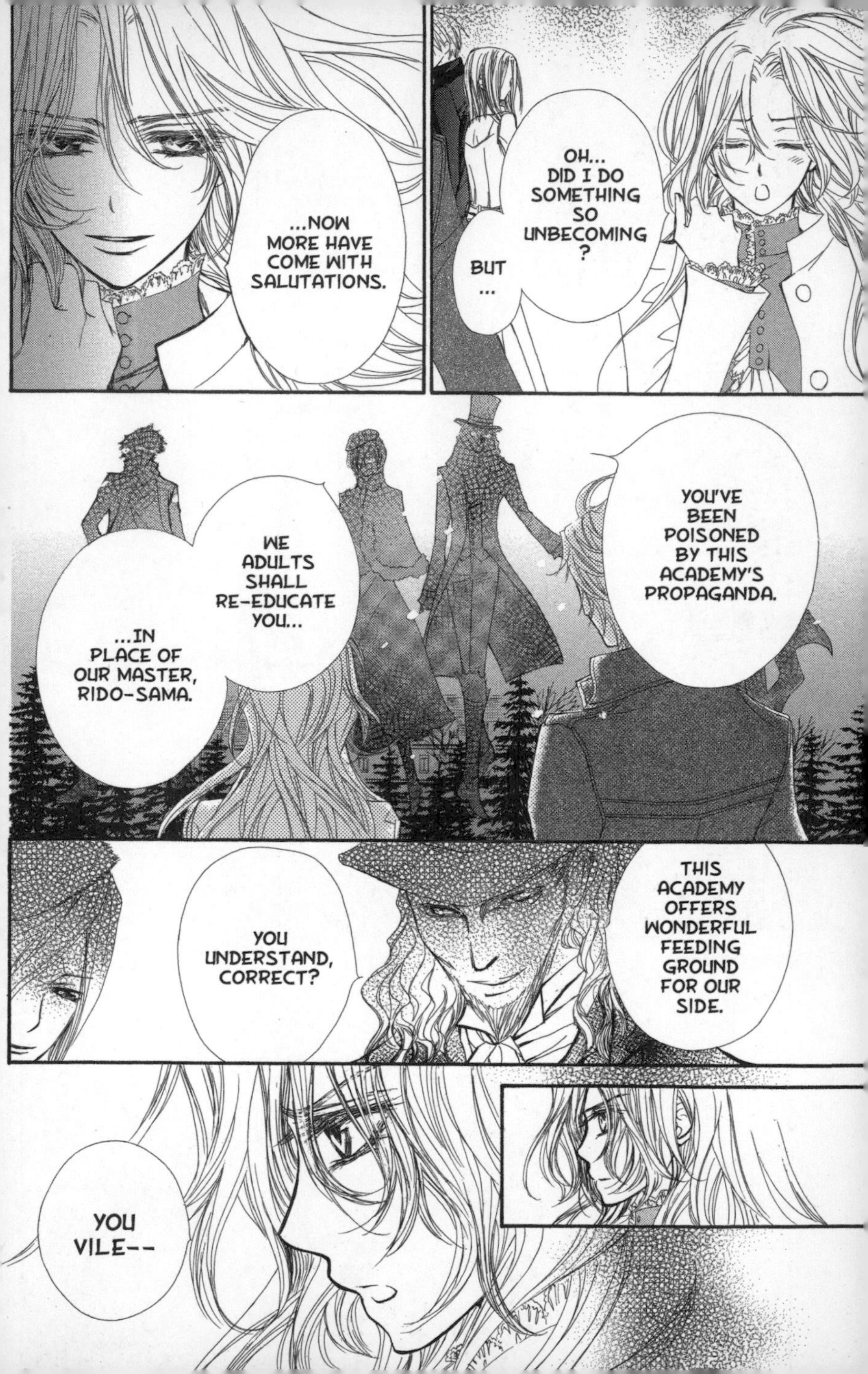
OH... DID I DO SOMETHING SO UNBECOMING?
BUT...
...NOW MORE HAVE COME WITH SALUTATIONS.
YOU'VE BEEN POISONED BY THIS ACADEMY'S PROPAGANDA.
WE ADULTS SHALL RE-EDUCATE YOU...
...IN PLACE OF OUR MASTER, RIDO-SAMA.
THIS ACADEMY OFFERS WONDERFUL FEEDING GROUND FOR OUR SIDE.
YOU UNDERSTAND, CORRECT?
YOU VILE--

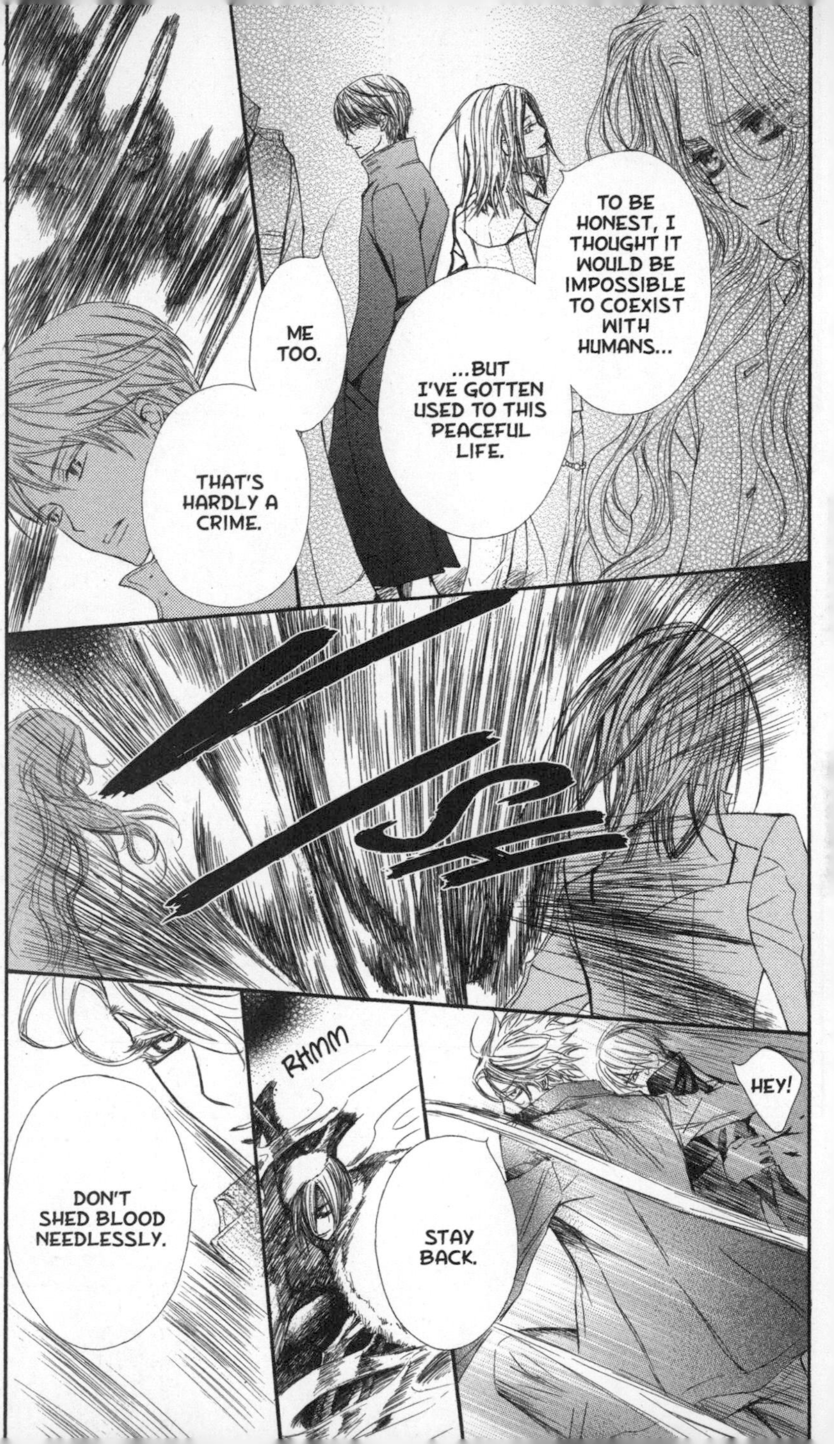
TO BE HONEST, I THOUGHT IT WOULD BE IMPOSSIBLE TO COEXIST WITH HUMANS...
...BUT I'VE GOTTEN USED TO THIS PEACEFUL LIFE.
ME TOO.
THAT'S HARDLY A CRIME.
HEY!
STAY BACK.
RHMM
DON'T SHED BLOOD NEEDLESSLY.

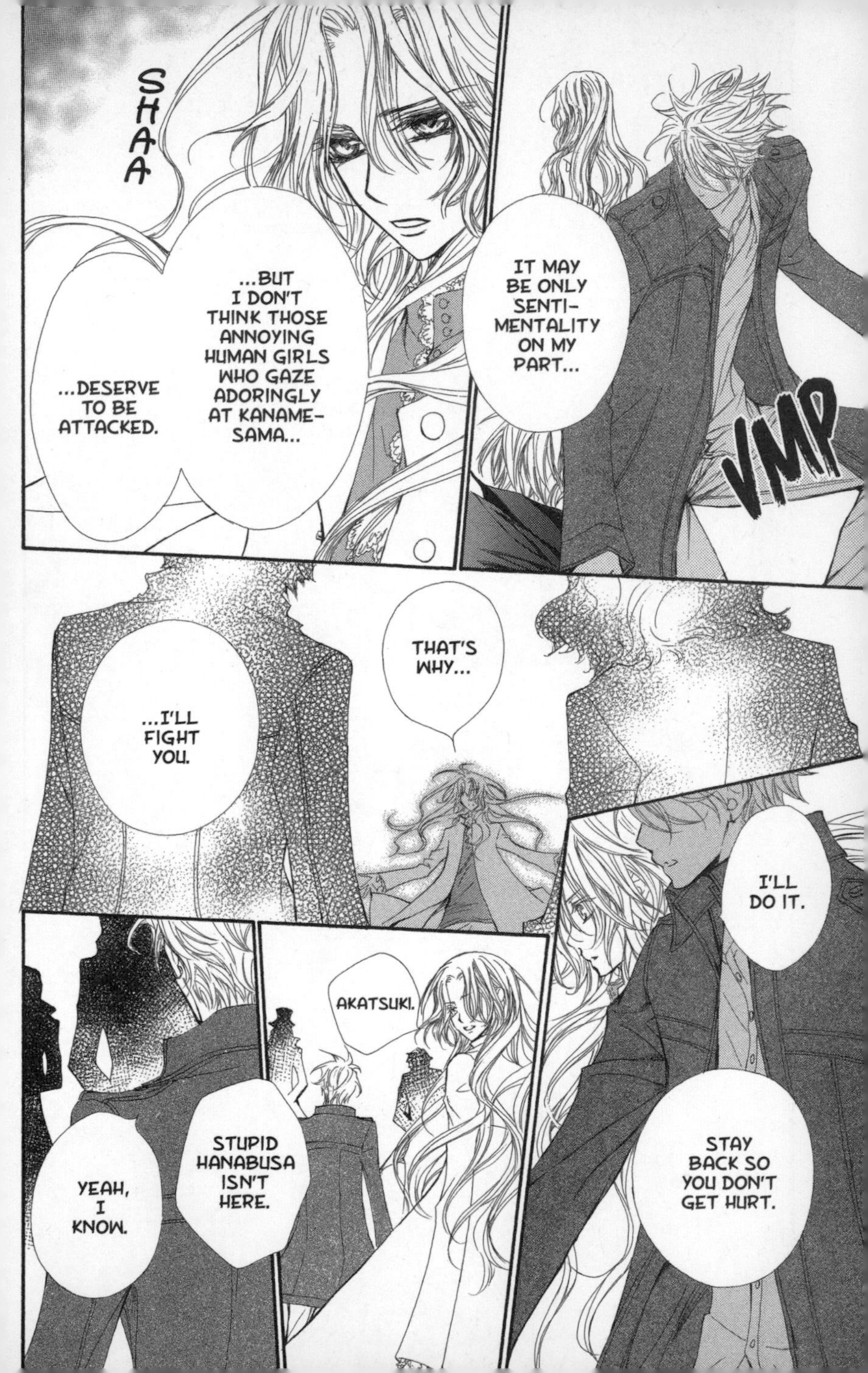
IT MAY BE ONLY SENTI-MENTALITY ON MY PART...
VMP
SHAA
...BUT I DON'T THINK THOSE ANNOYING HUMAN GIRLS WHO GAZE ADORINGLY AT KANAME-SAMA...
...DESERVE TO BE ATTACKED.
THAT'S WHY...
...I'LL FIGHT YOU.
I'LL DO IT.
STAY BACK SO YOU DON'T GET HURT.
AKATSUKI.
STUPID HANABUSA ISN'T HERE.
YEAH, I KNOW.

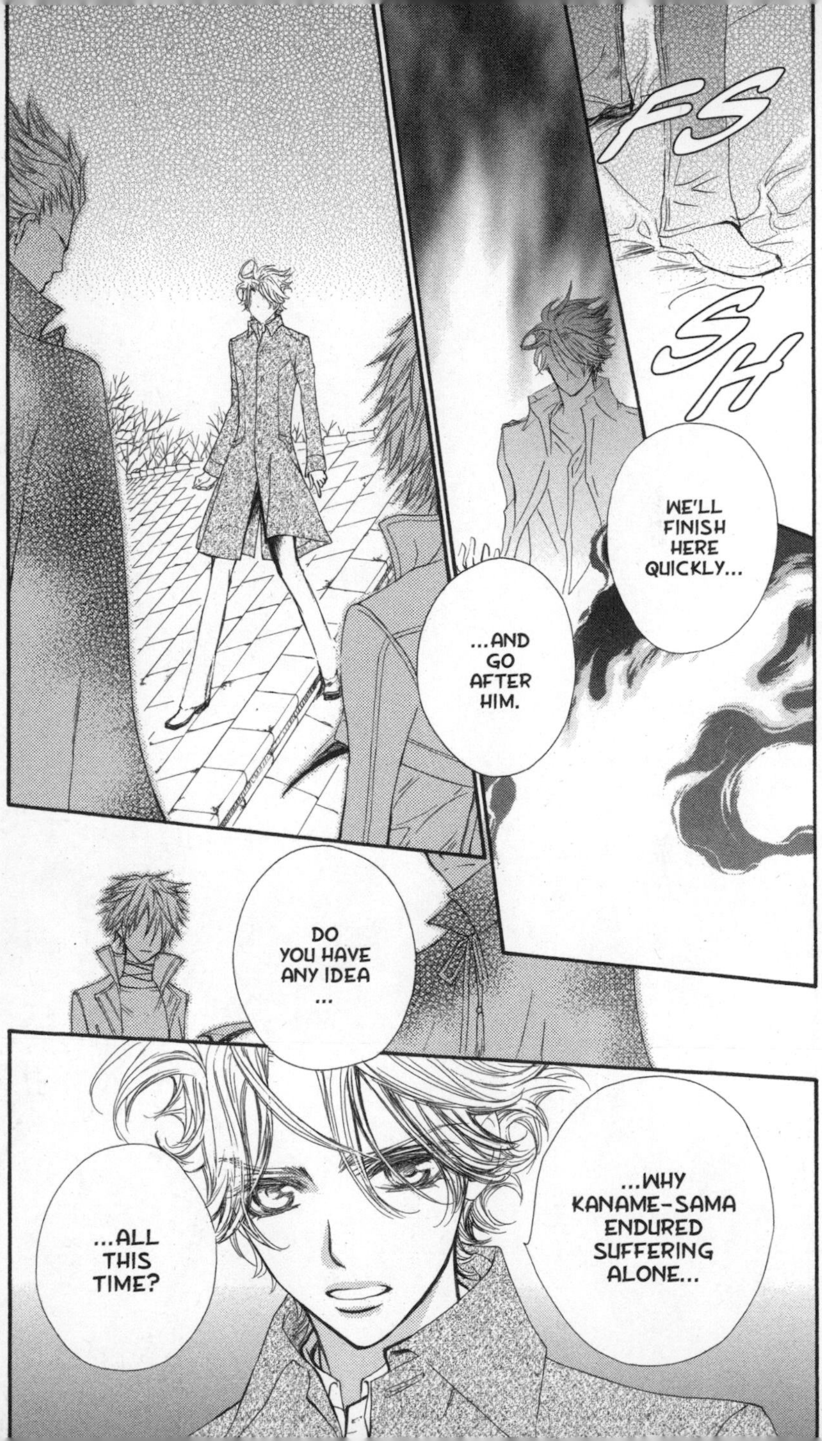
FS
SH
WE'LL FINISH HERE QUICKLY...
...AND GO AFTER HIM.
DO YOU HAVE ANY IDEA ...
...WHY KANAME-SAMA ENDURED SUFFERING ALONE...
...ALL THIS TIME?

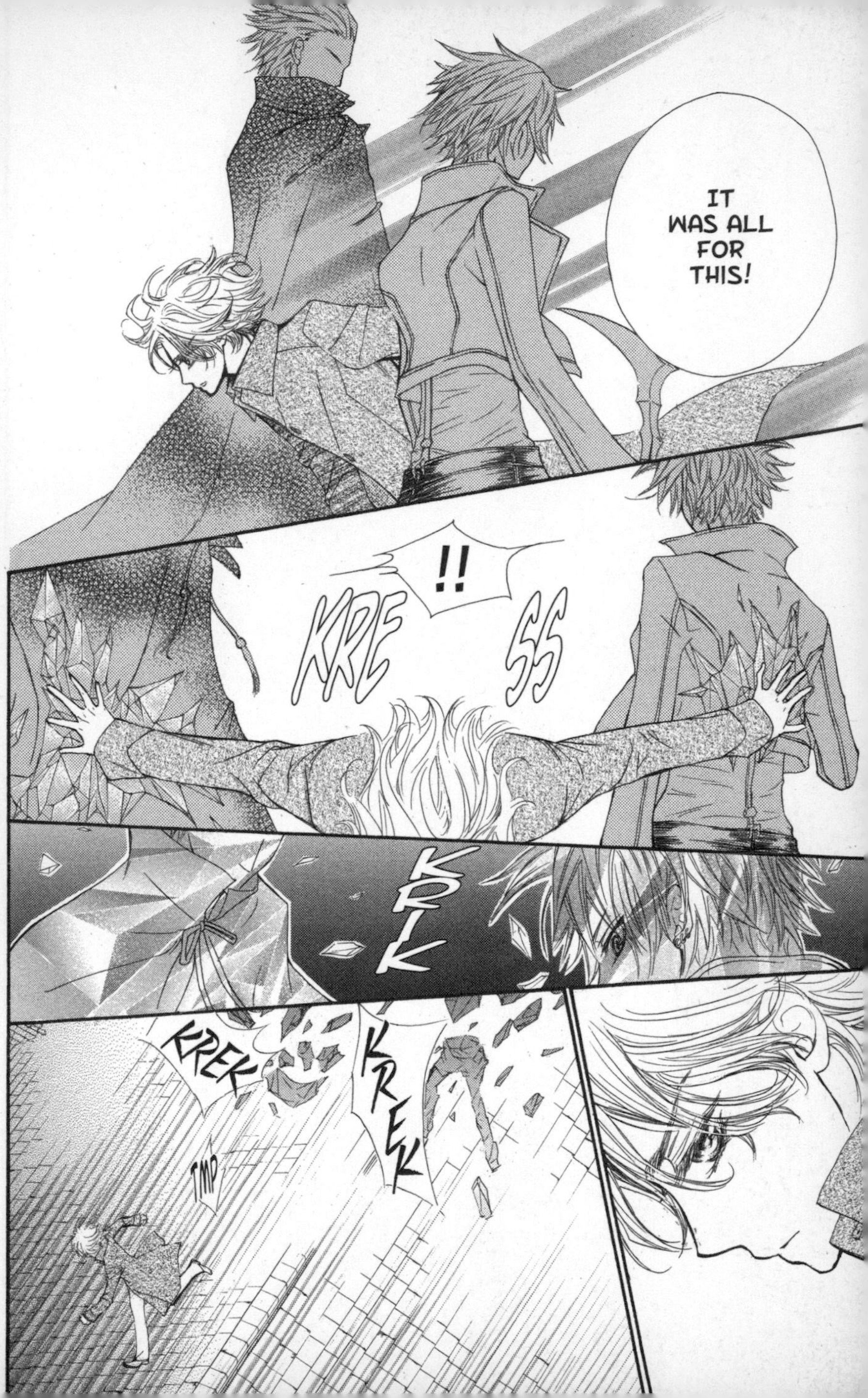
IT WAS ALL FOR THIS!
!!
KRE SS
KRIK
KREK
KREK
TMP

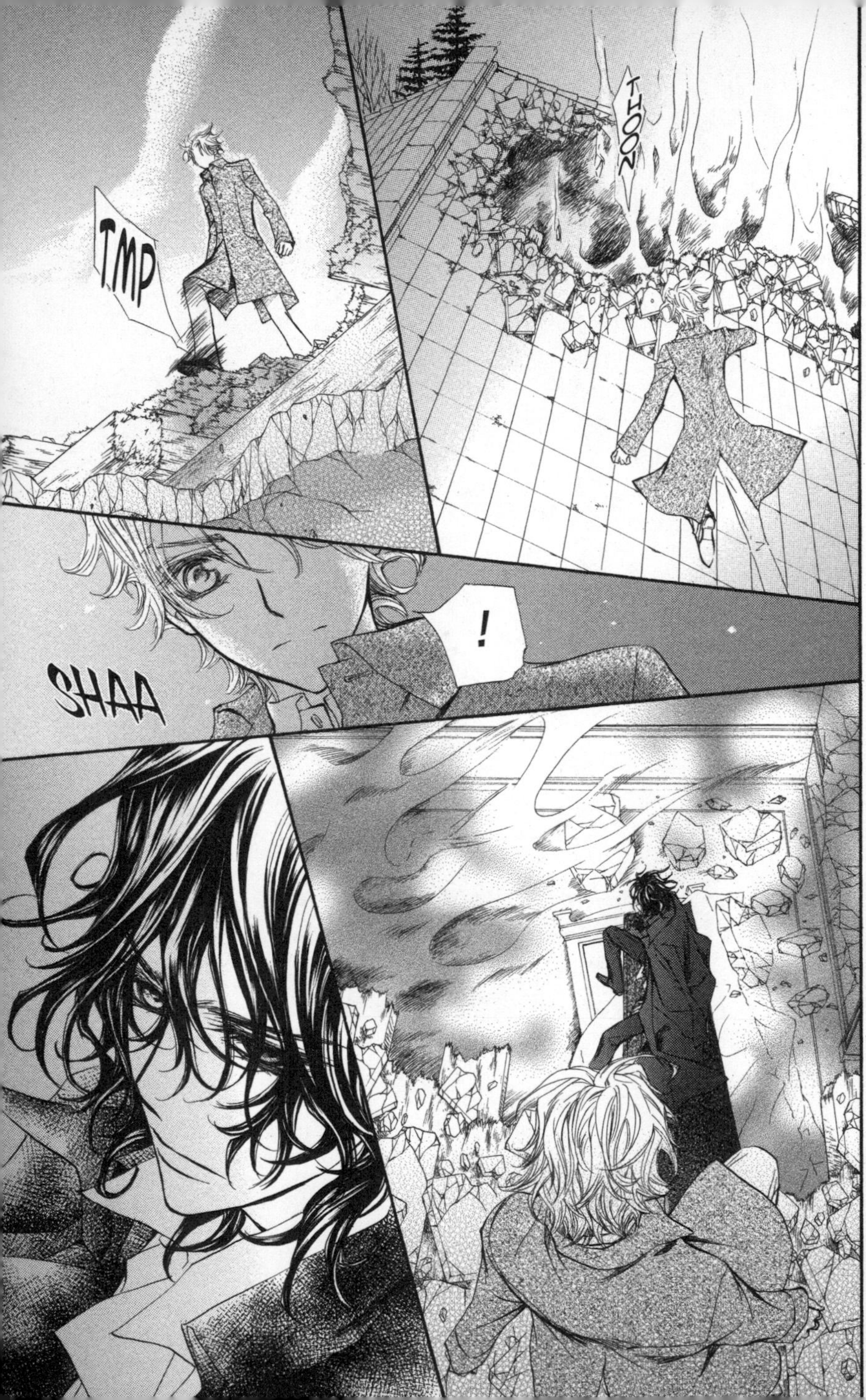
THOON
TMP
!
SHAA

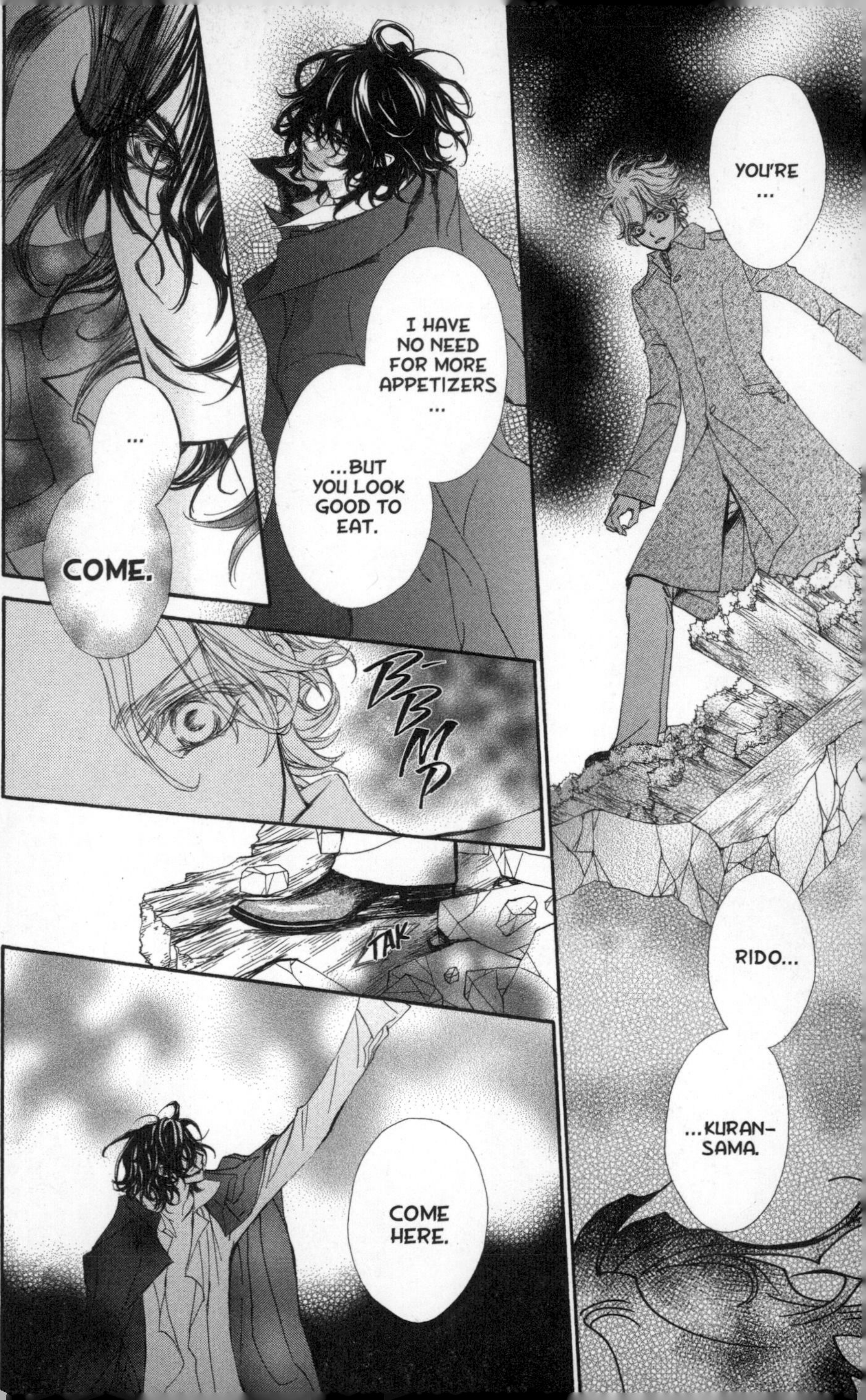
YOU'RE ...
RIDO...
...KURAN-SAMA.
I HAVE NO NEED FOR MORE APPETIZERS ...
...BUT YOU LOOK GOOD TO EAT.
...
COME.
B-BMP
TAK
COME HERE.

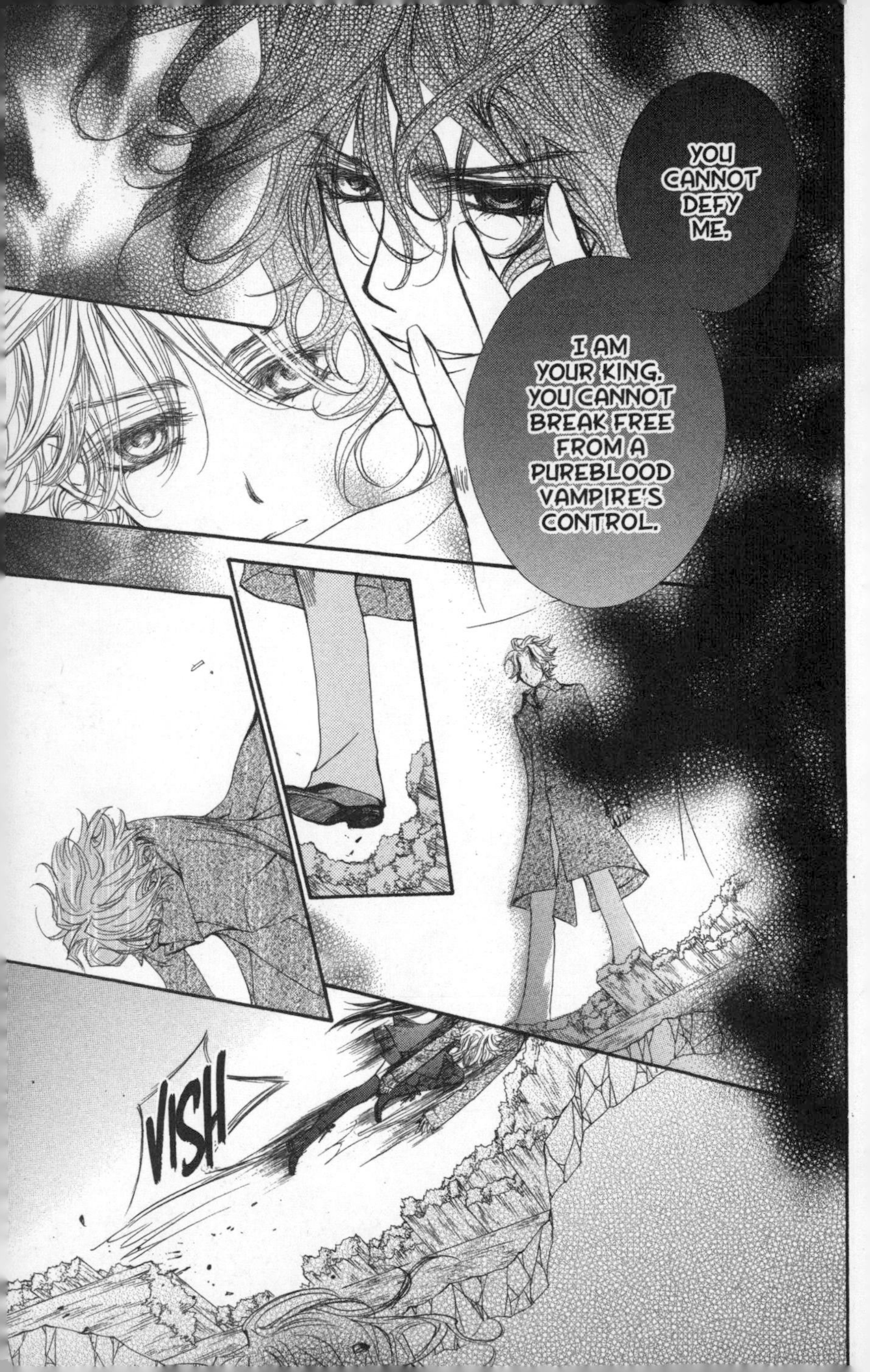
YOU CANNOT DEFY ME.
I AM YOUR KING. YOU CANNOT BREAK FREE FROM A PUREBLOOD VAMPIRE'S CONTROL.
VISH

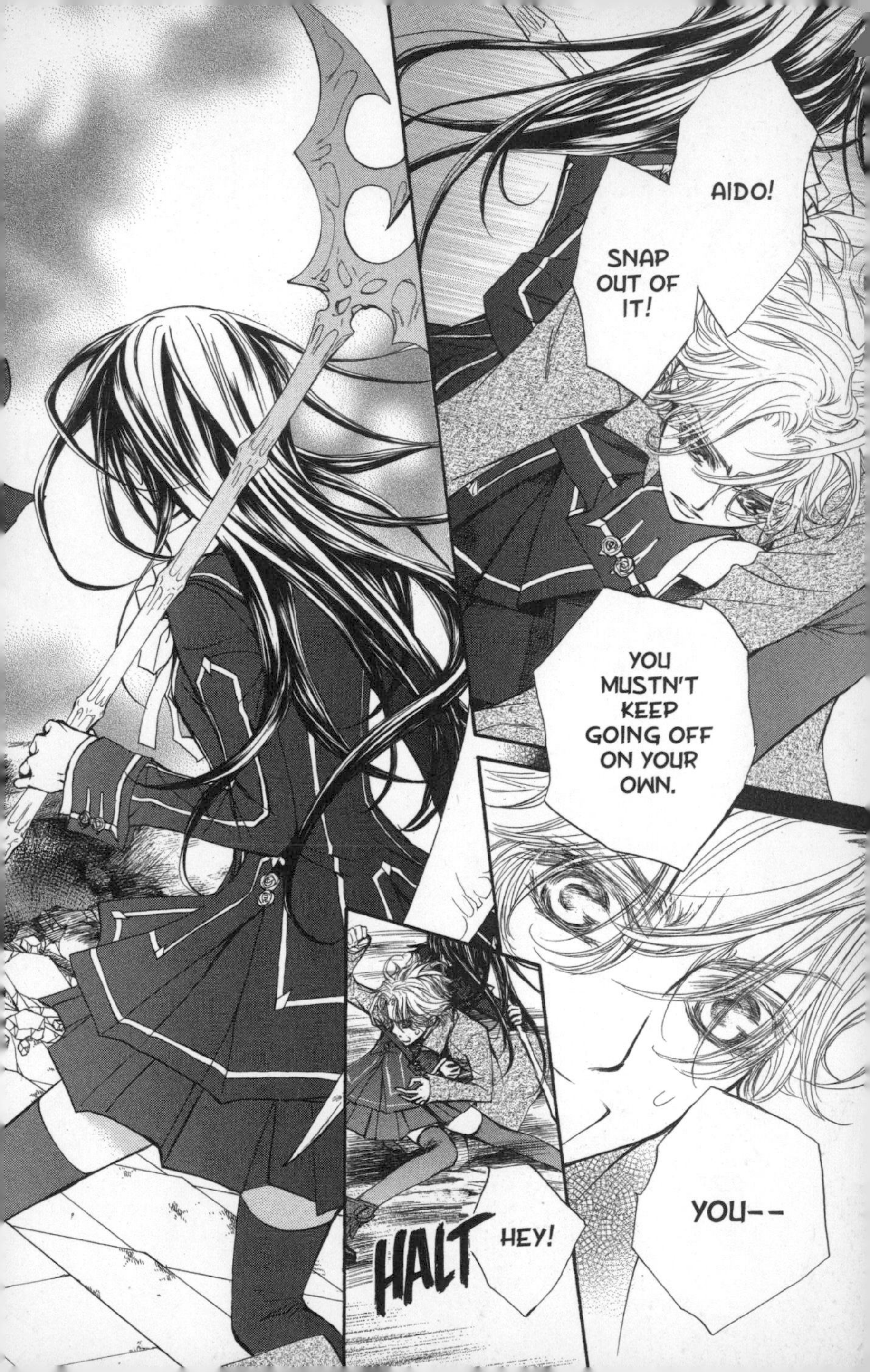
AIDO!
SNAP OUT OF IT!
YOU MUSTN'T KEEP GOING OFF ON YOUR OWN.
YOU--
HEY!
HALT

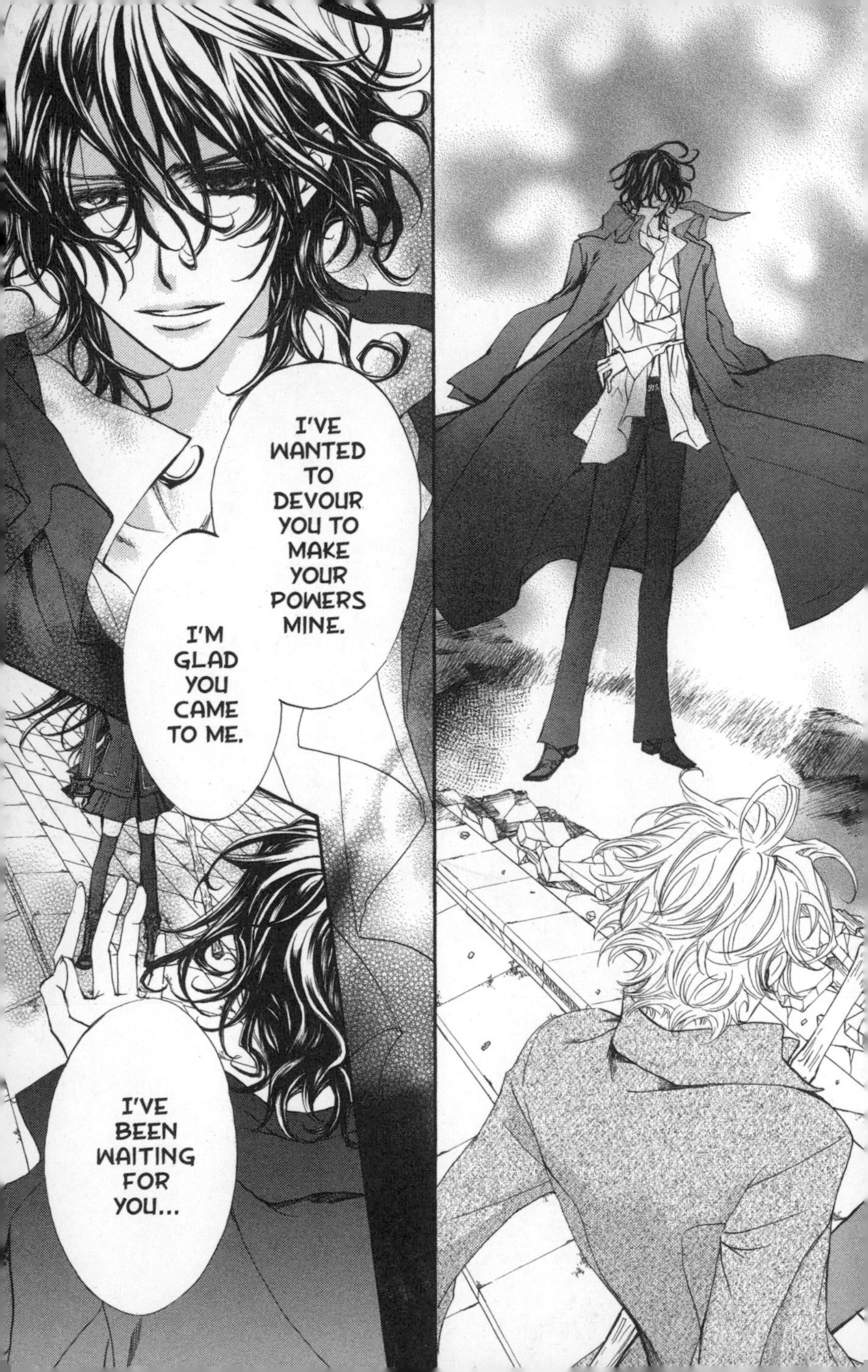
I'VE WANTED TO DEVOUR YOU TO MAKE YOUR POWERS MINE.
I'M GLAD YOU CAME TO ME.
I'VE BEEN WAITING FOR YOU...

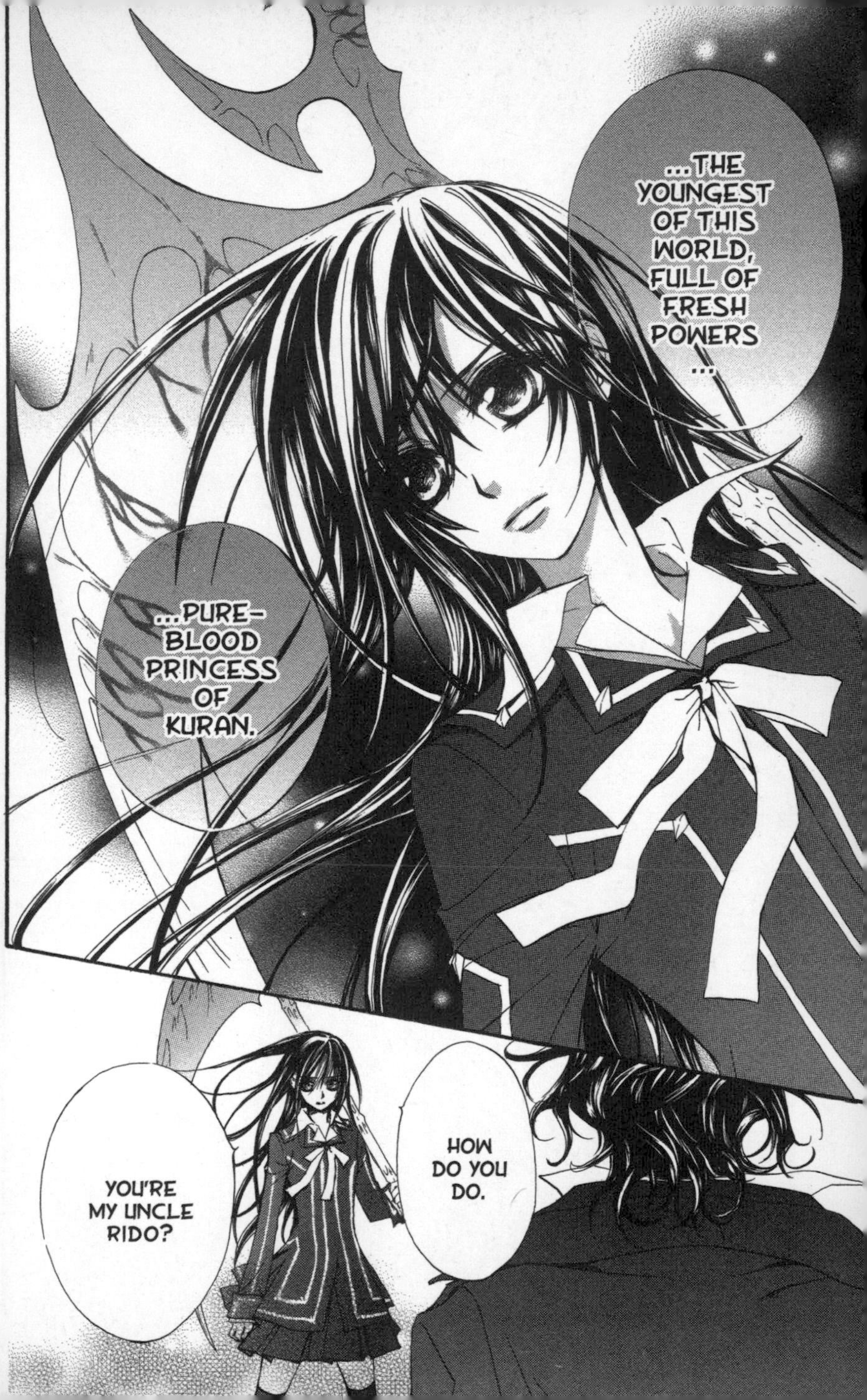
...THE YOUNGEST OF THIS WORLD, FULL OF FRESH POWERS ...
...PURE-BLOOD PRINCESS OF KURAN.
HOW DO YOU DO.
YOU'RE MY UNCLE RIDO?

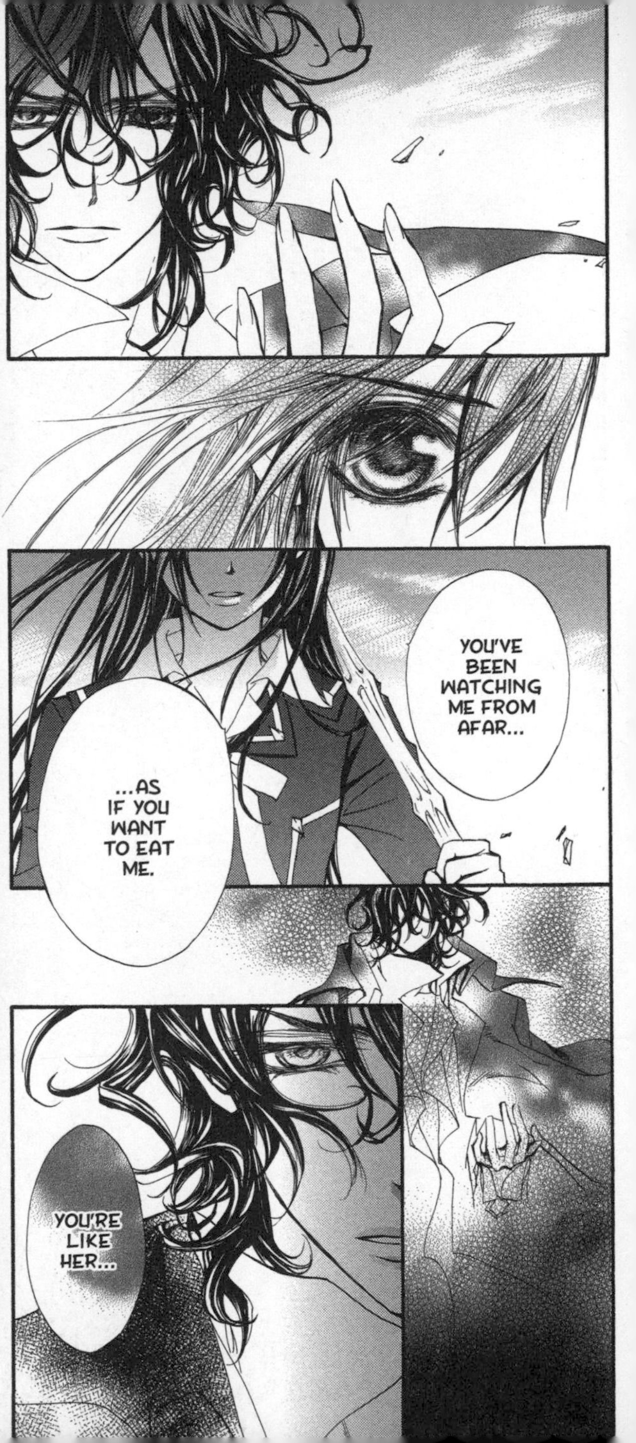
YOU'VE BEEN WATCHING ME FROM AFAR...
...AS IF YOU WANT TO EAT ME.
YOU'RE LIKE HER...

IV

Storyboard materials: B4-size paper, MONO eraser, Pilot mechanical pencils (clutch point), Pentel HI-POLYMER FOR PRO (0.5mm), and a Kutsuwa ruler.

Black-and-white manuscript materials: IC B4-size manuscript paper (rough sketch 110kg/inking 135kg), MONO NON DUST eraser, Pilot mechanical pencil (S Series), Pentel HI-POLYMER FOR PRO (0.3mm), drafting rulers, templates, Pilot drafting ink, Tokyo Slider pen-holder (SL3100 cork handle), Nikko round nip pen, Misunon correcting fluid, 3M masking tape, Iken putty rubber, MONO KNOCK 3.8 eraser, Pentel Clic Eraser (eraser for oil-based ballpoint pens), uni PROCKEY (thin/thick, very thin/thin), Mitsubishi Shin-mohitsu brush-tip pen, Pilot Kohitsu-nanhitsu brush-tip pen, COPIC Multi-liners, Rotring Rapidograph pens (0.2/0.8), NT Cutter (D-400/45 degrees), Too Rub Tone spatula, Light blue and other colored pencils, various screentones...

Color manuscript materials: The basic tools are the same as when I work on my black-and-white manuscripts. The paper is Muse Board (BB Kent smooth, CANSON Kent, Pastel color board), NITTO masking tape, TORICON masking sheet, air-brush and compressor. The main lines are NOUVEL's color ink (burnt sienna and warm gray). Colors are mainly COPIC (and other materials). Dr. Martin's Bleedproof White, BUNSEIDO Woody fit brush (2/0). That's all.

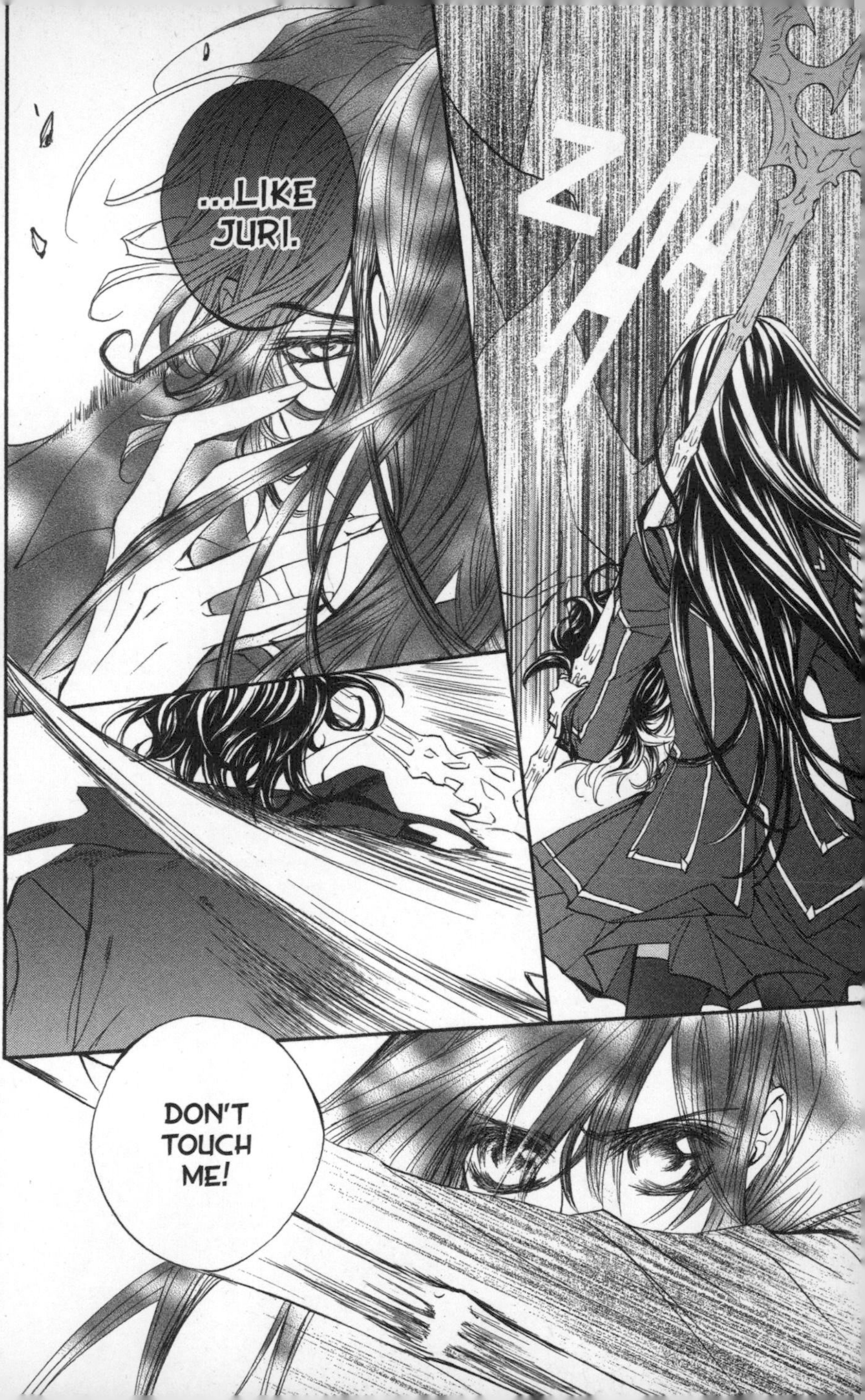
ZAA
...LIKE JURI.
DON'T TOUCH ME!

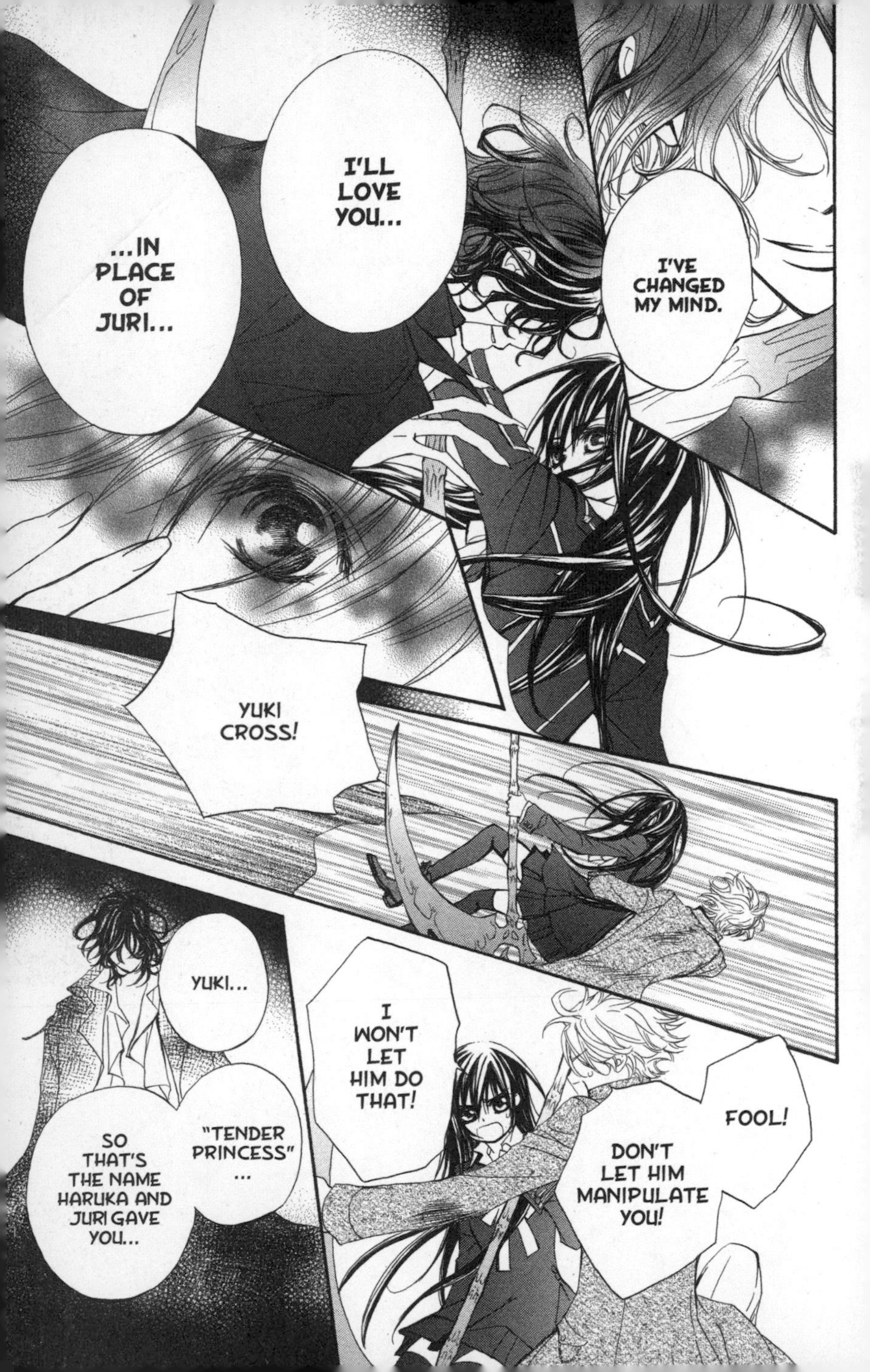
I'VE CHANGED MY MIND.
I'LL LOVE YOU...
...IN PLACE OF JURI...
YUKI CROSS!
FOOL!
DON'T LET HIM MANIPULATE YOU!
I WON'T LET HIM DO THAT!
YUKI...
"TENDER PRINCESS" ...
SO THAT'S THE NAME HARUKA AND JURI GAVE YOU...

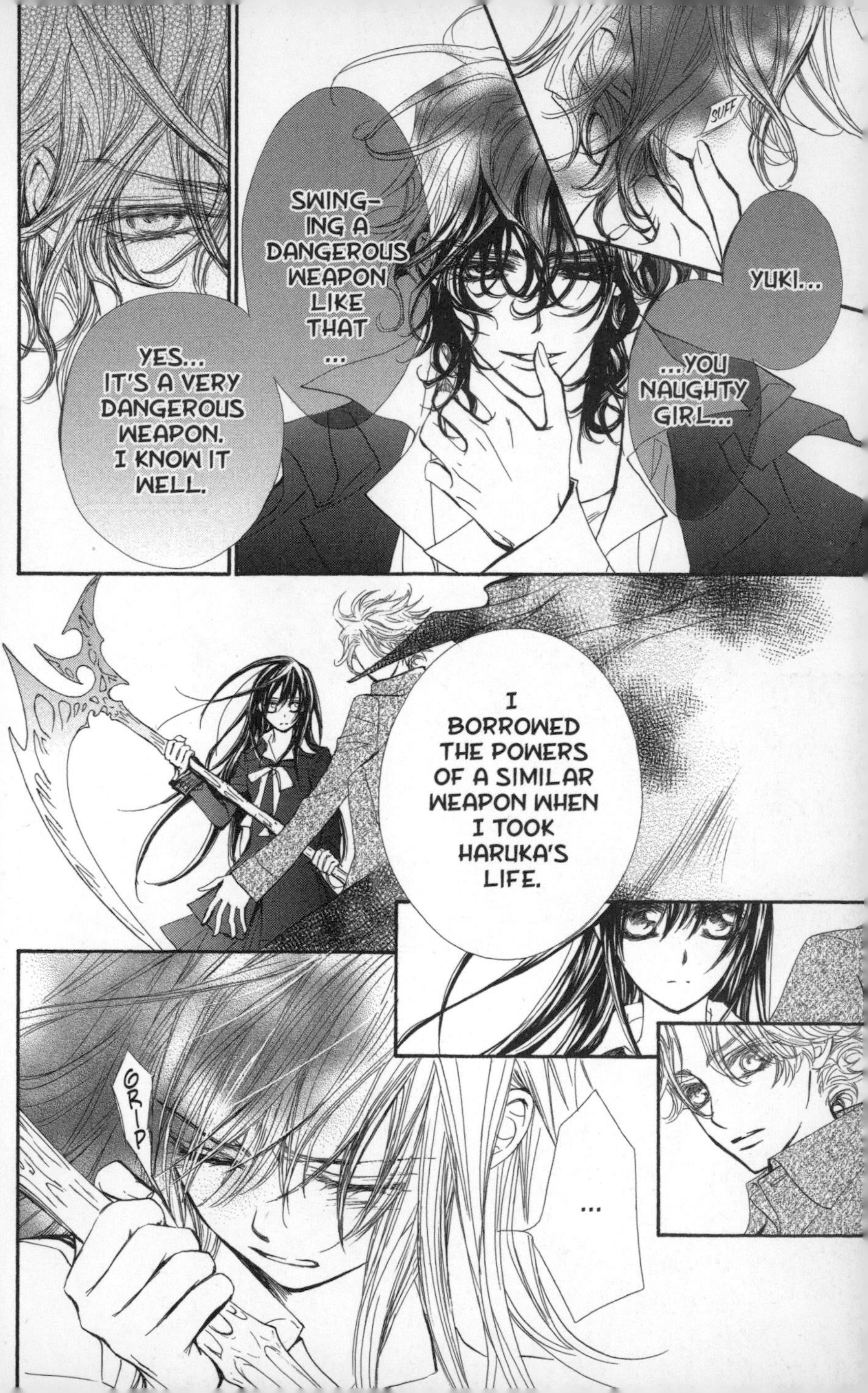
SUFF
YUKI...
...YOU NAUGHTY GIRL...
SWING-ING A DANGEROUS WEAPON LIKE THAT...
YES... IT'S A VERY DANGEROUS WEAPON. I KNOW IT WELL.
I BORROWED THE POWERS OF A SIMILAR WEAPON WHEN I TOOK HARUKA'S LIFE.
...
GRIP

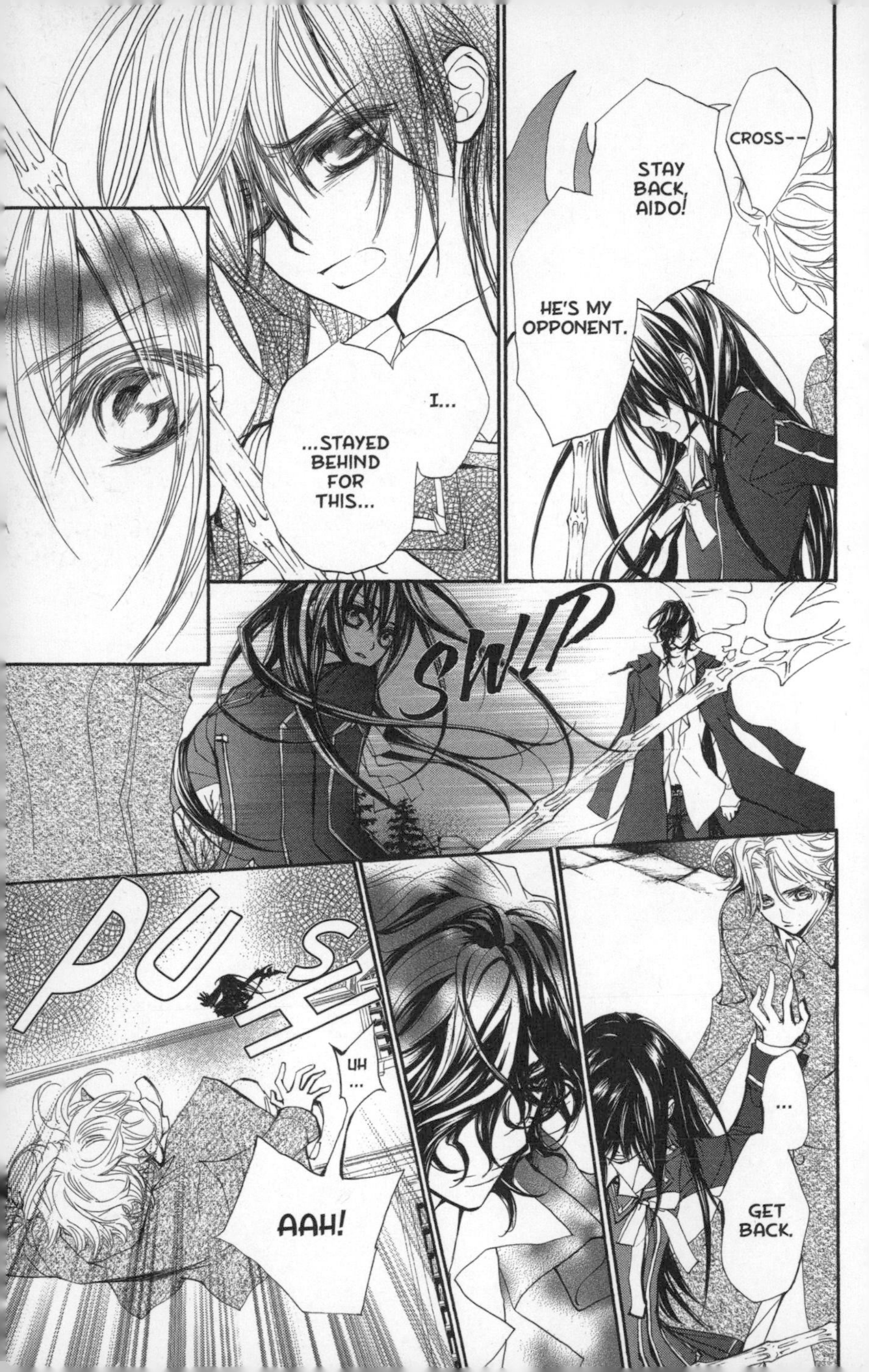
CROSS--
STAY BACK, AIDO!
HE'S MY OPPONENT.
I...
...STAYED BEHIND FOR THIS...
SWIP
...
GET BACK.
PUSH
UH ...
AAH!

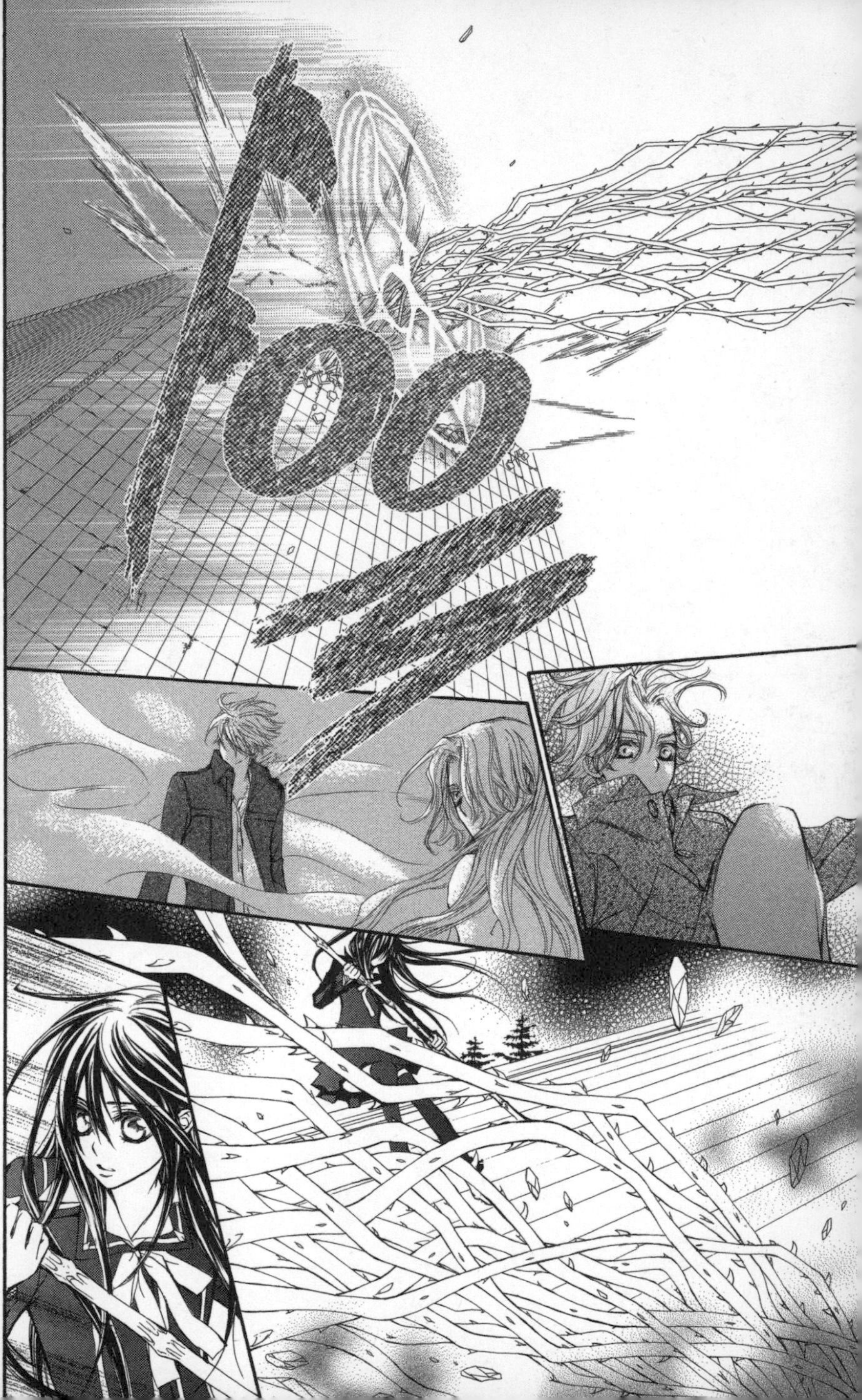
FOOM

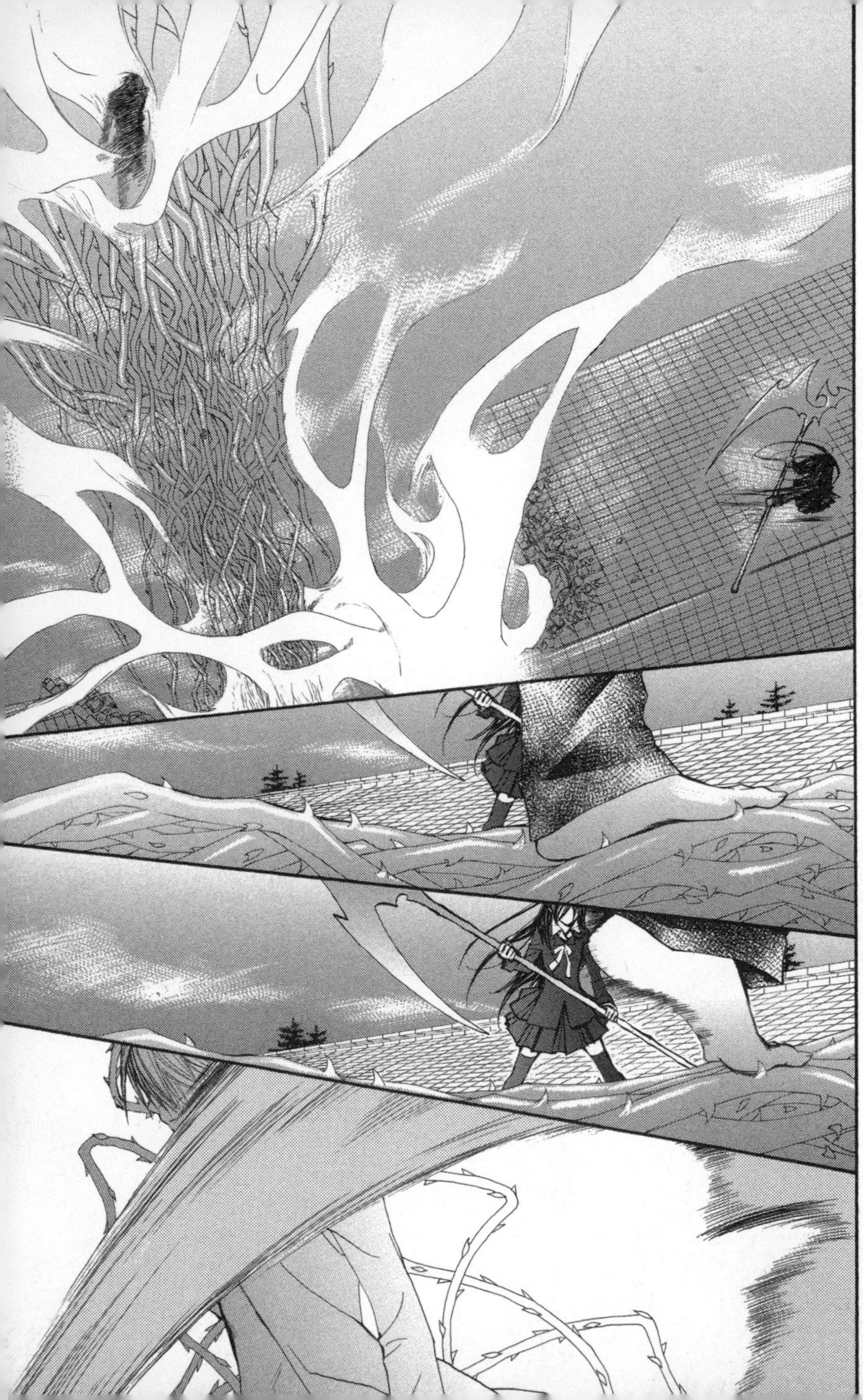

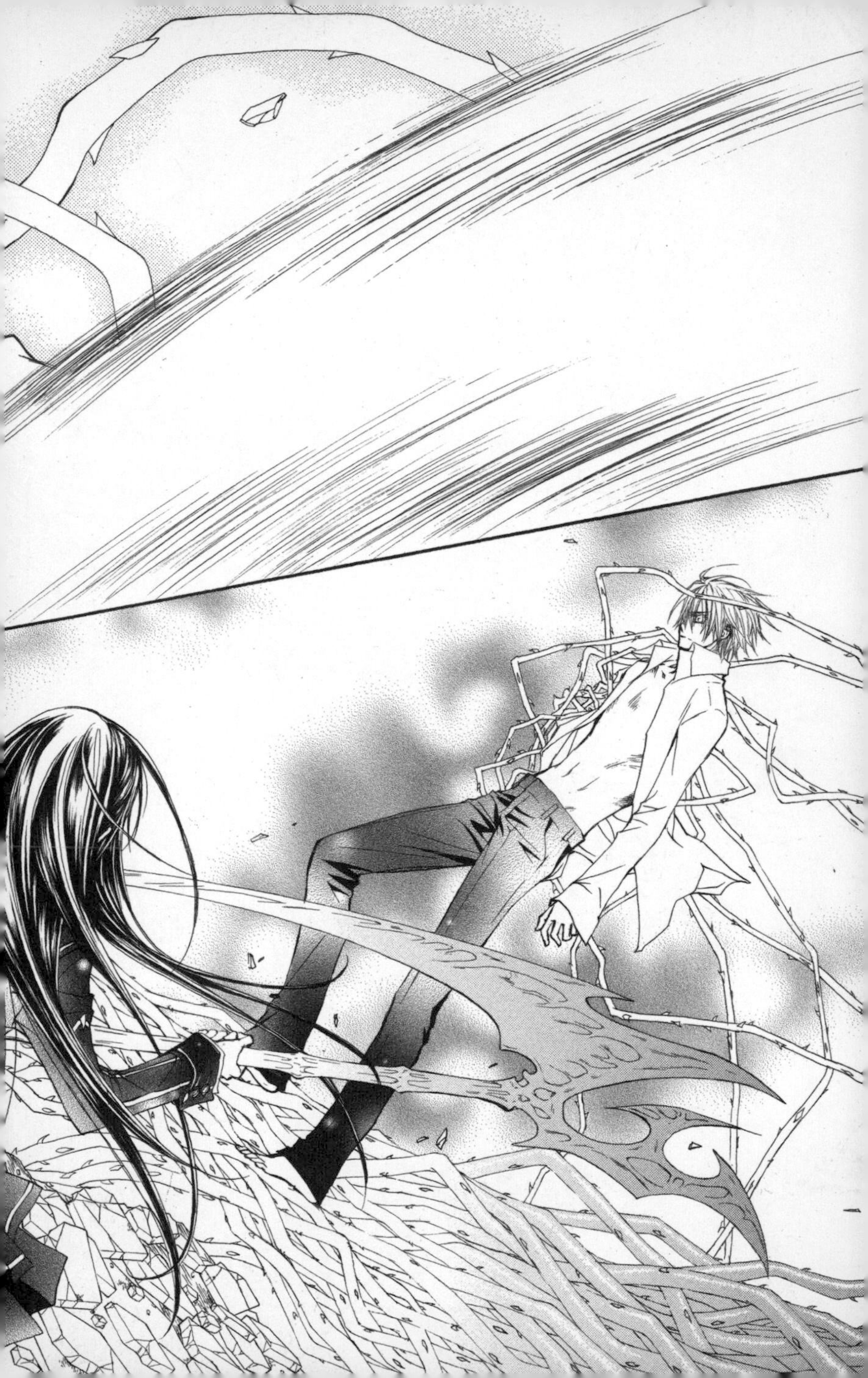

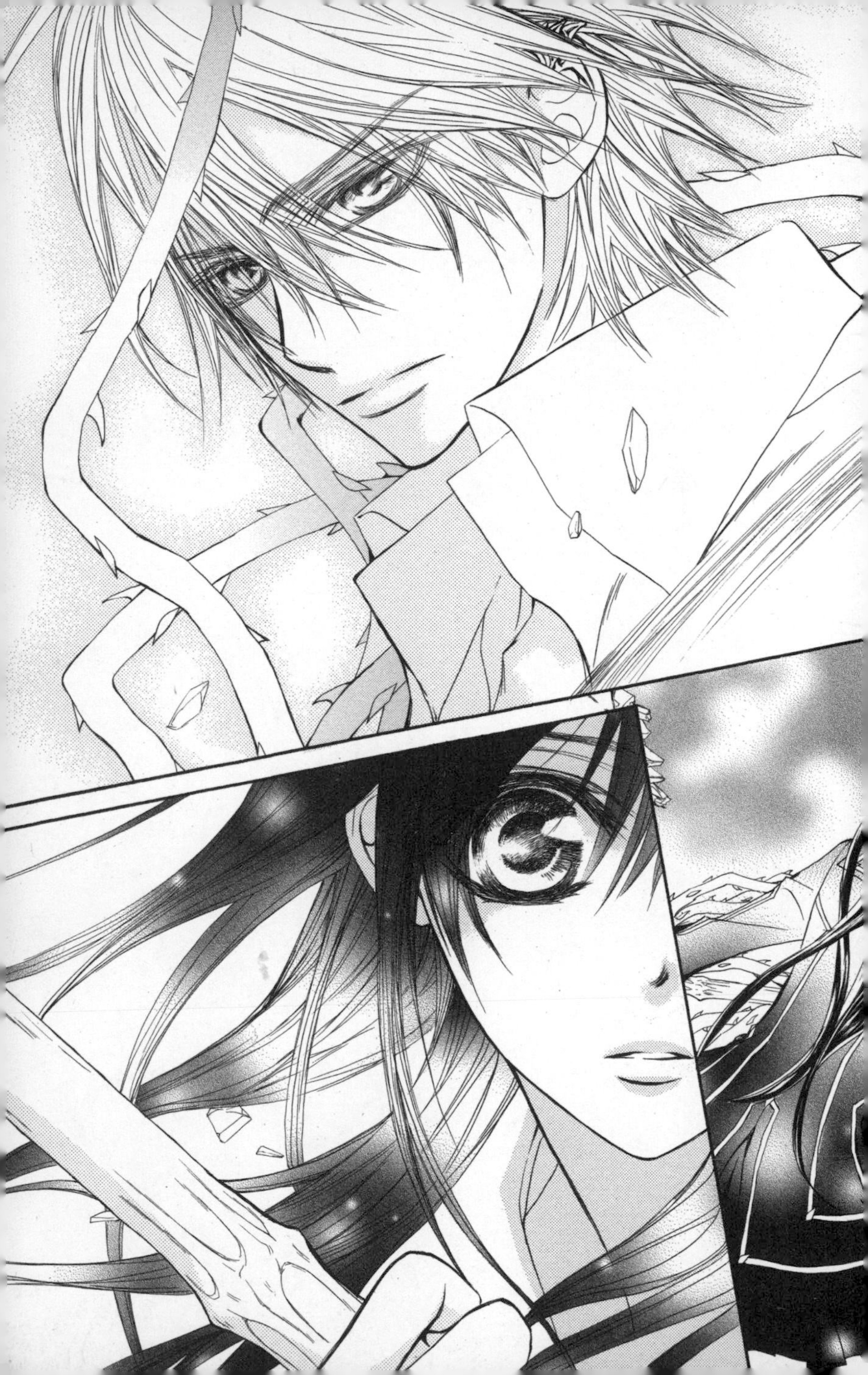

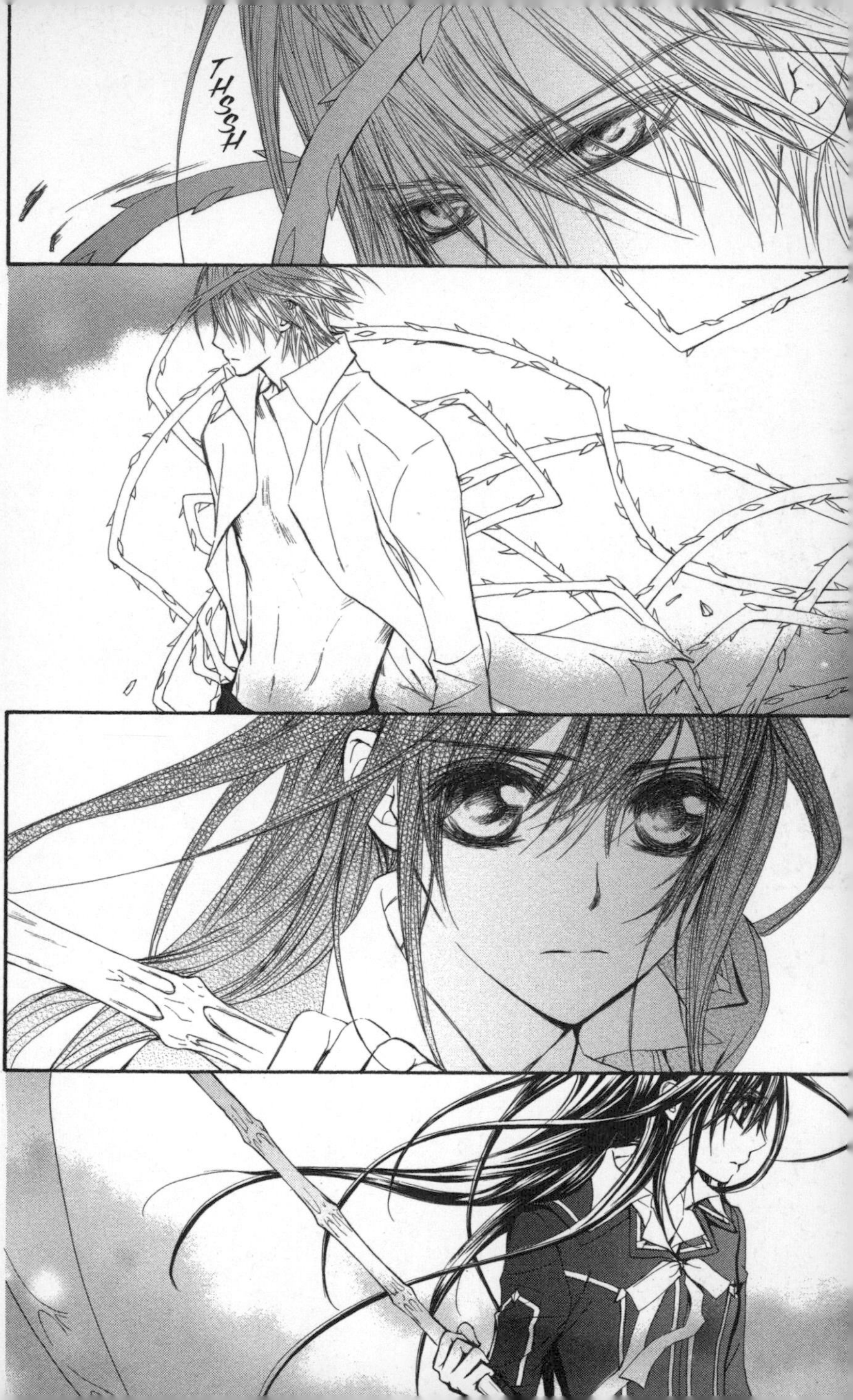
THSSH

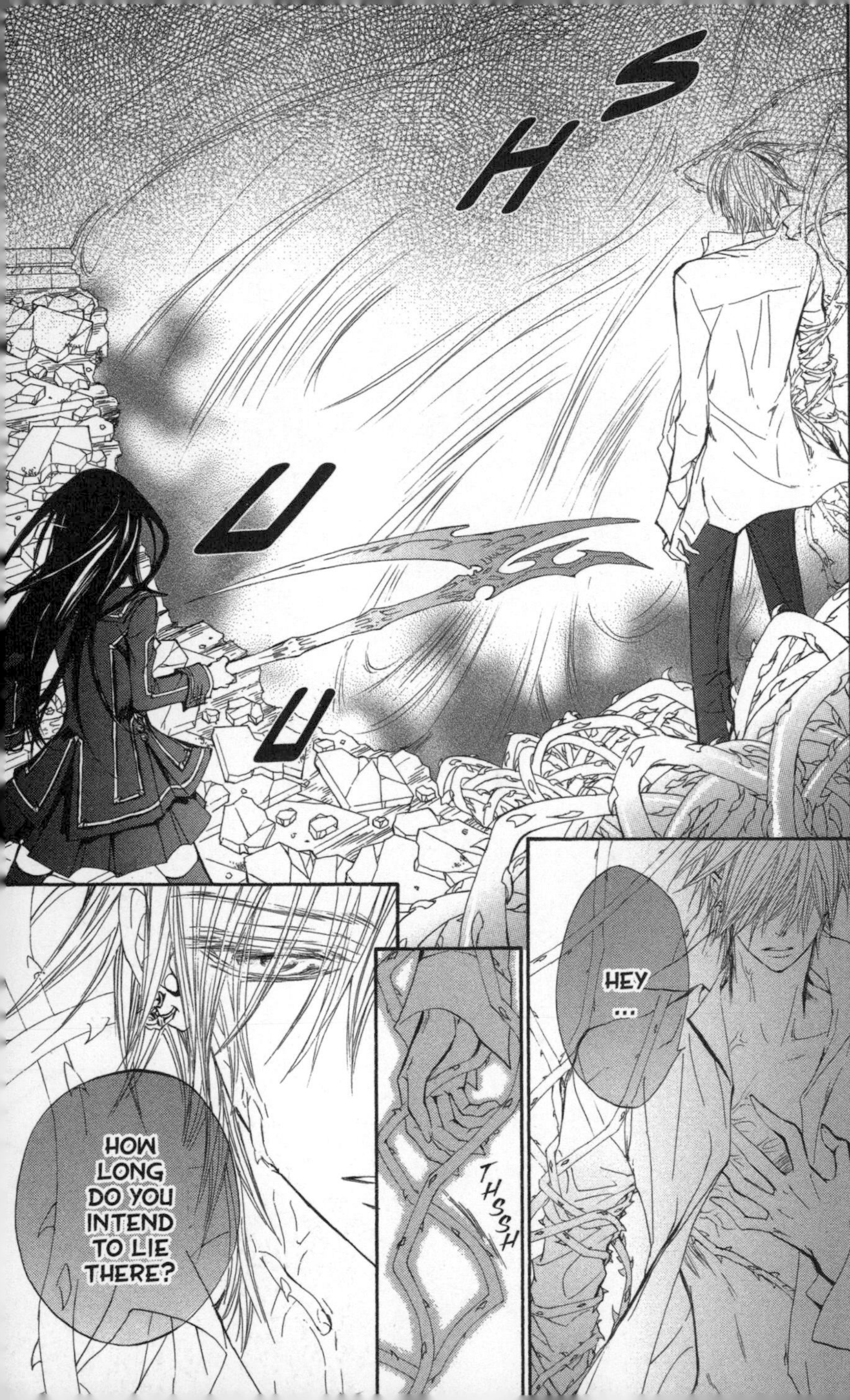
SHUU
HEY ...
THSSH
HOW LONG DO YOU INTEND TO LIE THERE?

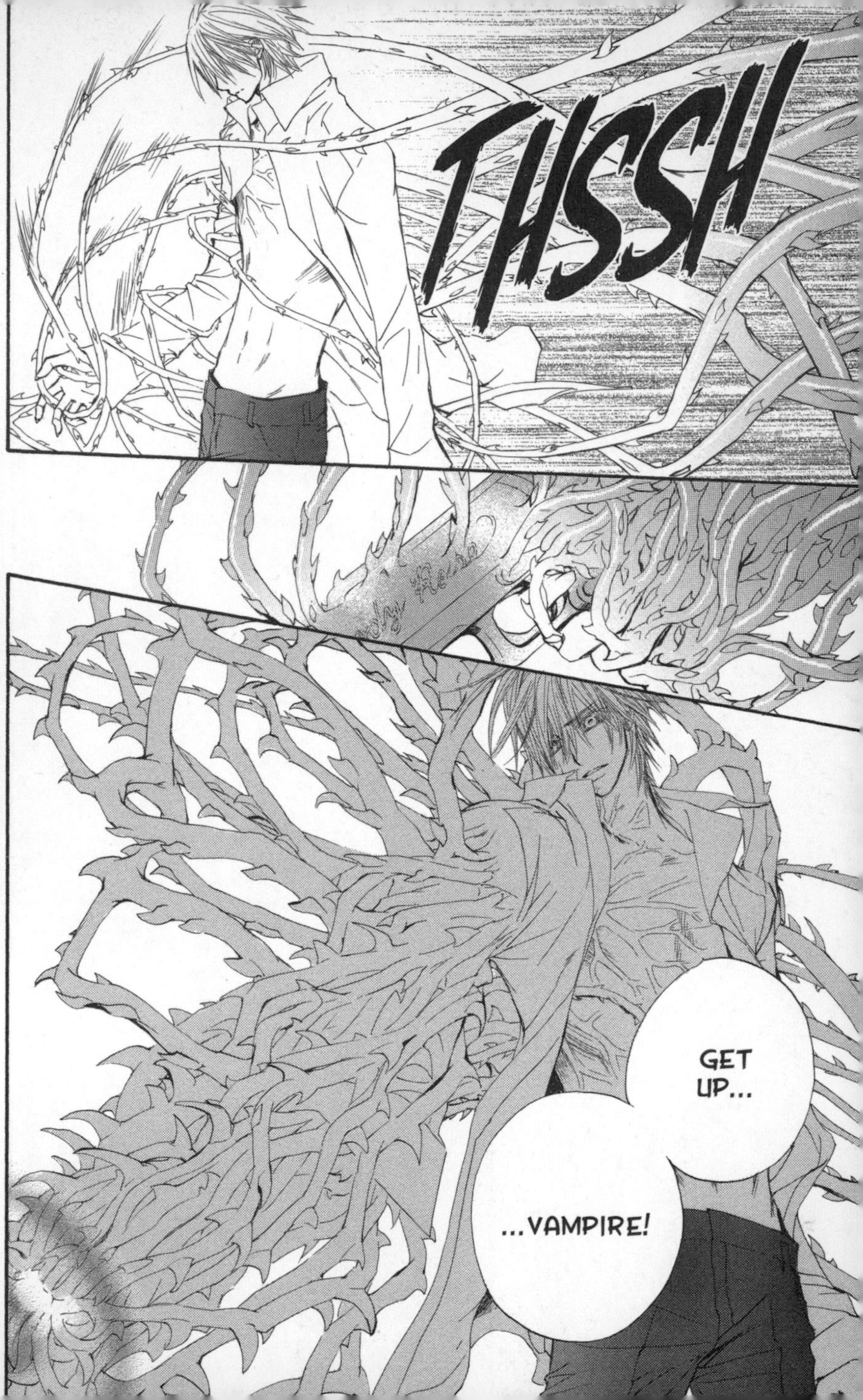
THSSH
GET UP...
...VAMPIRE!

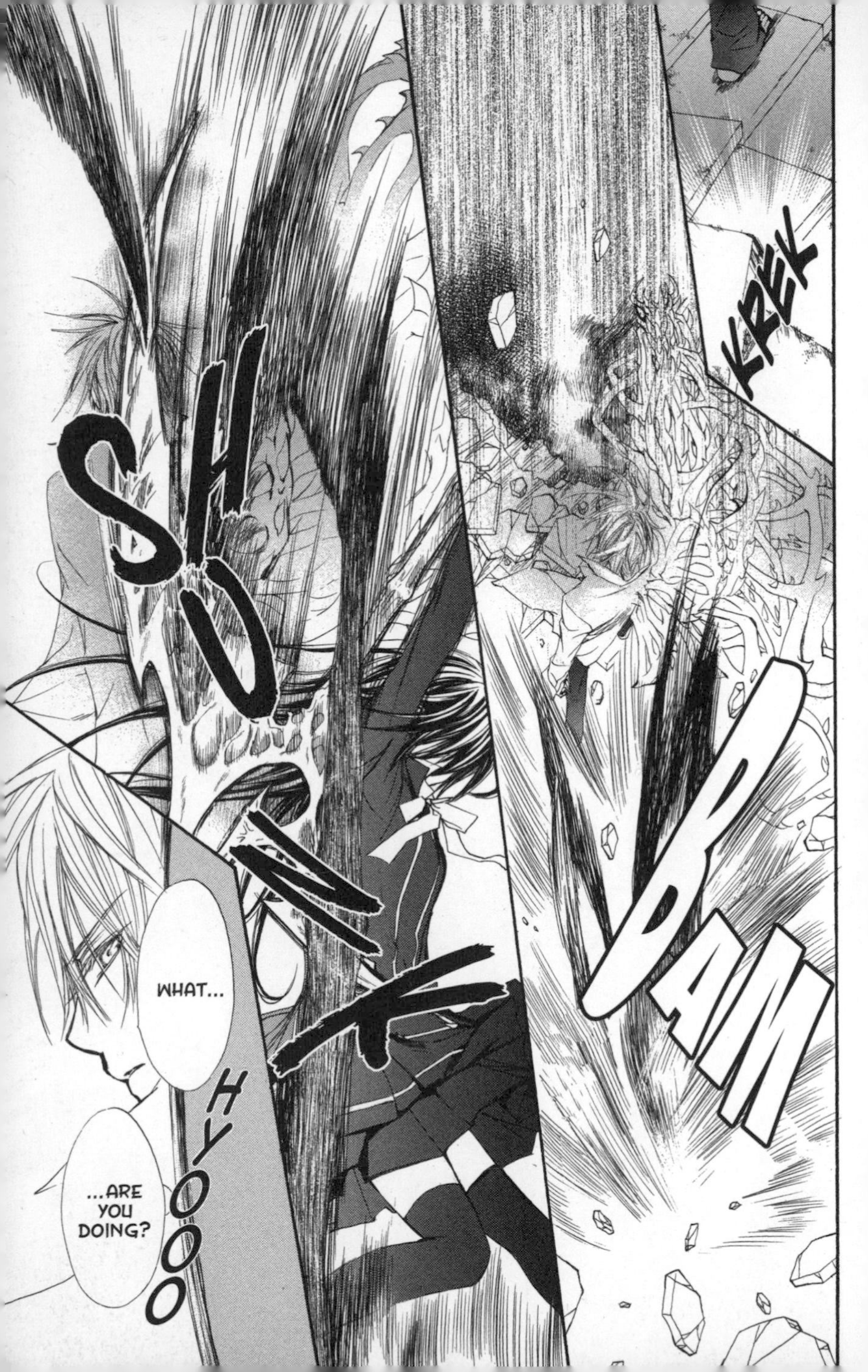
KREK
BAM
SHUNK
WHAT...
...ARE YOU DOING?
HYOOOO

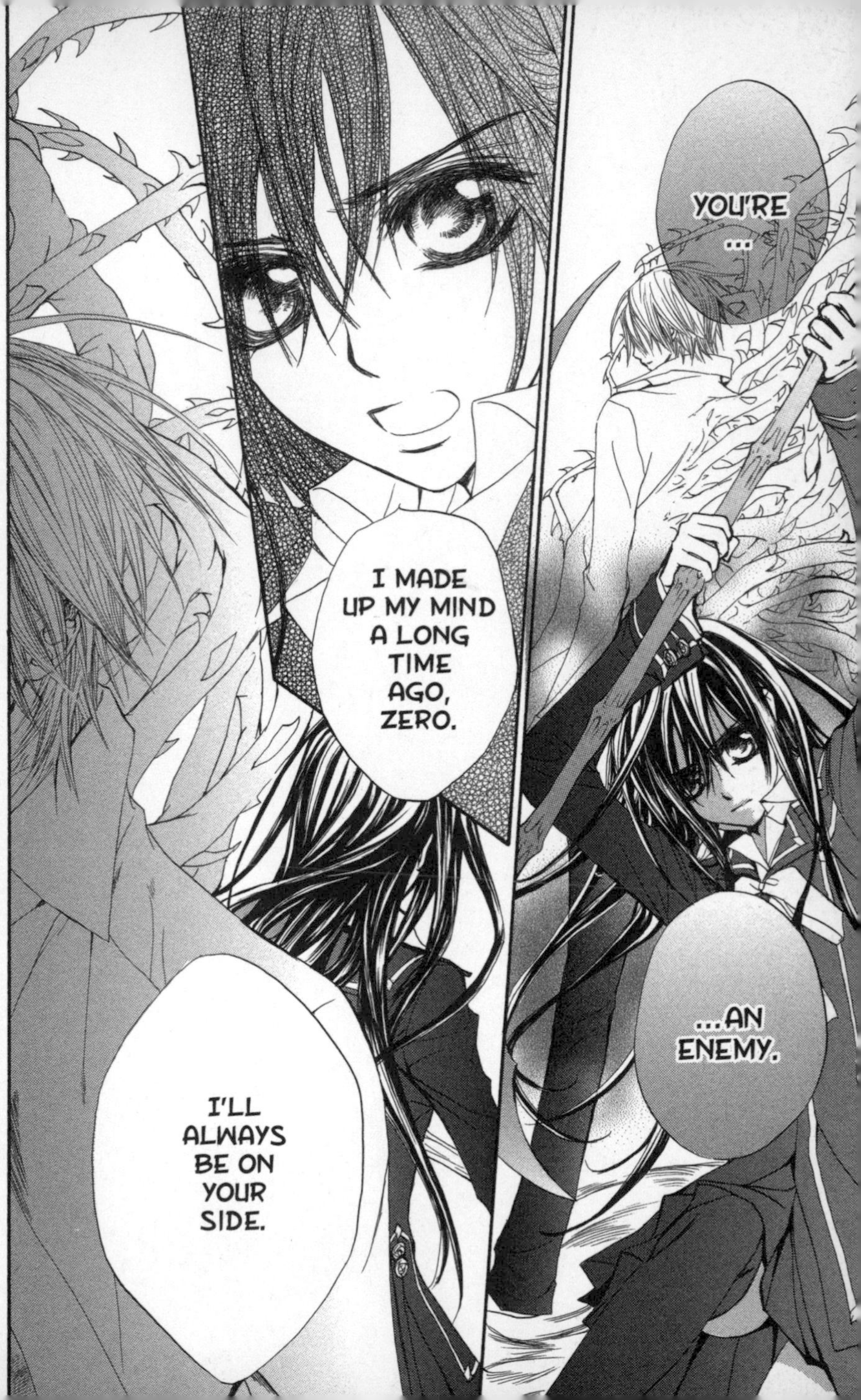
YOU'RE ...
...AN ENEMY.
I MADE UP MY MIND A LONG TIME AGO, ZERO.
I'LL ALWAYS BE ON YOUR SIDE.

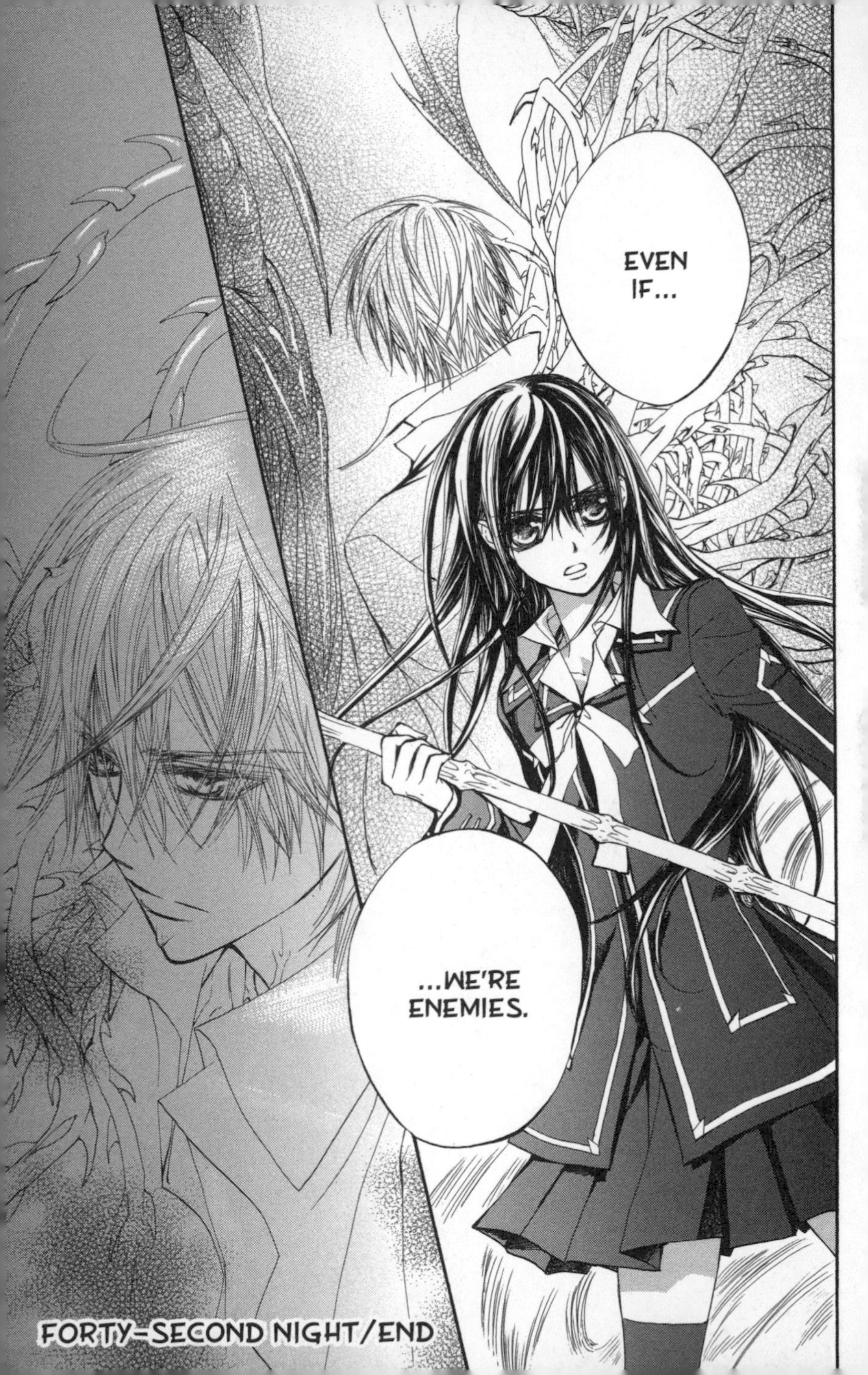
EVEN IF...
...WE'RE ENEMIES.
FORTY-SECOND NIGHT/END

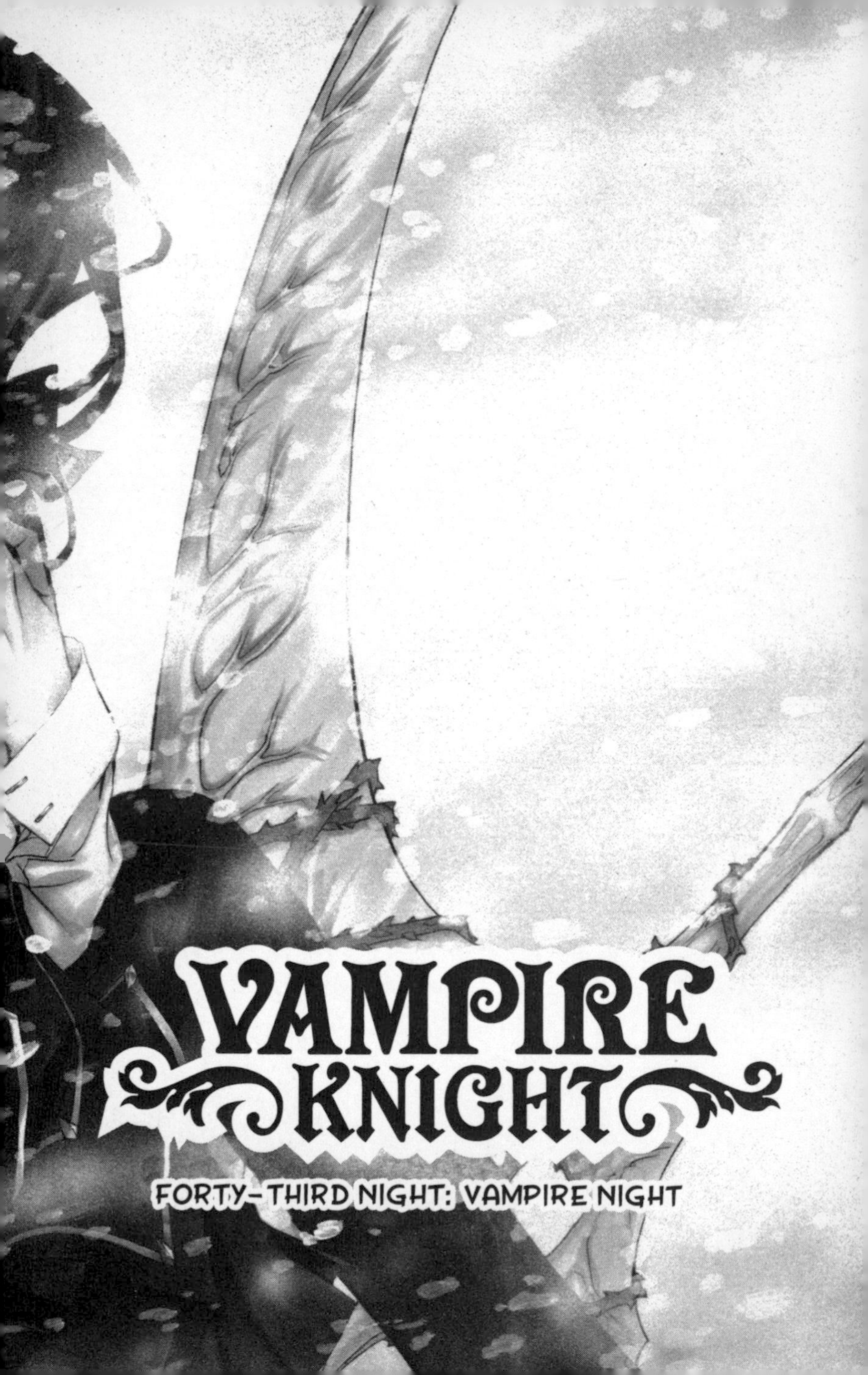
VAMPIRE
KNIGHT
FORTY-THIRD NIGHT: VAMPIRE NIGHT

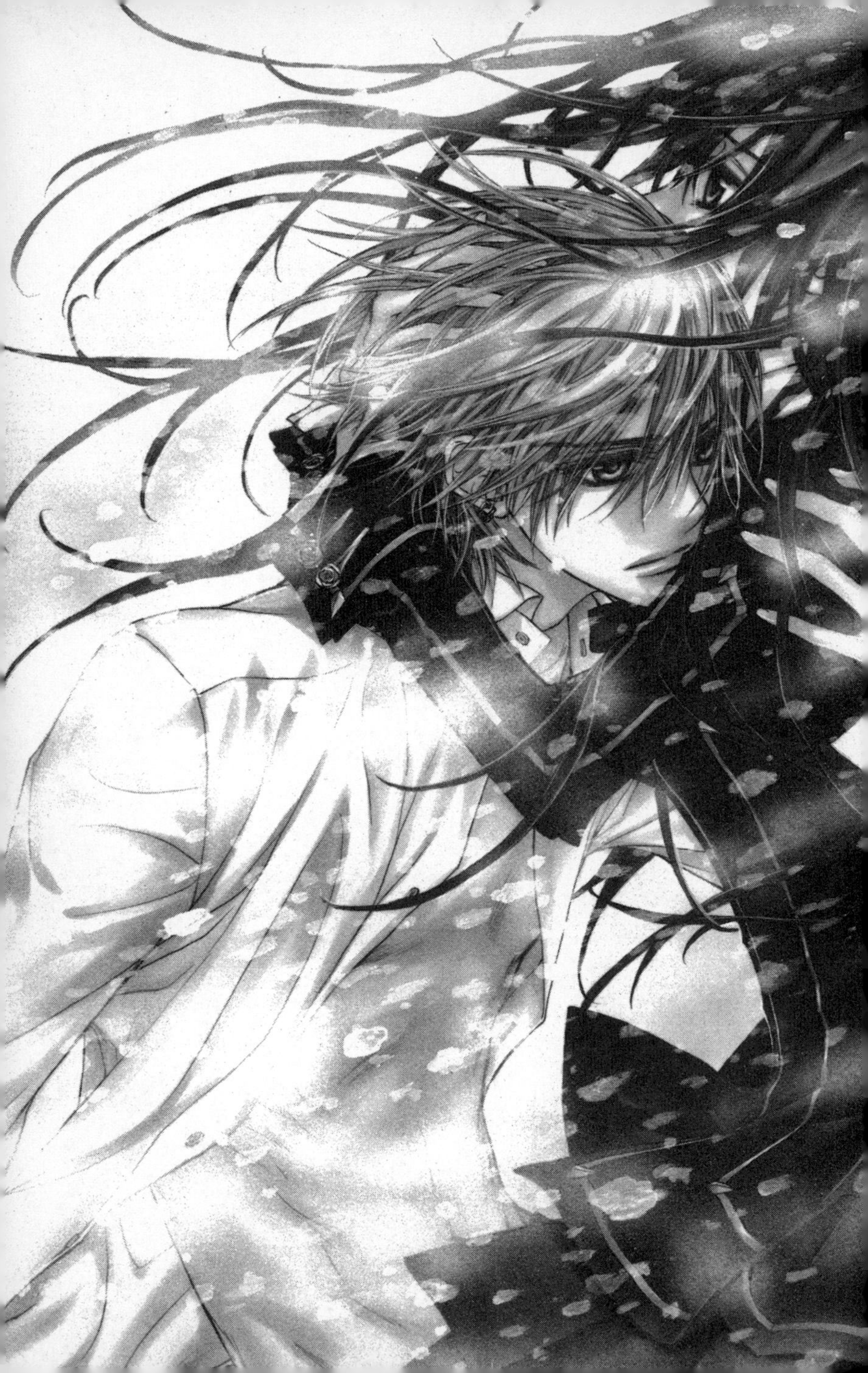

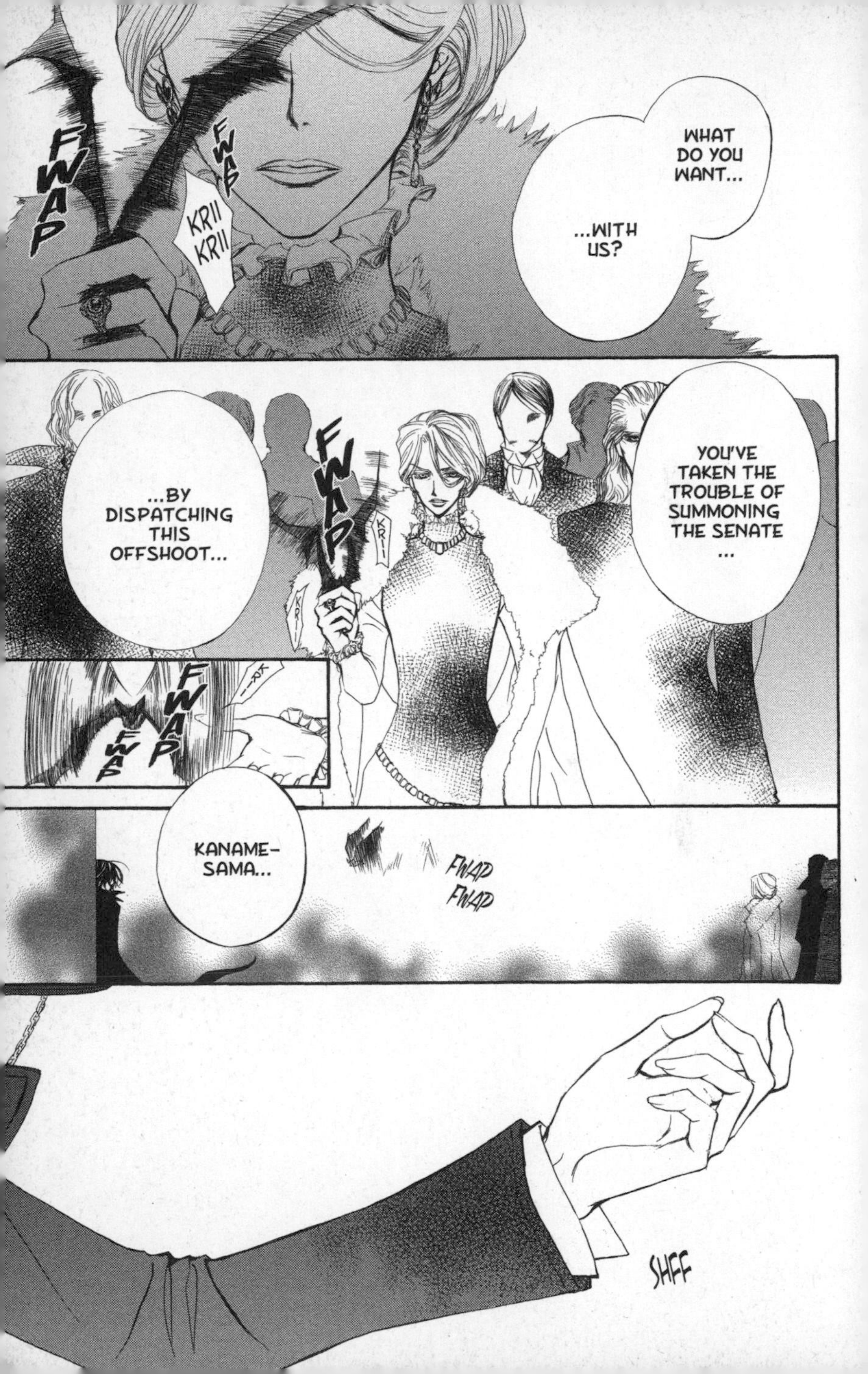
WHAT DO YOU WANT...
...WITH US?
FWAP
FWAP
KRII KRII
YOU'VE TAKEN THE TROUBLE OF SUMMONING THE SENATE ...
FWAP
...BY DISPATCHING THIS OFFSHOOT...
FWAP
FWAP
FWAP FWAP
KANAME-SAMA...
SHFF

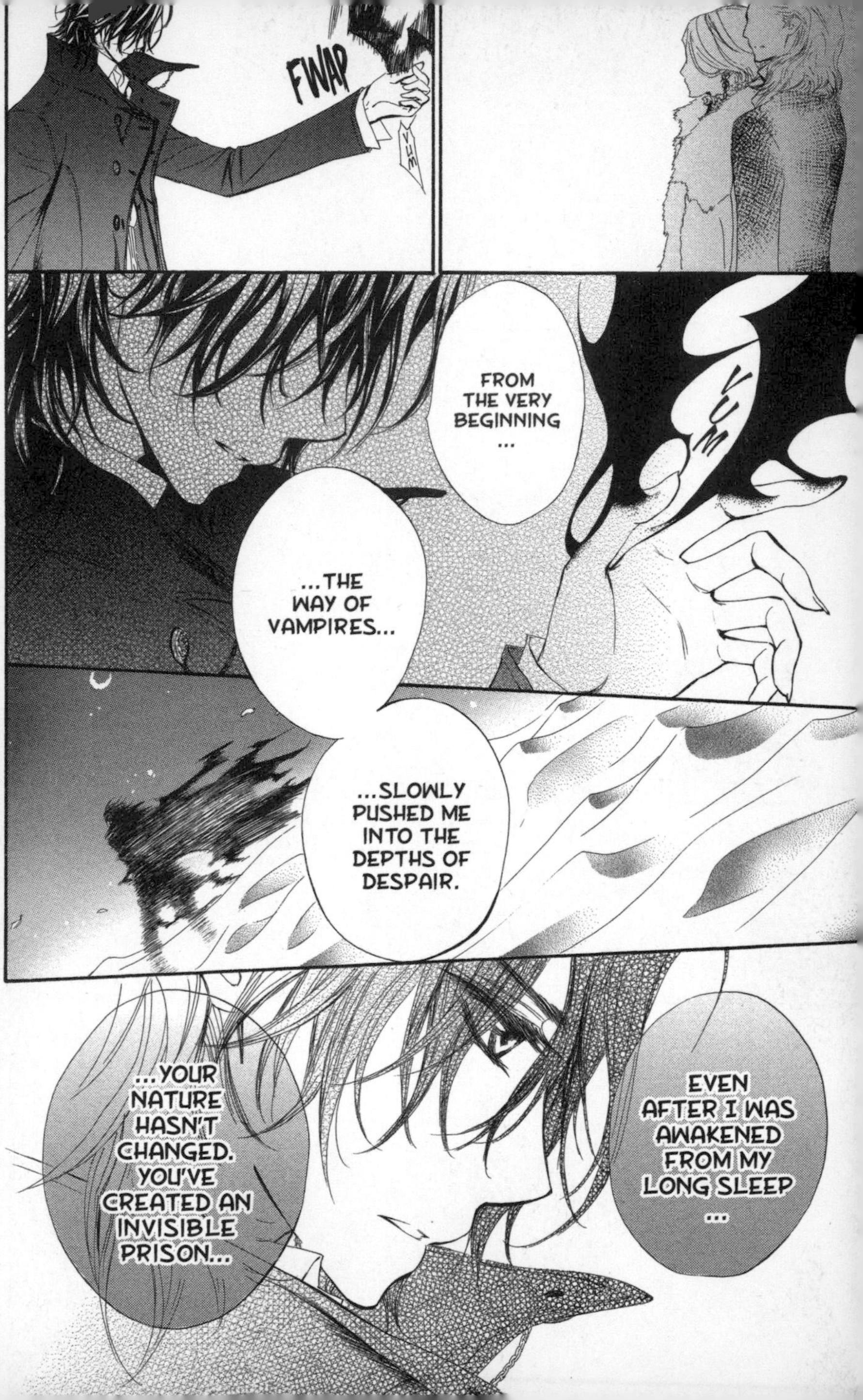
FWAP
VUM
VUM
FROM THE VERY BEGINNING ...
...THE WAY OF VAMPIRES...
...SLOWLY PUSHED ME INTO THE DEPTHS OF DESPAIR.
EVEN AFTER I WAS AWAKENED FROM MY LONG SLEEP ...
...YOUR NATURE HASN'T CHANGED. YOU'VE CREATED AN INVISIBLE PRISON...

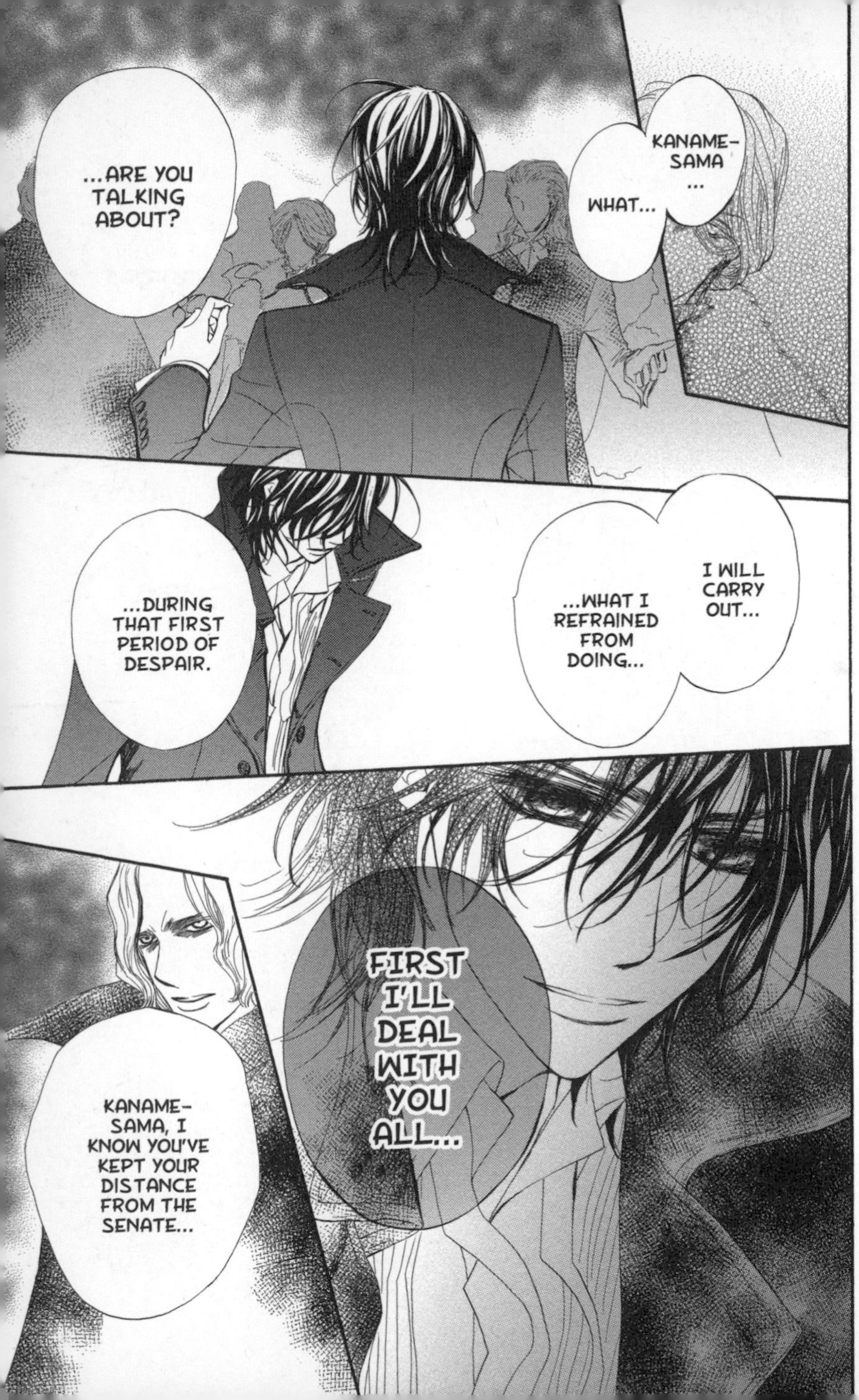
KANAME-SAMA ... WHAT...
...ARE YOU TALKING ABOUT?
I WILL CARRY OUT...
...WHAT I REFRAINED FROM DOING...
...DURING THAT FIRST PERIOD OF DESPAIR.
FIRST I'LL DEAL WITH YOU ALL...
KANAME-SAMA, I KNOW YOU'VE KEPT YOUR DISTANCE FROM THE SENATE...

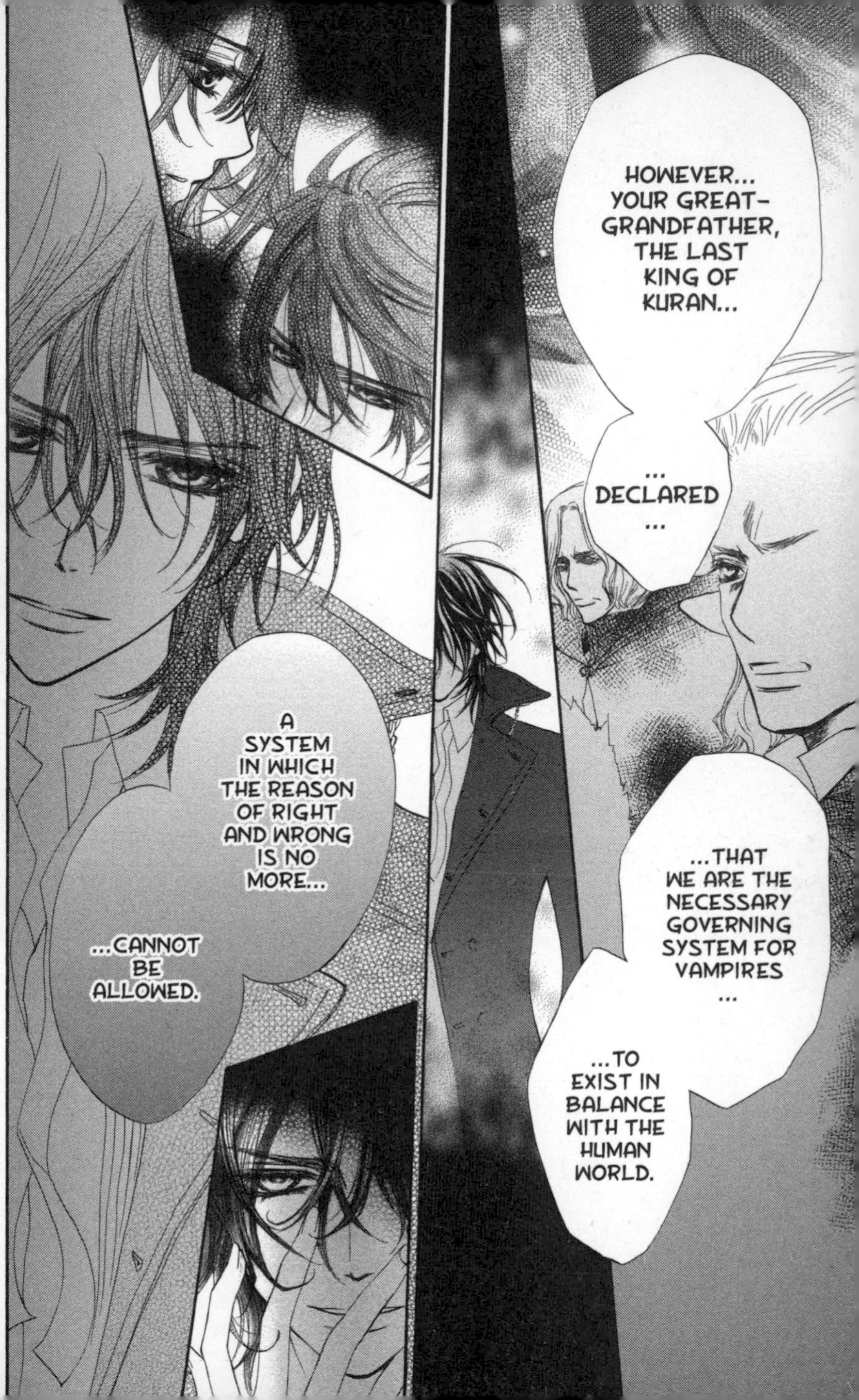
HOWEVER... YOUR GREAT-GRANDFATHER, THE LAST KING OF KURAN...
...DECLARED...
...THAT WE ARE THE NECESSARY GOVERNING SYSTEM FOR VAMPIRES...
...TO EXIST IN BALANCE WITH THE HUMAN WORLD.
A SYSTEM IN WHICH THE REASON OF RIGHT AND WRONG IS NO MORE...
...CANNOT BE ALLOWED.

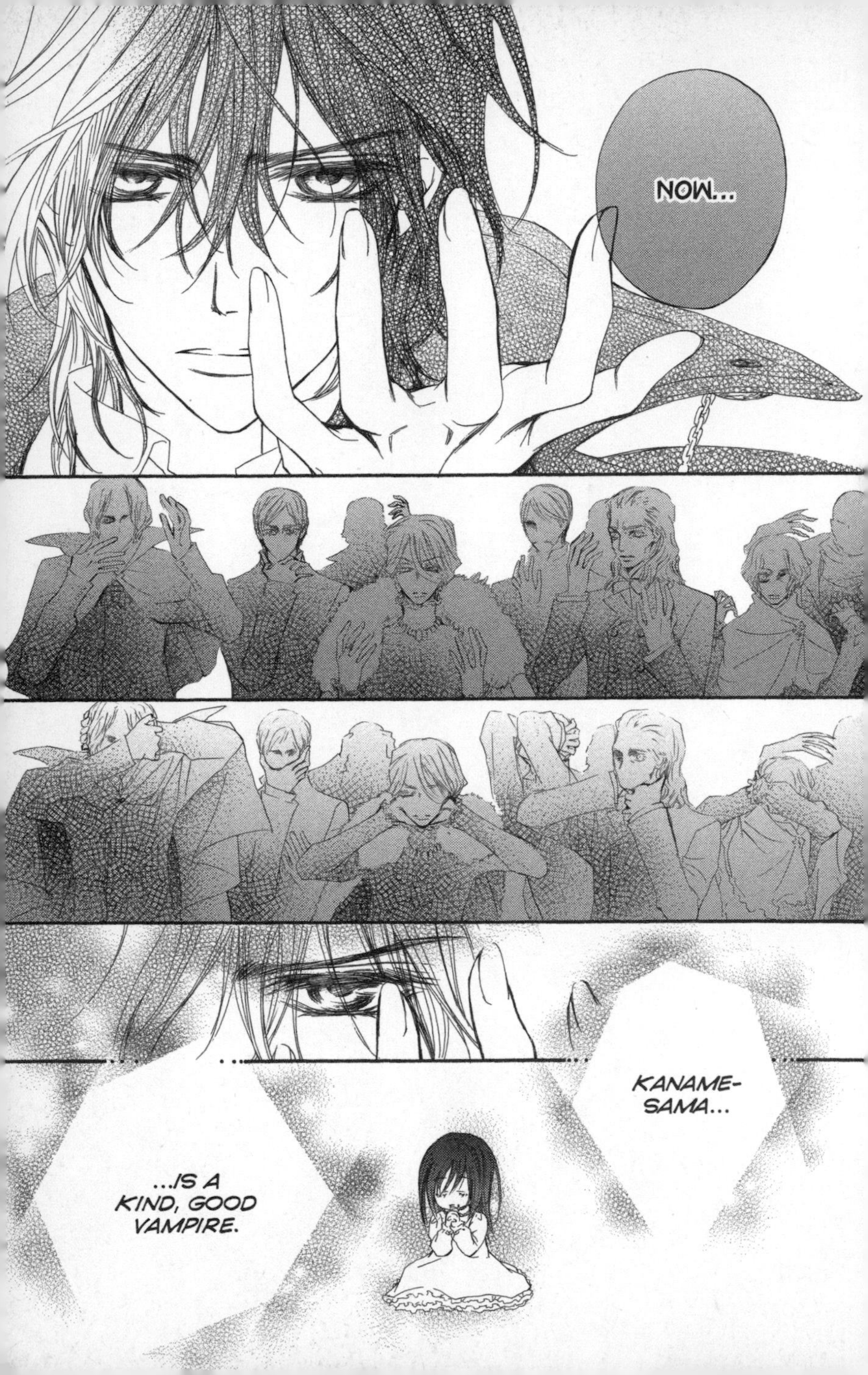
NOW...
KANAME-SAMA...
...IS A KIND, GOOD VAMPIRE.

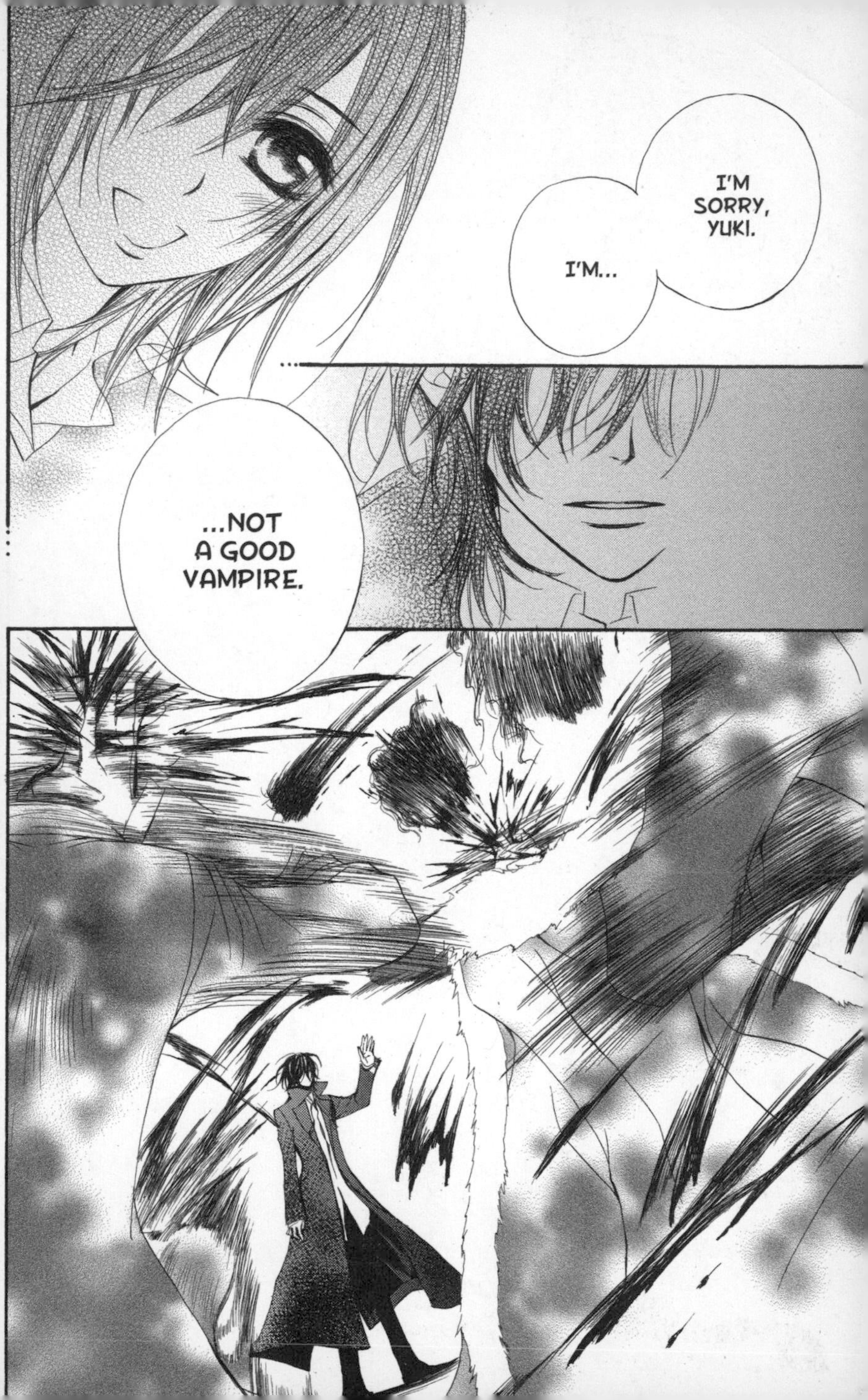
I'M SORRY, YUKI.
I'M...
...NOT A GOOD VAMPIRE.

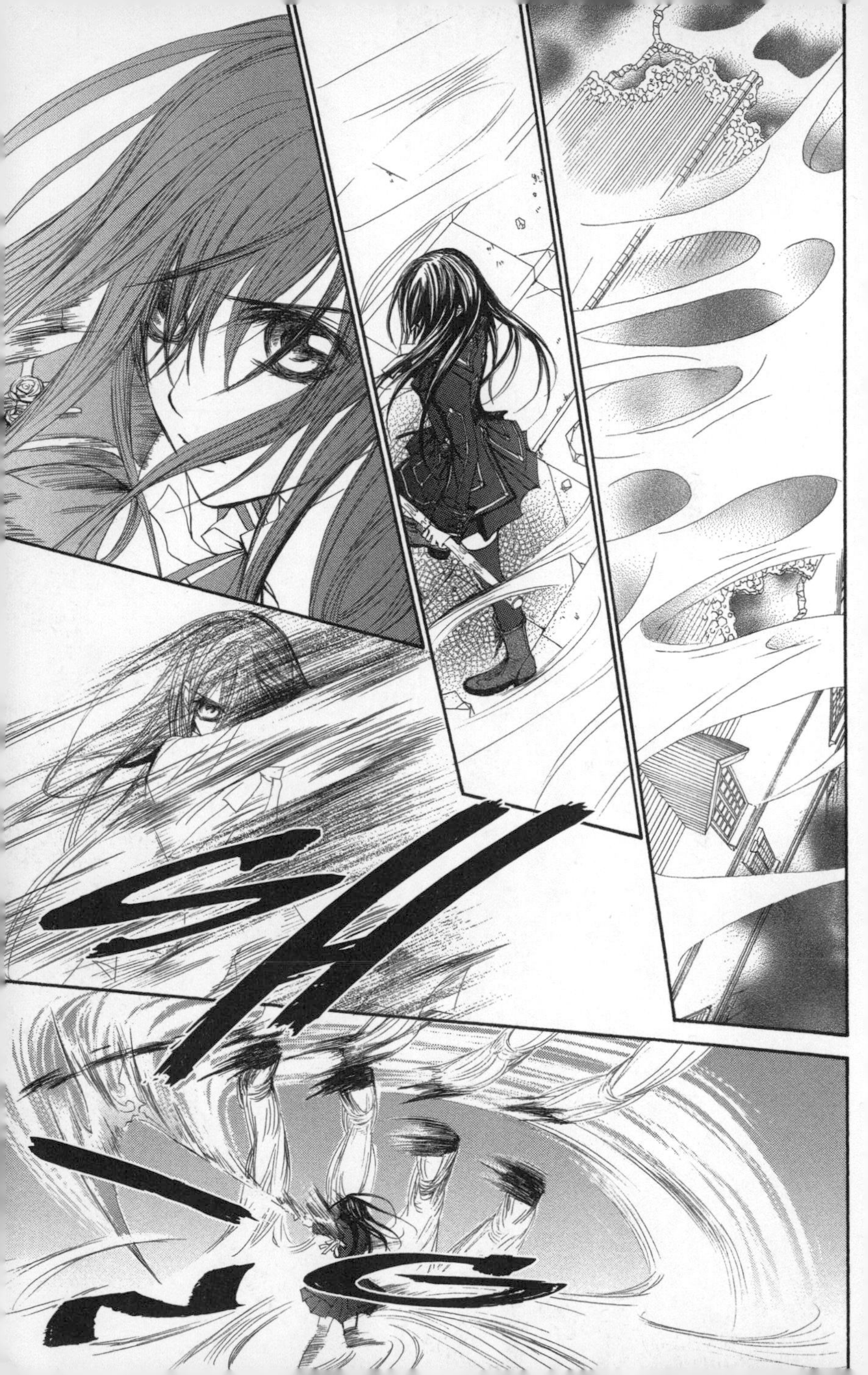

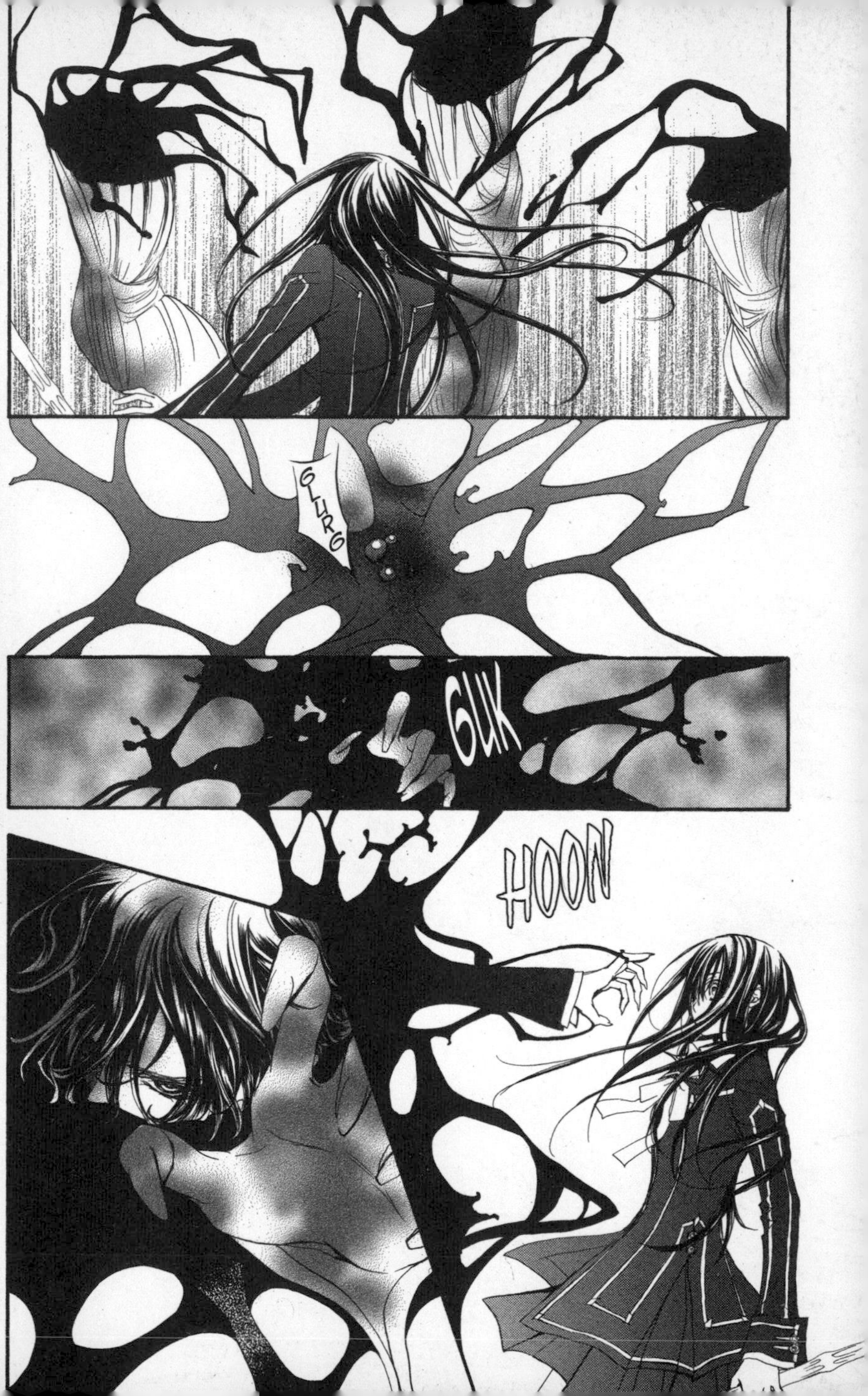
GLURG
GUK
HOON

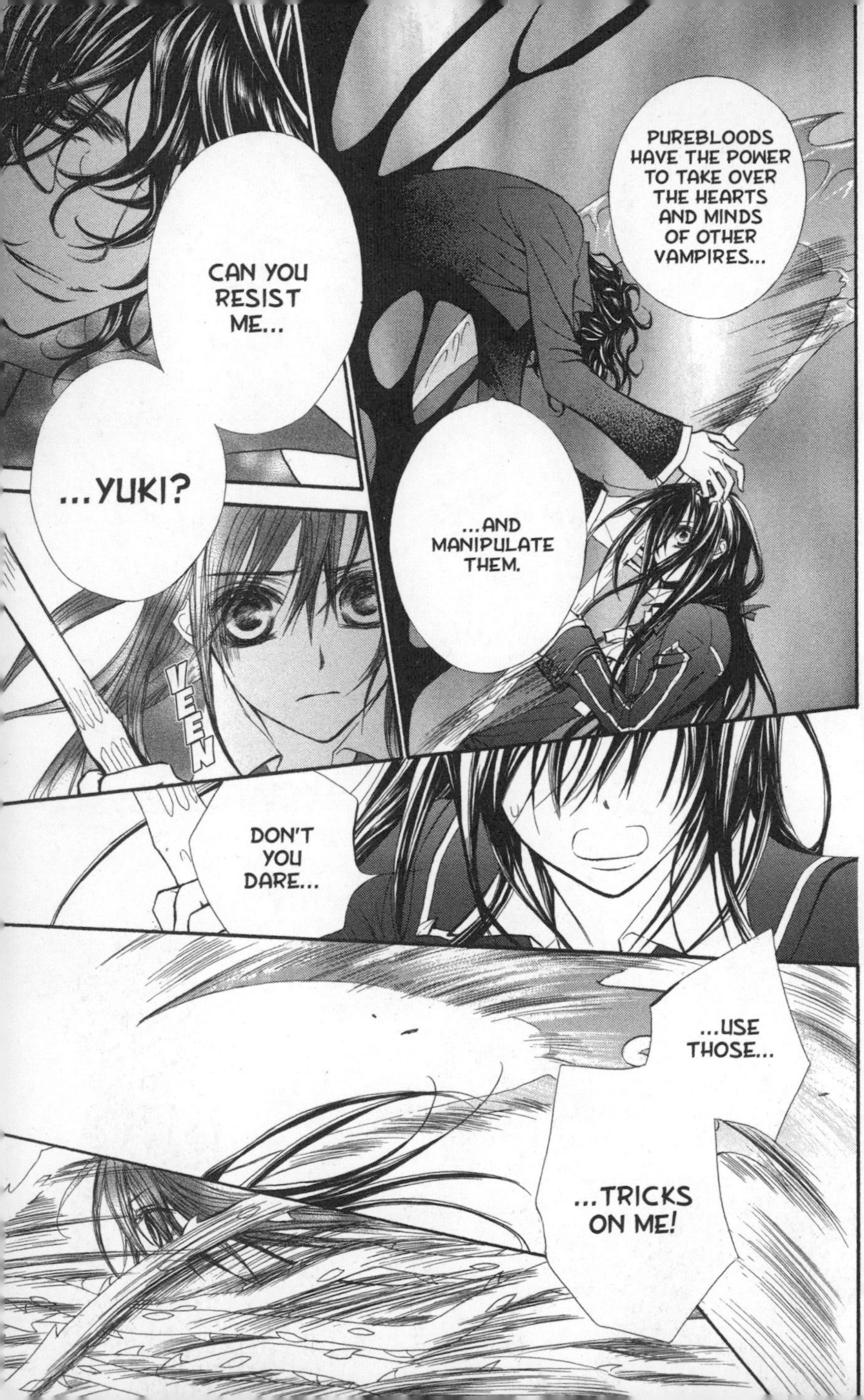
PUREBLOODS HAVE THE POWER TO TAKE OVER THE HEARTS AND MINDS OF OTHER VAMPIRES...
...AND MANIPULATE THEM.
CAN YOU RESIST ME...
...YUKI?
VEEN
DON'T YOU DARE...
...USE THOSE...
...TRICKS ON ME!

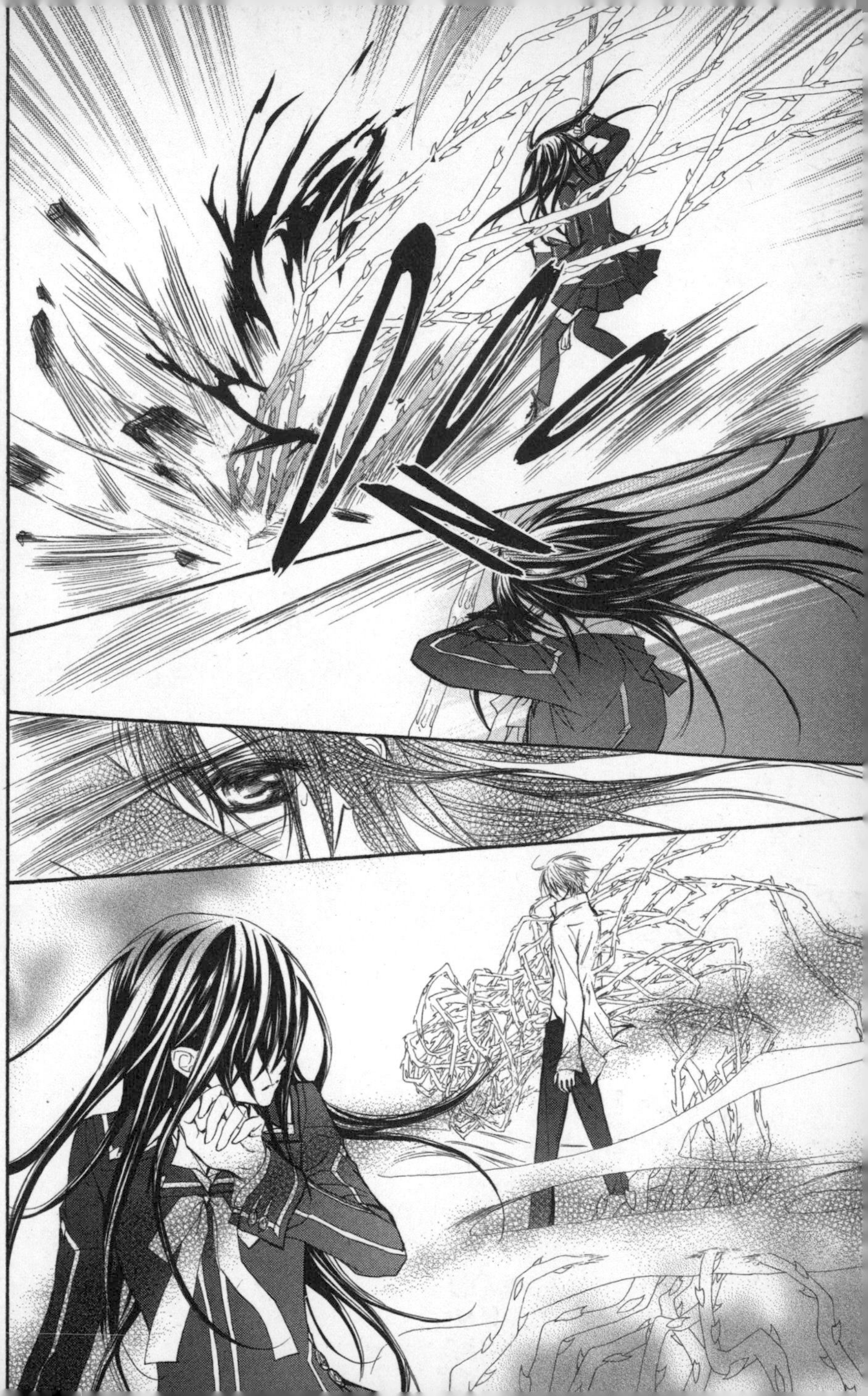

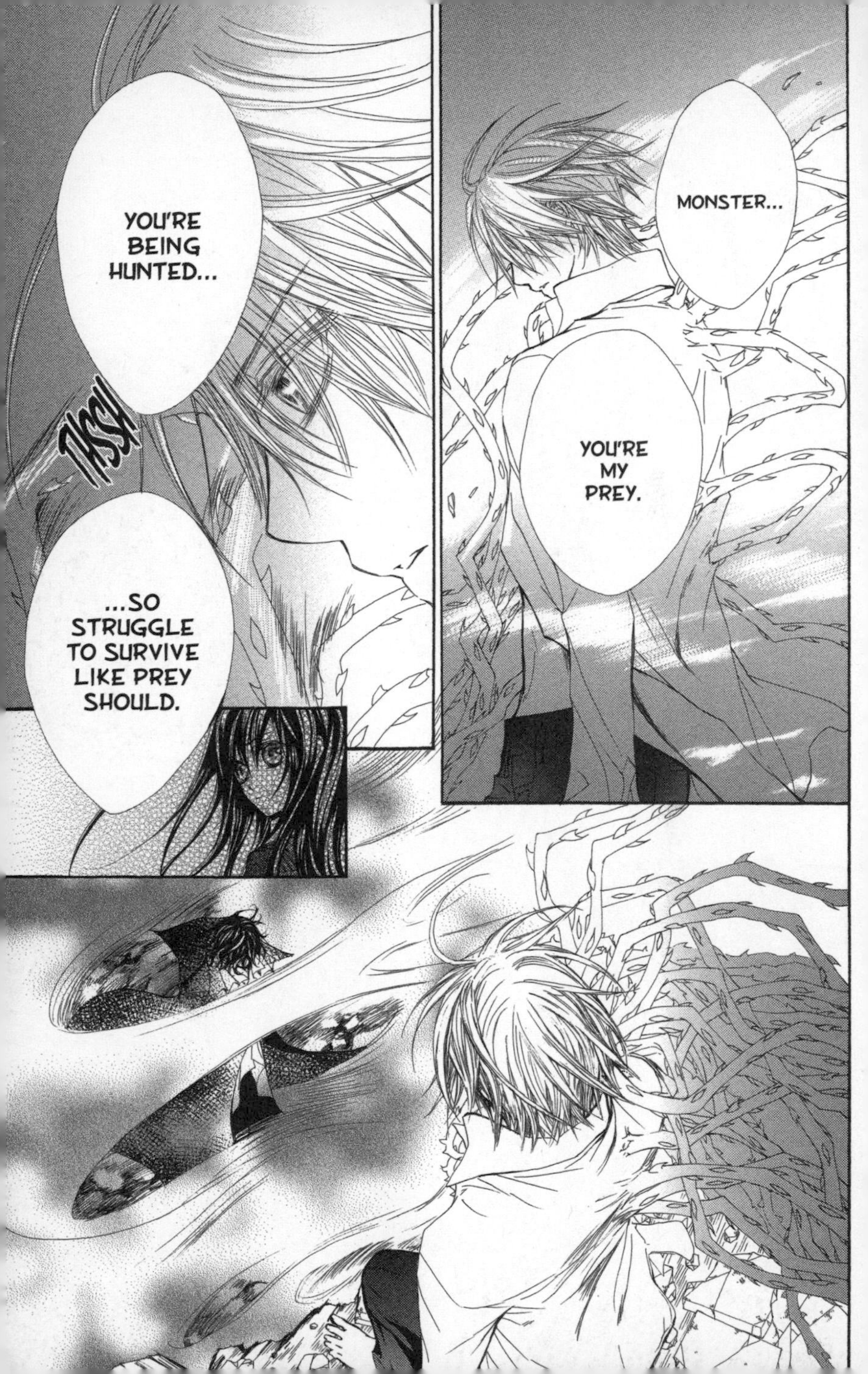
MONSTER...
YOU'RE MY PREY.
YOU'RE BEING HUNTED...
THSH
...SO STRUGGLE TO SURVIVE LIKE PREY SHOULD.

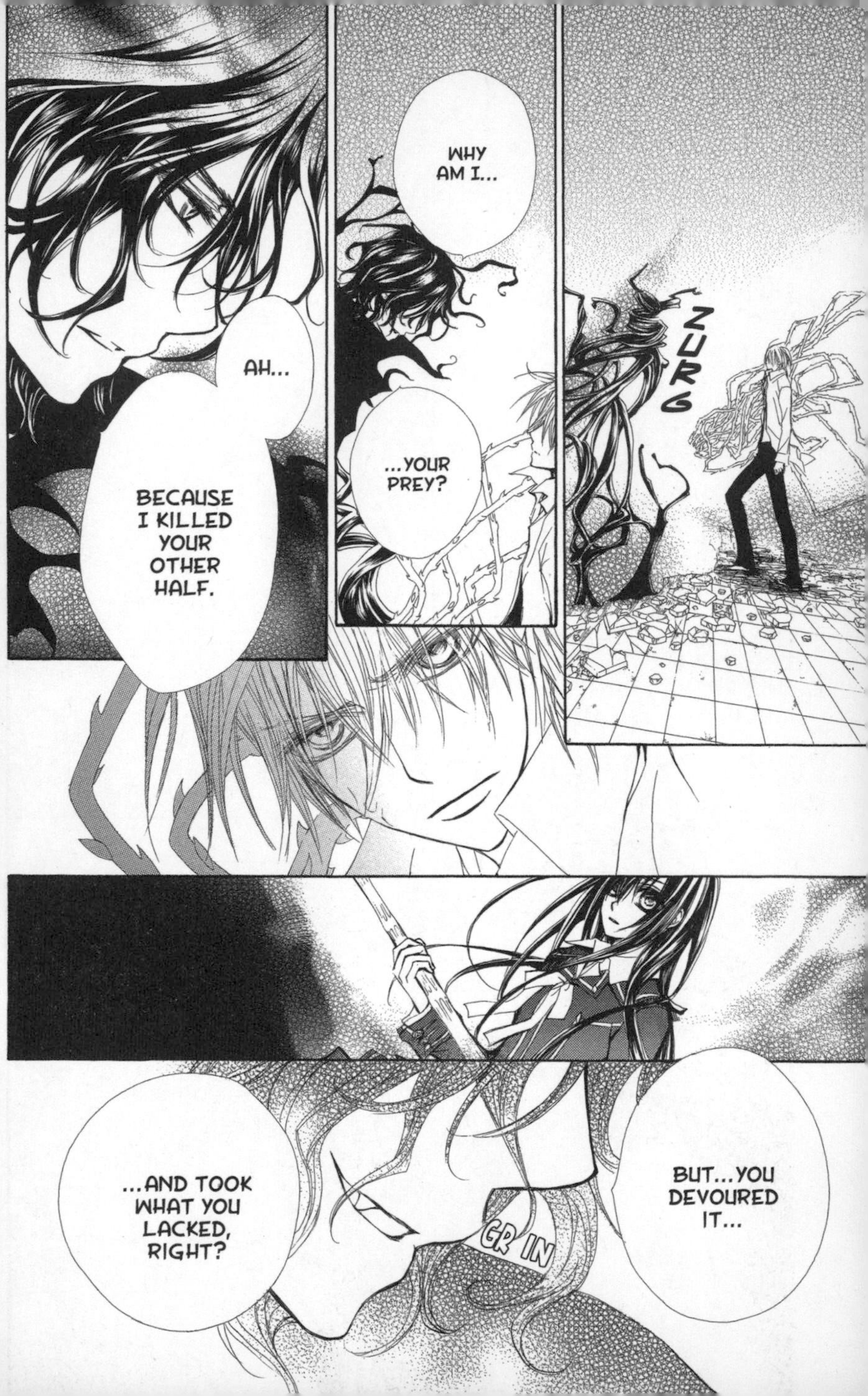
ZURG
WHY AM I...
...YOUR PREY?
AH...
BECAUSE I KILLED YOUR OTHER HALF.
BUT...YOU DEVOURED IT...
GR IN
...AND TOOK WHAT YOU LACKED, RIGHT?

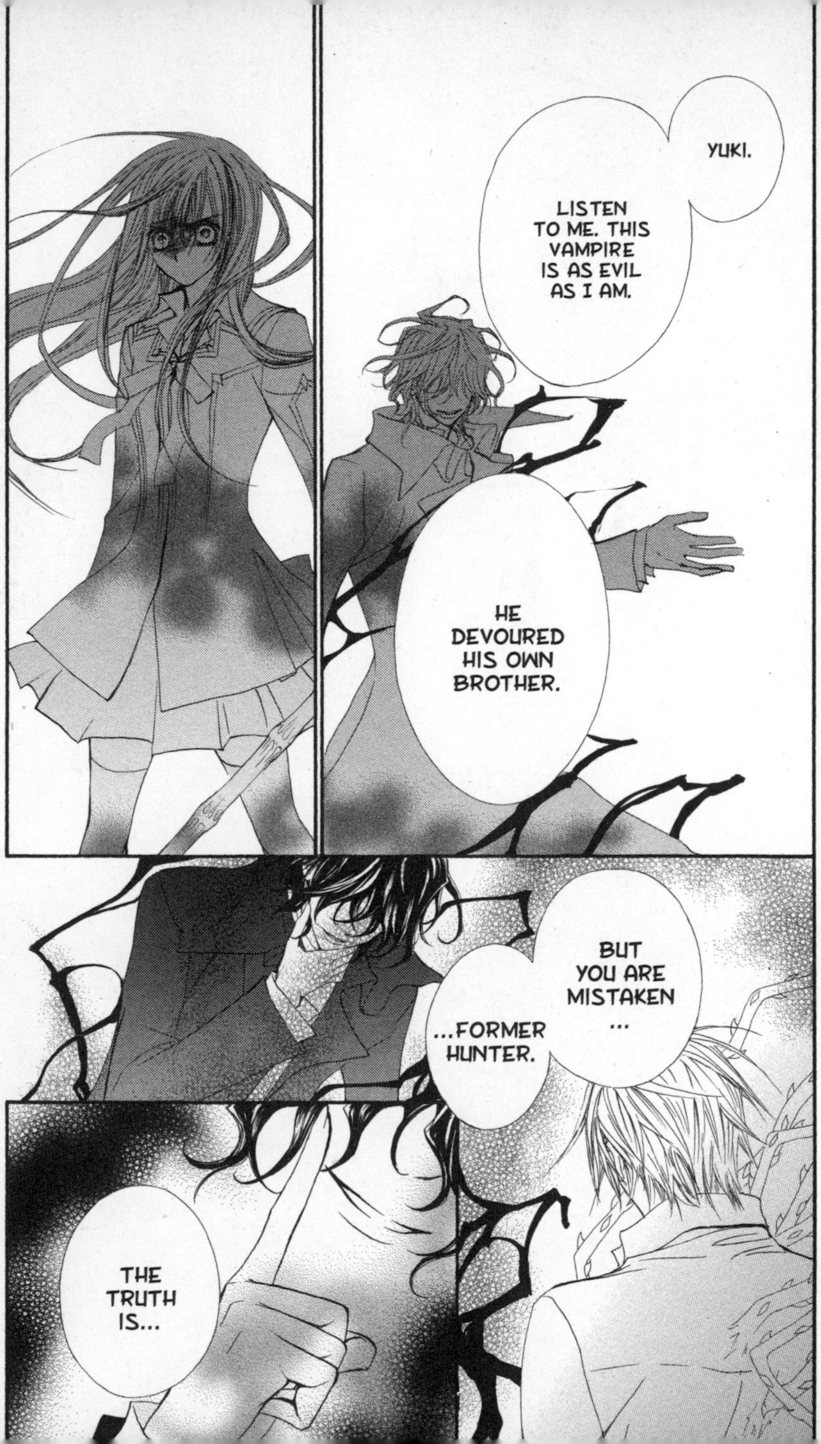
YUKI.
LISTEN TO ME. THIS VAMPIRE IS AS EVIL AS I AM.
HE DEVOURED HIS OWN BROTHER.
BUT YOU ARE MISTAKEN ...
...FORMER HUNTER.
THE TRUTH IS...

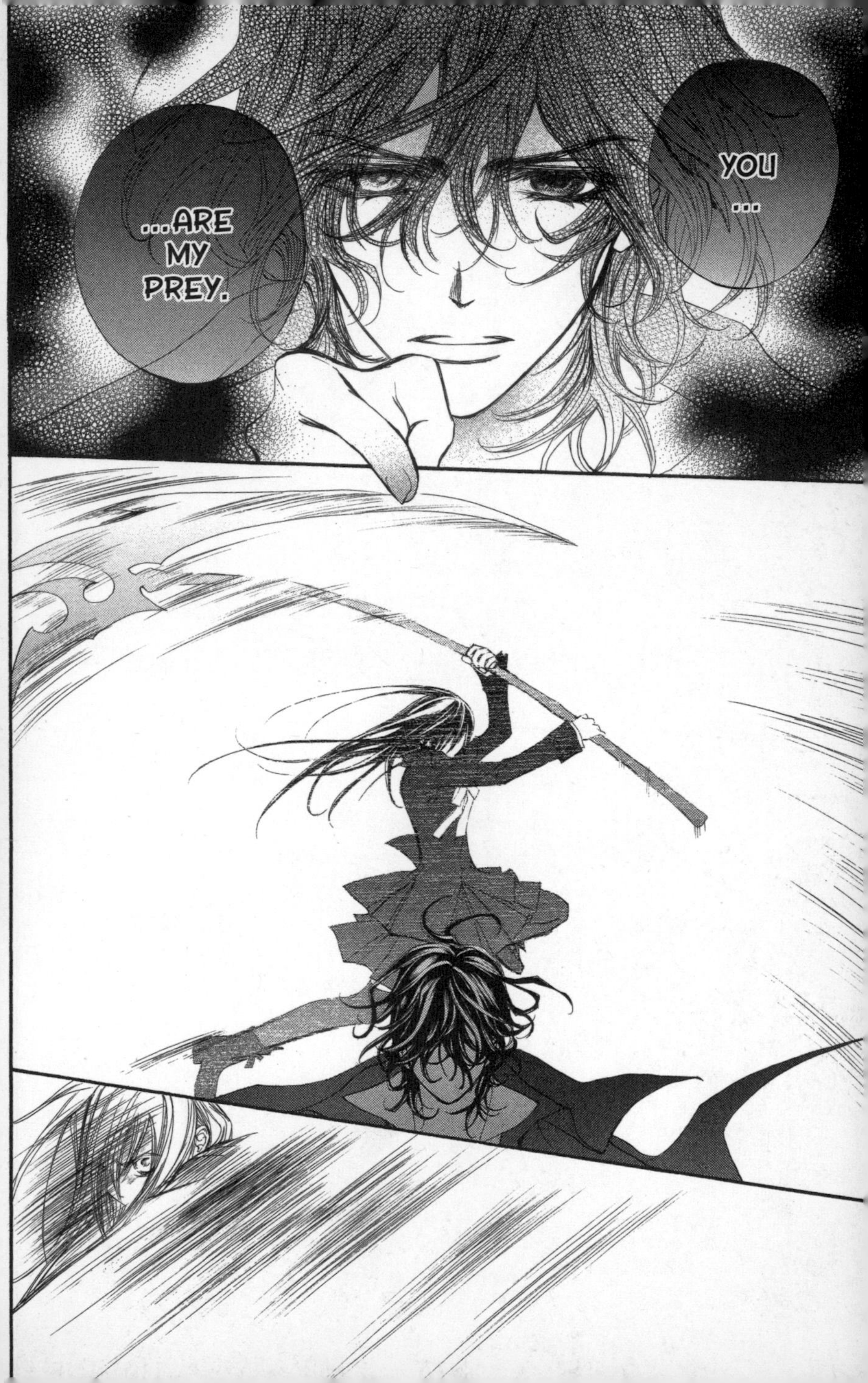
YOU ...
...ARE MY PREY.

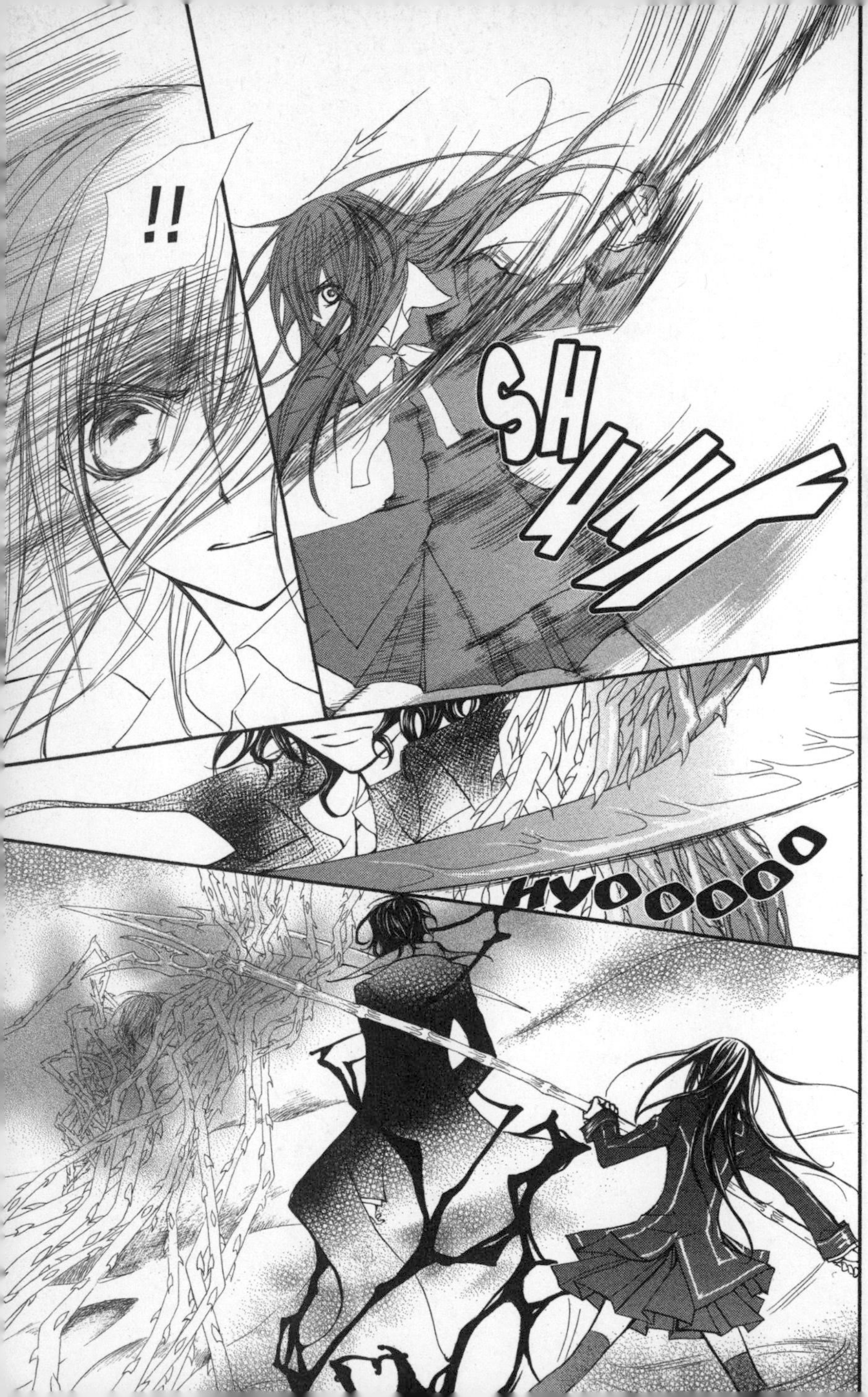
!!
HYOOOOOO

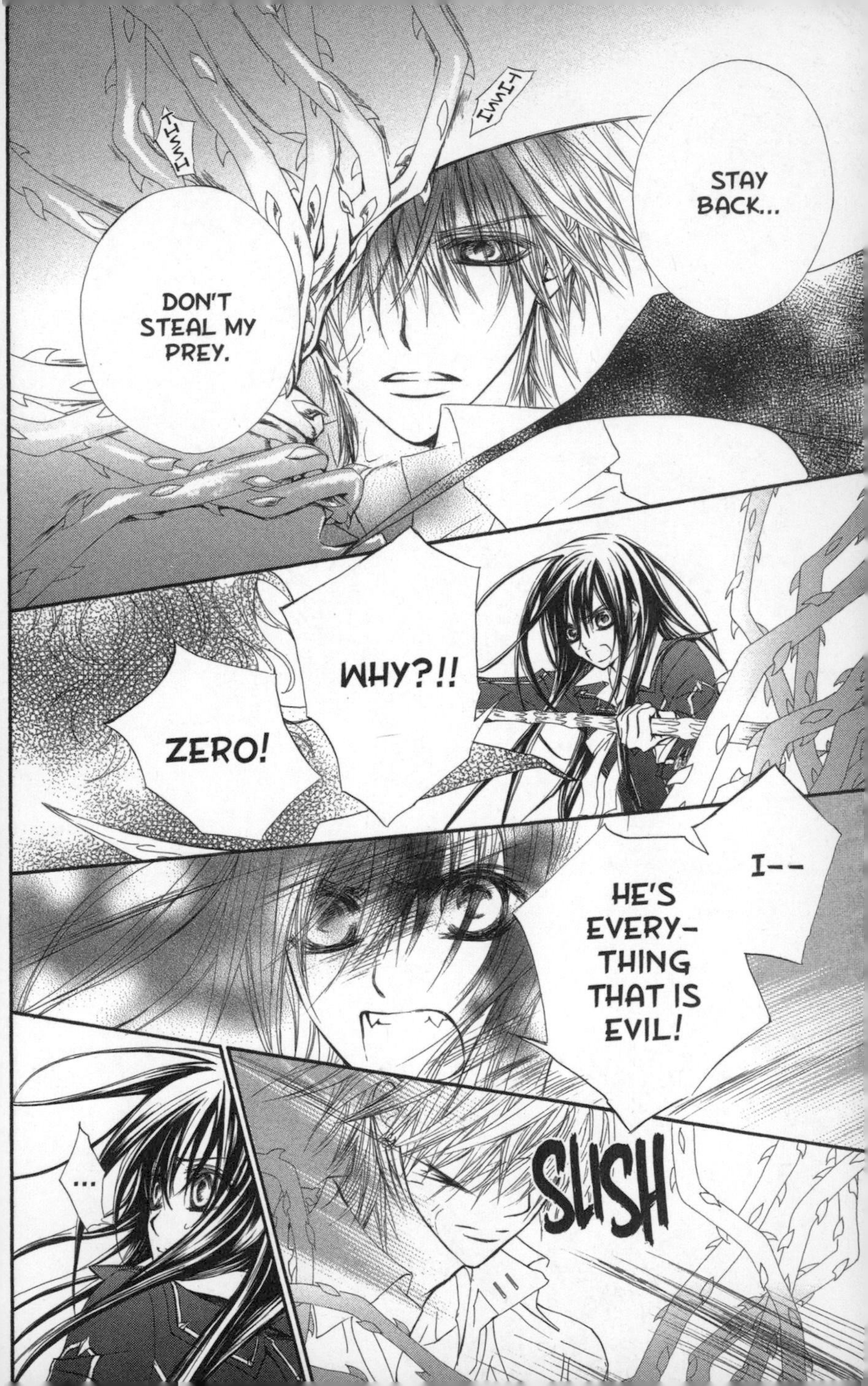
TWIST
TWIST
STAY BACK...
DON'T STEAL MY PREY.
WHY?!!
ZERO!
I--
HE'S EVERYTHING THAT IS EVIL!
SLISH
...

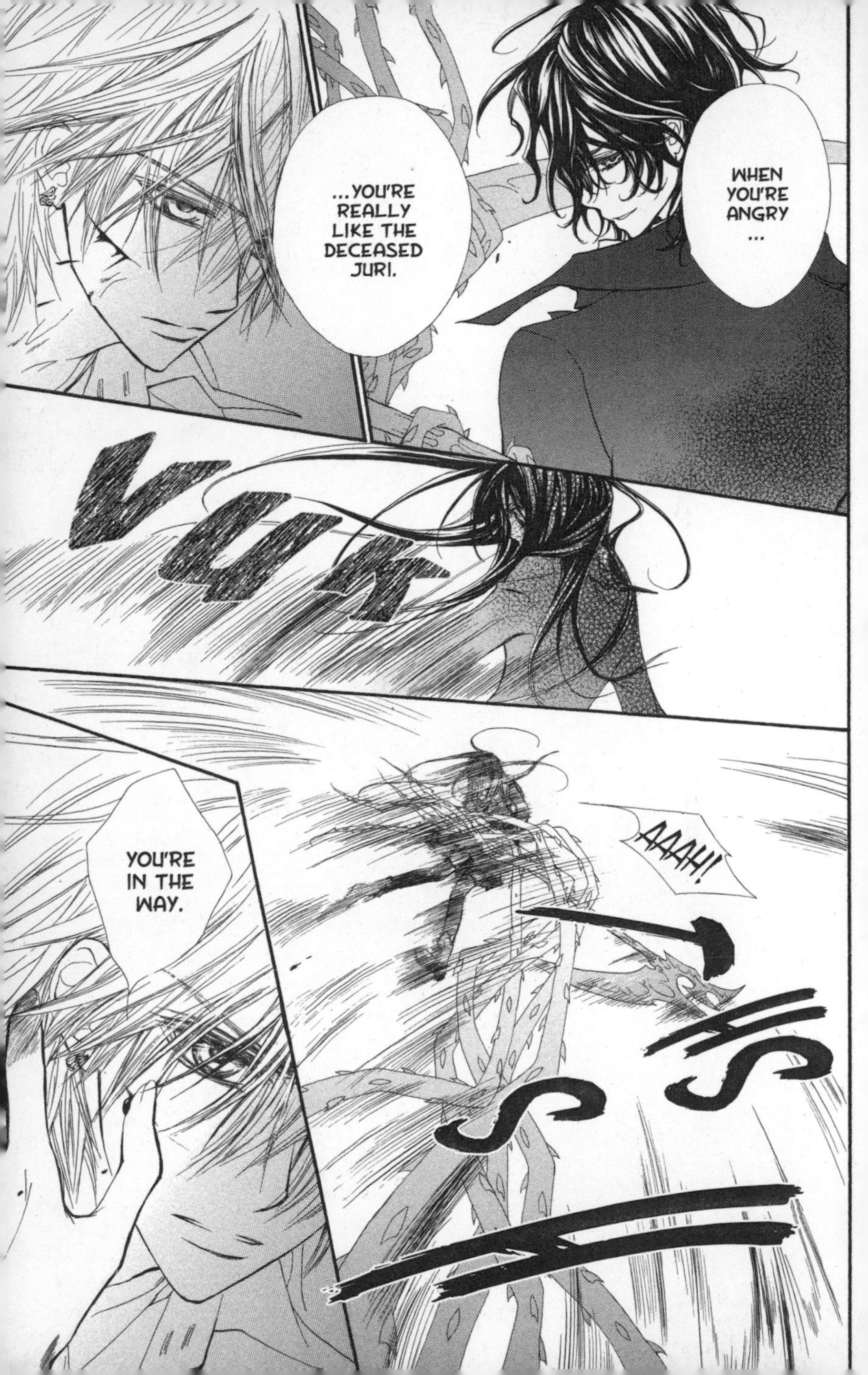
WHEN YOU'RE ANGRY ...
...YOU'RE REALLY LIKE THE DECEASED JURI.
VUM
AAAH!
YOU'RE IN THE WAY.

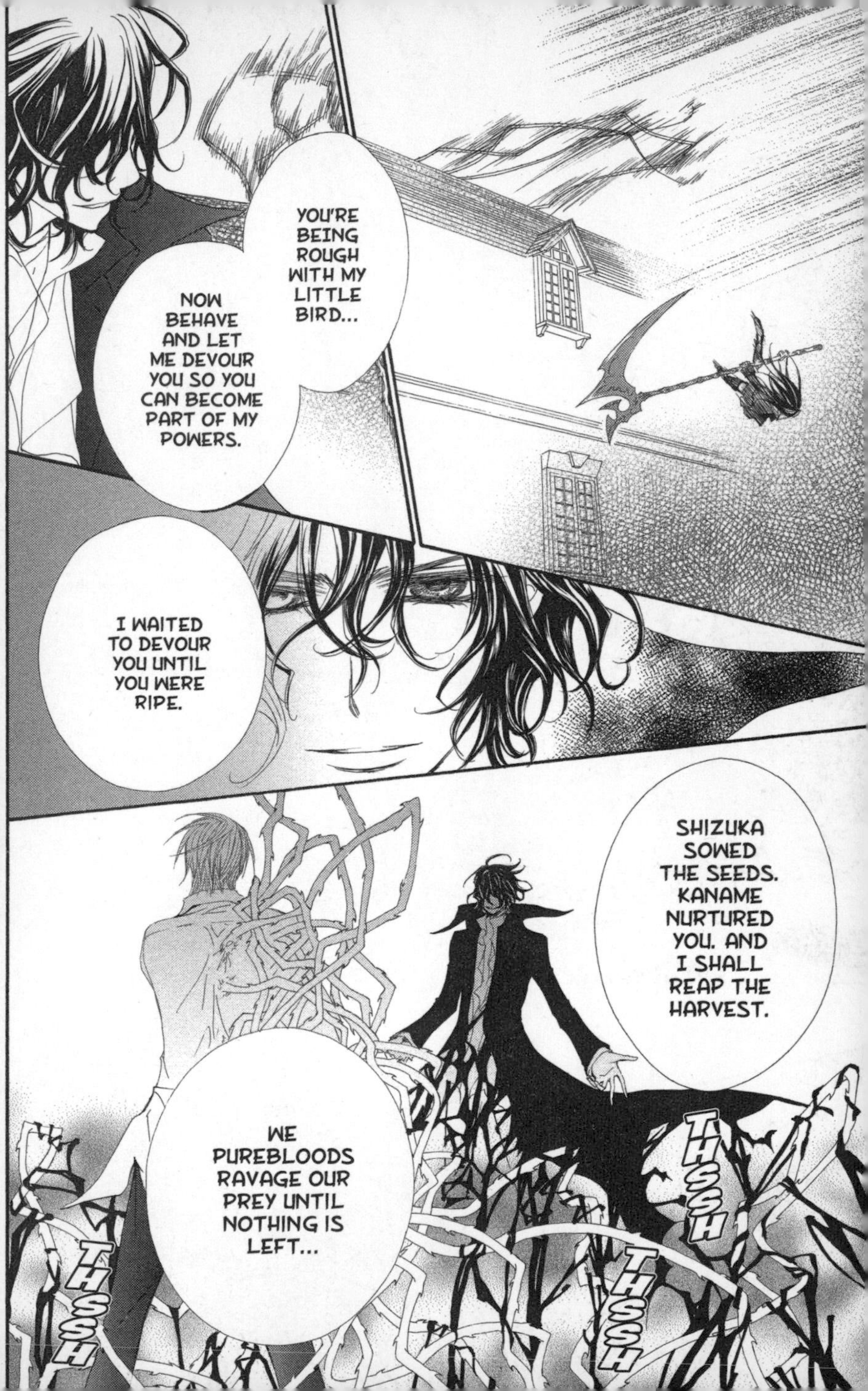
YOU'RE BEING ROUGH WITH MY LITTLE BIRD...
NOW BEHAVE AND LET ME DEVOUR YOU SO YOU CAN BECOME PART OF MY POWERS.
I WAITED TO DEVOUR YOU UNTIL YOU WERE RIPE.
SHIZUKA SOWED THE SEEDS. KANAME NURTURED YOU. AND I SHALL REAP THE HARVEST.
THSSH
WE PUREBLOODS RAVAGE OUR PREY UNTIL NOTHING IS LEFT...
THSSH
THSSH

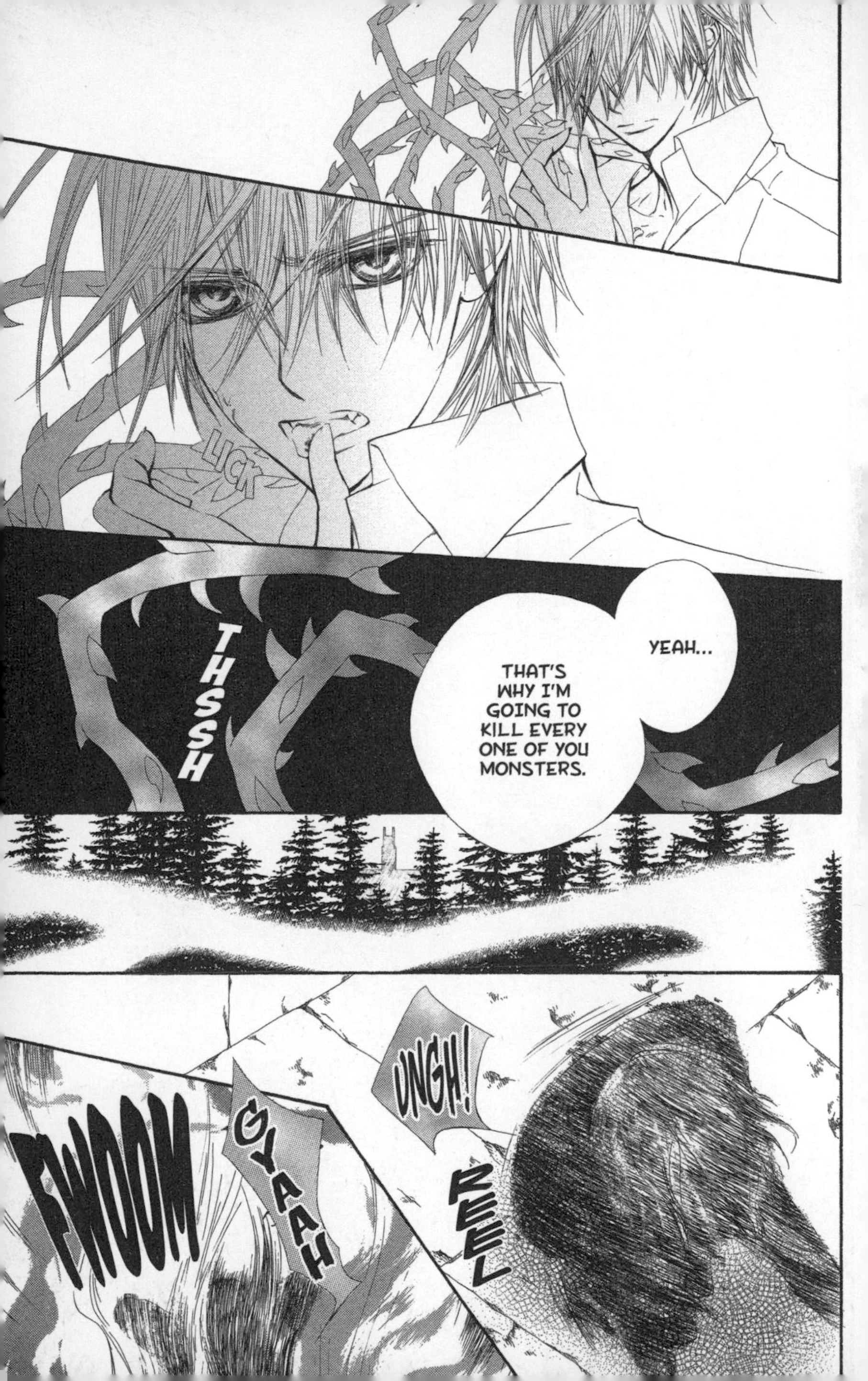
LICK
YEAH...
THAT'S WHY I'M GOING TO KILL EVERY ONE OF YOU MONSTERS.
THSSH
UNGH!
REEL
GYAAH
FWOOM

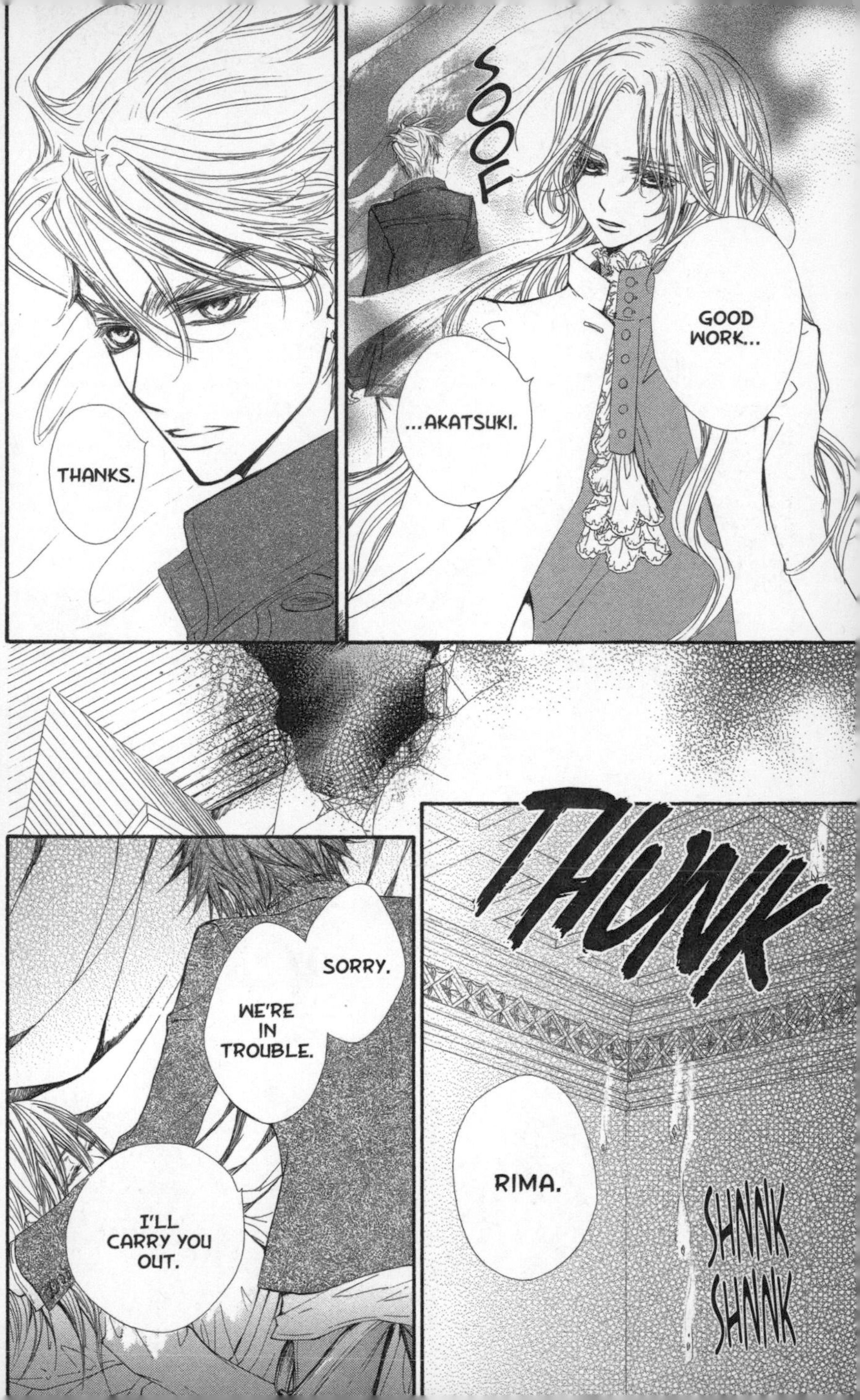
FOOOS
GOOD WORK...
...AKATSUKI.
THANKS.
THUNK
RIMA.
SHNNK SHNNK
SORRY.
WE'RE IN TROUBLE.
I'LL CARRY YOU OUT.

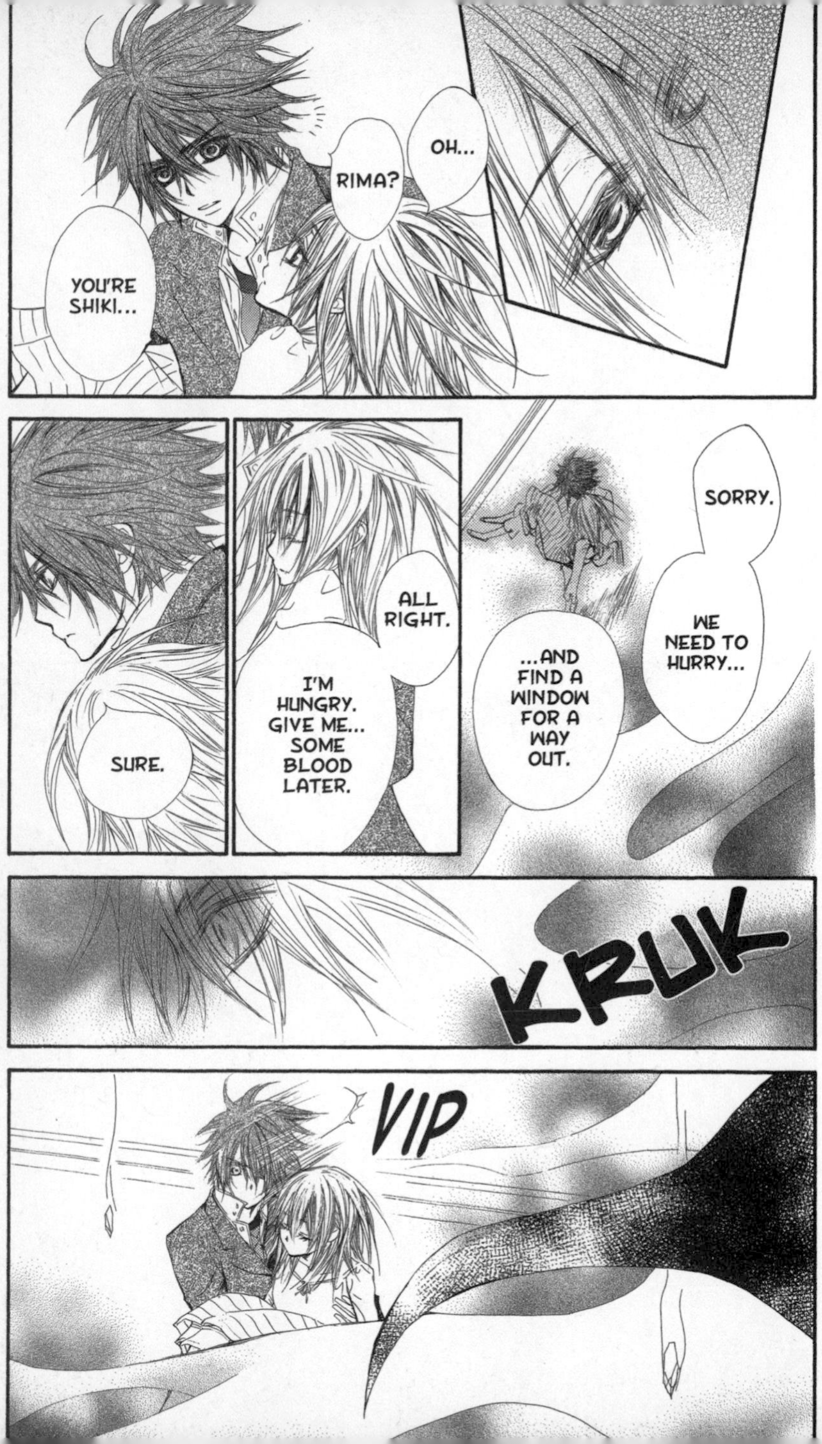
OH...
RIMA?
YOU'RE SHIKI...
SORRY.
WE NEED TO HURRY...
...AND FIND A WINDOW FOR A WAY OUT.
ALL RIGHT.
I'M HUNGRY. GIVE ME... SOME BLOOD LATER.
SURE.
KRUK
VIP

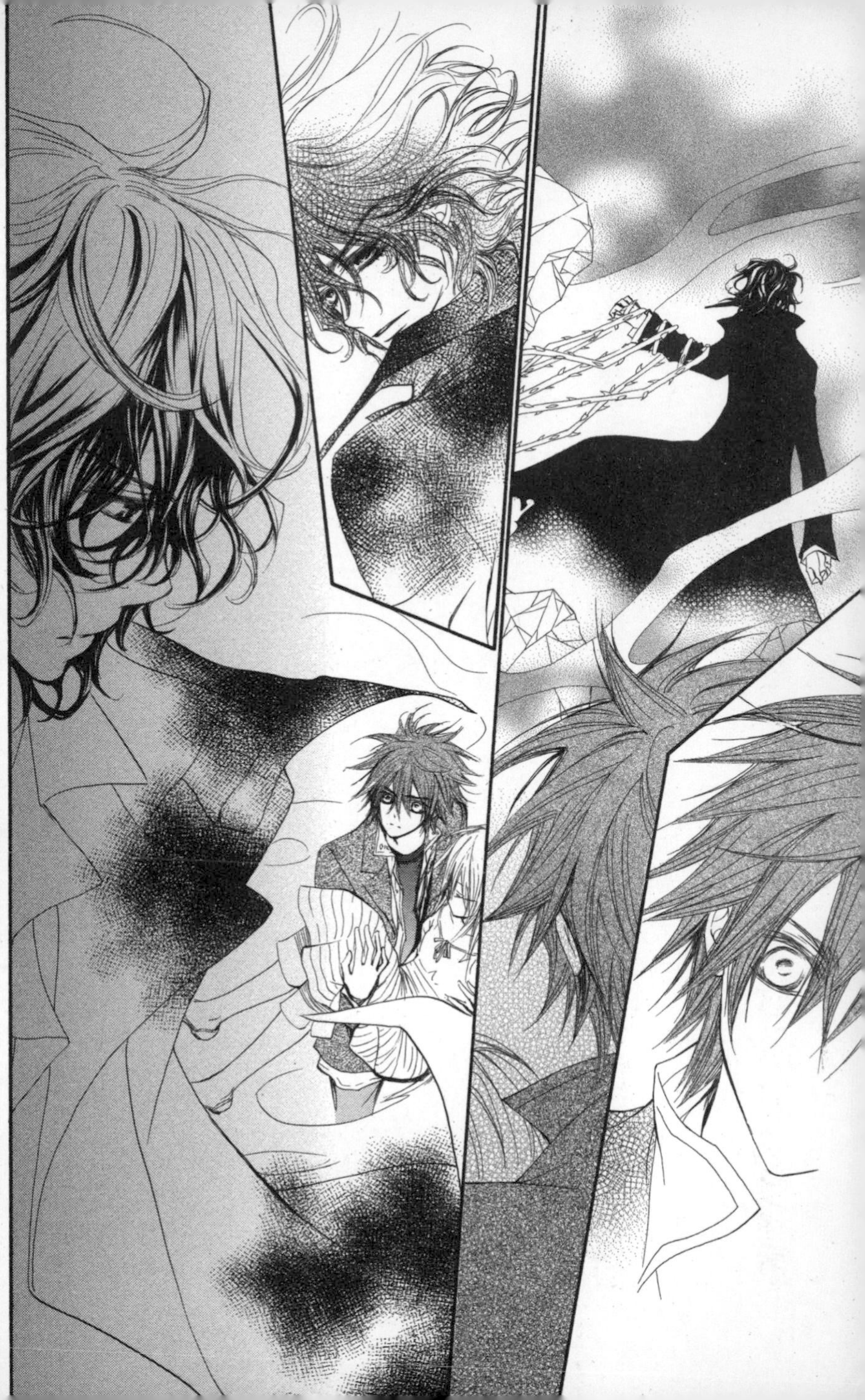

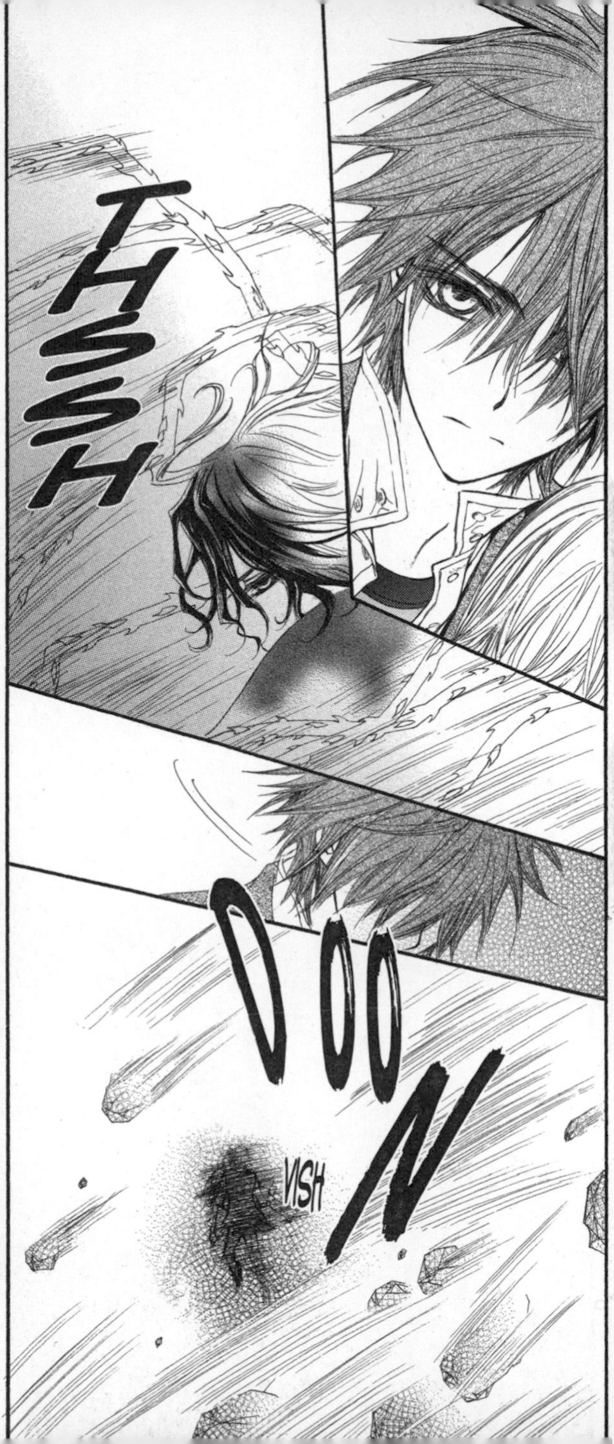
THSH
DOON
VISH

V

The writing for the sidebar IV was too small. I'm sorry. Well, some people might have noticed, but Hino is a stationery otaku. When something new comes out, I can't help trying it. Yes... I want to write a report on a blog or something every time a new product is released. For about a year now, I've been staying at home most of the time, so I don't do as many otaku things as before...

No, no. Now it's manga more than stationery! I made various mistakes, recovered, and learned from *Vampire Knight*. The next volume number will be in double-digits! I'd like to use what I've learned to draw the continuation, so please look forward to it...!!

Matsuri Hino
樋野まつり

O. Mio-sama.
K. Midori-sama. (Congratulations on your debut in *Hana to Yume Stars*!!!)
I. Asami-sama.
And H-sama, Y-sama. And to my mother, thank you!

I'll do my best so I can answer your letters...!!!

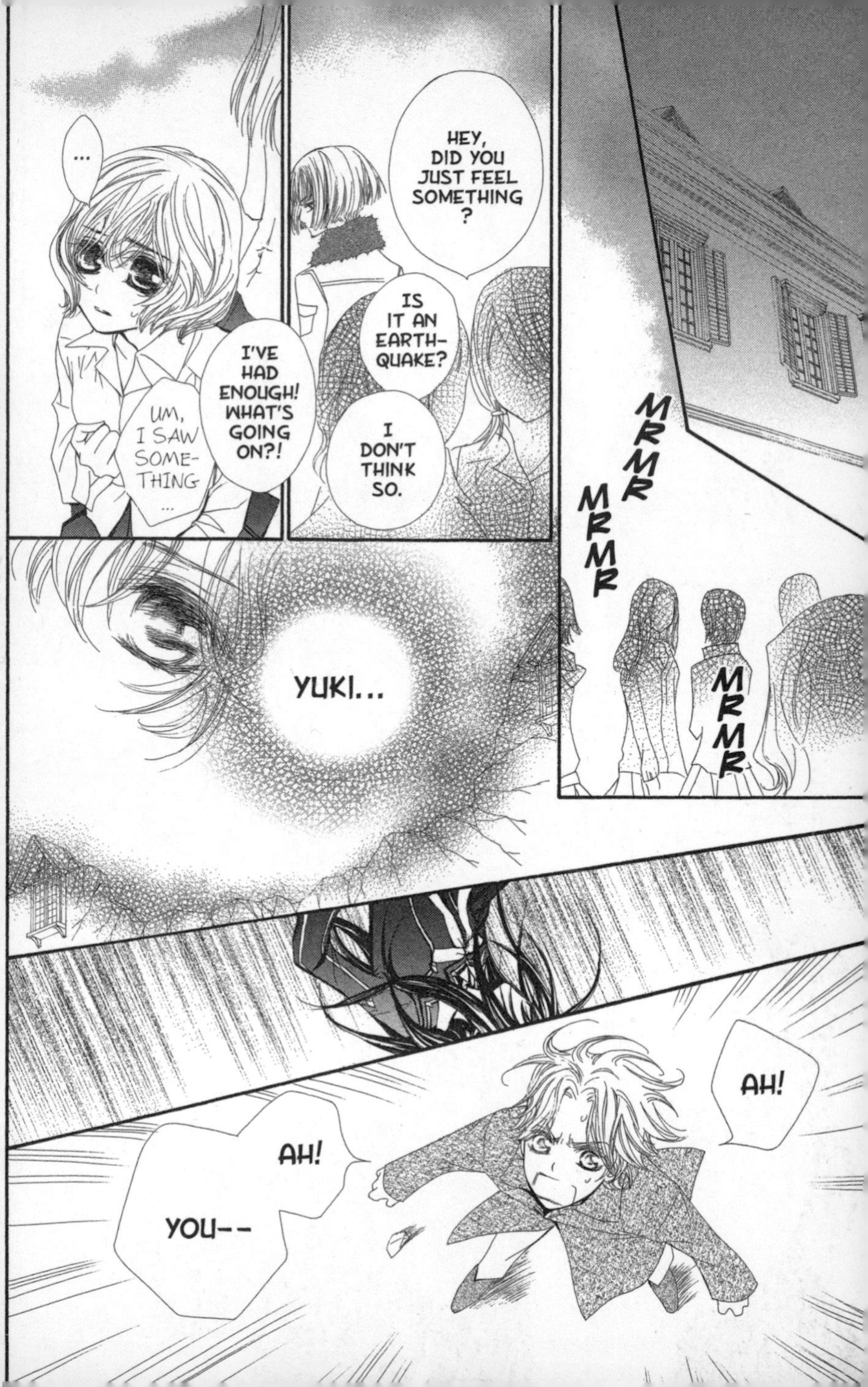
MRMR
MRMR
MRMR
HEY, DID YOU JUST FEEL SOMETHING?
IS IT AN EARTHQUAKE?
I DON'T THINK SO.
...
I'VE HAD ENOUGH! WHAT'S GOING ON?!
UM, I SAW SOMETHING...
YUKI...
AH!
AH!
YOU--

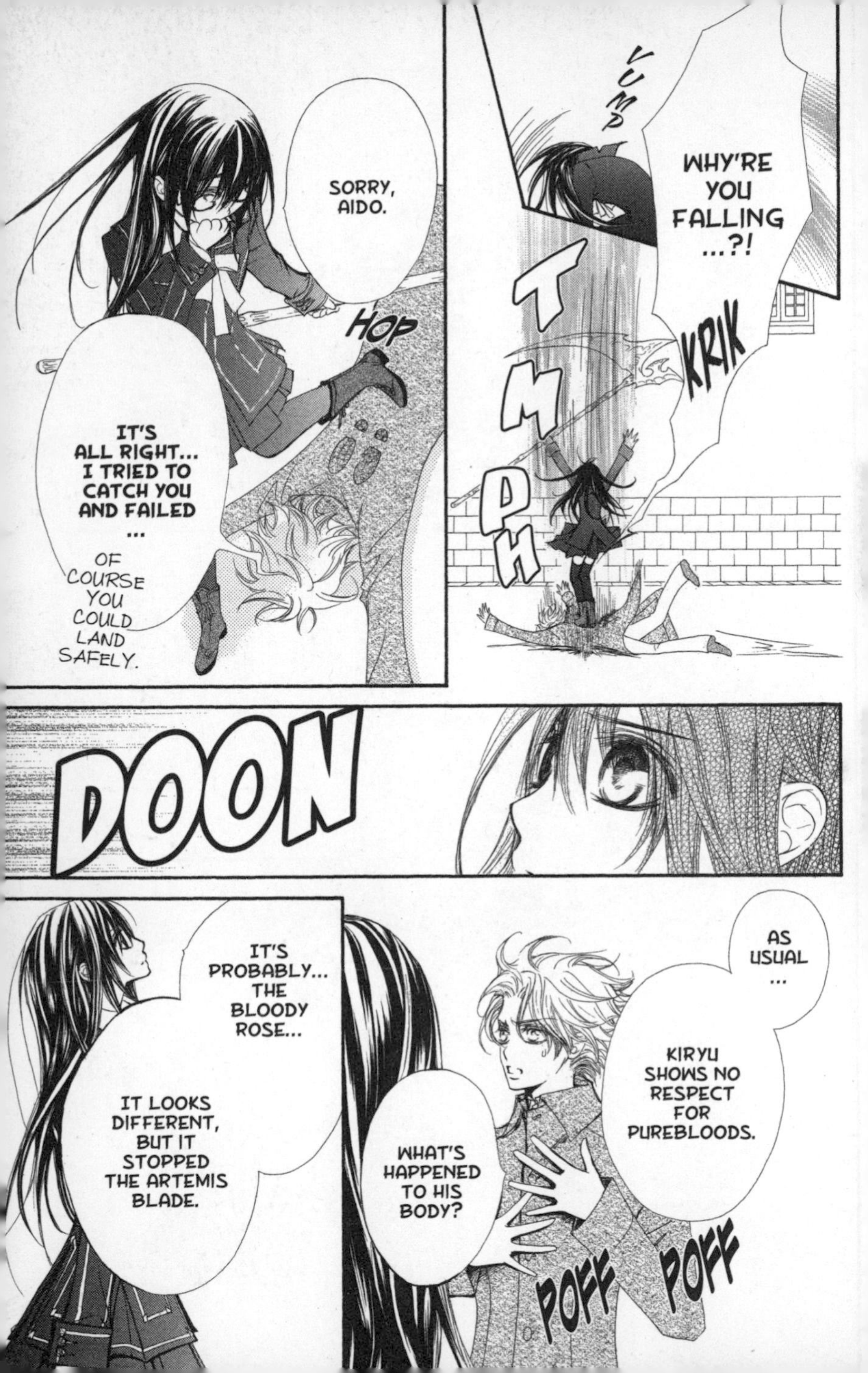
VUMP
WHY'RE YOU FALLING ...?!
KRIK
TMPH
SORRY, AIDO.
HOP
IT'S ALL RIGHT... I TRIED TO CATCH YOU AND FAILED ...
OF COURSE YOU COULD LAND SAFELY.
DOON
AS USUAL ...
KIRYU SHOWS NO RESPECT FOR PUREBLOODS.
POFF
POFF
WHAT'S HAPPENED TO HIS BODY?
IT'S PROBABLY... THE BLOODY ROSE...
IT LOOKS DIFFERENT, BUT IT STOPPED THE ARTEMIS BLADE.

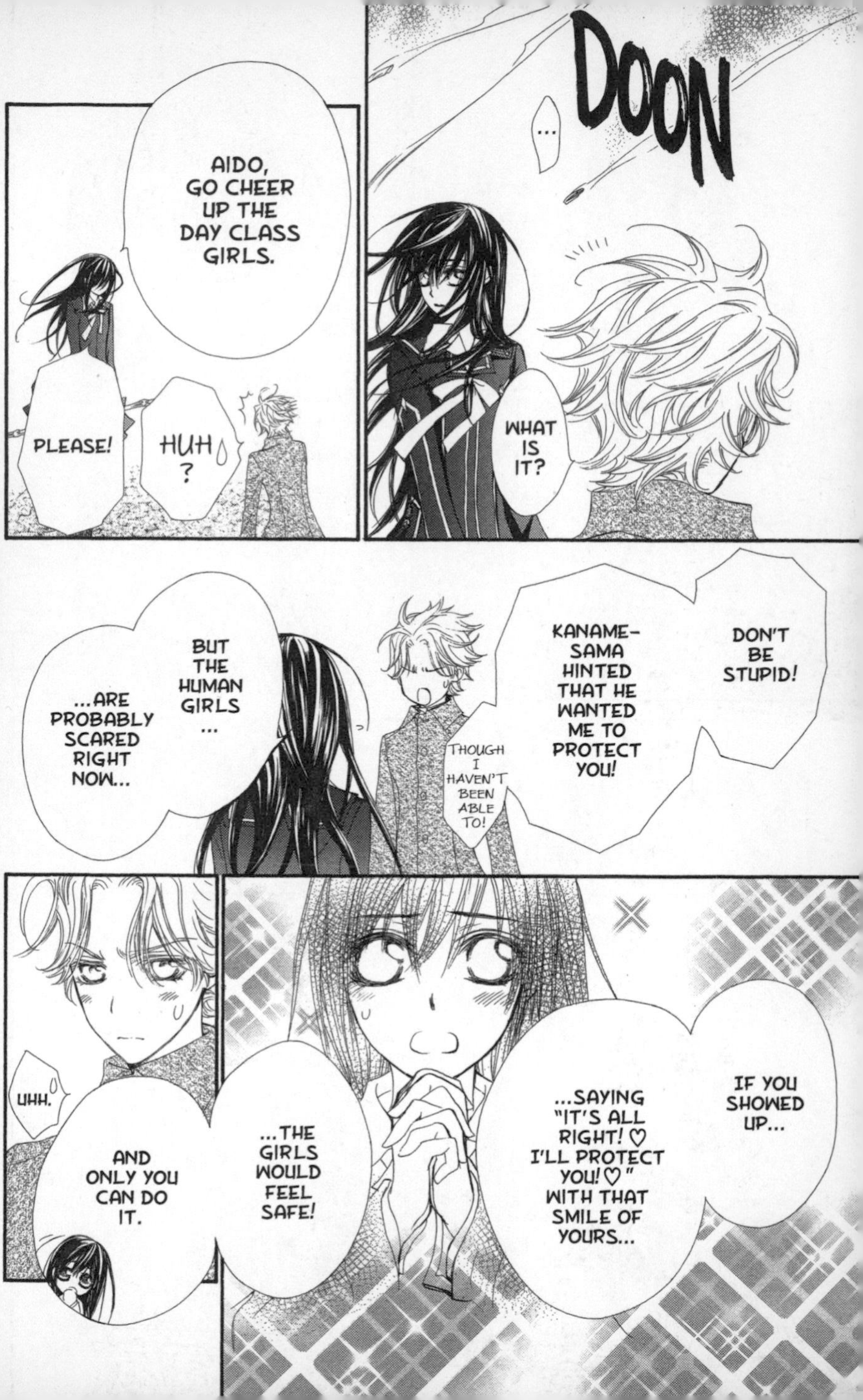
DOON
...
WHAT IS IT?
AIDO, GO CHEER UP THE DAY CLASS GIRLS.
HUH?
PLEASE!
DON'T BE STUPID!
KANAME-SAMA HINTED THAT HE WANTED ME TO PROTECT YOU!
THOUGH I HAVEN'T BEEN ABLE TO!
BUT THE HUMAN GIRLS...
...ARE PROBABLY SCARED RIGHT NOW...
IF YOU SHOWED UP...
...SAYING "IT'S ALL RIGHT! ♡ I'LL PROTECT YOU! ♡" WITH THAT SMILE OF YOURS...
...THE GIRLS WOULD FEEL SAFE!
UHH.
AND ONLY YOU CAN DO IT.

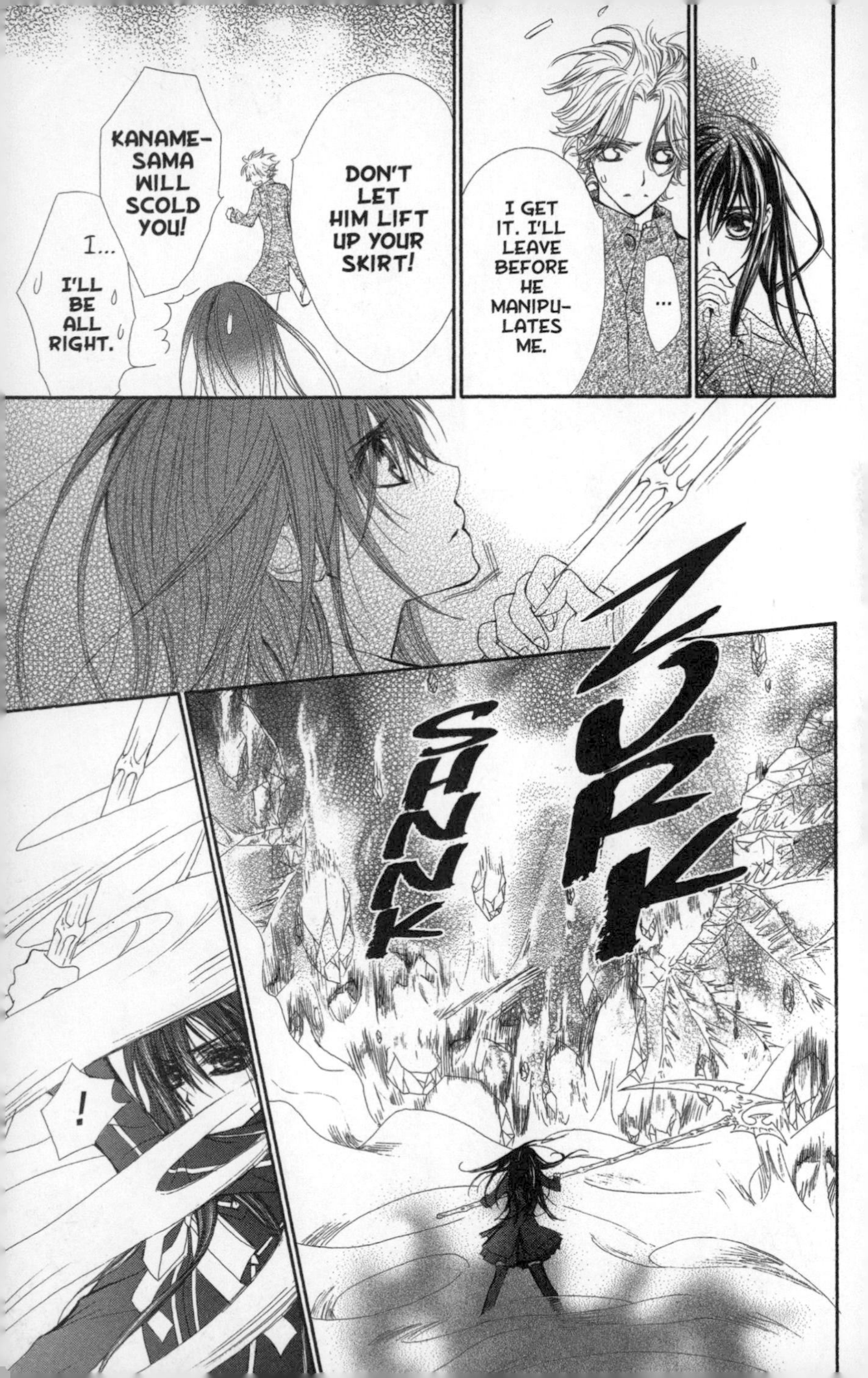
I GET IT. I'LL LEAVE BEFORE HE MANIPULATES ME.
...
DON'T LET HIM LIFT UP YOUR SKIRT!
KANAME-SAMA WILL SCOLD YOU!
I...
I'LL BE ALL RIGHT.
ZRK
SHNNK
!

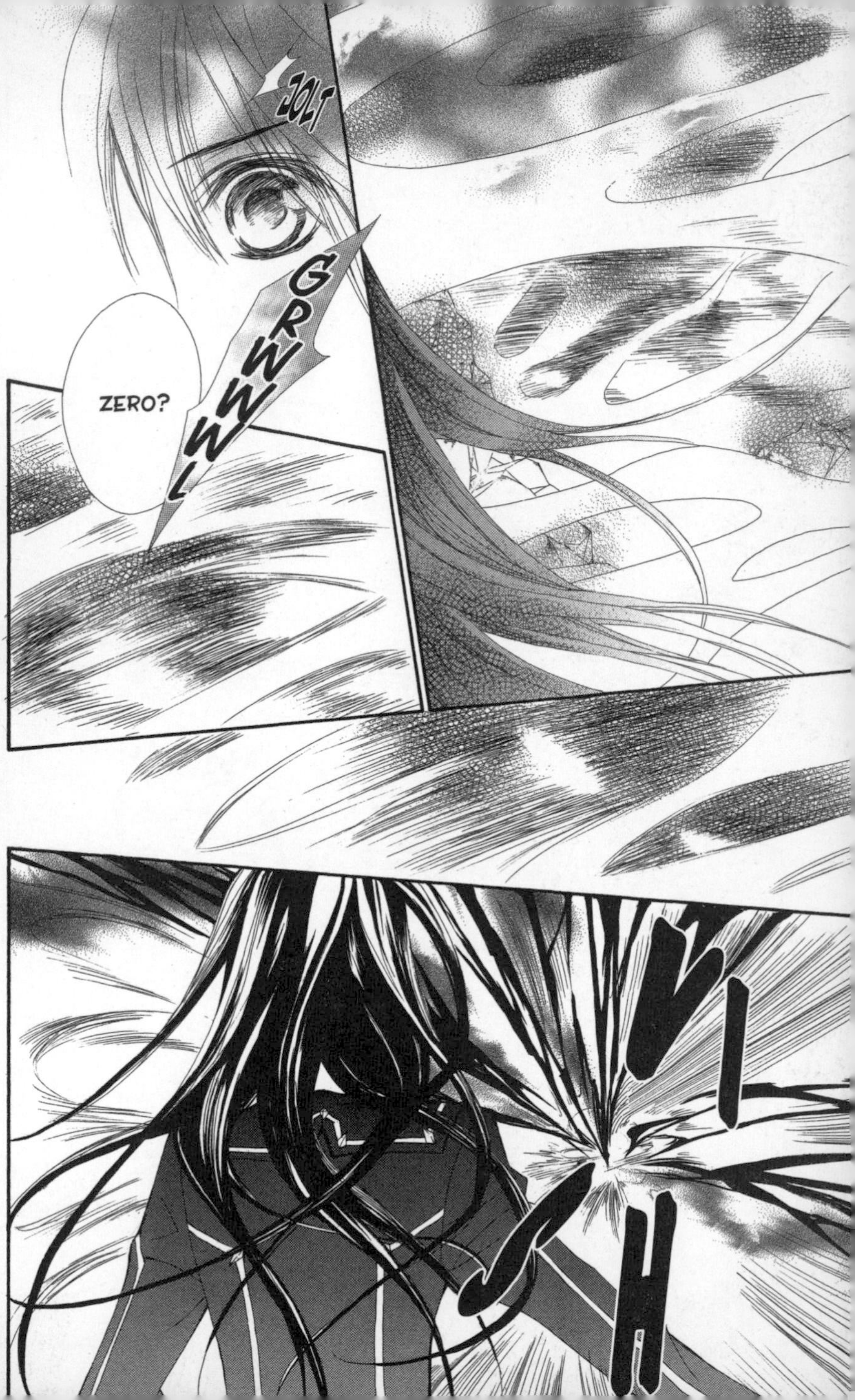
JOLT
ZERO?
GRWWL

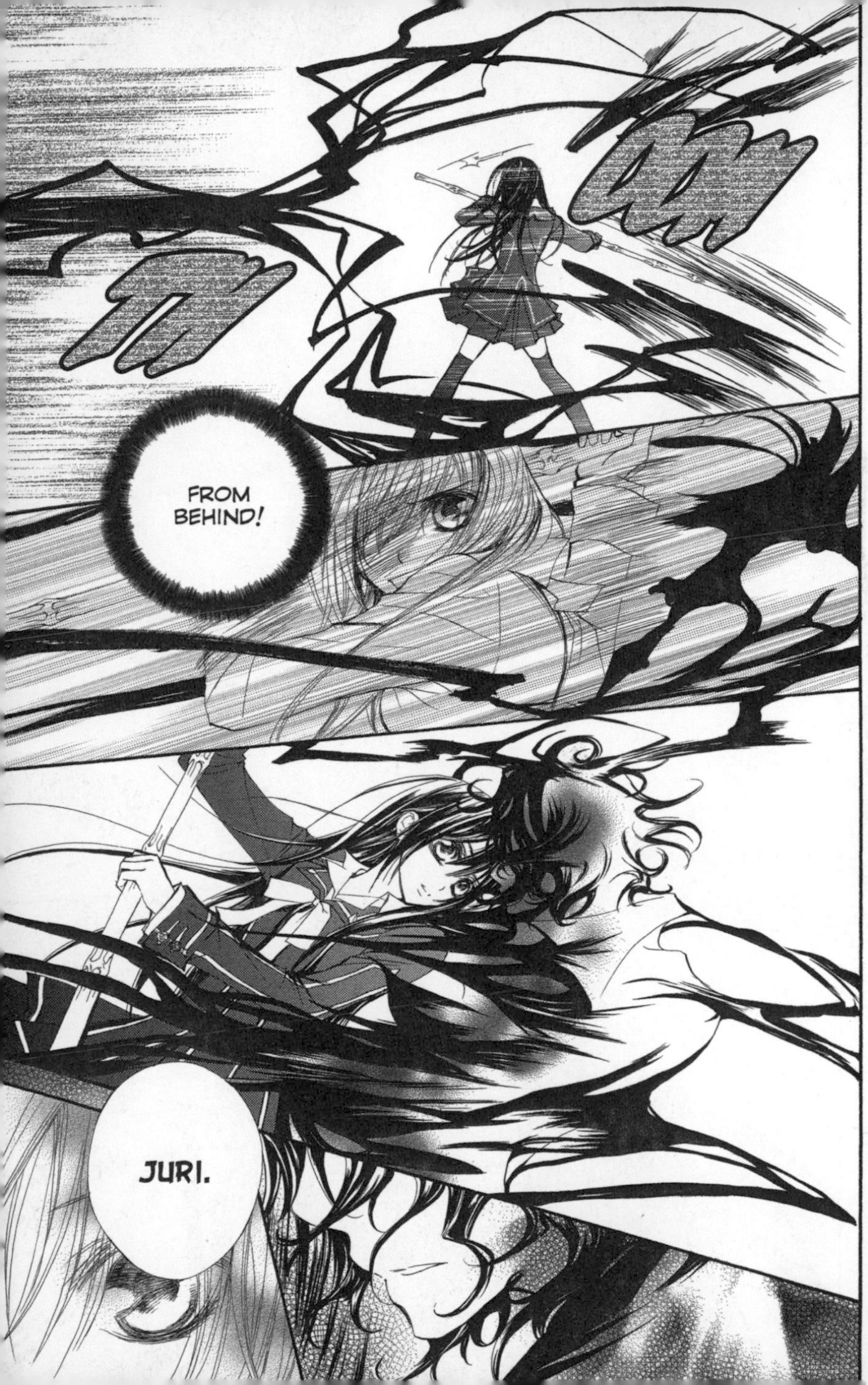
FROM BEHIND!
JURI.

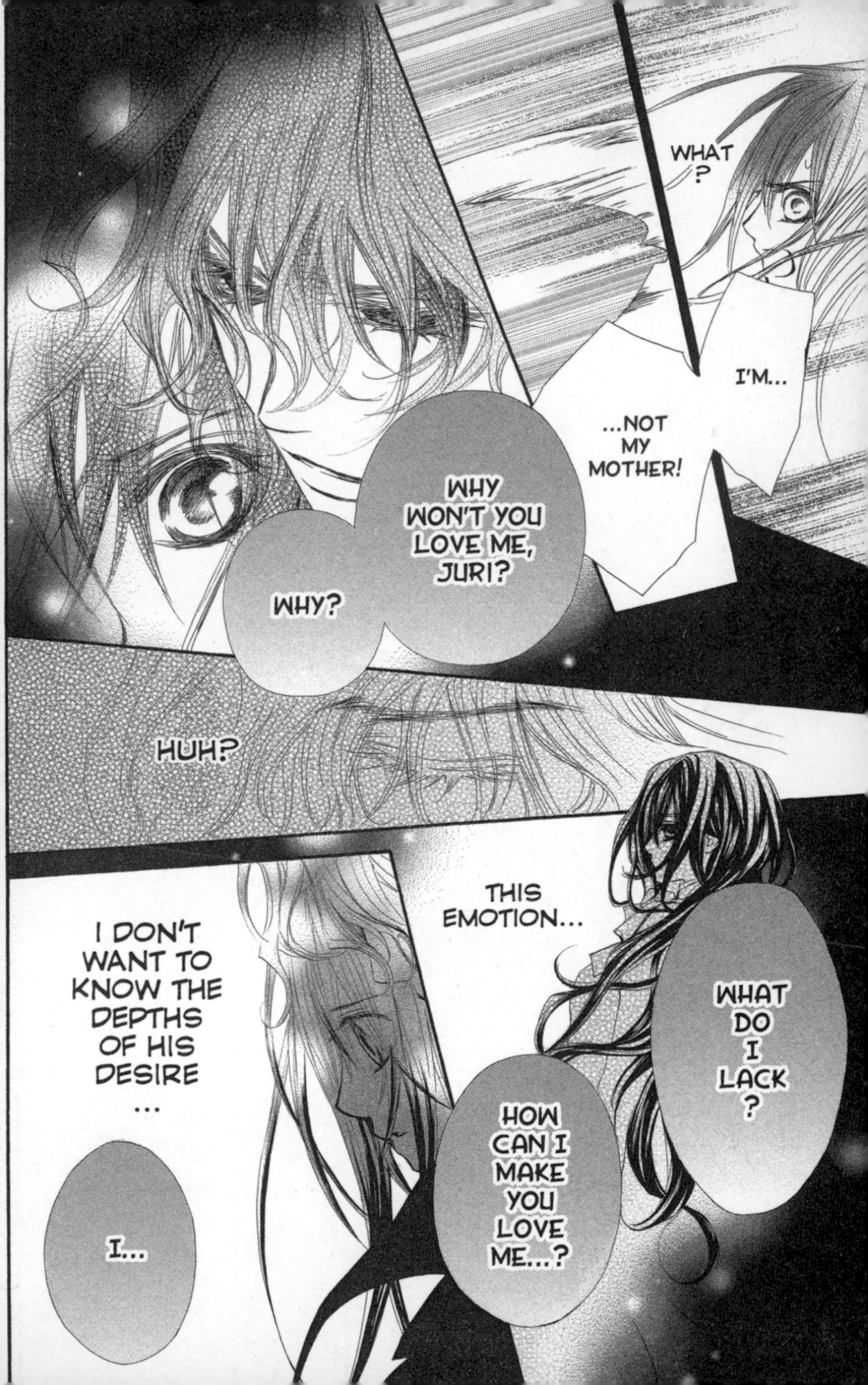
WHAT?
I'M...
...NOT MY MOTHER!
WHY WON'T YOU LOVE ME, JURI?
WHY?
HUH?
THIS EMOTION...
WHAT DO I LACK?
HOW CAN I MAKE YOU LOVE ME...?
I DON'T WANT TO KNOW THE DEPTHS OF HIS DESIRE...
I...

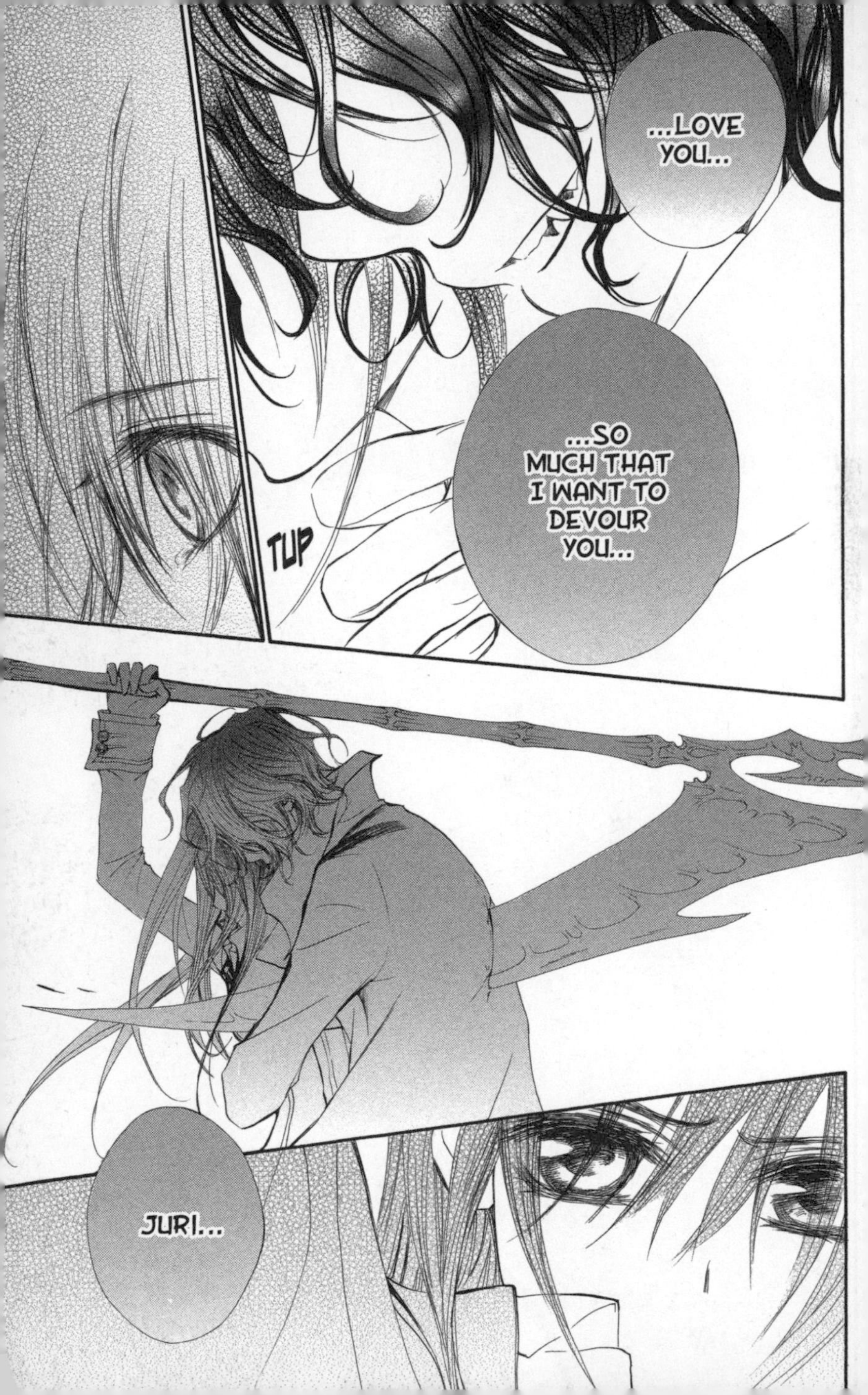
...LOVE YOU...
...SO MUCH THAT I WANT TO DEVOUR YOU...
TUP
JURI...

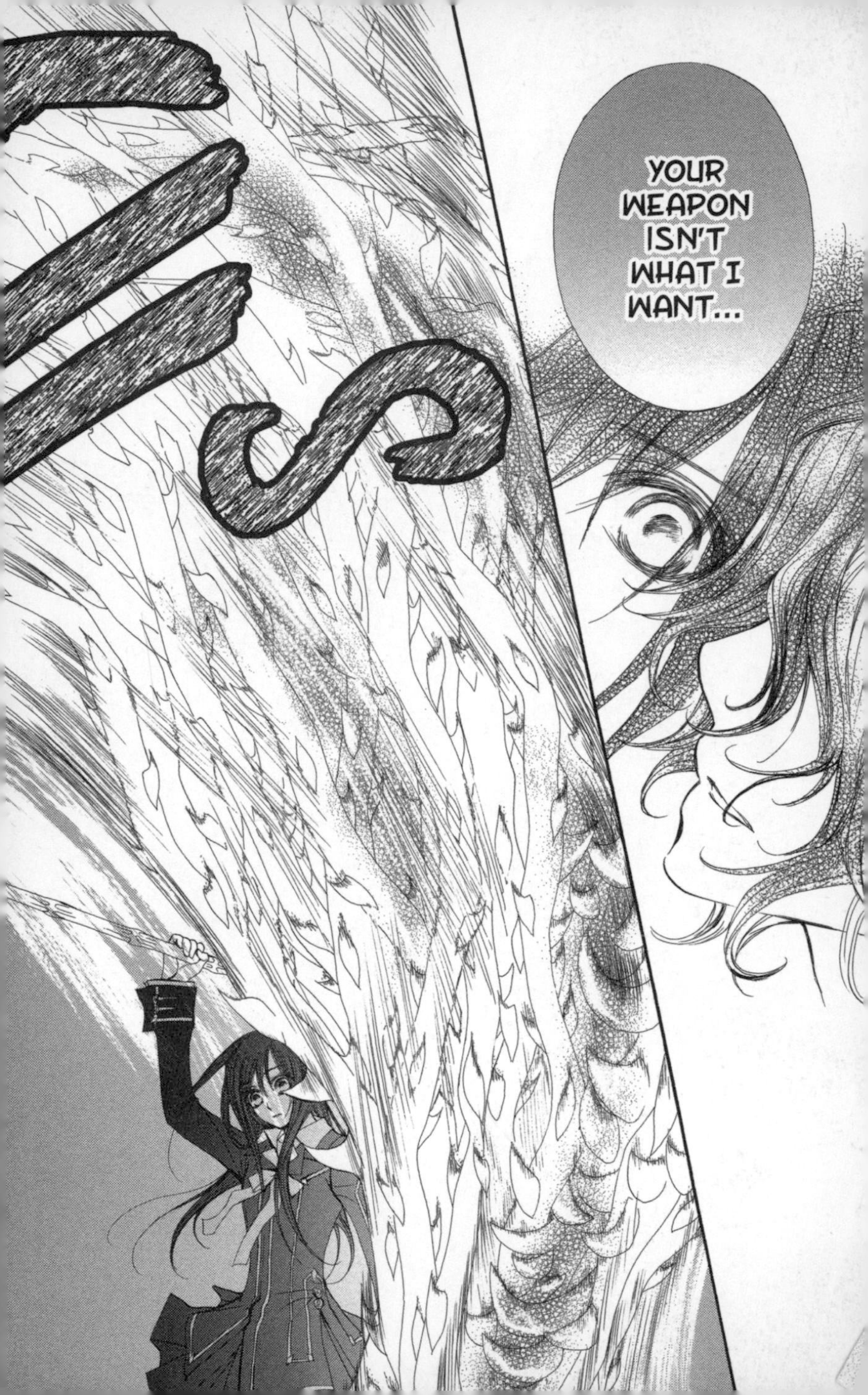
YOUR WEAPON ISN'T WHAT I WANT...

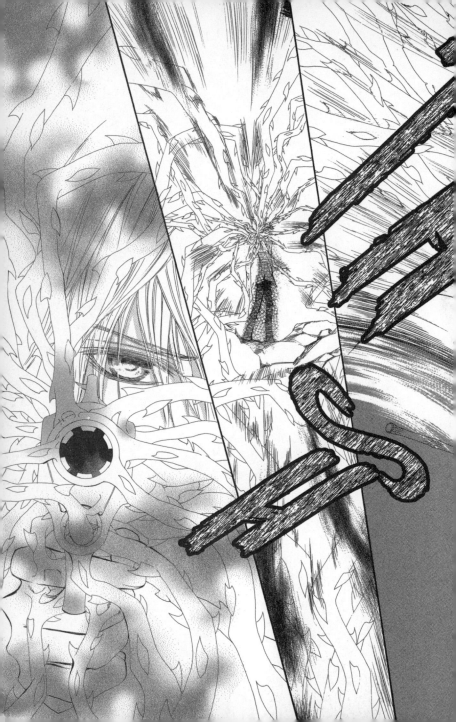

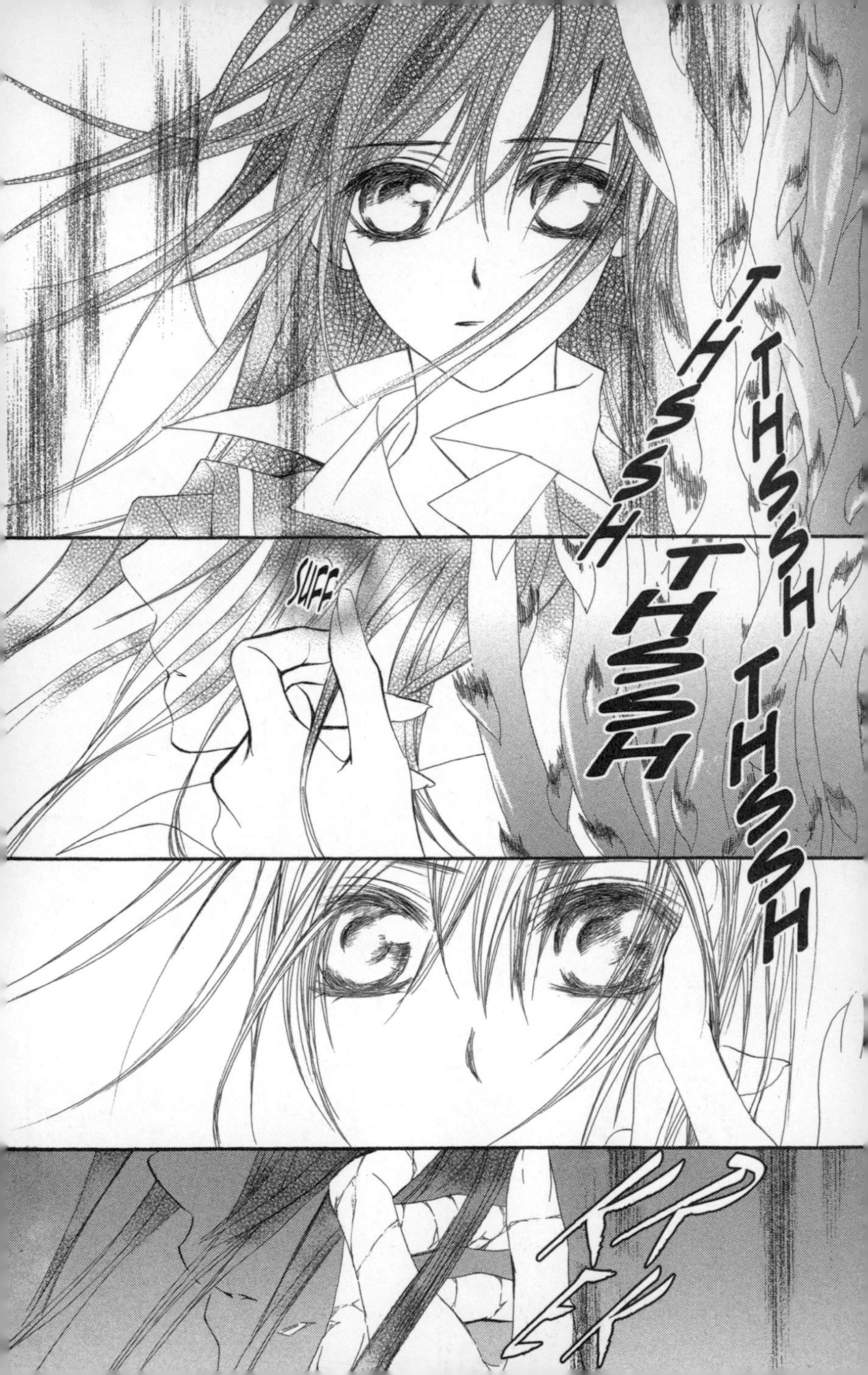
THSSH THSSH
THSSH
THSSH
SUFF

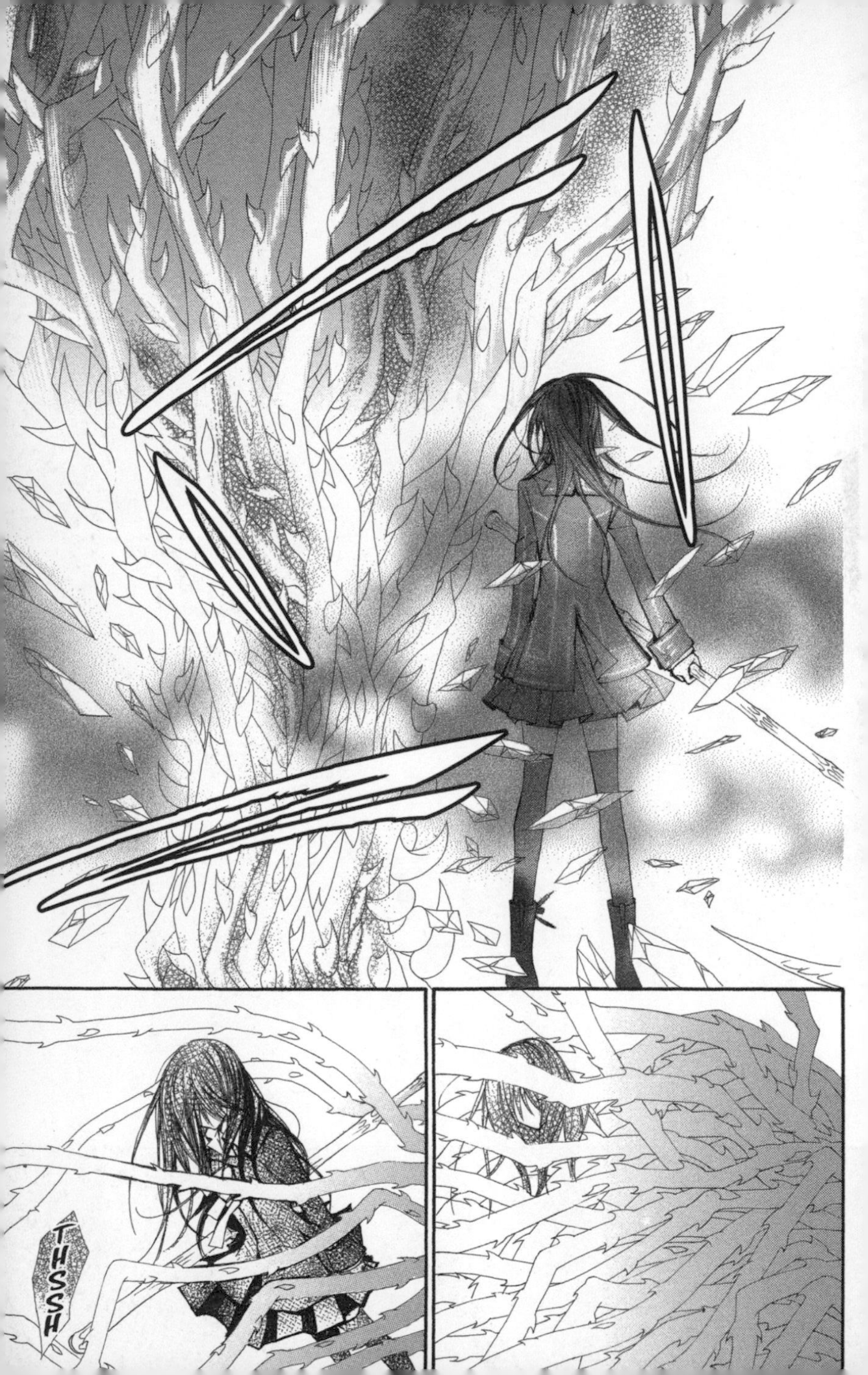
THSSH

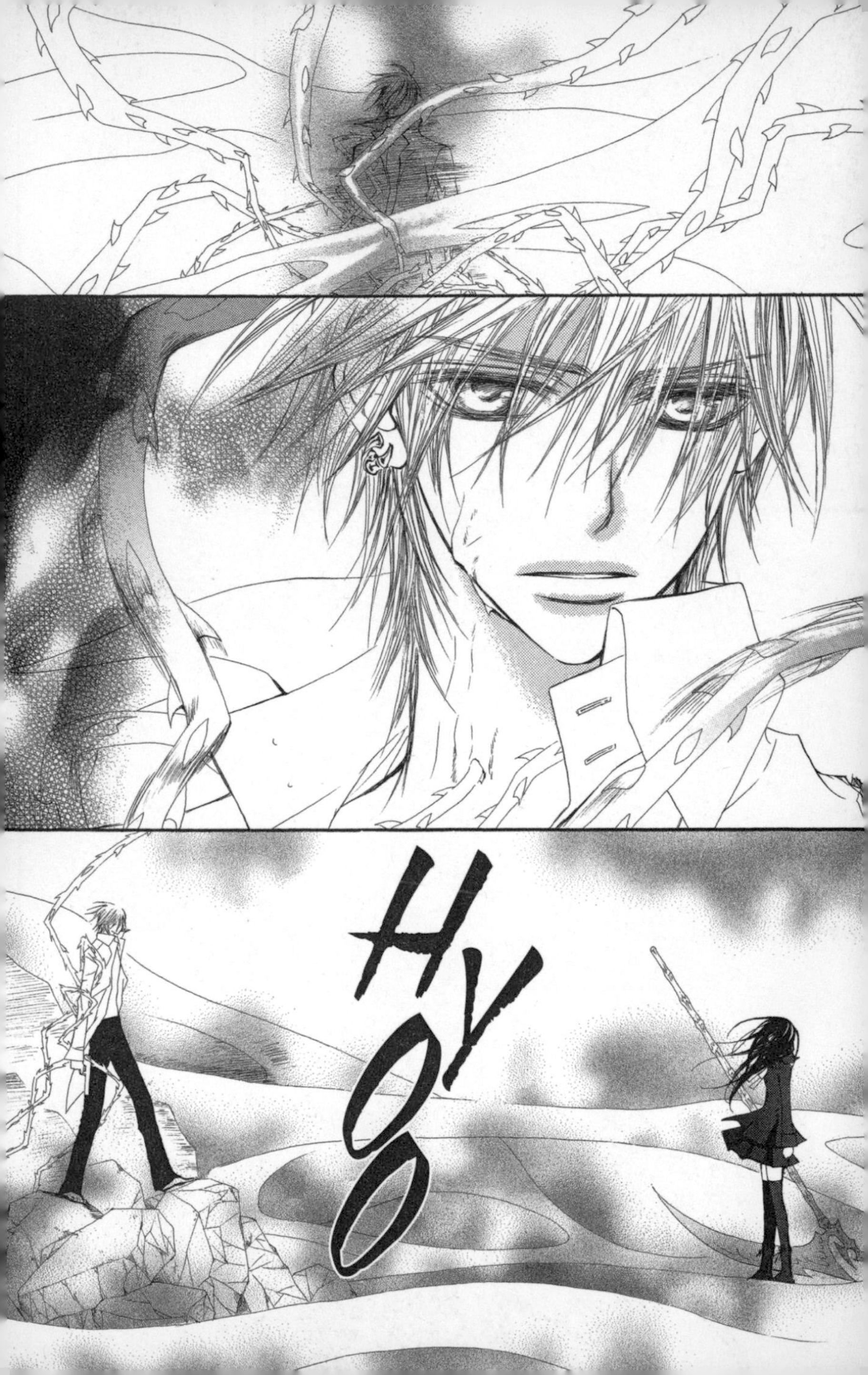
HYGO

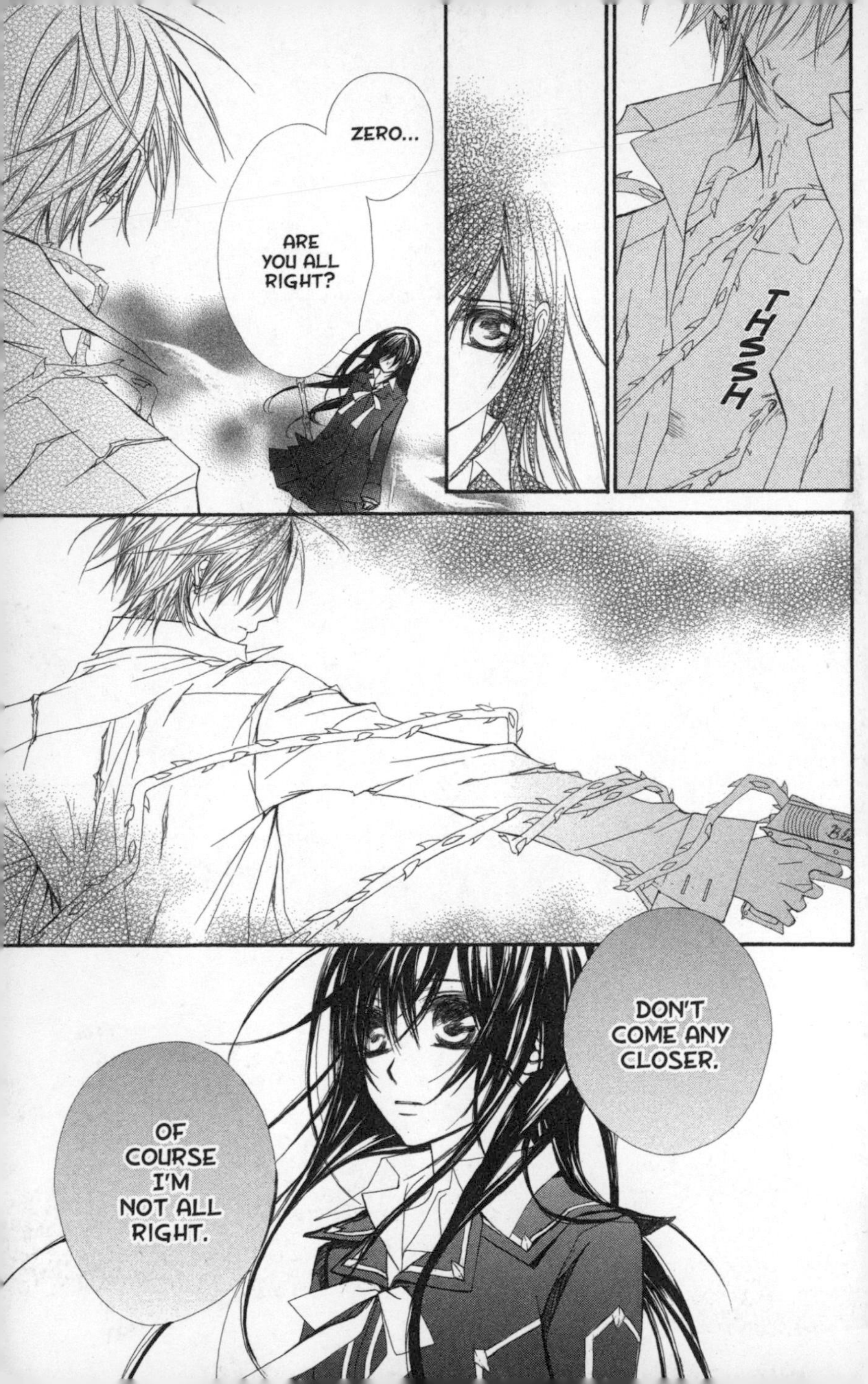
THSSH
ZERO...
ARE YOU ALL RIGHT?
DON'T COME ANY CLOSER.
OF COURSE I'M NOT ALL RIGHT.

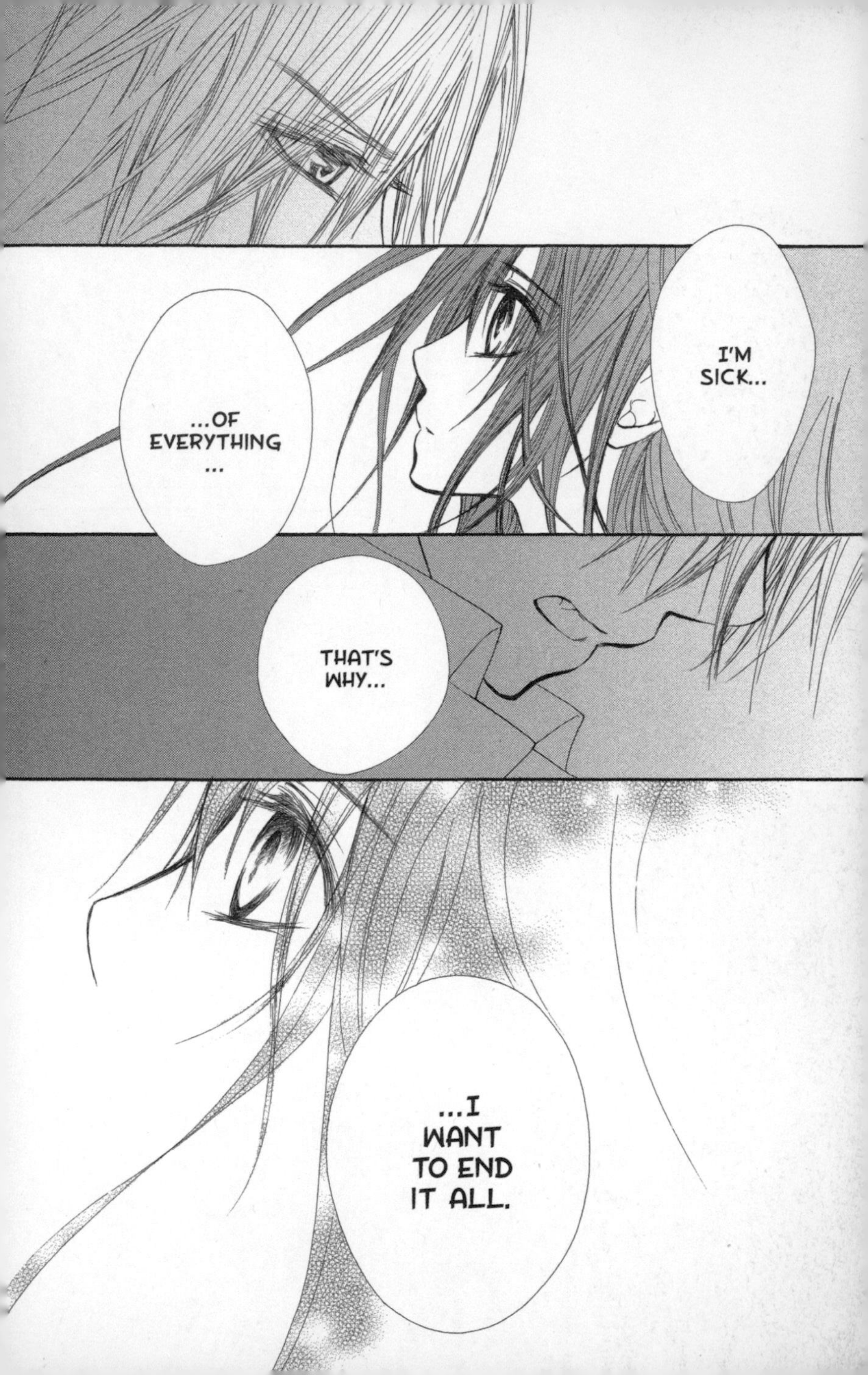
I'M SICK...
...OF EVERYTHING ...
THAT'S WHY...
...I WANT TO END IT ALL.

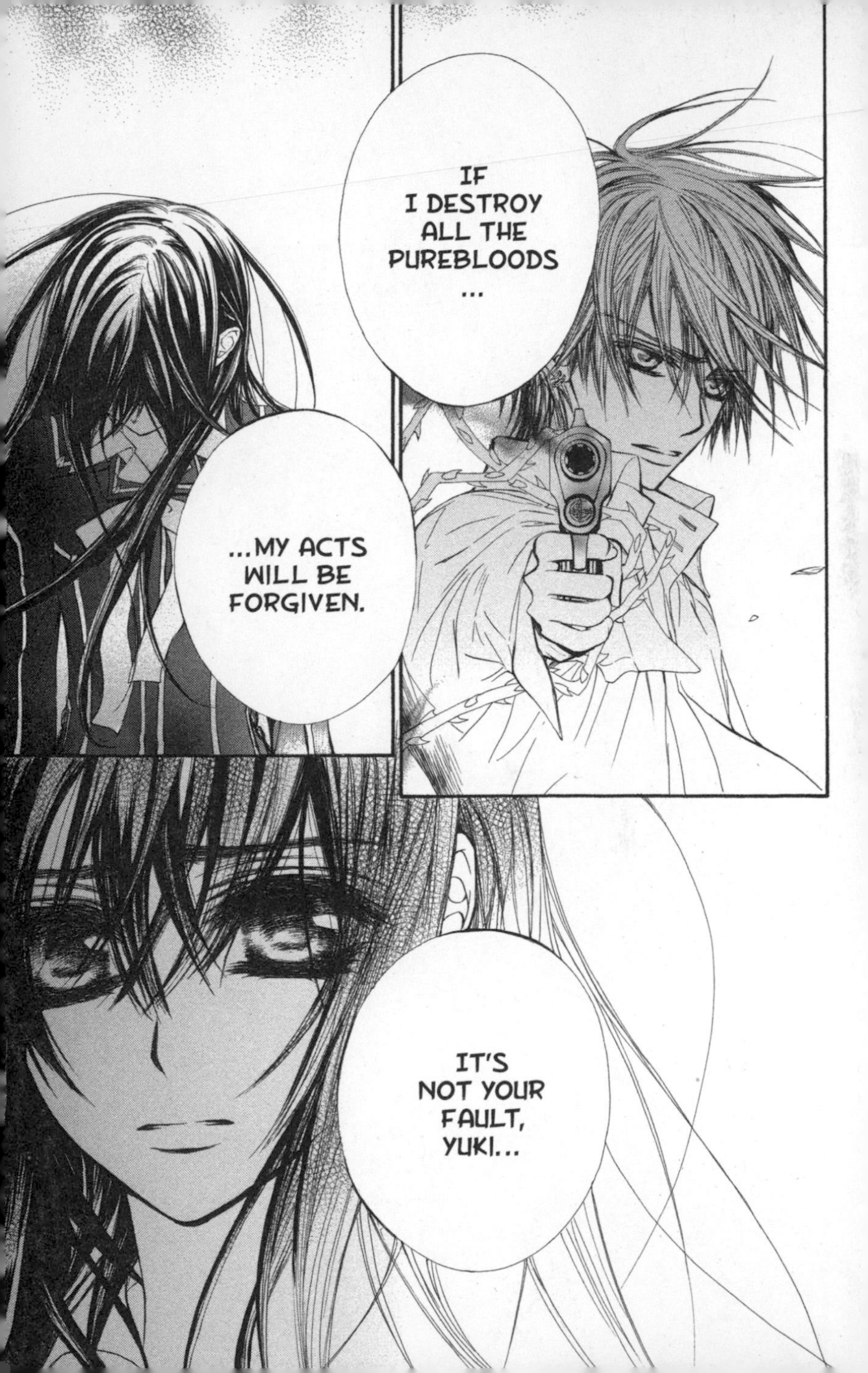
IF I DESTROY ALL THE PUREBLOODS ...
...MY ACTS WILL BE FORGIVEN.
IT'S NOT YOUR FAULT, YUKI...

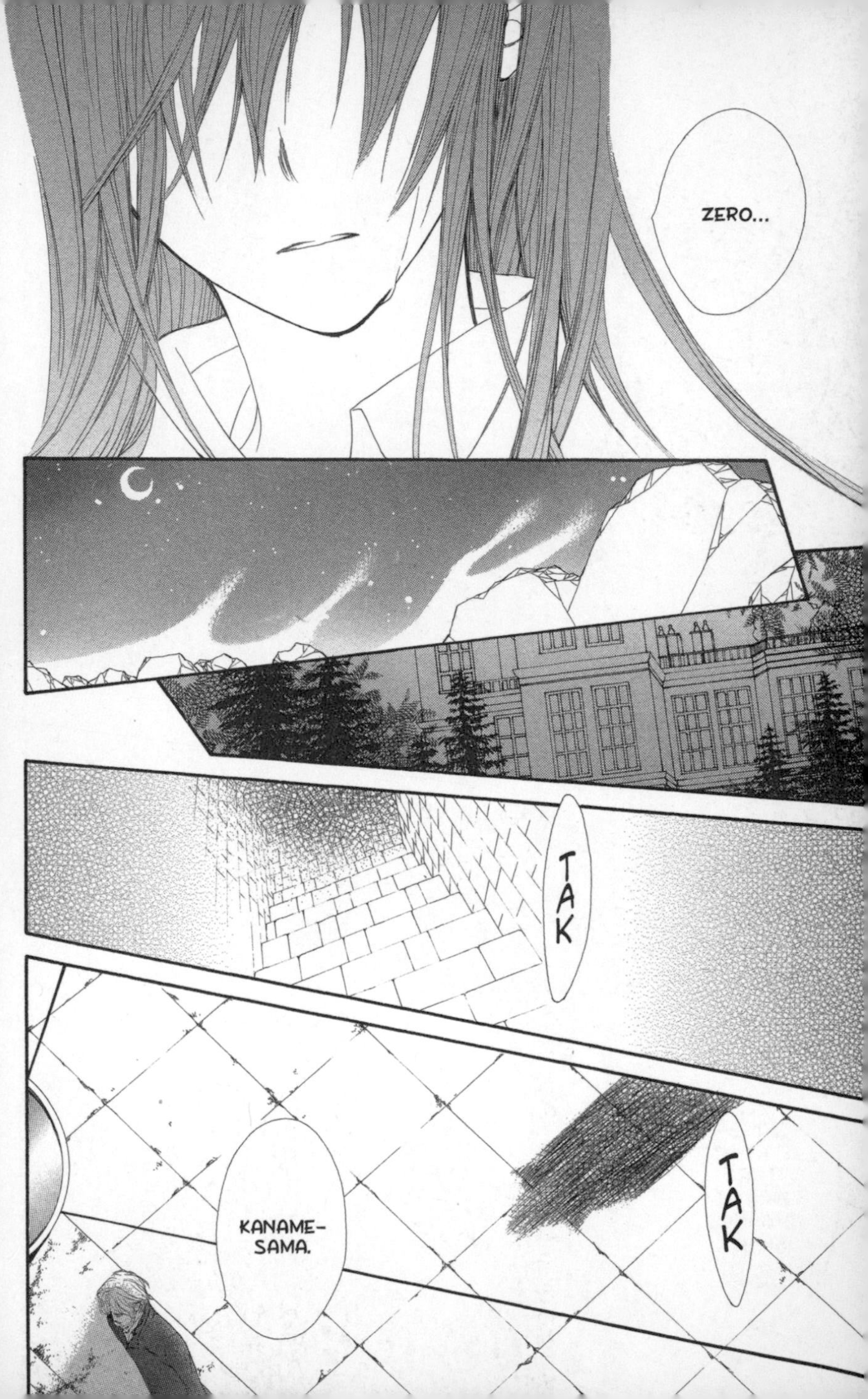
ZERO...
TAK
TAK
KANAME-SAMA.

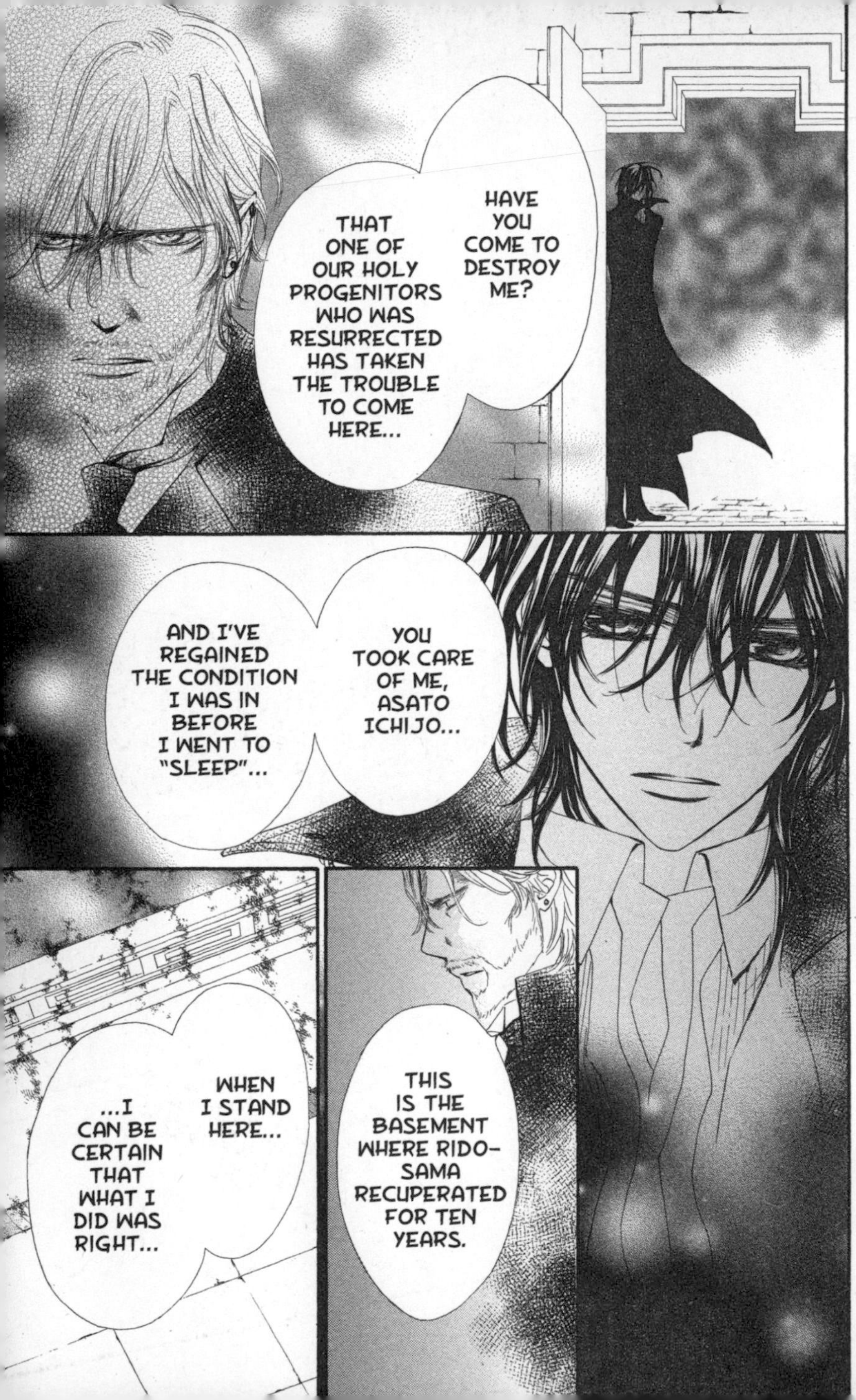
HAVE YOU COME TO DESTROY ME?
THAT ONE OF OUR HOLY PROGENITORS WHO WAS RESURRECTED HAS TAKEN THE TROUBLE TO COME HERE...
YOU TOOK CARE OF ME, ASATO ICHIJO...
AND I'VE REGAINED THE CONDITION I WAS IN BEFORE I WENT TO "SLEEP"...
THIS IS THE BASEMENT WHERE RIDO-SAMA RECUPERATED FOR TEN YEARS.
WHEN I STAND HERE...
...I CAN BE CERTAIN THAT WHAT I DID WAS RIGHT...

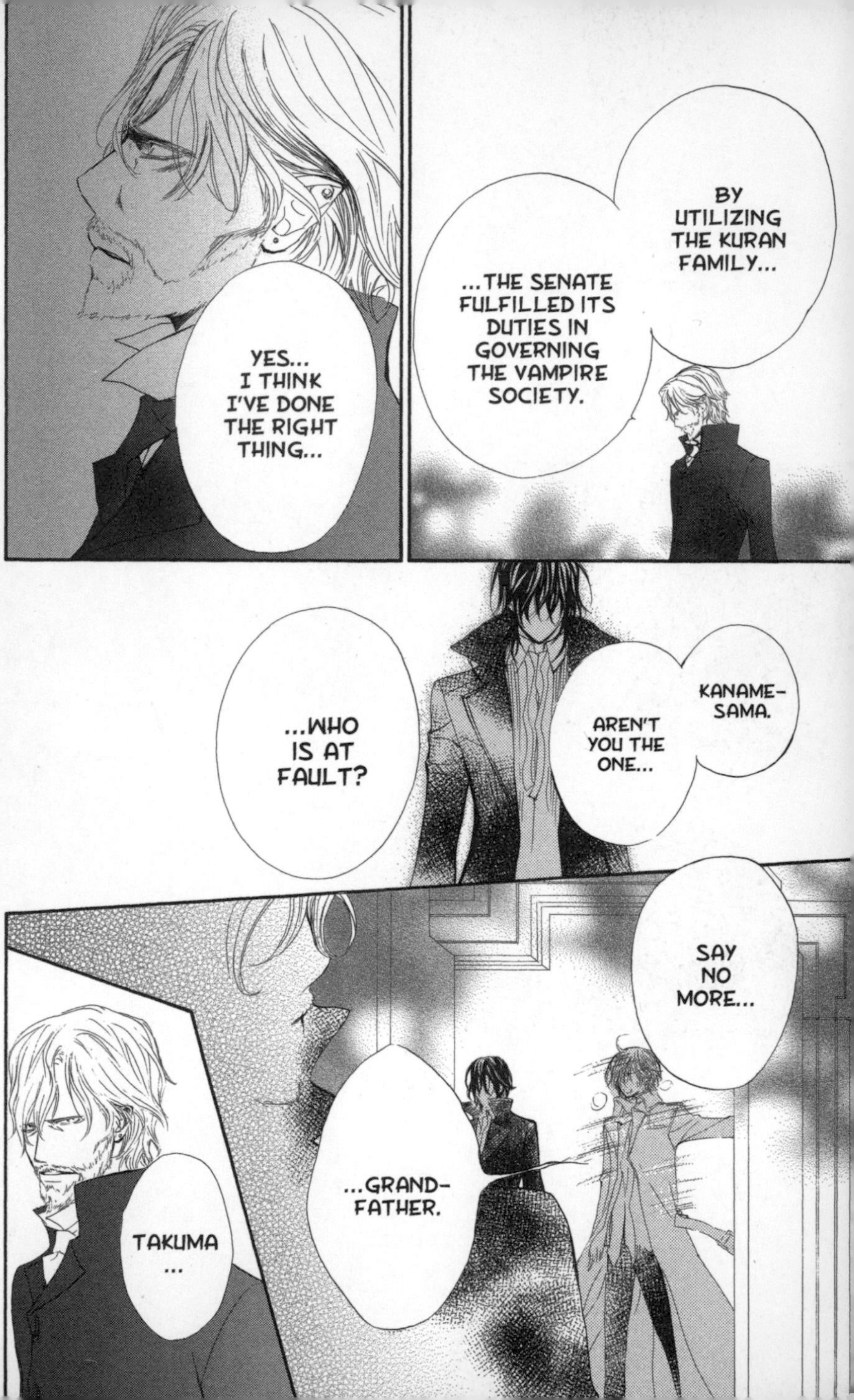
BY UTILIZING THE KURAN FAMILY...
...THE SENATE FULFILLED ITS DUTIES IN GOVERNING THE VAMPIRE SOCIETY.
YES... I THINK I'VE DONE THE RIGHT THING...
KANAME-SAMA.
AREN'T YOU THE ONE...
...WHO IS AT FAULT?
SAY NO MORE...
...GRAND-FATHER.
TAKUMA ...

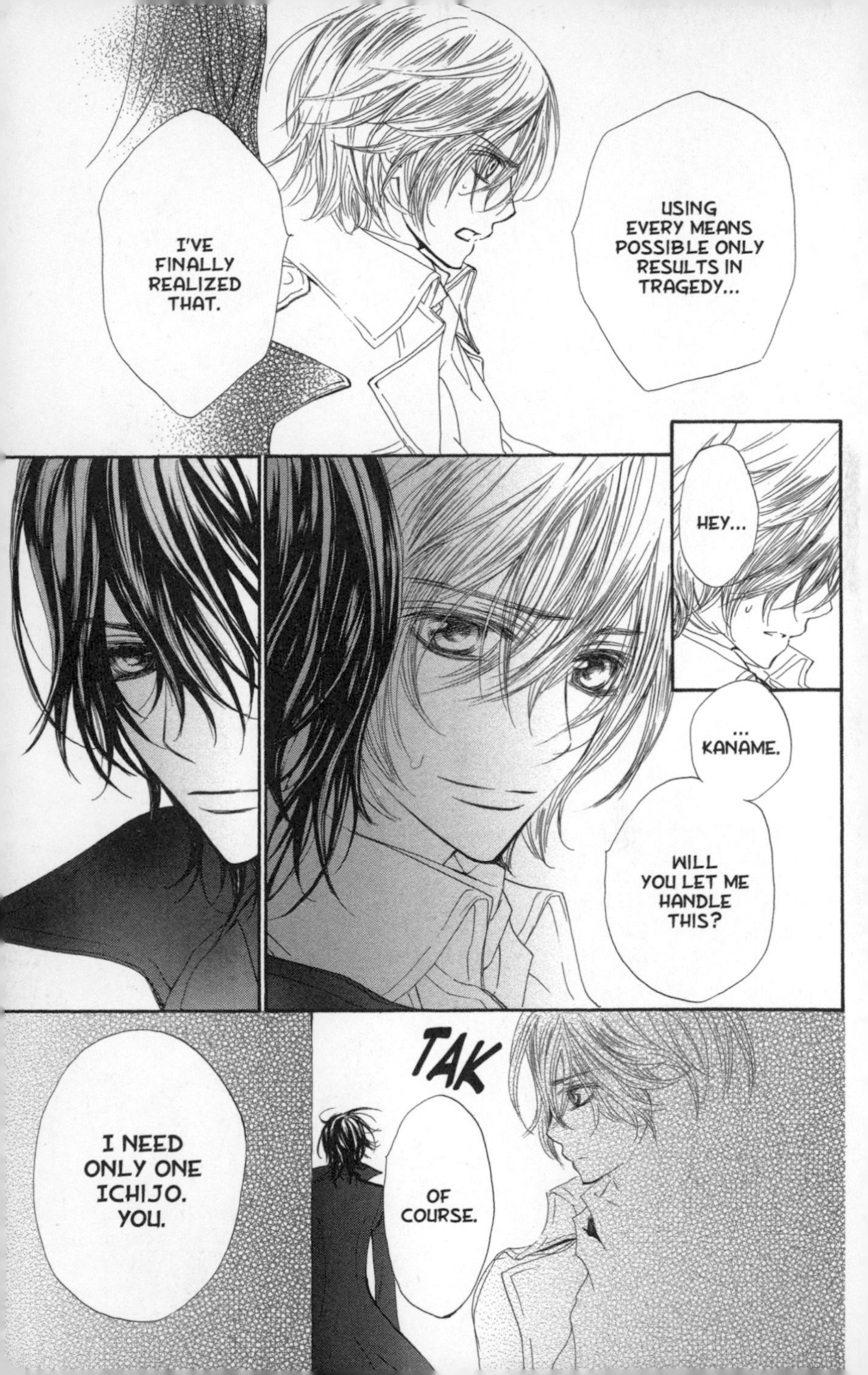
USING EVERY MEANS POSSIBLE ONLY RESULTS IN TRAGEDY...
I'VE FINALLY REALIZED THAT.
HEY...
... KANAME.
WILL YOU LET ME HANDLE THIS?
TAK
OF COURSE.
I NEED ONLY ONE ICHIJO. YOU.

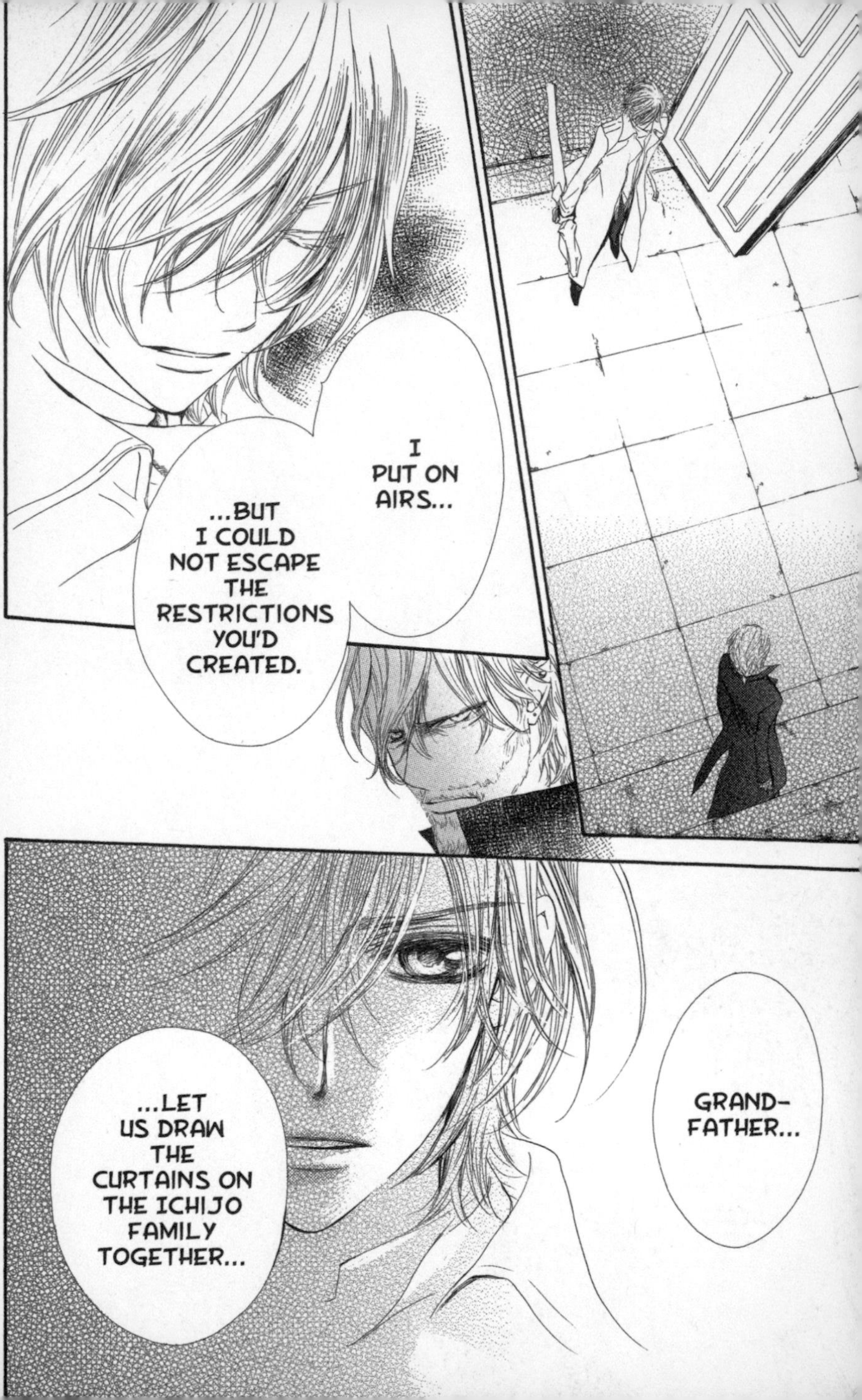
I PUT ON AIRS...
...BUT I COULD NOT ESCAPE THE RESTRICTIONS YOU'D CREATED.
GRAND-FATHER...
...LET US DRAW THE CURTAINS ON THE ICHIJO FAMILY TOGETHER...

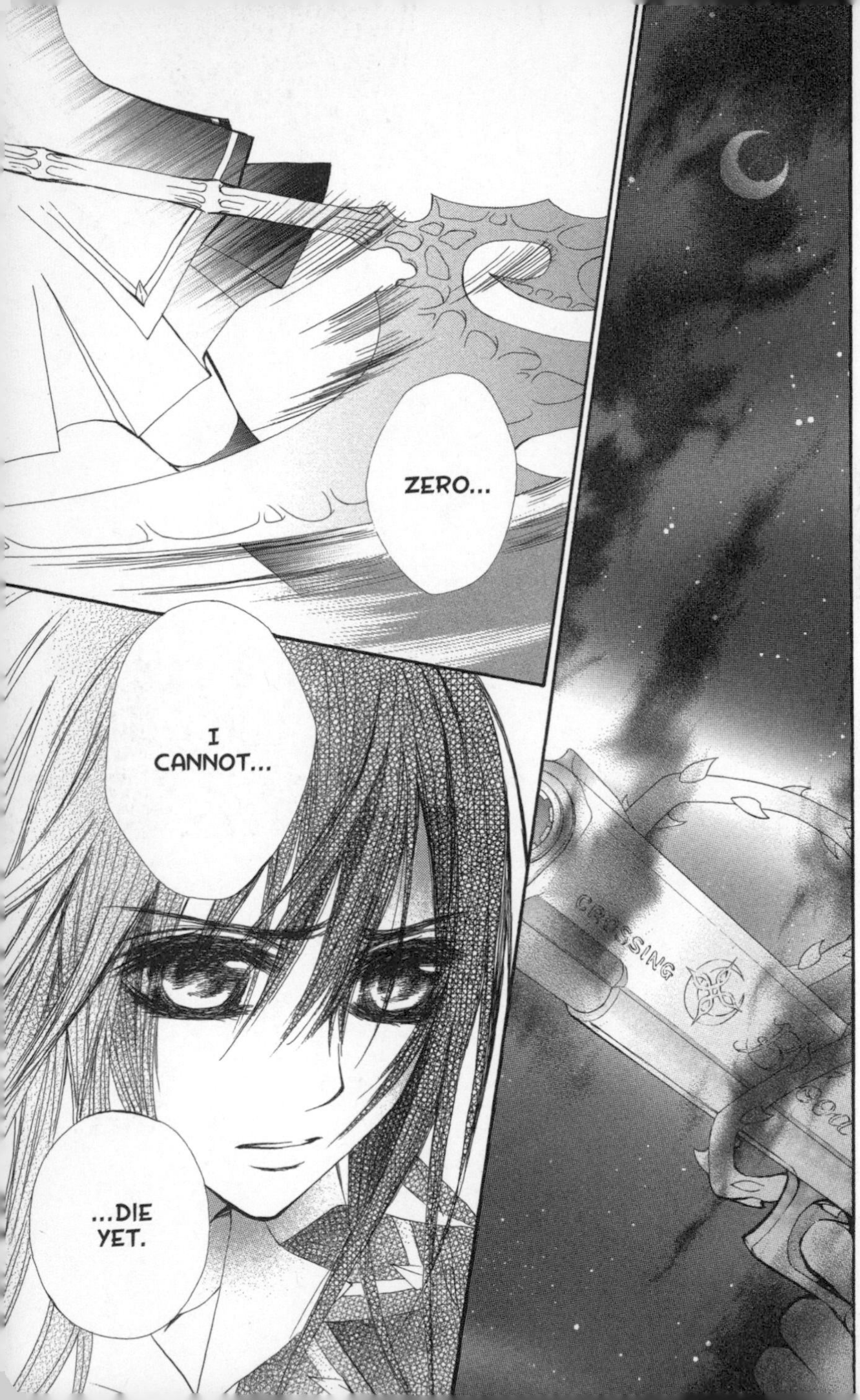
CROSSING
ZERO...
I CANNOT...
...DIE YET.

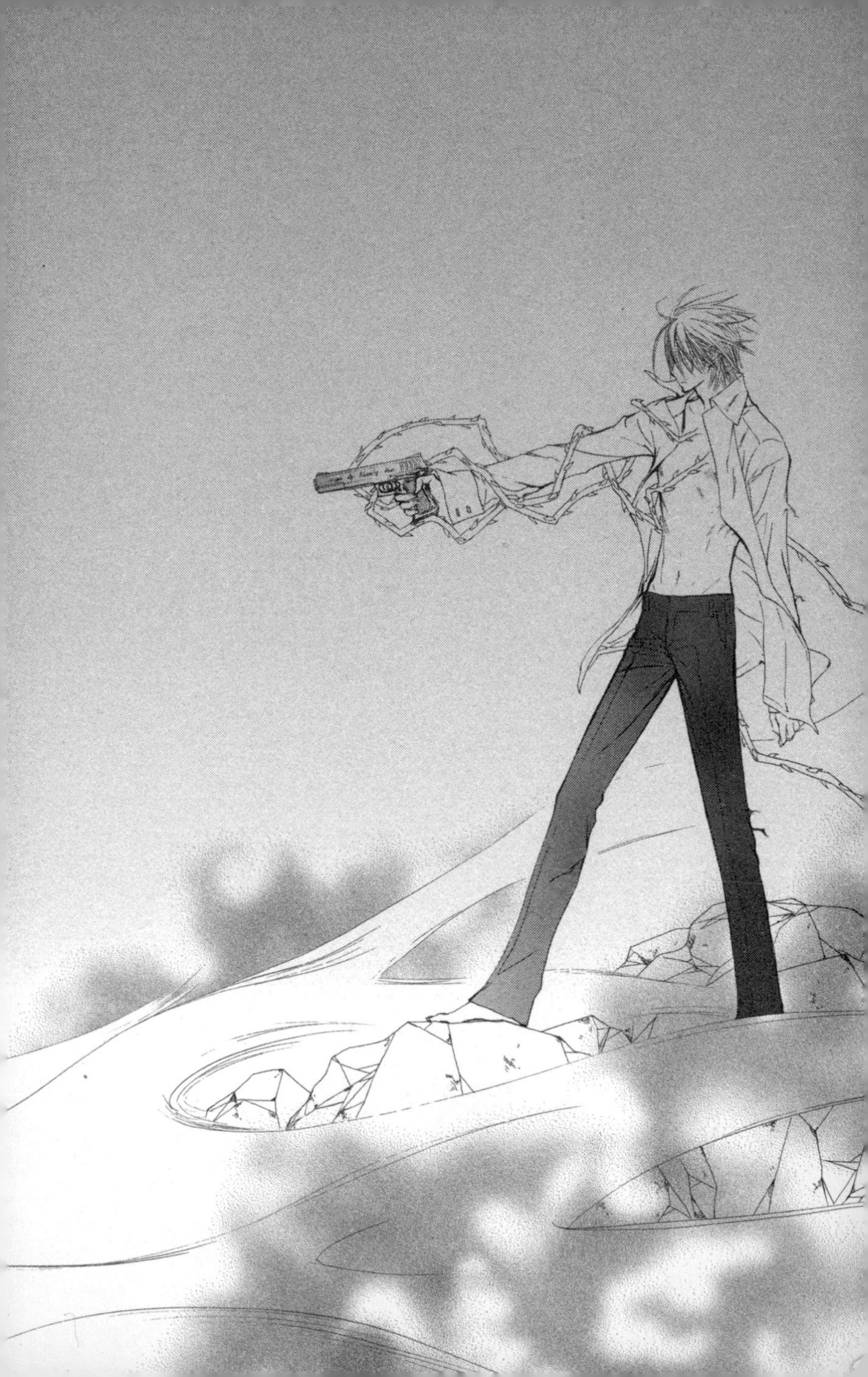

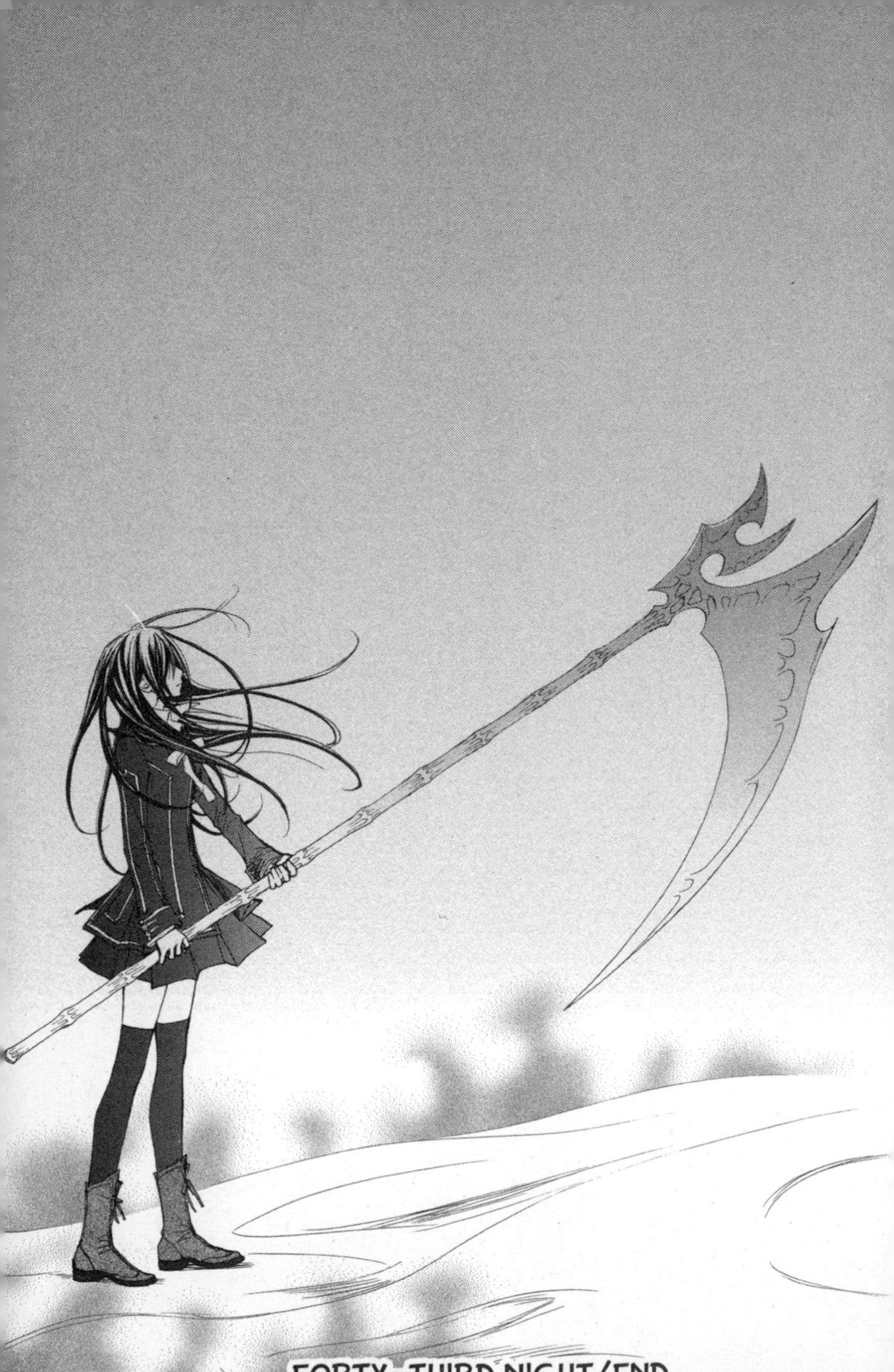

FORTY-THIRD NIGHT/END

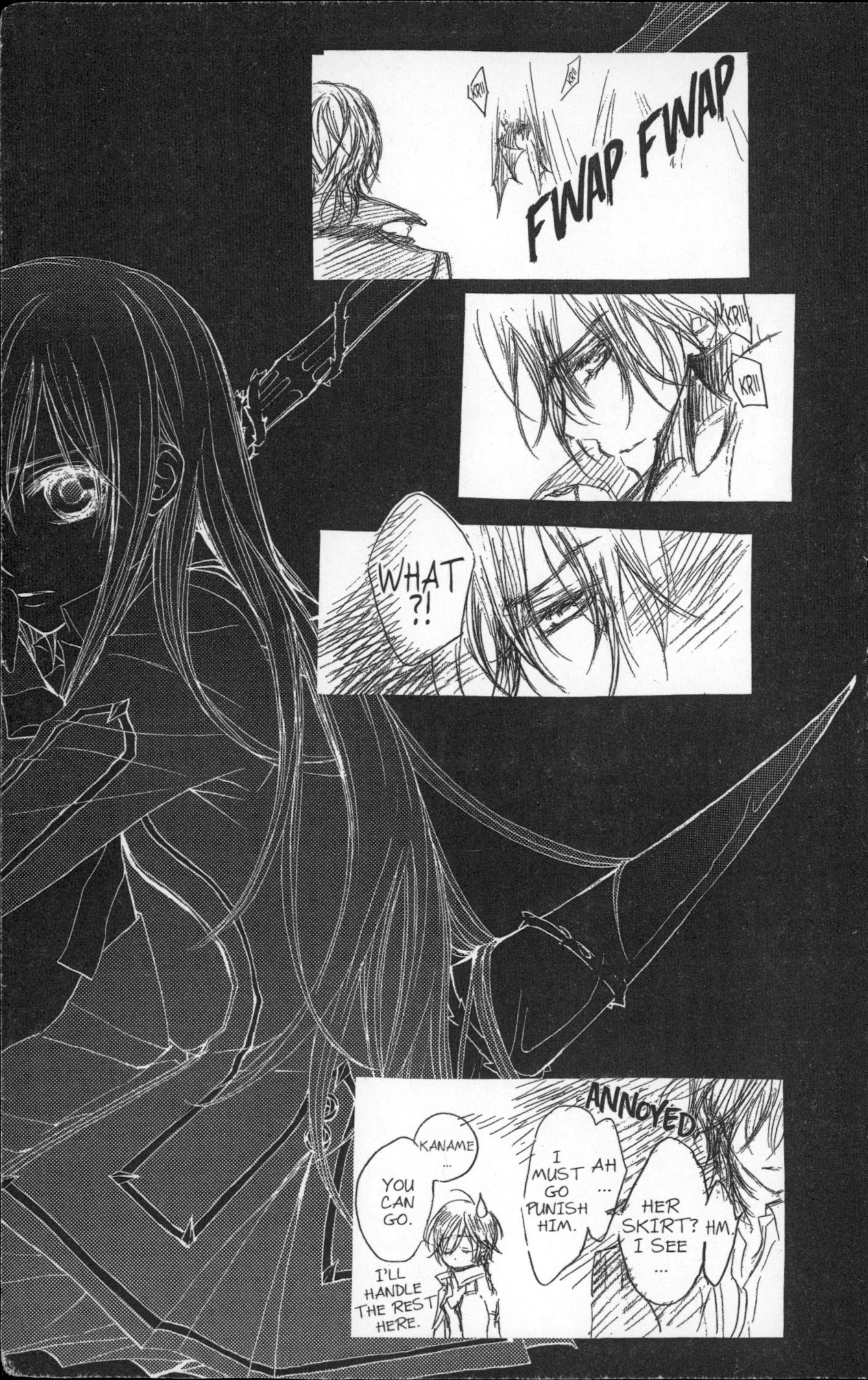
KRII
KRII
FWAP FWAP
KRII
KRII
WHAT ?!
ANNOYED.
HM.
HER SKIRT? I SEE ...
AH ...
I MUST GO PUNISH HIM.
KANAME ... YOU CAN GO.
I'LL HANDLE THE REST HERE.

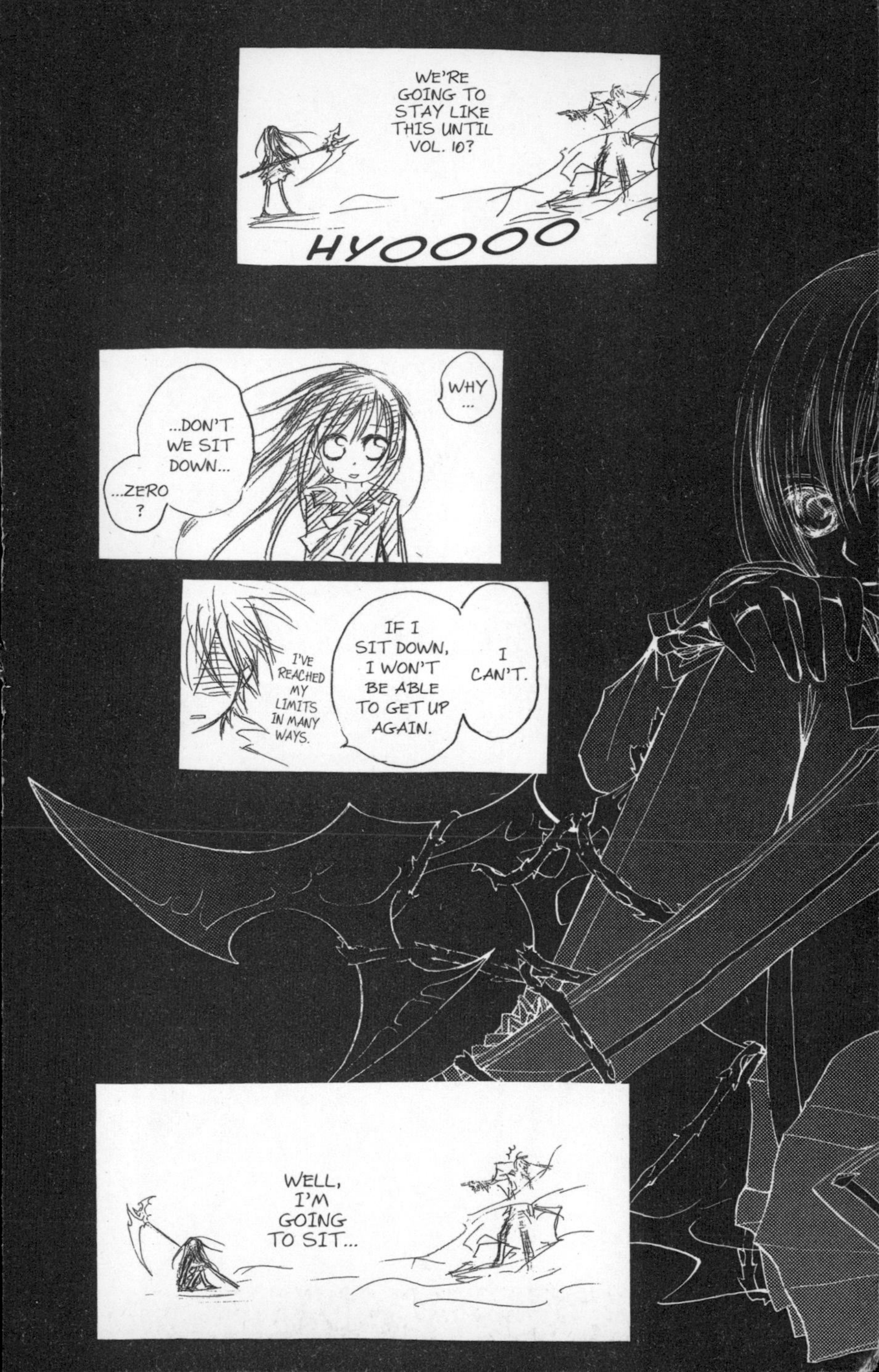
WE'RE GOING TO STAY LIKE THIS UNTIL VOL. 10?
HYOOOO
WHY ...
...DON'T WE SIT DOWN...
...ZERO ?
I CAN'T.
IF I SIT DOWN, I WON'T BE ABLE TO GET UP AGAIN.
I'VE REACHED MY LIMITS IN MANY WAYS.
WELL, I'M GOING TO SIT...

EDITOR'S NOTES

Characters

Matsuri Hino puts careful thought into the names of her characters in *Vampire Knight*. Below is the collection of characters through volume 9. Each character's name is presented family name first, per the kanji reading.

黒主優姫

Cross Yuki

Yuki's last name, *Kurosu*, is the Japanese pronunciation of the English word "cross." However, the kanji has a different meaning—*kuro* means "black" and *su* means "master." Her first name is a combination of *yuu*, meaning "tender" or "kind," and *ki*, meaning "princess."

錐生零

Kiryu Zero

Zero's first name is the kanji for *rei*, meaning "zero." In his last name, *Kiryu*, the *ki* means "auger" or "drill," and the *ryu* means "life."

玖蘭枢

Kuran Kaname

Kaname means "hinge" or "door." The kanji for his last name is a combination of the old-fashioned way of writing *ku*, meaning "nine," and *ran*, meaning "orchid": "nine orchids."

藍堂英

Aido Hanabusa

Hanabusa means "petals of a flower." *Aido* means "indigo temple." In Japanese, the pronunciation of *Aido* is very close to the pronunciation of the English word *idol*.

架院暁

Kain Akatsuki

Akatsuki means "dawn" or "day-break." In *Kain, ka* is a base or support, while *in* denotes a building that has high fences around it, such as a temple or school.

早園瑠佳

Souen Ruka

In *Ruka*, the *ru* means "lapis lazuli" while the *ka* means "good-looking" or "beautiful." The *sou* in Ruka's surname, *Souen*, means "early," but this kanji also has an obscure meaning of "strong fragrance." The *en* means "garden."

一条拓麻

Ichijo Takuma

Ichijo can mean a "ray" or "streak." The kanji for *Takuma* is a combination of *taku*, meaning "to cultivate" and *ma*, which is the kanji for *asa*, meaning "hemp" or "flax," a plant with blue flowers.

支葵千里

Shiki Senri

Shiki's last name is a combination of *shi*, meaning "to support" and *ki*, meaning "mallow"—a flowering plant with pink or white blossoms. The *ri* in *Senri* is a traditional Japanese unit of measure for distance, and one *ri* is about 2.44 miles. *Senri* means "1,000 *ri*."

夜刈十牙
Yagari Toga

Yagari is a combination of *ya*, meaning "night," and *gari*, meaning "to harvest." *Toga* means "ten fangs."

一条麻遠, 一翁
Ichijo Asato, aka "Ichio"

Ichijo can mean a "ray" or "streak." Asato's first name is comprised of *asa*, meaning "hemp" or "flax," and *tou*, meaning "far off." His nickname is *ichi*, or "one," combined with *ou*, which can be used as an honorific when referring to an older man.

若葉沙頼
Wakaba Sayori

Yori's full name is Sayori Wakaba. *Wakaba* means "young leaves." Her given name, *Sayori*, is a combination of *sa*, meaning "sand," and *yori*, meaning "trust."

星煉

Seiren

Sei means "star" and *ren* means "to smelt" or "refine." *Ren* is also the same kanji used in *rengoku*, or "purgatory."

遠矢莉磨

Toya Rima

Toya means a "far-reaching arrow." Rima's first name is a combination of *ri*, or "jasmine," and *ma*, which signifies enhancement by wearing away, such as by polishing or scouring.

紅まり亜

Kurenai Maria

Kurenai means "crimson." The kanji for the last *a* in Maria's first name is the same that is used in "Asia."

錐生壱縷
Kiryu Ichiru

Ichi is the old-fashioned way of writing "one," and *ru* means "thread."

緋桜閑, 狂咲姫
Hio Shizuka, Kuruizaki-hime

Shizuka means "calm and quiet." In Shizuka's family name, *hi* is "scarlet," and *ou* is "cherry blossoms." Shizuka Hio is also referred to as the "Kuruizaki-hime." *Kuruizaki* means "flowers blooming out of season," and *hime* means "princess."

藍堂月子
Aido Tsukiko

Aido means "indigo temple." *Tsukiko* means "moon child."

白蕗更

Shirabuki Sara

Shira is "white," and *buki* is "butterbur," a plant with white flowers. *Sara* means "renew."

黒主灰闇

Cross Kaien

Cross, or *Kurosu*, means "black master." Kaien is a combination of *kai*, meaning "ashes," and *en*, meaning "village gate." The kanji for *en* is also used for Enma, the ruler of the Underworld in Buddhist mythology.

玖蘭李土

Kuran Rido

Kuran means "nine orchids." In *Rido*, *ri* means "plum" and *do* means "earth."

玖蘭樹里

Kuran Juri

Kuran means "nine orchids." In her first name, *ju* means "tree" and a *ri* is a traditional Japanese unit of measure for distance. The kanji for *ri* is the same as in Senri's name.

玖蘭悠

Kuran Haruka

Kuran means "nine orchids." *Haruka* means "distant" or "remote."

Terms

-sama: The suffix *sama* is used in formal address for someone who ranks higher in the social hierarchy. The vampires call their leader "Kaname-sama" only when they are among their own kind.

Matsuri Hino burst onto the manga scene with her series *Kono Yume ga Sametara* (When This Dream Is Over), which was published in *LaLa DX* magazine. Hino was a manga artist a mere nine months after she decided to become one.

With the success of her popular series *Captive Hearts* and *MeruPuri*, Hino has established herself as a major player in the world of shojo manga. *Vampire Knight* is currently serialized in *LaLa* magazine.

Hino enjoys creative activities and has commented that she would have been either an architect or an apprentice to traditional Japanese craft masters if she had not become a manga artist.

VAMPIRE KNIGHT
Vol. 9
Shojo Beat Edition

STORY AND ART BY
MATSURI HINO

Translation & English Adaptation/Tomo Kimura
Touch-up Art & Lettering/Rina Mapa
Graphic Design/Amy Martin
Editor/Nancy Thistlethwaite

VP, Production/Alvin Lu
VP, Sales & Product Marketing/Gonzalo Ferreyra
VP, Creative/Linda Espinosa
Publisher/Hyoe Narita

Printed in Canada

Published by VIZ Media, LLC
P.O. Box 77010
San Francisco, CA 94107

10 9 8 7 6 5 4 3 2 1
First printing, February 2010

www.viz.com

www.shojobeat.com

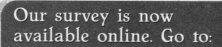